DOCUMEN

An Invitation to a Critical Humanism

KEN PLUMMER

SAGE Publications
London • Thousand Oaks • New Delhi

© Ken Plummer 2001

First published 2001

Apart from any fair dealing for the purposes of research or private study, or criticism or review, as permitted under the Copyright, Designs and Patents Act 1988, this publication may be reproduced, stored or transmitted in any form, or by any means, only with the prior permission in writing of the publishers or, in the case of reprographic reproduction, in accordance with the terms of licences issued by the Copyright Licensing Agency. Inquiries concerning reproduction outside those terms should be sent to the publishers.

 SAGE Publications Ltd
6 Bonhill Street
London EC2A 4PU

SAGE Publications Inc
2455 Teller Road
Thousand Oaks, California 91320

SAGE Publications India Pvt Ltd
32, M-Block Market
Greater Kailash – I
New Delhi 110 048

British Library Cataloguing in Publication data

A catalogue record for this book is available
from the British Library

ISBN 0 7619 6131 3
ISBN 0 7629 6132 1 (pbk)

Library of Congress catalog card number 133467

Typeset by Mayhew Typesetting, Rhayader, Powys
Printed in Great Britain by Athenaeum Press, Gateshead

IN MEMORY OF MY DEAR MUM AND DAD
LEONARD S. PLUMMER (1904–1979)
ETHEL PLUMMER (1914–2000)

Contents

List of Tables, Figures and Boxes

Preface to the Fully Revised and Expanded Edition of *Documents of Life*

An earlier version of this book, *Documents of Life*, was originally written some twenty years ago, at a time when the approach to social science it advocated was very marginal. Since that time, there has been a major cultural boom in life story and auto/biographical work, though such ideas are very far from being mainstream and are often still shunned within the social or human 'sciences'. In revising this book, I have tried to maintain the feel of the original wherever I could, whilst taking into account many of the important developments that have happened since the early 1980s. This has led not to just a few changes here and there, as is often the case with second editions. Rather it has led to a substantial rewrite – significantly longer with many new chapters and a stream of new arguments and examples.

When *Documents of Life* (hereafter *Documents-1*) was first published in the early 1980s, it had four central arguments. The first suggested that life stories had a minor, 'underground' history in the social sciences – and it was one that needed to be made prominent and developed. Whatever sense that claim made then, it makes less sense now. For the past twenty years has seen considerable development in life story work: biography, narrative, lives, oral histories, subjectivity, telling tales – all these have now developed into a wide network of research. Indeed, whereas in *Documents-1* one of my goals was to introduce and discuss every life history study of which I was aware, today such a task would be a nonsense. There are many journals devoted to this field; books are legion; and there are also many more popular versions. So in twenty years, it could be suggested that a marginal method has come out of the closet and become a major one. I would of course be very pleased if this was true. Yet despite its prominence with certain groups – like symbolic interactionists, oral historians and some feminists – it still remains at the margins of mainstream academic research. At the same time, in the process of becoming more widespread, the whole approach has also become much more theoretically sophisticated. So the aim of this book now is much more to review and clarify some of the debates and issues that have been raised during the growth of a method: to take stock of this developing field.

If my first argument has become less in need of saying, my second argument is paradoxically needed more. In *Documents-1*, I argued for a *humanist method*: it is there in the subtitle of the book ('An introduction to the problems and literature of a humanistic method') and the case is argued throughout for a need to take seriously human subjects. Whilst humanism may never be the mainstream of sociology (for various logical reasons to do with the discipline's nature), I suggested that it had an important corrective role to play, and life stories were a key exemplar of this approach. Yet over the past twenty years, there has been a major onslaught on the very ideas of humanism: for many it has indeed become a bad word. Very few social scientists these days own up to any kind of humanism at all. Attacked by structuralists, poststructuralists, postmodernists, postcolonialists and multiculturalists alike, 'humanists' are often seen as the ideological carriers of western colonization and tyranny: symbols of the west's dominance by white men. Theoretically, the language has turned to 'discourses of the subject', 'decentred identities', 'polyvocal voices' but rarely these days to the living and breathing, embodied and feeling *human being*; this is an idea that has had its day. Yet it is slightly paradoxical that this attack should increase at the very time when talk of lives, life stories and auto/biography should be escalating. A problem for this book then is to continue to re-assess the attacks made on humanism and to see whether it is still a viable philosophical backdrop. What I will argue here is that it is still important, but in a carefully modified, cautious and critical way. Hence, this is a case for a critical humanism as a ceaselessly nagging tradition to undermine mainstream positions. To this end, I have seen the need to include an epilogue which aims to defend my position more strongly.

My third argument was concerned with showing that this humanistic concern with life stories had indeed itself a history: one that could be traced through the west's embracing of both individualism and the self; and more recently in the sociological work of the Chicago School of symbolic interactionism. Critics have alleged that this has become a canonical or foundational orthodoxy that is simply not true. They have argued for other roots: from voices hidden from history (slave narratives, for instance), from feminism (with a somewhat different slant on biography), and from other roots. I have to agree with this, whilst not dismissing my own earlier view entirely. I would now argue that there are multiple histories of the preoccupation with life story, self and auto/ biography: there is no one unified route through to our present. The work at 'Chicago' remains a major route into sociological life stories, but there are certainly other pathways to examine. Hence this book will aim to chart a range of histories rather than one.

My fourth concern was to provide something of a 'how to manual', taking the reader through five stages of life history research – in order to achieve the best possible stories. Lurking behind much of this (as some critics like Norman Denzin have noted) was a thinly disguised positivistic concern with getting at the truth. I think this was a major problem with the first edition, a matter about which I was not a little confused!

For my own position of being a symbolic interactionist clearly does not lead me to any straightforward sense of empirical reality, though empirical reality there is. The world is constituted through multiple refracted perspectives: it is indeed a 'plural world', one that is constantly changing and never fixed, and one where meanings are always being negotiated. In such a world, meanings and truth never arrive simply. Whenever I talked of the meanings of lives being 'simply accessible' I was in error: they are not. They are always accessed via a hallway of mirrors and signification best understood as complex semiotic systems composed of narratives, stories and the like (cf. Plummer, 1995a, 1995b, 1999, 2000). Hence, in this revised edition, I will be giving a much stronger focus to these problems and worries.

In short, this book has the same concerns as the first edition, and includes parts of the original text. But the debates have become sharpened and the examples have proliferated and often been updated. Further, although my key concern in both books is with sociology, this book, I hope, will be a little more interdisciplinary: I ponder aspects of psychology, anthropology, history, feminist, queer and cultural studies along the way. I am convinced more and more that whilst disciplines are much needed (each bringing their own special understandings), they must also be porous: seeping into each other to weaken boundaries and broaden understandings.

A brief comparison with the earlier edition may be in order. There are five wholly new chapters in this book: the chapters on history (Chapter 4), writing (Chapter 8), narratives (Chapter 9), memory and truth (Chapter 11) and critical humanism (Chapter 12). Chapter 2 of the original has grown into two chapters, as has the original Chapter 5. All chapters have been updated, and only Chapters 1, 2 and 3 of the original have remained recognizable as significantly unmodified though updated. The original Chapters 4 and 6 (on theory and uses) have been cut as chapters, though parts of their arguments have been moved elsewhere.

The chapters can be read individually and separately, but taken together there is a logical flow to an argument. I move from detailing the background and histories of the method, on to matters of 'doing life stories', and end by championing the method on moral and political grounds. Chapter 1 sets the scene on the need for a humanistic social studies that takes the life story seriously; and is followed by two chapters that provide examples of the method at work. Chapters 4 and 5 aim to provide some elements of the history of the method, and claim that the method is part of a wider social process we could call the rise of the Auto/Biographical Society. Chapters 6 to 10 then look at various problems in doing life history work – from establishing problems and doing interviews (Chapter 6), through analysis and theory (Chapter 7), and on to matters of writing and narrative (Chapters 8 and 9). The book then considers the issue of ethics and morality in life story work (Chapter 10).

Issues of memory and truth are raised in Chapter 11. Finally, the arguments made in Chapter 1 for a humanistic social studies are revisited and the claim is made for a new kind of critical humanism (Chapter 12).

Many changes have happened which have had an impact on this new book. Thus, when I wrote *Documents-1*, 'videos' were just making an appearance in retail outlets and the idea of a personal computer was unknown; now they are a feature of everyday life and bring their own ways of capturing life stories. Likewise, when I first wrote this book, non-sexist writing was only starting to become widespread: it now is. This means that I have corrected the text with this in mind, and I have also taken the liberty of correcting many of the quotes used. Intellectually, the wave of theory and approaches commonly known as 'postmodernism' had not really been announced; now it is omnipresent, and has to be recognized. These are just three of the many 'happenings' that I have had to taken into account. In the end what started as 'just a few changes to the original edition' has ended up as a major rewrite. I hope it will still prove to be of some value.

A book like this that enters a second edition nearly twenty years after it first appeared owes a lot of debts to a lot of people. Rather than separate them out by time, place, or priority I would simply like to provide an alphabetical listing of people who have provided support or encouragement or direct help at some point. I know I must have overlooked too many! Thanks to Chris Allen, Sue Aylott, Ted Benton, Martin Bulmer, Stan Cohen, Brenda Corti, Ian Craib, Norman Denzin, Jean Duncombe, Annabel Faraday, Dwight Fee, John Gagnon, Jeffrey Geiger, Mary Girling, Marion Haberhauer, Helen Hannick, Nerida Harrowing, Vanessa Harwood, Susie Home, Randal Kinkead, George Kolankiewicz, Elaine Leek (copyeditor), Mary McIntosh, Dennis Marsden, Harvey Molotch, Joan Murdoch, Stephen Murray, Dan Mahoney, Lydia Morris, Peter Nardi, Paul Rock, Mike Roper, Colin Samson, Beth Schneider, Suzie Scott, Bill Simon, Agnes Skambolis, Nigel South, Arlene Stein, Rob Stones, Jon Stratton, Diane Streeting, Terry Tostevin, Paul Thompson, Jeffrey Weeks, Glenn Wharton, Emma Wildsmith, Tony Woodiwiss, Stephen York (proofreader) and Jock Young. I dedicated the first edition to my mum and dad, as I do this one. And thanked my 'bestest friend in all the world', Everard Longland, then as I do now, but even more so.

Ken Plummer
Wivenhoe

Every morning before I open my eyes, I know I am in my bedroom and my bed. But if I go to sleep after lunch in the room where I work, sometimes I wake up with a feeling of childish amazement – *why am I myself*? What astonishes me, just as it astonishes a child when he [*sic*] becomes aware of his own identity, is the fact of finding myself here, and at this moment, deep in this life and not in any other. What stroke of chance has brought this about? If I look at it from outside, my birth in the first place seems unlikely. The penetration of that particular ovum by that particular spermatozoon, with its implications of the meeting of my parents and before that of their birth and the births of all their forebears, had not one chance in hundreds of millions of coming about. And it was chance, a chance quite unpredictable in the present state of science, that caused me to be a woman. From that point on, it seems to me that *a thousand different futures might have stemmed from every single movement of my past*; I might have fallen ill and broken off my studies, I might not have met Sartre; anything at all might have happened. Tossed into the world, I have been subjected to its laws and its contingencies, ruled by wills other than my own, by circumstances and by history: it is therefore reasonable for me to suggest that *I am myself contingent*. What staggers me is that at the same time I am *not* contingent. If I had not been born no question would have arisen: I have to take the fact that I do exist as my starting point. To be sure, the future of the woman I have been may turn me into someone other than myself. But in that case it would be this other woman who would be asking herself who she was. Or the person who says 'Here am I' there is no other coexisting possibility. Yet this necessary coincidence of the subject and his [*sic*] history is not enough to do away with my perplexity. My life: it is both intimately known and remote: it defines me and yet I stand outside it. Just what, precisely, is this curious object?

(Simone de Beauvoir, 1974 emphasis added)

It is difficult not to notice a curious unrest in the philosophical atmosphere of the time, a loosening of old landmarks, a softening of oppositions, a mutual borrowing on the part of systems anciently closed, and an interesting new suggestion, however vague, as if the one thing sure were the inadequacy of the extant solutions. The dissatisfaction with these seems due for the most part to a feeling that they are too abstract and academic. Life is confused and superabundant, and what the younger generation appears to crave is more of the temperament of life in its philosophy, even though it were at some cost of logical rigor and of formal purity . . .

(William James, 1997: 194)

1 For a Humanistic Way in Social Science

Now the blindness in human beings . . . is the blindness with which we are all inflicted in regard to the feelings of creatures and people different from ourselves. We are practical beings, each of us with limited functions and duties to perform. Each is bound to feel intensely the importance of his [sic] own duties and the significance of the situations that these call forth. But this feeling is in each of us a vital secret, for sympathy with which we vainly look to others. The others are too much absorbed in their own vital secrets to take an interest in ours. Hence the stupidity and injustice of our opinions, so far as they deal with the significance of their lives. Hence the falsity of our judgments, so far as they presume to deal in an absolute way on the value of other person's conditions or ideals . . .

What is the result of all these considerations . . .? It is negative in one sense, but positive in another. It absolutely forbids us to be forward in pronouncing on the meaninglessness of forms of existence other than our own; and it commands us to tolerate, respect, and indulge those whom we see harmlessly happy and interested in their own ways, however unintelligible they may be to us. Hands off: neither the whole truth nor the whole of good is revealed to any single observer, although each observer gains a partial superiority of insight from the peculiar position in which he [sic] stands . . .

(William James, 'On a certain blindness in human beings', 1899/1913)

. . . writing a personal narrative is perhaps worth a try because the prize is very great: that of some degree of transcendence of difference, of reaffirmation of common humanity . . .

(Pat Caplan, 1997: 17)

. . . although the field of qualitative research is defined by constant breaks and ruptures, there is a shifting centre to the project: the avowed humanistic commitment to study the social world from the perspective of the interacting individual . . .

(Norman Denzin, 1997: xv)

A major theme haunts this book. It is a longing for social science to take more seriously its humanistic foundations and to foster styles of thinking that encourage the creative, interpretive story tellings of lives – with all the ethical, political and self-reflexive engagements that this will bring. I will give lots of examples of such work, try to show that such concerns have a long history, that they straddle many 'disciplines' and indeed have accelerated in recent years. I will give something of the 'feel' for doing such work – though in no sense is this a 'methods primer'. And I will focus quite a lot on the difficulties of such approaches. In a way, I am simply advocating getting close to living human beings, accurately yet imaginatively picking up the way they express their understandings of the world around them, perhaps providing an analysis of such expressions, presenting them in interesting ways, and being self-critically aware of the immense difficulties such tasks bring.

This is a style which now constitutes a large and growing underbelly of social science research. Classically, almost 'canonically', it was exemplified in the 300-page 'life story' of Wladek, a Polish peasant arriving in Chicago from Poland at the start of the twentieth century and written as part of Thomas and Znaniecki's major work *The Polish Peasant in Europe and America*. But it is there too in the intensive life stories of delinquents gathered by Clifford Shaw in Chicago in the late 1920s; in the famous if controversial studies by Oscar Lewis of family life and poverty in Mexico and Puerto Rico; in the *vox populi* gathered together in the studies by Tony Parker and Studs Terkel of workers, the elderly, murderers, soldiers, lighthousekeepers, unmarried mothers and sex offenders; and in the startling films of organizational life produced by Frederick Wiseman – of schools, hospitals, welfare, army. More recently, since the 1970s, there seems to have been a renaissance and renewal of interest in the approach. As Paul Atkinson remarked in 1999: 'Having for some time been eclipsed and all but excluded from the methodological canon, the biographical perspective has enjoyed a significant revival in recent years' (Atkinson, 1999: 191; cf. Miller, 2000: vii).

Thus, the approach can now be found in the extensive local development of 'oral history', 'oral testimony' and 'popular memory groups' in many parts of the world; in the proliferating debates over 'auto/ biographical' method; in the rise of new forms such as video diaries, camrecording groups, and life story web sites; in the 'confessional' and 'self-help' literatures; in the so-called 'narrative turn' and much self-reflective 'biography from below' – ranging through post-colonial tales of enslavement through 'gay and lesbian coming out tales' and on to feminist concerns as shown in books like Carolyn Steedman's *Landscape for a Good Woman* and Mary Catherine Bateson's *Composing a Life*. It is to be found in the narratives of illness told by 'wounded story tellers' – from diaries of AIDS to 'cancer journals'. It is there in the politics of a book like *I, Rigoberta Menchú* – a young Guatemalan revolutionary who might have stood for 'all poor Guatemalans'. It is there in the writing styles of those like Robert Coles who provide a mix of psychodynamics, fieldwork and literary flare – in the five volumes of *Children of Crisis*, or his more literary excursions into *The Call of Stories*. And it is to be found in growing numbers of innovations around the personal life such as 'reminiscence work' for the elderly, 'narrative therapy' for the troubled, and 'story telling' in schools. Everywhere it seems the 'own story', the 'personal tale' is being told.

Whilst most life story research throughout the twentieth century was characterized by a lack of pomposity and pretension about methods (the researcher was merely there in the first instance to give 'voice' to other people; in some circumstances the voices may have then been interpreted), some of the newer work has been marked by an altogether more abstract turn. In a route that takes in Nietzsche's *Ecce Homo*, Freud's *The Interpretation of Dreams*, Sartre's *Words*, *Barthes by Barthes*, Derrida and many others, some of the more recent work has rendered any claims that you can simply 'tell it as it is', or 'simply record people's experiences' much more problematic. Thankfully there are still many studies which refuse to get bogged down in these abstract methodological and theoretical debates which characterize so much social science today: there are still folk for whom 'methodology' and 'theorizing' is something simply done with a firm problem in mind; for whom there is far too much talk and far too little action. I continue to think there is a great need for such studies. But at the same time, and without going too far, this whole way of thinking has been dramatically re-shaped – sometimes invigoratingly so – by the newer awareness of life story and auto/biographical form. This book will aim to walk a balance between the older tradition of action and the newer concerns with understanding the mechanisms through which stories and lives are composed.

This particular methodological style has gone by various names – personal documents, the documentary tradition, oral history; and it connects to an array of different styles of qualitative talk that have been developing over the past century (Gubrium and Holstein, 1997). But for sociologists it has most regularly, since Thomas and Znaniecki, been identified as 'human documents': 'account[s] of individual experience which reveal the individual's actions as a human agent and as a participant in social life' (Blumer, 1979: 29). These accounts embrace a wide range of forms (to be discussed in Chapters 2 and 3): letters and diaries, biographies and life histories, dreams and self-observation, essays and notes, photographs and film. There was a moment in sociological history, roughly between 1920 and 1935, when it looked as if such documents would finally establish themselves as a central sociological resource; I will discuss this early stage in its history in Chapter 5. But that moment has come and gone and, whilst it may have gathered strength elsewhere, still today most contemporary sociologists would not be expected to have even the most passing acquaintance with this research style. It remains the 'outsider' of much social science research. Who, for example, ever reads Thomas and Znaniecki these days?

The reasons for this historical neglect are not hard to find, and they echo the famous critiques of C. Wright Mills nearly half a century ago. He claimed then, and it is probably as true today, that there were two dangerous but popular trends in social science. One trend worshipped at the altar of 'methodology'; the other at the altar of 'high theory'. At the first, a special place is given to a hard-line scientific approach in human affairs; strong and generalizable, bold and countable. Whilst the much 'softer' human documents are certainly concerned with the observable facts of social life, they are rarely committed to this 'unity' of science, the search for generalizable laws and the quantification that characterizes positivism. If they find unity at all, it is with the humanities; literature and the arts not science and the experiment become the model for personal document research. At the second altar, there is the counter-prevailing trend away from positivism towards realism, rationalism and the theoretical heavens, a view that sees a concern with mere epiphenomena such as life stories as marginal. Such 'data' require well-developed theoretical problematics before they may be interpreted; for these critics, the epistemological status of personal documents becomes highly suspect because they cannot embody 'objective truth' and are mere surface scratchings. To a considerable extent, both these counter-positions – positivism and realism – converge in their refutation of the life story as a cornerstone of social science work.

More recently there has also been a trend towards post-structuralism and postmodernism, a trend that rejects any grand claims to truth and all the big stories of the recent past – such as Marxism, feminism or, indeed, humanism. Whilst some aspects of this approach certainly favour the telling of life stories, taken as a whole it is generally 'against humanism' and unsympathetic to the modernist tale of the human being. The extremely influential work of the French philosopher of ideas Michel Foucault is depressingly bleak on the value of human stories, seeing them as little more than instances of power/knowledge at work in the disciplining and surveillance of life. If he takes a life to look at – and he does in the cases of Herculine Barbine and Pierre Rivière – he does so only to see how their lives are constituted through talk, writing and discourse; and how power relations inevitably constitute this process (Foucault, 1978, 1980). He, along with others, pronounces the very end of the 'human subject' which is the abiding concern of this book. I want to look a little more closely at this rejection of the human (see also the Epilogue).

Social actions and human structures revisited

This rejection of the human subject highlights one of sociology's core contradictions: an interminable tension between the subjectively creative individual human being acting upon the world and the objectively given social structure constraining him or her. As Alan Dawe rightly commented over twenty years ago, it is a tension to be found not only through 'all varieties of Western social, political, moral and creative thought and work, from philosophy and ethics to the novel and the film', it is also 'a problem central to our everyday experience in vast industrial societies' (Dawe, 1978: 364). Just how can we reconcile our own human creativity with a coercive and dehumanizing social order? The problem is posed over and over again throughout the history of sociology from Marx to discourse theory, and almost invariably the answer is finally achieved by giving primacy to social structure over human agency; the humanistic Marx becomes the scientific Marx, the voluntaristic Parsons becomes the Parsonian System, the 'breaching' Garfinkel becomes the 'deep-ruled' Cicourel. For the contemporary theorist Anthony Giddens it lies in a process which he calls 'structuration' (Giddens, 1986). But it remains a constant tension. Nor is this surprising for:

> . . . Although sociology has many potential uses and has been enlisted in support of various political faiths, it is by the nature of its key concepts and approaches intrinsically oriented toward the group rather than the individual, toward the herd rather than the lone stray. In connection with this emphasis, sociology stresses the notion of order, of collectivity, of social organization, irrespective of political labels such as 'Left' or 'Right'. Thus sociology has an anti-liberal twist, and may even be considered as a critique of the traditional liberal idea of individualism . . . few sociologists have been distinguished by their concern for the individual as opposed to their preoccupation with social disintegration . . . A sociologist who is also a liberal–individualist, then, may encounter theoretical difficulties and contradictions. (Bramson, 1961: 16–17)

The logics of both sociology and anthropology strain towards the systems side of the individualist–collectivist tension. Indeed, some have gone so far as to eliminate 'the subject' altogether, the human being becoming an epistemological disaster (an 'idealism of the essence' (Althusser, 1969: 228) and a 'myth of bourgeois ideology' (Althusser, 1976: 52–3)) and humanism becoming little more than an ideological construct, which along with bourgeois notions like democracy and freedom permits the maintenance and reproduction of the late capitalist hegemonic state. There is no human being independent of the material and ideological forces that construct 'it'. In such views, 'the final goal of human sciences is not to constitute man, but to dissolve him' (Levi-Strauss, 1966).

Dissolve the subject! Although such statements are supported by very sophisticated arguments, they do bring with them the spectre of a dehumanized collectivist idealism which can kill off any concern for the concrete joys and suffering of active, breathing, bodily human beings; they bring with them a denial of the root tension that has existed within sociology since its earliest days by co-opting 'the subject' into an ideology; they harbour a myopia which can deny insights of other approaches and contrary discipline. In short, they encourage a premature theoretical closure and a tottering towards sure, safe absolutism, denying the role of active human beings and their lived experiences. (An important critique and defence of humanism may be found in E.P. Thompson, 1978: 193–399.) Again, it is the Marxist inspired C. Wright Mills who provides the classic humanistic statement about the need for a triple concern with biography, structure and history – one we do well to keep in mind:

> Always keep your eyes open to the image of man – the generic notion of . . . human nature – which by your work you are assuming and implying; and also to the image of history – your notion of how history is being made. In a word, continually work out and revise your views of the problems of history, the problems of biography, and the problems of a social structure in which biography and history intersect. Keep your eyes open to the varieties of individuality, and to the modes of epochal change. Use what you see and what you imagine as the clues to your study of the human variety . . . know that many personal troubles cannot be solved merely as troubles, but must be understood in terms of public issues – and in terms of the problems of history making. Know that the human meaning of public issues must be revealed by relating them to personal troubles and to the problems of individual life. Know that the problems of social science, when adequately formulated, must include both troubles and issues, both biography and history, and the range of their intricate relations. Within that range the life of the individual and the making of society occur; and that within that range the sociological imagination has its chance to make a difference in the quality of human life in our time. (Mills, 1970: 247–8)

This triple focus, on biography, history and structure, which is sociology's heritage, can be denied by an exclusive focus on structure; human joy and suffering can simply be left out. But it is in deep opposition to such anti-humanist views that the main justification for this small study lies. For to resolve the central contradiction of sociology by taking one side and denying the other – of championing system over agency, discourse over doing, structure over consciousness – runs the risk of developing accounts of the world that are simply wild and wrong, untempered as they are with the concrete historical yet human experiences out of which societies are invariably composed.

Sociology is not alone in these divides. There are parallel splits and movements in both psychology and anthropology to remove the human subject – classically from Skinner's behaviourism and Lacan's structuralism to the structural anthropologies of Levi-Strauss. Interestingly, again, in recent years there have been strong movements within each of these disciplines to restore the human and the human being. In psychology, for example, a strand of thought stretching back to at least William James with his concern for the 'tough' and 'tender' minded has been furthered in the work of Jerome Bruner's 'two modes of thought': a logico-scientific one which stresses 'formal mathematical systems of description and explanation', and an 'imaginative, narrative' mode which 'leads to good stories, gripping drama, believable (though not necessarily 'true') historical accounts' (Bruner, 1986: ch. 2). Likewise, the early personality studies of Henry Murray, Gordon Allport and Abraham Maslow, championing the study of personal and human lives, has seen more recently a concern within psychology to recognize the 'duality of human experience' between agentic (or action) and communion (or social) theories (Bakan, 1969, 1996). And in the 'feminist' psychology of Carol Gilligan and her colleagues we start to sense a whole world of analysis rooted in the complexities of narratives, stories and an attentive listening to the voices of connection and care; in contrast with earlier more abstract theories of human development (Gilligan, 1982, 1990). In anthropology too, there has been growing interest in autobiography, stories and 'the transcendent individual' – whereby 'the particularities of individualized experiences are not eclipsed by generalization, or otherwise abstracted, reduced, typified by totalization (Rapport, 1997: 29).

I must be clear. I am not making a case here for a sociology without society; or for an imaginative, narrative psychology alone; or for a preoccupation with individuals or individualism. It is not my task to challenge the helpfulness of much of the mainstream of social science in its various guises. Nor am I rejecting many structural accounts, or 'scientific' and realist modes of thinking. Certainly the concrete human must always be located within this historically specific culture – for 'the individual' becomes a very different animal under different social orders. This is not a book that champions looking at the wonderful solitary human being: my conception of the human subjects and their experiences is one that cannot divorce them from the social, collective, cultural, historical moment. But in the face of the inherent society–individual dualism of sociology, I argue that there must surely always remain a strand of work that highlights the active human subject? And in the face of a constant tendency towards the abstract and the linear in modern thought, surely there is also always a need for the creative, imaginative and concrete? The need for a bit of a protest against the 'typical, the classifiable' (Jackson, 1989: 2)? The need to see experience and life as a fluctual praxis, always in flow and ever messy. These may strain against major tendencies, but to keep them in mind will be a positive, if minor, check on the worst excesses of the human sciences. Much of this echoes the new sensibility arising through postmodern thought – a concern with the local and a shunning of grander tendencies. I will return to all this later.

Reclaiming the humanities for the 'human sciences'

So how are we to proceed? In his study of *Sociology as an Art Form*, Robert Nisbet reflects 'How different things would be . . . if the social sciences at the time of their systematic formation in the nineteenth century had taken the arts in the same degree they took the physical science as models'

(Nisbet, 1976: 16). More recently, Pierre Bourdieu notes that while there may be 'significant differences between sociology and literature . . . we should be careful not to turn them into an irreconcilable antagonism . . . [Sociologists] can find in literary works research clues and orienations that the censorship specific to the scientific field tend to forbid to them or to hide from them' (Bourdieu and Wacquant, 1992: 206). Many sociologists have indeed taken the humanities and literature very seriously in their work. Yet from most angles it does seem that the two cultures have grown irrevocably apart: facts, generalizations and abstractions have become divorced from the imaginative, the inspirational and the idiographic, and – for all its critical pondering on 'positivism' – it is clear for all to see the path by which sociology has been most moulded. Its major journals speak to abstractions, hypotheses, explanations, proof, samples, theory, objectivity, distance – and although it is constantly at war with the enemy of positivism, in the very battle it reveals what ultimately matters to it. Nobody wages war with Dostoevsky or Dickens, Balzac or Bellow, Austen or Auden. Their mode of experiencing, feeling, interpreting and writing sets no standards, provides no models, makes no sense to a discipline that has always aspired to science. As Arthur Bochner and Carolyn Ellis have recently remarked in the introduction to a study of 'fiction and social research', we need to

> explore the intersection of fiction and social research, offering a corrective to the traditional polarization of the literary and the scientific . . . In short stories, ethnographic fictions, poems, plays and other narrative forms, [we should] experiment with modes of storytelling that consciously attempt to bridge the gaps between author and reader, between fact and truth, between cool reason and hot passion, between the personal and the collective, and between the drama of social life, and the legitimized modes of representing it . . . *No longer [should] we see literary and personal genres of writing as too subjective, too soft and too emotional to qualify as legitimate social research, but rather we might judge monographs lacking literary and subjective qualities as too impersonal, too distanced, and too unimaginative to be taken seriously.* (Ellis and Bochner in Banks and Banks, 1998: 7–8, emphasis added)

From all this, we might say that there are then 'two orders . . . separate but unequal' (Gouldner, 1962: 210). Such differences (documented in Table 1.1) are very broad: it is the chasm between a *compassion* for the sufferer and a *neutrality* towards him or her; between looking inside, exploring, feeling and imagining, or recording externals, measuring, generalizing and theorizing. The images are starkly opposed: one 'falls in love', the other 'observes love'. In a still powerful display of this contrast, *Redeeming the Sin*, Audrey Borenstein remarks:

> Just as genes are not always expressed in material form, so, too, the silent workings of feelings and thought are often hidden from appearance. From the outside looking in, an observer might see a 'common' condition: a son is killed

in Vietnam, a daughter's mind is destroyed by LSD, a woman is widowed, a man becomes subject to mandatory retirement, there is a divorce. Yet, in interior life, what happens to one is unique. Life histories, like snowflakes, are never of the same design. The social terrain surveyed by the sociologist is criss-crossed with pathways, each with its crusaders beckoning, its pied pipers and sirens making their invitational music. But it is not given to the social scientist to say which path is to be followed. Nor is it given to anyone to say what another shall make of the journey. In inner life, each of us is solitary . . . Wherever one begins, the task is always the same: to follow the labyrinthine corridors between inner and outer reality, without losing one's integrity, one's selfhood, in either. (1978: 30)

The sensitive scientific sociologist has generally acknowledged the need for the inner to be scrutinized with the outer, and the unique with the general (cf. Bruyn, 1966); but in the end, it is always clear that the final solutions lie in grasping general laws from the outside. Ultimately, to side with the uniquely subjective is to dismantle the model of social science – and to favour the model of the humanities. Here again, as in the structure–action dichotomy, sociology is lodged in a twist – and the logic of sociology is ultimately to side with science. But here again, there must be virtue in sustaining an undercurrent of sociological work that strains against the dominant tendencies and persistently reminds the scientific sociologist that for all his or her neat abstractions, concrete human beings may not tidily bend before them.

TABLE 1.1 **A bridgeable divide?**

	Towards the humanities	Towards the sciences
Foci	Unique and idiographic Human-centred The inner: subjective, meaning, feeling experience	General and nomothetic Structure-centred The outer: objective, 'things', events facts
Epistemology	Phenomenalist Relational/relativist Perspectivist/pragmatist	Realist Absolutist/essentialist Logical positivist
Task	Interpret, understand Describe, observe Appreciate	Causal explanation Measure Theorize
Style	'Soft', 'warm' Imaginative Valid-'real', 'rich' Personal research	'Hard', 'cold' Systematic Reliable, 'replicable' Large-scale funding
Theory	Inductive and grounded 'Story telling'	Deductive and abstract 'Operationalism'
Values	Ethically and politically committed Egalitarianism	Ethically and politically neutral 'Expertise and elites'

Evoking the humanities – not the sciences – as an imagery to think about social life, we can find many pathways: poetry and poetics, drama and performance, portraits and photography, video and film, narrative and stories. Turning to these could provide a very different model for the human sciences. I wonder, for example, if it goes too far to suggest that many of our earlier literary classics are versions of ethnography and life story? Long before the days of social science, many of the most astute social observers were surely the 'authors' of their day? The stories of Dante, Boccaccio, Chaucer push us to see the lives of the day told in the words of their time: and often, as in the case of the twenty-four pilgrims in Geoffrey Chaucer's (1340–1400) *The Canterbury Tales* wandering the English countryside on the way to Thomas à Becket's shrine, telling the stories of their lives. Throughout the second millennium these tales continued being told, and the history of writing is the history of telling stories: from the grand epic tales lodged in the past of Milton, through to the satires of Voltaire, Rousseau or Diderot's *Encyclopaedia* (1751–76); and on to the age of the novel, where big sweeping tales are told in the first person and seen as 'the life and adventures of' many folk. From Daniel Defoe's *Life and Adventures of Mrs Duncan Campbell* (1720), through Henry Fielding's *Tom Jones* (1749) and *Joseph Andrews* (1742), and on to Tobias Smollett's *Roderick Random* (1748), *Frederick Pickle* (1751) and *Sir Launcelot Graves* (1762), we keep finding the tales of lives reflecting their times. And then there is Balzac, Dickens or even Proust? Or sensitive novels such as George Eliot's *Middlemarch* (1870–2), which weaves its ethnographic web – a 'keen vision and feeling of all ordinary human life' (cf. Clark, 1997). The list could go on and on. None of these, of course, is a real life story: they are all fictions. But they may well harbour clues and signs for the modern humanistic social 'science'.

A very engaging metaphor for social science has to be that of 'drama'. It is probably used to greatest effect in the studies of Erving Goffman (1922–82), whose *The Presentation of Self in Everyday Life* (1959) provides a kind of handbook for a 'dramaturgical sociology' – an analysis of the workings of day-to-day interactions, selves and situations as a mode of stagecraft (Goffman, 1959). In this it re-works some celebrated ideas of Shakespeare:

All the world's a stage,
And all the men and women merely players:
They have their exits and their entrances;
And one man in his time plays many parts,
His acts being seven ages . . . (*As You Like It*, Act 2: scene vii)

We could also turn to Luigi Pirandello's *Six Characters in Search of an Author* (1922), to Nikolas Evreinoff's idea of 'theotocracy', or Kenneth Burke's 'dramatism' to see that social and political life is a perpetually scripted and enacted drama. More recently, Lyman and Scott's (1975) *The*

Drama of Social Reality treats the reader to ponderings on Shakespeare's *Macbeth*, *Hamlet*, *Troilus and Cressida* and *Antony and Cleopatra* as a baseline for discussing society; John Gagnon and William Simon (1973) suggest the telling idea that our sexualities are scripted; and Victor Turner (1981) sees drama as a major metaphor for anthropology. And the wider imagery of performance (and performativity) has also started to shape social analysis (e.g. Butler, 1991). All this can now be closely linked to 'performance theory', where performance art of various kinds (body sculptures, choreography, body art and even 'sex work') can be seen as bridges to linguistics, anthropology, ethnography, sociology (cf. Carlson, 1996). We start to enter worlds where 'good ethnographic theater stirs the critical, emotional imagination of the audience' (Denzin, 1997: 97).

From the perspective of this book, my entré into the humanities comes through the metaphors of 'narrative' and 'story' – two images with a wider currency these days. In a now very famous passage, Roland Barthes (1977: 79) caught the pervasiveness of narrative:

> The narratives of the world are numberless. Narrative is first and foremost a prodigious variety of genres, themselves distributed amongst different substances . . . Able to be carried by articulate language, spoken or written, fixed or moving images, gestures, and the ordered mixture of these substances, narrative is present in myth, legend, fable, tale, novella, epic, history, tragedy, drama, comedy, mime, paintings . . . stained glass windows, cinema, comics, news item, conversation. Moreover, under this almost infinite diversity of forms, narrative is present in every age, in every place, in every society; it begins with the very history of mankind and there nowhere is nor has been a people without narrative . . . Like life itself, it is there, international, transhistorical, transcultural.

This 'narrative turn' is well recognized across the social sciences. In psychology, there has been the emergence of 'historical psychology' (Sarbin, 1986), 'constructivist psychology' (Gergen, 1999) a concern with story-telling and 'life as narrative' (Bruner, 1987), with 'storied lives' (Rosenwald and Ochberg, 1992) and narrative itself (Polkinghorne, 1988). In psychoanalysis, the distinction has been clearly worked through between 'historical truth' and 'narrative truth', and there has been a growing interest in 'narrative means to therapeutic ends' (Mair, 1989; Schafer, 1992; White and Epston, 1990). And within sociology (Atkinson, 1990; Maines, 1993; Plummer, 1995b; Van Maanen, 1988), anthropology (Davies, 1999: 34; Rosaldo, 1989), history (White, 1987), law (on legal story telling see the special issue of *Michigan Law Review*, 1989) and even economics (McCloskey, 1985), stories and narratives have become also self-conscious metaphors. These days, and with good reason, the idea of narrative – and its close companion 'story' – have become major concerns in the human sciences, and they will appear as guiding motifs regularly throughout this book.

Symbolic interactionism and the rise of a late or post modern sensibility

The interest in 'stories' and 'narratives' is often linked to the so-called postmodern turn, a turn which, ironically, is usually seen to be strongly anti-humanist. Over the past fifteen years or so (but in actuality since the earlier part of the twentieth century), there have been steady changes in many social forms – from architecture and literature, through social theory and analysis, and on to culture in general, and society in particular – which have been increasingly identified as 'postmodern'. I see most of this as simply accelerating many of the changes that were taking place in the modern capitalist world ('to make it new'), and hence it may be more appropriate to view this as a 'late modern turn' rather than a postmodern one (cf. Giddens, 1991). At the heart of all this is the breakdown of a traditional form of society, one which was usually authoritarian with strong religious commitments to an overarching belief system. Bit by bit we see the arrival of a more provisional world, one where there is an increased sensitivity to diversities, differences, differentiations – to what has been called the 'pluralization ethos' (Connolly, 1995). In this view the world becomes less dominated by generalities and 'master narratives', and there is a turn towards 'local cultures' and their 'multiplicty of stories'. Gianni Vattimo captures postmodernism as

> . . . the liberation of differences, of local elements, of what could generally be called dialect. With the demise of the idea of a central rationality of history, the world of generalised communication explodes like a multiplicity of 'local' rationalities – ethnic, sexual, religious, cultural or aesthetic minorities – that finally speak up for themselves. They are no longer repressed and cowed into silence by the idea of a single pure form of humanity that must be realised irrespective of particularity and individual finitude, transience and contingency . . . (1992: 8–9)

All this has created a newish approach in social science which Rob Stones has suggested takes three major forms:

> Postmodernists argue, respectively, for: (1) respecting the existence of a plurality of perspectives, as against a notion that there is one single truth from a priviliged perspective; (2) local, contextual studies in place of grand narratives; and (3) an emphasis on disorder, flux and openness, as opposed to order, continuity and restraint. (1996: 22)

I think this is a useful characterization (though there are many, many others: see, for examples: Denzin, 1997; Dickens and Fontana, 1994; Gubrium and Holstein, 1997: ch. 5) and I think Rob Stones (1996) is also right to point out that if taken to extremes such a position harbours many dangers (not least that of an extreme relativism). But what we find here is really compatible with the humanistic arguments I will be making in this book – that is, the need for *grounded, multiple and local studies of lives in all their rich flux and change*. Further, as I see it, there is little in this characterization that has not been prefigured in debates and discussions within the theory of symbolic interactionism over the past one hundred years. Indeed, this description of postmodern theory even contains the words of interactionism. It was William James who talked of a 'plurality of perspectives' and we find in the work of John Dewey the claims that we live in 'a universe which is not all closed and settled, which is still in some respects indeterminate and in the making . . . an open universe in which uncertainty, choice, hypotheses, novelties, and possibilities are naturalised . . .' (1991).

Many symbolic interactionists, then, have sensed this broad affinity between some of the themes of postmodern thought and their own theory, and hence probably alone amongst the more 'traditional sociologies' (who have tended to reject it) symbolic interactionists have over the past decade had ongoing debates with it. As Dmitri Shalin remarked: 'The issues that symbolic interactionism has highlighted since its inception and that assured its maverick status in American sociology bear some uncanny resemblance to the themes championed by postmodernist thinkers' (1993: 303). He shows how both reject subject–object dualism and the over-reliance on positivism–scientism whilst championing 'the marginal, local, everyday, heterogeneous and indeterminate' alongside the 'socially constructed, emergent and plural' (p. 304). Likewise, David Maines has argued that 'symbolic interactionism, by virtue of its interpretive centre, finds an easy affinity with much of postmodernism, but, because of that same centre, has no need for it'. He finds valuable the resurgence of interest in interpretive work, the importance now given to writing 'as intrinsic to method', the concern over multiple forms of presentation, and the reclaiming of value positions and 'critical work' (Maines, 1996: 325). But he is unhappy with the wider and wilder positions of the postmodern project – when they start simply highlighting the new, or claiming to abandon all claims to truth.

This is all taken much further in the work of the main champion of the link between symbolic interactionism and postmodern theory, Norman K. Denzin. He has been at the forefront to defend postmodernism within sociology/cultural studies and symbolic interactionism in numerous books and papers (e.g. Denzin, 1989, 1991, 1992, 1995, 1996, 1997). He argues that researchers should take sides; should study experiences that are biographically meaningful for the researcher; should attend to pivotal turning point experiences; should uncover and display models of truth, accuracy and authenticity; should privilege languages of feelings and emotions over those of rationality and science; should examine multiple discourses and should write multivoiced polyphonic texts, which includes the researchers' own experience. Further, suggesting that social science writing has passed through various waves, he sees it as now entering a new stage where there surely is a 'crisis of representation'.

But this must lead to a renewed passionate commitment to a self-reflexive, moral and political project in the human and social sciences. Much of the past work has seriously failed us. He sees the need for new and experimental modes of seeing the social world and writing about it. He sees cinema, television and other forms of electronic culture as new forms of reality demanding our attention. And he advocates a strong humanistic commitment merging with a radical and liberal politics of action linked to feminist, queer, postcolonial concerns. It is important to note that this is far from the relativist impasse which some suggest postmodernism leads us towards. Indeed, what is suggested here is a strong political linkeage – a broad affinity – between a post- (or late) modern sensibility, a humanistic orientation, and the theoretical perspective of symbolic interactionism grounded in pragmatism (cf. Plummer, 2000). It is an argument to which I will return later.

An opening conclusion: a critical humanistic social science

For the time being, I wish to call this corrective social and human approach to both society and knowledge a *critical humanism*, and it has at least five central criteria. First, it must pay tribute to *human subjectivity and creativity* – showing how individuals respond to social constraints and actively assemble social worlds. It must deal with concrete human experiences – talk, feelings, actions – through their *social and economic organization* (and not just their inner, psychic or biological structuring). It must show a naturalistic *'intimate familiarity'* with such experiences – abstractions untempered by close involvement are ruled out. There must be a self-awareness by the sociologist of their ultimate *moral and political role* in moving towards a social structure in which there is less exploitation, oppression and injustice and more creativity, diversity and equality. Recognizing an inherent ambivalence and ambiguity in human life (and that there can be no 'final solutions' only damage limitations in public policy), it walks a tightrope between a situated ethics of care (recognition, tolerance, respect for persons, love) and a situated ethics of justice (redistribution, equality). And finally, in all of this it espouses an epistemology of *radical, pragmatic empiricism* which takes seriously the idea that knowing – always limited and partial – should be grounded in experience (cf. Jackson, 1989). One of the founders of this tradition of thought, William James, puts it very well:

> Pragmatism reflects a perfectly familiar attitude in philosophy, the empiricist attitude, but it represents it, as it seem to me, both in a more radical and in a less objectionable form than it has ever assumed. A pragmatist turns his [*sic*] back resolutely and once for all upon a lot of inveterate habits dear to professional philosophers. He turns away from abstraction and insufficiency,

from verbal solutions, had a priori reasons, from fixed principles, closed systems, and pretended absolutes and origins. He [sic] turns towards concreteness and adequacy, towards facts, towards actions, and towards power. That means the empiricist temper regnant and the rationalist temper sincerely given up. It means the open air and possibilities of nature, as against dogma, artificiality and the pretense of finality in truth. (James, 1907/1955: 379)

Much more will be said about critical humanism in the epilogue, but this provisional listing will guide us through the book. It is open to detailed extension and revision, but it is hard to imagine a humanistic sociology or analysis that is not at least minimally committed to these criteria.

Guide to further reading

(Full references are given in the Bibliography at the end of the book.)

Important general guides to current debates in **qualitative method** include Jaber Gubrium and James Holstein's *The New Language of Qualitative Method* (1997), which – read in connection with Norman Denzin and Yvonne Lincoln's monumental edited collection *The Handbook of Qualitative Research* (1994), Norman Denzin's *Interpretive Ethnography* (1997) and John Cresswell's *Qualitative Inquiry and Research Design: Choosing among Five Traditions* (1998) will together provide an excellent overview of the field at the end of the twentieth century. There is also much of help in feminist methodology that complements the approach taken here: see, for example, most recently Marjorie L. DeVault's *Liberating Method: Feminism in Social Research* (1999).

Opening introductions to the field of **life documents and life story research** include Norman Denzin's *Interpretive Biography* (1989), Robert Atkinson's *The Life Story Interview* (1998), William McKinley Runyan's *Life Histories and Psychobiography* (1982) and Paul Thompson's *The Voice of the Past* (3rd edn, 2000).

The classic introductions to **humanistic method** in social science are to be found in Peter Berger's *Invitation to Sociology* (1966) and C.W. Mills's, *The Sociological Imagination* (1970). The latter contains a diatribe against the tendencies in sociology towards both grand theory (which now moves in the name of post-structuralism not Parsons) and abstracted empiricism (which remains strong). A key statement of humanism in sociology is Alfred McLung Lee's *Sociology for Whom* (1978), and a very central text on methodology and humanism is S.T. Bruyn's, *The Human Perspective in Sociology*, which although published in only 1966, seems to have already become a forgotten classic. It is a gold mine of analysis and advice and strongly recommended (even though its main technical concern is participant observation). More recent espousals of imagination and humanism in sociology include David Morgan's Presidential Address to the British Sociological Association 'Sociological imaginings

and imagining sociology: bodies, auto/biographies and other mysteries'
(1998); Harvey Molotch's 'Going out' (1994), and Charles Lemert's
excellent introduction *Social Things* (1997). For anthropology some of the
humanist arguments are played out in Nigel Rapport's *Transcendent
Individual: Towards a Literary and Liberal Anthropology* (1997), although I
think he takes his argument too far in almost denying the role of the
social. Another important contribution to this debate is Michael Jackson's
defence of radical empiricism – *Paths Toward a Clearing: Radical
Empiricism and Ethnographic Inquiry* (1989).

On the **humanities and social science** in general see Wolf Lepenies,
Between Literature and Science: the Rise of Sociology (1988); Robert Nisbet,
Sociology as an Art Form (1976); Audrey Borenstein, *Redeeming the Sin*
(1978); Pierre Bourdieu and Loic J.D. Wacquant, *An Invitation to Reflexive
Sociology* (1992) esp. pp. 202–15; and Anna and Stephen Banks (eds),
Fiction and Social Research: By Ice or Fire (1998). A delightful 'coffee table'
guide to literature is Malcolm Bradbury's *The Atlas of Literature* (1996).

On **pragmatism**, the foundational text is William James's *Pragmatism*
(1907). His collected works have been published by University of
Chicago Press (1997; originally published by Random House, 1967). A
useful overview of the Big Four – Mead, James, Dewey and Peirce – can
be found in Scheffler's *Four Pragmatists* (1974). Contemporary accounts of
pragmatism include Giles Dunn, *Thinking Across the American Grain*
(1992) and Morris Dickstein's edited *The Revival of Pragmatism* (1998).

On **symbolic interactionism and postmodernism**, see Norman K.
Denzin, *Symbolic Interactionism and Cultural Studies* (1992). The classic
source for interactionism is Herbert Blumer, *Symbolic Interactionism*
(1969); I have collected papers on it in Ken Plummer, *Symbolic Interactionism*, Vols 1 & 2 (1991) as well as analysing its recent manifestations
in Ken Plummer, 'Symbolic interactionism at the end of the twentieth
century' in Bryan S. Turner (ed.), *The Blackwell Companion to Social Theory*
(2nd edn, 2000). On postmodernist social theory, a good introductory
guide is George Ritzer's *Postmodern Social Theory* (1997). On **Queer
theory**, see Eve Kosofsky Sedgwick's *Epistemology of the Closet* (1990) and
Steven Seidman's *Difference Troubles: Queering Social Theory and Sexual
Politics* (1997).

2 Sighting a Diversity of Life Stories: From Resource to Topic

1712–1719: I have resolved on an entrerprise which has no precedent and which, once complete, will have no imitator. My purpose is to display to my kind a portrait in every way true to my nature, and the man I shall portray will be myself. Simply myself. I know my heart and understand my fellow man. But I am made unlike any one I have ever met; I will even venture to say that I am like no one in the whole world. I may be no better, but at least I am different. Whether Nature did well or ill in breaking the mould in which she formed me, is a question which can only be resolved after the reading of my book. Let the last trump sound when it will, I shall come forward with this work in my hand, to present myself before my Sovereign Judge and proclaim aloud: 'Here is what I have done . . .

(Jean-Jacques Rousseau, opening lines to his *Confessions* . . ., 1781)

In the life history is revealed, as in no other way, the inner life of the person, his [*sic*] moral struggles, his successes and failures in securing his destiny in a world too often at variance with his hopes and ideals.

(Ernest Burgess, as quoted by Clifford Shaw, 1966: 4)

The world is crammed full of human, personal documents. People keep diaries, send letters, make quilts, take photos, dash off memos, compose auto/biographies, construct web sites, scrawl graffiti, publish their memoirs, write letters, compose CVs, leave suicide notes, film video diaries, inscribe memorials on tombstones, shoot films, paint pictures, make tapes and try to record their personal dreams. All of these expressions of personal life are hurled out into the world by the millions and can be of interest to anyone who cares to seek them out. They are all in the broadest sense 'documents of life', and the aim of the next few chapters is to explore a little of this diversity and to see what they have to offer.

One feature of this diversity is the sheer range of approaches and disciplines with divergent aims that take life documents seriously. There is the oral historian, often using documents to throw some light upon the past; the psychiatrist using documents to probe the dynamic repressed unconscious; the anthropologist making the prime target of investigation the culture of which the document is a part; and the video diarist trying to visually record a life fragment. For the sociologist, the human document is 'an account of individual experience which reveals the individual's actions as a human agent and as a participant in social life' (Blumer, 1939: 29); for the literary biographer the prime task is to explore the relationship of the self to the past life and the outer world; for the genealogist, as in Alex Haley's *Roots* (1977), the task is to dig out the ancestral history (Steel, 1980); and for the 'new autobiographer' the task is to explore something of the inner storying of a life (Rainer, 1998). Sometimes the approach is broadly interdisciplinary, attempting to establish general criteria for the appraisal of life histories that cross academic boundaries – particularly those of sociology, anthropology, medicine and psychiatry (Dollard, 1935). Sometimes it is simply eclectic – many literary biographies for example nowadays have to be heavily researched and rely on 'psychological, medical, economic, political, geographical and religious' materials (Gittings, 1978, ch. 2: 63). Sometimes, too, the discipline may be a new hybrid: like the 'literature of fact' (Weber, 1981) where real life events may be fictionalized, as in Truman Capote's *In Cold Blood* (1966), or in the vox populi of simply recorded voices, as in the works of 'popular' oral historians Tony Parker and Studs Terkel. Although each of these approaches may differ, they all have in common a concern to present the subjective point of view of a participant. There are many definitions of the field, but Robert Redfield's sensitizing one will suffice:

> the essential element in every definition is the same: a human or personal document is one in which the human and personal characteristics of somebody who is in some sense the author of the document find expression, so that through its means the reader of the document comes to know the author and his or her views of events with which the document is concerned. (Redfield, in Gottschalk et al., 1942: vii)

I am taking the vagueness and openness of Redfield's classic statement to be a virtue, allowing this book to move freely between a range of contrasting forms. It is, however, clear what they are not: they refuse to be social scientists' own second-order constructs – accounts of accounts – that claim to be external and objective truth (though this is not to say that life documents cannot ultimately be used for such purposes). They are all first-order accounts which attempt to enter the subjective world of informants, taking them seriously on their own terms and thereby providing first hand, intimately involved accounts of life. The prime example of this is the life story.

The varieties of life stories

At the heart of personal document research is the life story – an account of one person's life in his or her own words. Life stories come through many blurred sources: biographies, autobiographies, letters, journals, interviews, obituaries. They can be written by a person as their own life story (autobiography) or as a fiction by themselves; they can be the story coaxed out of them by another, or indeed their 'own story' told by someone else (as in biography). They can exist in many forms: long and short, past and future, specific and general, fuzzy and focused, surface and deep, realist and romantic, ordinary and extraordinary, modernist and postmodernist. And they are denoted by a plethora of terms: life stories, life histories, life narratives, self stories, 'mystories', autobiographies, auto/biographies, oral histories, personal testaments, life documents. (For a discussion of this diversity, see Denzin, 1989: 27–49.) At its simplest, a life story is

> the story a person chooses to tell about the life he or she has lived, told as completely and honestly as possible. What is remembered of it, and what the teller wants to know of it, usually as a result of a guided interviewer by another. (Atkinson, 1998: 8)

For Robert Atkinson, it is 'a fairly complete narrating of one's entire experience of life as a whole, highlighting the most important aspects'. Although this is a good, practical, working definition of a social science life story – and one that clearly has guided Atkinson's own work – he soon reveals the complexities of this when he adds: 'In a life story interview, the interviewee is a storyteller, the narrator of the story being told, whereas the interviewer is a guide, or director, in this process. The two together are collaborators, composing, constructing a story the teller can be pleased with' (1998: 9). As soon as this language is entered – directors, narrating, stories, collaborators, constructions, composing – a more complex account of life stories is under way (and one that I will develop throughout this book). Liz Stanley even finds that so many of the most common distinctions that are made – for example between biography and autobiography – are false: 'telling apart fiction, biography and autobiography is no easy matter' (Stanley, 1992: 125). Because of this she carves out yet another word: 'auto/biography' – 'a term which refuses any easy distinction between biography and autobiography, instead recognising their symbiosis' (Stanley, 1992: 127). Whilst I like this term and will use it often, my aim in this chapter is to make a few rough and ready distinctions within life story research before making my account more complicated.

The long and the short

An initial simple but helpful contrast is between 'long' and 'short' life stories. *Long life stories* are perhaps seen as the key to the method – the full-length book account of one person's life in his or her own words. By contrast, *short life stories* take much less time (half an hour to three hours or so), tend to be more focused, and are usually published as one in a series.

The long life story   Usually, this is gathered over a longish period of time with gentle guidance from the researcher, the subject either writing down episodes of life or tape-recording them. At its richest, it will be backed up with keeping diaries, intensive observation of the subject's life, interviews with friends, the perusals of letters and photographs. It is, of course, a purely subjective account – a detailed *perspective* on the world – and requires serious examination on its own terms. It does not matter if the account can later be shown to be false in particulars – most accounts, even so-called 'scientific' ones, are context-bound and speak to certain people, times and circumstances. What matters, therefore, in life history research is the facilitation of as full a subjective view as posible, not the naive delusion that one has trapped the bedrock of truth. Given that most social science seeks to tap the 'objective', the life history reveals, like nothing else can, the subjective realm.

Symbolically at any rate, the first sociological use of life histories in this way is generally credited to the publication of W.I. Thomas and F. Znaniecki's massive *The Polish Peasant in Europe and America*, first published between 1918 and 1920, which makes the famous claim that life histories 'constitute the perfect type of sociological material' (Thomas and Znaniecki, 1918–21; 1958: 1832–3). One volume of this study provides a 300-page story of a Polish emigré to Chicago, Wladek Wisniewski, written in three months before the outbreak of the First World War. In his story, Wladek describes the early phases of his life in the Polish village of Lubotyn where he was born, the son of a rural blacksmith. He talks of his early schooling, his entry to the baker's trade, his migration to Germany to seek work, and his ultimate arrival in Chicago and his plight there. Twenty years on this 'classic' study was honoured by the Social Science Research Council 'as the finest exhibit of advanced sociological research and theoretical analysis' (cf. Blumer, 1979: vi; Plummer, 1991). Following from this classic work, life histories became an important tool in the work of both Chicago and Polish sociologists (cf. Shaw, 1931, 1938, 1966; and Chalasinski in Bertaux, 1981: 120). Some of the major instances of this approach are chronicled in Table 2.1.

Other disciplines have their life stories too. Within anthropology there is a well-established tradition of presenting the fullest accounts of Native Americans and their problems of acculturation. Paul Radin's Winnebago autobiography of *Crushing Thunder* (Radin, 1926) is generally taken to mark 'the beginning of rigorous work in this field' (Kluckhohn, 1942: 87), and was followed by many others (see Table 2.2). In psychology, the situation is a little different. Whilst there has been an interest in 'life course' development and life stories, the major interest has been in presenting biographies to the reader not as personal narratives but as 'translations' by the analyst or psychologist. Thus, Freud's accounts of

TABLE 2.1 Some 'classics' of social science life stories

Agnes	A male to female hermaphrodite (Garfinkel, 1967)
Mrs Abel	A woman dying of terminal cancer (Strauss and Glaser, 1977)
Herculine Barbin	A nineteenth-century hermaphrodite (Foucault, 1980)
Chic Conwell	A professional thief (Sutherland, 1937)
Jane Fry	A male to female transsexual (Bogdan, 1974)
Pierre Rivière	A nineteenth-century French family murderer (Foucault, 1978)
The Martin Brothers	Five delinquent brothers in Chicago in the 1920s (Shaw, 1938)
The Martinez Family	A poor rural Mexican family (Lewis, 1964)
The Sanchez Family	A poor urban Mexican family (Lewis, 1979a)
Stanley	A Chicago delinquent in the 1920s (Shaw, 1966)
James Sewid	A Kwakiutl Indian (Spradley, 1969)
Sidney	Another Chicago delinquent (a rapist) (Shaw, 1931)
Vincent Swaggi	A professional fence (Klockars, 1975)
Don Talayesa	A Hopi Indian chief (Simmons, 1942)
Wladek Wisniewski	A Polish emigré to Chicago (Thomas and Znaniecki, 1958)

TABLE 2.2 Some classic anthropological life stories

1920	Paul Radin, *The Autobiography of a Winnebago Indian*, later published as *Crashing Thunder* (1926)
1938	Walter Dyk, *Son of Old Man Hat: A Navaho Autobiography*: a classic and still quite a lively read
1942	Leo W. Simmons, *Sun Chief: The Autobiography of a Hopi Indian*
1960	Joseph B. Casagrande, *In the Company of Men: Twenty Portraits of Anthropological Informants*: a collection of 20 life histories recorded by well known anthropologists
1960	Sidney Mintz, *Worker in the Cane*: a life history of a Puerto Rican sugar cane worker
1961	Theodore Kroeber Ishi, *In Two Worlds*
1964	Theodore Kroeber Ishi, *Last of His Tribe*: A 'wild' American Yahi Indian. The first is a biography, the second more like a novel
1954	Mary Smith, *Baba of Karo: A Woman of the Nigerian Hausa*
1985	Vincent Crapanzano, *Tuhami: Portrait of a Moroccan*: a Moroccan tilemaker's life, though with a concentration on his sexuality and spirituality
1978	James Freeman, *Untouchable*: the life of Muli, an Indian transvestite
1981	Marjorie Shostak, *Nisa: the Life and Words of a !Kung! Woman*: a woman, about 50 years old, tells her story as a member of one of the last remaining traditional hunter–gatherer societies (the Zhun/twasi – 'the real people') in isolated areas of Botswana, Angola and Namibia
1982	Kevin Dwyer, *Moroccan Dialogues: Anthropology in Question*: a life story set in dialogical mode
1984	Elisabeth Burgos-Debray, *I, Rigoberta Menchú: An Indian Woman in Guatemala*: a politically active 23-year-old woman tells her 'revolutionary' story, one which led to her being awarded a Nobel Laureate
1991	Richard Werbner, *Tears of the Dead*: histories and multiple discourses of the Kalanga family in Zimbabwe
1997	Pat Caplan, *African Voices, African Lives*: story and diaries of Mohammed, told in a rich 'dialogic' fashion in four interweaving parts

'Dora', 'The Rat Man', 'Little Hans' – as well as the psychobiographies of Leonardo da Vinci, Moses and Doestoevsky – come not in the subjective voice, but so heavily overlaid with the interpretation of Freud they do not really count as documents of life, as defined here.

TWO EXEMPLARS: JANE FRY, A TRANSSEXUAL, AND RIGOBERA MENCHÚ, A GUATEMALAN WOMAN   Consider two examples of the long life history. The first is the story of Jane Fry, a transsexual born a 'biological male' but believing she was in fact a woman. (It is one of many transsexual biographies.) It was gathered by Robert Bogdan in the early 1970s, largely through a hundred hours of informal and unchronological discussions with Jane Fry, several times a week for three months. The discussions were recorded, transcribed into 750 pages, and then edited by Bogdan to exclude materials that seemed either repetitious or of little sociological value. The work thus becomes a collaboration – Jane's words are filtered through Bogdan's sociology. In the final book, Jane's story has been organized into seventeen chapters and 200 pages. It takes the reader through her life – from her earliest memories of herself and her family to her life in high school, the navy and psychiatric hospitals, and on to marriage, suicide attempts and her involvement in the gay movement. Like all such documents, the importance of Jane's story lies in the text, no summary can do it justice. Here are two extracts to convey the flavour:

> I'm not very moralistic concerning other people's sex. If it turns you on, do it – as long as it doesn't hurt anybody. Life among the freaks and the people at the Crisis [centre] was a beautiful thing. It is really a nice thing they had going, and it was only through my own choice that I was left out. It was because of the situation I was in. For one thing, I just couldn't participate in sex. l couldn't go to bed with a female because I am not 'homosexual', and I couldn't go to bed with a male because he would treat me as if I was a male. There is no way I could function as a female in bed, so I wouldn't be satisfied. So, therefore, I just steer clear of all sex. (Bogdan, 1974)

Such a quote opens up the significance of people's subjective interpretations of sexuality: no matter that Jane was an 'objective' male – subjectively, she was female: and her actions followed from this. Or consider this almost classical illustration of the self-fulfilling prophecy:

> Society is funny – first people put you in a position to make you withdraw, and the people get angry because you are withdrawing. That getting angry with you builds a higher wall between you and the society. The person who is pushed out has a tough time seeing what was happening. That's what was happening to me at this point. I was being tormented by the kids for being feminine so I withdrew, but the more I tried to withdraw the odder I became, and the more they tormented me the more I withdrew. An eight year old kid doesn't have the knowledge to understand what is happening to him – why he does what he does. Somebody might have pointed it out to me, and that might

have helped. Well anyway, these are my first feelings of being pushed out of society. (Bogdan, 1974: 41)

The two quotes above are fairly random: the biography is splattered with such insights and the whole story has to be read for the greatest understanding.

The second story is that of Rigoberta Menchú, a twenty-three-year-old Quiché Indian woman who speaks of her experience as a member of one of the largest of twenty-two ethnic groups in Guatemala; speaking for all the Indians of the American continent, she talks of her relationship with nature and and of her community's discriminations, oppression, defeat and genocide. The story was gathered by Elisabeth Dubray-Burgos, in Spanish, over a period of a week in her Paris flat in 1982. It started with a schematic outline – the usual chronology from childhood onwards, but was soon deflected into much more political issues, and indeed a centrepiece of the book becomes the torturing, death and funeral of members of her family at the hand of the government. As with Bogdan above, the discussions were recorded, transcribed and edited into 500 pages of transcript. All Burgos's questions were deleted as the material was turned into thirty-four chapters (and 250 pages of book) – starting with 'The family' and 'Birth ceremonies', and moving through such topics as 'Life in the community', 'Attack on the village by the army', 'The torture and death of her little brother, burnt alive in front of members of his family and the community', 'In hiding in the capital. Hunted by the army'. The work seems less of a collaboration than the Jane Fry book: Rigoberta's words are less filtered, the relationship between the two was less developed, and the whole project was done much more quickly. Again, here are two extracts to convey a little of the flavour:

> I worked from when I was very small, but I didn't earn anything. I was really helping my mother because she had to carry a baby, my little brother, on her back as she picked coffee. It made me very sad to see my mother's face covered in sweat as she tried to finish her workload, and I wanted to help her. But my work wasn't paid, it just contributed to my mother's work. I either picked coffee with her or looked after my little brother, so she could work faster. My brother was two at the time . . . (Menchú, 1984: 33)

Much of the story is given over to detailed cultural description of daily life in the village – of work, religious ritual, family and children. Curiously at one point she speaks of the importance of not disclosing the village secrets – 'Indians have been very careful not to disclose any details of their communities, and the community does not allow them to talk about Indian things. I too must abide by this' (p. 9; cf. p. 188). This is either hard to reconcile with the vivid descriptions she supplies, or it suggests that what she has told in the story is heavily screened by this taboo. Another quote:

It was in 1979, I remember that my younger brother died, the first person in my family to be tortured. He was sixteen years old, . . . It's an unbelievable story. We managed to find out how he died, what tortures were inflicted on him from start to finish. They took my brother away, bleeding from different places. When they'd done with him, he didn't look like a person any more. His whole face was disfigured from beating, from striking against stones, the tree-trunks; my brother was completely destroyed. His clothes were torn from his falling down. After that they let the women go. When he got to the camp, he was scarcely on his feet, he couldn't walk any more. And his face, he couldn't see any more, they'd even forced stones into his eyes, into my brother's eyes. Once he arrived in the camp, they inflicted terrible tortures on him to make him tell where the guerilla fighters were and where his family was . . . [a long description of torture follows]. (Menchú, 1984: 174)

The tale of Rigoberta Menchú has rapidly become a classic: noted for the account of the way the Guatemalan Army killed her two brothers and parents. A better 'seller' than most 'life stories', it has made her a hero of the international human rights movement, led to her being awarded a Nobel Peace Prize in 1992; and has brought a storm of controversy – the relationship between Elisabeth Burgos and Rigoberta Menchú has been questioned, the veracity of her story has been challenged and the potential use of such stories for political ends has been put under scrutiny. I shall return to all this later (cf. Newsweek, 21 June 1999; Stoll, 1999).

Short life stories   These are more common and very different. They are usually gathered through in-depth interviews, with open-ended questionnaires, requiring gentle probes and taking somewhere between half an hour and three hours. Sometimes, they are first person documents found in autobiographical collections or letters. The stories here usually have to be more focused than the long life histories. They are not published in book-length form, but are more likely to appear as one in a series. They are altogether more truncated versions of the above.

A classic example of this is Ronald Blythe's *Akenfield: Portrait of an English Village* (1969), which was also made into a TV drama. The book pieces together the stories of many people from the same small village under themes such as 'God', 'The Forge', 'The Craftsmen', 'The School', providing some 40 or more voices, all of whom tell their own stories in their own words – 'Fred Mitchell, horseman'; 'Alan Mitton, orchard foreman'; 'Terry Lloyd, pig farmer'. As Blythe says of the study:

This book is the quest for the voice of Akenfield, Suffolk, as it sounded during the summer and autumn of 1967. The talk covers half a century of farming slump and the beginnings of what is being called the second agricultural revolution. It begins with the memories of men who were children when much of the land changed toward the end of the twentieth century . . . (Blythe, 1969: 19)

A major recent example of this can be found in the large-scale French project *La Misère du monde*, which was a best seller in France and became translated as *The Weight of the World: Social Suffering in Contemporary Society* (Bourdieu, 1999). This massive book overflows with first person accounts – elicited through interviews and fieldwork descriptions – of the little daily sufferings of work and family, town and country, illness and solitude. Each segment comes with a brief contextualization before the first person 'story' is told. But the isolated short tales are not enough:

> To understand what happens in places like 'projects' or 'housing developments' as well as in certain kinds of schools, places which bring together people who have nothing in common and force them to live together either in mutual ignorance and incomprehension or else in latent or open conflict – with all the suffering this entails – it is not enough to explain each point of view separately. All of them must be brought together as they are in reality, not to relativize them in an infinite number of cross-cutting images, but quite to the contrary, through simple juxtaposition, to bring out everything that results when different or antagonistic visions of the world confront each other – that is, in certain cases, the tragic consequences of making incompatible points of view confront each other, where no concession or compromise is possible because each of them is equally founded in social reason. (Bourdieu et al., 1999: 3)

Here, then, short life stories are weaved together to create a larger map of social suffering. Other studies may take a smaller number of lives. The recent work of Leon Pettiway, for instance, has told the five lives of 'black, gay, transgendered hustlers' in *Honey, Honey, Miss Thang* (1996) and the five lives of 'black, heroin using women' in *Working It: Women Living Through Drugs and Crime* (1997). In these studies, he takes 'cases' from a much bigger project involving the interviewing of some 431 individuals, narrowed down to 48 more detailed interviews, narrowed still further to a small cluster published in these books. Apart from an introduction, however, Pettiway's voice is largely absent as his subjects tell their stories. In other studies – like Arlene Stein's (1997) account of changing lesbian identities in the postwar period, drawing from forty-one women's 'self stories' as they relay generation differences; or Bob Blauner's (1989) account of three decades of race relations in the USA told through the stories of sixteen blacks and twelve whites – the focus is on a number of life stories that are then pieced together into a wider account. These are all powerful studies using life story methods, but the styles and shapes of these books is very different indeed from that of the single life story. Short stories are relatively more common than long ones, and are often – as with Stein and Blauner above – more likely to be edited down into the researcher's 'story'. The extent of coverage and degree of editing hence raises another simple but useful distinction between comprehensive, topical or edited life stories.

Comprehensive, topical or edited?

Making another set of distinctions, some time ago Gordon Allport (1942) suggested three main forms of life history writing: the comprehensive, the topical and the edited. For him, the most generally useful way of distinguishing life documents was to focus on whether it was purporting to grasp the comprehensive *life*, or to grasp a particular *topic*. And in each, it could be edited or not.

The *comprehensive life document* is the rarest document to come by: it purports to grasp the totality of a person's life – the full sweep – from birth to their current moment. It has no sharp focus but tries to capture the essence of the development of a unique human being. Such a goal of course is strictly impossible: wholes and totalities must always be arranged from a particular perspective. Nevertheless, the kind of work that approaches this is typified by the story of Jane Fry described above, as well as Stanley, the delinquent boy (Shaw, 1966). It is also to be found in psychology in the work of Robert White and his study *Lives in Progress: A Study of the Natural Growth of Personality* (1975). In this book he presents in considerable detail the lives of only three people. Hartley Hale, physician and scientist, Joseph Kidd, businessman, and Joyce Kingsley, housewife and social worker. He tries to bring together within the volume the perspectives of biology, psychology and sociology but the focus throughout is on the overall flow of the life. Among other studies which have produced this pattern are the Grant study of adaptation to life and the work of Kimmel (see Kimmel, 1989; Vaillant, 1977; White, 1975), as well as the re-publication of *The Life Stories of (Undistinguished) Americans as Told by Themselves* (Holt, 1906/1990).

The *topical life document* does not aim to grasp the fullness of a person's life, but confronts a particular issue. Here are some of the the most famous of all the life history documents: the study of Stanley in the late 1920s focuses throughout upon the delinquency of his life, the study of Janet Clark in the 1960s focuses throughout upon the theme of her drug use, and the study of Jane Fry in the early 1970s focused throughout upon her transsexuality (see Shaw, 1966; Hughes, 1961; Bogdan, 1974 respectively). Sometimes the material around a special theme is not related to an overall life. With these personal documents the full flow of a life is not necessary; the document is used to throw light upon a particular topic or issue. Sutherland's *The Professional Thief* (1937/1967) is the classic instance of this, although it is often quite mistakenly called a life history. It was gathered during the early 1930s (through responses to a written questionnaire and long discussions) and tells neither the life story of its author, Chic Conwell, nor of his personal qualities; indeed, what it does provide on this score may even be false or fictitious (cf. Snodgrass, 1973). But this is not important. For its main concern lies with the detailed descriptions of the workings of professional thieves, a picture further clarified and updated by *The Box Man* in the 1970s (cf. Chambliss, 1972). *The Professional*

Thief details the strategies of various rackets like picking pockets, shoplifting, confidence tricks and passing illegal cheques; it describes the characteristics of the 'profession', including its understandings, agreements, rules, codes of behaviour and language; and reveals 'the fix', the widespread practice of arranging immunity for a thief on a criminal charge. As Chic Conwell says on the latter:

> In order to send a thief to the penitentiary, it is necessary to have the cooperation of the victim, witnesses, police, bailiffs, clerks, grand jury, prosecutor, judge, and perhaps others. A weak link in the chain can practically always be found and any of the links can be broken if you have pressure enough. There is no one who cannot be influenced if you go at it right and have sufficient backing, financially and politically. It is difficult if the victim is rich or important, it is more difficult in some places than others. But it can practically always be done. (Sutherland, 1967: 82–3)

A topical life document then will usually have the task of throwing light on a highly focused area of life.

Finally, the *edited life document* does not leave the story quite so clearly in the subject's voice. Rather, here, the author speaks and edits his subjects into his account – they are often used more for illustration. The classic version of this is William James's *The Varieties of Religious Experience: A Study in Human Nature* (1902/1952). Here, in a book-length study organized though themes such as 'Conversion', 'Saintliness', 'Mysticism', James draws from a series of case studies of religious experience. No one life dominates – instead extracts appear in many places.

Naturalistic, researched, reflexive

A third key distinction lies in what I will call *'naturalistic'*, *'researched'* and *'reflexive'*, though there can be overlaps between them.

Naturalistic life stories   Stories that naturally occur, stories that people just tell as part of their everyday life. They are simply present as part of a society, and have not been shaped by the social analyst. Yet they can be read in their own right, or gathered to become the objects of social science study. Naturalistic life stories are not artificially assembled, but just happen *in situ*. They tell it as it is: with such voices there is a natural fidelity to the world as the life story tellers find it (cf. Gubrium and Holstein, 1997: ch. 2). Such stories can be heard in everyday settings by fieldworkers – when the elderly reminisce, when teenagers chat on the phone, when the criminal confesses, when the job applicant is interviewed; and they may also be heard increasingly as media voices: on talk radio, in the letters pages, on chat shows. They are omnipresent in those most popular forms of publishing – confessions, personal testaments, biographies and autobiographies. They are found in popular publications such as the US monthly *Biography* (which has its slogan: 'Every life has a story') and in UK radio and TV programmes like *This is Your Life* and Anthony Clare's *In the Psychiatrist's Chair*. These tales are occurring everywhere in social worlds, and it is open for the social scientist to inspect them.

A core of such stories can be found in the autobiography – literally the description of one's own life. And they have provided many a wonderful source for analysis. The oral historian Paul Thompson, for example, was able to locate a cross-section of autobiographies of men and women living in England between the 1830s and 1870s, and analyse them to suggest what life was like being old in the nineteenth century; Diane Bjorklund was able to gather some 200 North American autobiographies written over two hundred years and analyse their content, themes and links to the historical and cultural moment; whilst Wendy Simonds has studied the self-help confessional tales that abound in North American culture (Bjorklund, 1999; Simonds, 1992; Thompson et al., 1990). In a culture such as ours, flooded with biographical musings, here indeed is a rich mine for the researcher.

Researched and solicited stories   By contrast, life stories that are researched are specifically gathered by researchers with a wider usually social science goal in mind. These do not naturalistically occur in everyday life: rather they have to be seduced, coaxed and interrogated out of subjects, often in special settings using special implements (tape recorders, videos, psychiatric couches). Oral history, sociological life history, literary bio-graphies, psychological case studies – all these can bring life stories into being that would not otherwise have happened in everyday life. The role of the researcher is crucial to this activity: without them there would be no life story.

Amongst the range of solicited stories are:

ORAL HISTORY AND TESTAMENTS   One of the most commonly used 'researched' life stories is that of the oral history and testament – a major development in the postwar period. It is, of course, no new approach – being as old as history itself – but it is only since the 1940s (with the work of Allan Neins at Columbia University) that an oral history movement has emerged around tape-recordings. Oral history now has its own organizations (the Oral History Association was established in America in 1966 and had 1,300 active members within a decade; the Oral History Society was established in the UK in 1970, and now has well over 1,000 members); its own journals (like *Oral History Review* in the USA, and *Oral History* in the UK); and a truly vast outpouring of research. Much of this oral history work has recently been collated and reviewed in the latest edition of Paul Thompson's landmark study *The Voice of the Past* (2000, 3rd edition). In the first edition, he expresses how his interest grew from an interest in Edwardian life in England – a period still within 'living memory':

It was too recent a period for a satisfactory range of more personal documents to have reached the county record offices. I wanted to know what it was like to be a child or parent at that time; how young people met and courted; how they lived together as husbands and wives; how they found jobs and moved between them; how they felt about work; how they saw their employers and fellow workers; how they survived and felt when out of work; how class consciousness varied between city, country and occupations. None of these questions seemed answerable from conventional historical sources . . . (P. Thompson, 1978: 78)

And in his most recent edition he charts an impressive and enormous range of work that has contributed to economic, political, family and social history since its inception. Indeed, the range of research now covered by oral historians throughout the world is vast: from the legions of modest amateurs to the proliferating professionals – all of whom capture the rich, vivid voices of subjects in history who might otherwise have been lost. Thus, at one extreme oral history groups can be found in local communities all over the world – oral history workshops, memory groups, testimony groups, school oral history societies (the journals are full of listings of these). At another extreme, oral history has become an international academic discipline – hosting International World Conferences dedicated to issues like 'global remembering'. Oral history – the term itself remains in controversy – can now almost be seen as a global, fragmented social movement hell bent on tracking, retrieving, recording and archiving the multiple worlds of our recent past. In a time of immense and rapid change, in a world where it would be so easy to lose 'our past', such life stories take on an ever-increasing importance – not just in providing clues to the past, but also in gathering the voices of people who may well otherwise be lost for the future. Much of the work is 'bottom up' work: it records the words of people whose voices may well have been lost before, but who now can gain a permanent record. We now have thousands of stories in the UK alone: the lives of old criminals in East London Underworlds like 'Arthur Harding' (Samuels, 1981); the voices of the truly marginalized disabled people at the start of the twentieth century, often institutionalized and forgotten (Humphries and Gordon, 1992; Walmsley, 1998); the lives of both staff and their patients living and working in large mental hospitals through the twentieth century (Gittings, 1998) – stories that may never have been heard had not oral history taken a key interest. And often they become part of the newer video and CD-Rom projects, a point I will return to in Chapters 3 and 4 (see Dunaway and Baum, 1996: Part 4; Perks and Thompson, 1998; Stave et al., 1999).

PSYCHOBIOGRAPHIES AND PSYCHO-HISTORIES Using various psychodynamic models, the main concern with this approach is to take a life and analyse it for its psychological workings (Runyan, 1984). This may mean taking a contemporary life – the classic psychoanalytic field –, but often it has meant taking a life that has been documented in the somewhat distant past and then attempting to draw out the psychological workings of the life. The most famous case is probably Freud's *Leonardo da Vinci and a Memory of his Childhood* (1910/1963). Erik Erikson's own approach has been to take a life and link the historical moment (its culture and history) with a psychoanalytic moment, often seeing the great life as embodying a major 'crisis' of its time. Amongst the great lives studied by Erikson have been Luther, Gandhi and Hitler (Erikson, 1959, 1968, 1977: cf. Friedman, 1999). Often, though, these are not first person accounts. They are 're-readings' and interpretations, and hence largely outside the scope of this book.

COLLECTIVE AUTOBIOGRAPHIES AND THE 'COLLECTIVE STORY'   Sometimes detailed life stories are collected as part of a much broader, even collective, project. In the United States, for instance, there have been attempts to collect large numbers of slave narratives (e.g. Botkin, 1945/1994; Rawick, 1978). Likewise, a number of feminist groups have been concerned to document their shared and collective memories: Frigga Haug and her co-workers found 'sexuality' to be a 'crucial area of unhappiness (and of silence), an area where our speechlessness prevents us asking questions'. Aware of this, they started group discussions in which they aimed to 'identify the ways we live in bodily terms, the ways we live in our bodies, and in so doing define our relation to other human beings and the world' (Haug, 1983/1987: 29–30). On a much larger scale, a serious attempt has been mounted to obtain the testimonies of as many people as possible who survived the holocaust. Thus there are some 4,000 witness accounts – many of them on video – to be found in the Yale Fortunoff collection (Langer, 1991). And the film producer Steven Spielberg is recording all remaining survivors – some 50,000 – for his Survivors of the Shoah Foundation (much of which can be found in the US Holocaust Memorial Museum in Washington). There are also major collections of women's lives, gay and lesbian lives, and many 'postcolonial' lives which are being archived in this way.

A more general project can be found in the UK, in the Mass Observation project originally founded in 1936 by Tom Harrison (an anthropologist) and Charles Madge (a poet). Diaries, handwritten and typed notes, along with questionnaire replies, surveys and photographs were provided by hundreds of volunteers at regular intervals between 1937 and the early 1950s. They were asked to talk and write about everyday life in England. These were solicited documents of life, and led to studies of such matters as wartime diaries, sexual behaviour and pub life (Mass Observation, 1943; Stanley, 1996). This project was restarted in 1981, based at Sussex University since when 'some 400,000 pages of typed and handwritten material have been amassed' from over 2,500 volunteers. Each person sends in a set of written observations three times a year responding to broad suggestions. These observations are a mix of subjective writing ('I woke up feeling depressed today'), reportage ('The shops were crowded in Bolton today') and life cycle events – giving a sense of a life and a history. As Dorothy Sheridan puts it: 'Mass observation writing can be considered as a form of collective or multiple autobiography which draws on a very wide range of existing conventions: letter writings, answering questionnaires, being interviewed, keeping a diary, writing a life story' (Sheridan, 1993: 34).

It is a short step from these collective autobiographies into what Laurel Richardson has called the 'Collective Story' (Richardson, 1990: 25). Here, listening to many people speak about a common theme in their lives can lead to a sense that they have a common, collective tale to tell – one that perhaps the social scientist can help weave together. For example, in my own study, *Telling Sexual Stories* (1995a), I had little difficulty sensing something of a common voice in both gay and lesbian coming out stories, as well as in rape victim/survivor stories. The individual tale becomes a collective tale: the one voice may be the voice of many. There can of course be a serious problem with this – a shared tale may often serve to gloss over ambiguities and complexities, creating tales that hugely distort the differences.

GENEALOGICAL AND FAMILY STORIES   Close to the collective story lies both the 'family story' and its more objective partner 'genealogy', a common tool for both historians and anthropologists. Alex Haley's (in)famous study of his black slave history, *Roots*, brings together a great many family stories; whilst the leading French oral historian Daniel Bertaux, has designed a method called the 'Social Genealogies' in which he connects an individual life to the wider family across both time and space, establishing patterns of relationships (Bertaux and Bertaux-Wiame, 1981). In the United States there is now a big industry which deals with genealogy (cf. Watson, 1996).

THE ETHNOGRAPHIC AUTO/BIOGRAPHY   Many ethnographies may be seen as partly composed of the stories people tell of their lives. In the classic *Street Corner Society*, not only does the presence of 'Doc', the key informant, loom large – so too do the stories of Chick Morelli, Tony Cataldo, the Nortons and the Shelby Street Boys (Whyte, 1943). Tally figures prominently in the classic *Tally's Corner* (Liebow, 1967), whilst 'Slim' is at the heart of *Slim's Table*. Slim, for example, is 'a black mechanic in a back alley garage in the ghetto', a regular patron of the 'Valois' "See Your Food"' cafeteria in Chicago. He is contrasted in part with Bart: white, ten years older, a filing clerk who died alone in his small studio. The story is told by Mitch Duneier, the 'white' observer sociologist, as part of his wider ethnographic concerns with how some black men live their lives 'through little acts of caring' (Duneier, 1992: 20). Likewise, David Goode's study *A World Without Words* takes two children as its core, Christina and

Bianca, who were born deaf, 'dumb', blind and mentally disabled as a result of pre-natal German measles during the rubella epidemic of the 1960s. The study gets close to their experiences – and though they are the centre of the stories, they are linked to an array of significant others reacting to them: professionals, parents, other children. Here the focus is the ethnographic study of lives, whilst broad theoretical links are made to communication and ethnomethodology (Goode, 1994). (See also Vinitzky-Seroussi, 1998.)

THE SOCIAL SCIENCE AUTOBIOGRAPHY   Sometimes, the social scientist becomes his or her own object of study: it is their life which is the focus. As Robert Merton said classically, 'The sociological autobiography utilizes socio-logical perspectives, ideas, concepts, findings and analytical procedures to construct and interpret a narrative text that purports to tell one's own history within the larger history of one's times' (1988: 18). Here then the focus may be on the sociologist's own 'insider' life but it is connected through sociology to an 'outsider' world of wider social processes . . . 'full fledged sociological autobiographers relate their intellectual development both to changing social and cognitive micro-environments close at hand and to the encompassing macro-environments provided by the larger society and culture' (Merton, 1988: 19–20). There are now quite a few volumes where sociologists link up the story of their lives to their sociology. Bennet Berger's *Authors of Their Own Lives* (1990) provides intellectual life stories of twenty prominent American sociologists, often showing their specific pains and sufferings and how they linked to wider social orders (including David Riesman, Hebert Gans, Jessie Barnard, Nathan Glazer, John Gagnon, Alice Rossi and Barbara Rosenblum). The studies in *Qualitative Sociology as Everyday Life* (Glassner and Hertz, 1999) get a number of sociologists to write essays that impinge on their own sociological and personal lives (I found the story by Lillian Rubin on her ageing mother in a nursing home especially moving – as she brings her own special pains around this along an informed sociological sensibility. I read it at a time when my own mother had just entered a home, and although the experiences were obviously not the same, sociological and personal bells rang loud). And in a more theoretical fashion, Pierre Bourdieu 'objectizes' himself in a specific social space in his book *Homo Academicus* (1988).

Sometimes, such sociologically informed work has moved further into research where the social scientist, and his or her life, moves into the heart of a sociological study. Here the social scientist is writing about his or her life whilst including within it the sense of other concerns coming from the social science literature. Sometimes these are book length – as in the late Irving Zola's *Missing Pieces*: here he describes 'an unusual experiment in living' (1982: 5) as his own life in a wheelchair is recounted side by side with his visits to Het Dorp in the Netherlands (he calls it a social-autobiography (p. 6), documenting the trials and tribulations of daily living with severe disabilities – not just the cultural and religious needs, but also the daily trials around the need to dress and wash, to urinate and defecate (ch. 4: 65) and all the other 'little things that fill a day'. Likewise, in a moving account of depression, David Karp's *Speaking of Sadness* (1996) draws from his own life-long experiences of 'living with depression', which are then used as a springboard for entering the worlds of others. Yet, while he recognizes the power of others' autobiographies in this field – Sylvia Plath (*The Bell Jar*, 1972), William Styron (*Darkness Visible*, 1990), Elizabeth Wurtzel (*Prozac Nation*, 1994) for instance – he is also clear that 'they are not based on systematically collected data nor are they directed at discovering underlying patterns in the depression experience' (1996: 12). In this instance, he keeps his own experiences close to the surface of the text but restricts their full exploration to one opening chapter.

Taking all this just one step further is self-observation. Freud, of course, left a model for doing this in *The Interpretation of Dreams* (1976), and if Freud could turn his dreams into a masterpiece of understanding, why shouldn't other social scientists? Many linguists and child psychologists have taken their own children and families as basic units of study, creating detailed documents about them. Znaniecki argued the case for such work over sixty years ago (cf. 1934: ch. IV):

> When I wish to ascertain at first hand what a certain activity is . . . I try to experience it. There is only one way of experiencing an object; it is to *observe* it personally. There is only one way of experiencing an activity; it is to *perform* it personally. Practical men [*sic*] insist on this: they will tell you that you cannot fully realise what they are doing till you do it yourself. Scientists have come to recognise this . . . (1934: 49)

Slowly, Znaniecki's observation is coming true. We could now make a long list of sociologists in the past who have used their own experiences – Riemer (1977) calls this 'opportunistic research' and lists over twenty such researchers. Nels Anderson, for example, came from a hobo family and this informed much of his research for his monograph *The Hobo* (1961), a fact he concealed till much later (cf. Anderson, 1975: 170). As Jack Douglas says:

> I know of any number of studies in which the author's fundamental way of knowing the things he [*sic*] reports was through direct personal involvement, a fact that has been carefully hidden from the readers because revealing it would stigmatise him as a creep, a weirdo or maybe a criminal. In all instances I know of, these sociologists have been unhappy that they felt it necessary to do this and in each case with which I am familiar they have not lied. They have merely evaded the issue. (Douglas, 1976: xiii)

But the time has now arrived when a number of researchers are stopping this evasion. Largely shaped by arguments from feminist theories about the importance of personal experiences, different 'ways of knowing', and the recognition that knowledges are bound up with 'standpoints', more and more researchers are turning to their own and others' personal experiences as a basis for reflection and understanding. One strong strand of this feminist lineage has been a continuingly appropriate critique on 'male abstractions' and their often abstracted methods – i.e. those which seem to get cut off from 'experiences' or even seek to devalue human experiences as too subjective (Bowles and Klein, 1983; Harding, 1991; Reinharz, 1979; Stanley and Wise, 1981/1993). In all sorts of ways, which we are only just starting to recognize without apology, the documentation of our own experiences and life stories are excellent starting points for research, and are productive points to return to again and again. Many contemporary researchers now recognize this, from postcolonial studies to queer theorists. Life stories have, ironically, gone personal: reflexive and recursive.

Reflexive and recursive life stories: the drift to the postmodern?   Finally, then, and flowing from the above are the reflexive and recursive life stories – stories that bring with them a much greater awareness of their own construction and writing. This is a distinction in the form of the story: whilst most earlier life stories brought with them a sense that they were telling the story of a life, these latter kinds of stories become self-conscious and suggest that story telling is a fabrication, an act of speech, a mode of writing. Whatever else they may say, stories do not simply tell the tale of a life. Here a life is seen more richly as 'composed' (Bateson, 1989) or constructed, and the author becomes much more involved in 'messy texts' (Marcus, 1994: 567), making the writer a part of the writing. Sometimes, too, they are seen to be much more overtly political, as in Liz Stanley's understanding of feminist auto/biography (Stanley, 1992), which is strongly critical of many of the unreflective and apolitical distinctions made between biography, autobiography, self, other etc. All these distinctions start to collapse.

AUTO/ETHNOGRAPHY, OBSERVING THE SELF AND SOCIOLOGICAL INTROSPECTION   All this leads to a new kind of life story work, one that is very much in the making. 'Narratives of the self' (Ellis, 1991), 'mystories' (Ulmer, 1989), 'systematic sociological introspection' (Ellis, 1991), 'auto/ethnography' (Neumann, 1998; Okely and Callaway, 1992; Reed-Danahay, 1997) and even 'ethnographic biography' embody this new reflexivity (which is really just an extension of the old autobiographical reflection anyway). Take *'auto/ethnography'*, a term which seems to have been invented in the 1970s to capture the experience of the anthropologist looking at worlds of their 'own people'. Recently it has been developed to capture the breakdown in distance (and the complex relationship) between ethnographer, biographer, and subjects – bringing the accounts together. So now the term 'auto/ethnography' has come to have a double sense: 'referring either to the ethnography of one's own group or to autobiographical

writing that has an ethnographic interest. Thus either a self (auto)ethno
graphy or an autobiographical (auto)ethnography can be signalled by
'autoethnography' (Reed-Danahay, 1997: 2).

Sometimes, these 'autoethnographies' are short essays that ring out a
different style and sensitivity for doing social science. Carol Rambo Ronai
for instance tells several of her stories – of what it is like to be a student
who works as a striptease dancer (Ronai, 1992); and the anguish of being
the daughter of a 'mentally retarded' mother – teeming with her personal
resentments at pretending to be a 'normal family' with a mother 'not
taking care of me' (Ronai, 1996). She calls these 'layered accounts',
because her voice appears alongside the study and the analysis – merging
them altogether. Other voices have told of women engaged in religious/
spiritual self-discovery (Foltz and Griffin, 1996); of the shifting voices
around child sexual abuse (Fox, 1996); or of the feelings held about
motherhood (Ribbens, 1998). In the books of Susan Krieger (1991, 1996)
and Laurel Richardson (1998), we start to see 'the spectacle of a significant
number of critics getting personal in their writing'.

Carolyn Ellis's *Final Negotiations* (1995) has caused some controversy
because of the way she treads such a difficult line between the emo-
tionality of its author, its personal writing style and its links to social
science. Her book reads like a hybrid between a novel, a fiction, an
autobiography and a research tract. Officially she calls it 'experimental
ethnography', and it is based on 'daily field notes'. It is subtitled 'A Story
of Love, Loss and Chronic Illness' – which does not immediately suggest
a sociological treatise! And what it provides is a 350-page, first person
account of the sociologist author's experience of her relationship with a
teacher (the sociologist Gene Weinstein based at the University of New
York at Stony Brook). They first negotiate their attachment 'through a
maze of jealousy, attraction, love and arguments' (p. 10) with her in the
more subordinate role, and then find they have to renegotiate their
relationship as they come to terms with the impending death of Gene.
Within this study, the story is presented in the present tense – 'which
invites the reader to share in the immediacy'; whilst sociological commentaries and personal reflections are woven into the past tense. This is
an intriguing study – almost certainly unacceptable to the more formal
scientific academic community because it highlights both speaking of
personal experience alongside narrative prose as a way of knowing. But
the study takes us into the sociology of love, relationships, emotions and
death (Ellis, 1995).

Whilst only a relatively small amount of social science is taking this
personal, narrative path, there are nevertheless signs here of a shift. The
'autoethnography' brings the author firmly into the text, with a height-
ened self-consciousness of the textual production; once this happens it
may be only a small step away to the 'fictional autobiographical ethnography', where the distinction of forms becomes completely 'blurred'.
Indeed, what is 'fiction' and what is 'faction' is hard to distinguish.

When social science starts to write fiction, and fiction writers start to write biographies, distinctions around life stories become very tenuous.

The life story as resource and as topic

The distinction between 'naturalistic, researched and reflexive' life stories leads to a final important clarification: that between life stories as a *resource* and as a *topic*. Hence, in looking at phenomena as resources we come to use them to see what insights they may bring to understanding social life. We are interested in crime rates, for example, because they will tell us about crime. Likewise, we are interested in the story of Rigoberta Menchú because it will tell us about being a young revolutionary in Guatemala – the story aids, is a resource for understanding. In contrast, in looking at phenomena as *topics*, we come to see them as matters of investigation in their own right: as topics of interest in themselves. Thus, if we are looking at crime rates, we are now concerned about just how such rates get produced, what they mean, how they get organized, and used. The content is less significant. Likewise, with Rigoberta Menchú, seeing her life story as a topic to be investigated means that we ask questions about how she came to tell this story at this time in this place. Why and how and with what consequences? What she says is shaped by a certain social condition, and it is this which becomes our topic to study. This is where we ended the last section – once a life story is seen as a 'construction', it becomes a topic we can investigate in its own right. I will look briefly at each of these angles.

The life story as a resource

The classic use of life stories as a resource can be found in the first major social science life story – that of Wladek, *The Polish Peasant*. This 300-page story is one of five volumes which looks into the experiences of traditional village life in Poland, capturing the experience of migrating to a large American city (Chicago), examining problems and crises in close detail. In this huge volume (to which I will return in Chapter 5), the authors W.I. Thomas and Florian Znaniecki made a now much-cited remark:

> In analysing the experiences and attitudes of an individual, we always reach data and elementary facts which are not exclusively limited to this individual's personality, but can be treated as mere instances of more or less general classes of data or facts, and can thus be used for the determination of social becoming. Whether we draw our materials for sociological analysis from detailed life records of concrete individuals or from the observation of mass phenomena, the problems of sociological analysis are the same. We are safe in saying that personal life records, as complete as possible, constitute the perfect type of

sociological material, and that if social science has to use other materials at all it is only because of the practical difficulty of obtaining at the moment a sufficient number of such records to cover the totality of sociological problems, and of the enormous amount of work demanded for an adequate analysis of all the personal material necessary to characterise the life of a social group. If we are forced to use mass phenomena as material, or any kind of happenings taken without regard to the life histories of the individuals who participate in them, it is a defect, not an advantage, of our present sociological method. (Thomas and Znaniecki, 1958: 1832–3)

For Thomas and Znaniecki then, life histories are not merely useful for sociology, they are '*the perfect type of sociological material*'. For them, they enabled access to 'social becoming'. These days many other claims have been made for their value. So just what are life stories best at grasping? Just why can such a claim be made?

At the very core of life documents is a very problematic subject matter. We have here stories – discourses – that aim to capture the continuous, lived flow of historically situated phenomenal experience, with all the ambiguity, variability, malleability and even uniqueness that such experience implies. Whether this be the experience of being a nomadic hunter and gatherer or a North American prostitute (Heyl, 2000; Shostak, 1981); of being 'worried to death' in a nursing home for the elderly or working down a mine (Bulmer, 1978; Gubrium, 1993); of being a teacher or facing disablity (Goodson, 1992; Zola, 1982); of being workless or being a man (Connell, 1995; Marsden and Duff, 1974) – whatever may be of interest to the analyst, a key perspective is the participant's account of this experience. It may not be adequate on its own. But if a study fails to get this 'intimate familiarity' with a life, then such research must run the risk of simply getting it wrong: of speculating, abstracting and theorizing at too great a remove (cf. Lofland, 1976); and worst of all, of substituting the researcher's own view for that of the participant (what has been called the fallacy of objectivism; (Denzin, 1978a: 10). How can one theorize or interpret coalmining or transsexualism if there is no familiarity with what it all means to the participants themselves?

Such a position has a long and respectable social science pedigree. From Weber's '*verstehen*' (understanding), through the phenomenological and hermeneutic sociologies (of Dilthey and others) and on to the more recent qualitative and interpretive researchers (Gubrium and Holstein, 1997), there is a persistent strand of social science that is concerned with *meaningful, intersubjective social actions* (cf. Bruyn, 1966; Prus, 1996). One central, but today largely neglected, figure in clarifying this position was Florian Znaniecki. Both in his 'methodological note' to *The Polish Peasant* (with Thomas) and in his *The Method of Sociology* (1934), he presents a strong concern with the neo-Kantian distinction between two systems, natural and cultural. Natural systems are given objectively and exist independently of the experience and activity of people, while cultural systems are intrinsically bound up with the conscious experiences of human agents in interaction with each other. As he puts it:

> Natural systems are objectively given to the scientist as if they existed absolutely independently of the experience and activity of men. The planetary system, the geological composition and structure of the rind of the earth, the chemical compound, the magnetic field, the plant and the animal, are such as they appear to the student, without any participation of human consciousness; scientifically speaking, they would be exactly the same if no men existed. The essential characters of their elements . . . are such that they are apart from the question whether and how anybody experiences them; they are bound together by forces which have nothing to do with human activity . . . Very different appear such indubitably cultural systems as those dealt with by students of language and literature, art, religion, science, economies, industrial technique and social organisation. Generally speaking, every cultural system is found by the investigator to exist for certain conscious and active historical subjects, i.e. within the sphere of experience and activity of some particular people, individuals and collectivities, living in a certain part of the human world during a certain historical period. Consequently, for the scientist this cultural system is really and objectively as it was (or is) given to those historical subjects themselves when they were (or are) experiencing it and actively dealing with it. In a word, the data of the cultural student are always 'somebody's', never 'nobody's' data. This essential character of cultural data we call the humanistic coefficient, because such data, as objects of the student's theoretical reflection, already belong to someone else's active experience and are such as this active experience makes them. If the humanistic coefficient were withdrawn and the scientist attempted to study the cultural system as he studies a natural system . . . the system would disappear and in its stead he would find a disjointed mass of natural things and processes, without any similarity to the reality he started to investigate. (Znaniecki, 1934: 136–7)

One major tradition of social science, then, has always stressed the importance of studying this 'humanistic coefficient'; of getting at the ways in which participants of social life construct and make sense of their particular world – their 'definitions of the situation', their 'first level constructs'. Personal documents are bound to this broad tradition.

Consider, for example, one of the earlier anthropological case studies: that of Don, the Sun Chief, presented by Leo Simmons (1942). His life can only be adequately understood once the realness to him of an environment peopled with imaginary spirits is grasped: there is the Sun God, a 'strong, middle aged man who makes daily journeys across the sky, lights and heats the world and sustains all life'; the Moon and Star Gods, and the Eagle and the Hawk Deities who live in the sky and look after people; there are the lesser gods like the Wind, the Lightning, the Thunder and the Rain; as well as the Snake Gods who live in the water springs and who must be protected. If you kill them you will bring shame to yourself. Now without getting close to Don's life this fundamentally different way of organizing his world would not be grasped.

His cultural system may differ greatly from the researcher's cultural system but it has to be intimately entered if sense is to be made of his social world. Here, then, the life story is a source for understanding the workings of a life and the culture of which it is a part. Some of the many differing traditions of looking at these meanings are outlined in Table 2.3.

'Subjectivity' and 'meaning' thus represent one of the main ways life stories can be used as a resource. But there are many other features that they can tap into. Three more can be mentioned here.

1 A tool for history Life stories always hurl us into a dual focus on history: into a concern with time in the life – of how it is lived over phases, careers, cycles, stages; and with time outside the life – of how the 'historical moment' plays its role in any life's shape. Such a concern lies at the heart of Erik Erikson's 'psycho-history', though he adds to it a concern with the inner psychodynamics of a person too (1959, 1969, 1977). More broadly, life story research at its best always brings a focus on historical change, moving between the changing biographical history of the person and the social history of his or her lifespan. Invariably the gathering of a life history will entail the subject moving to and fro

---

TABLE 2.3   The layers of life story meanings

- *Sociology of knowledge*
  Meanings as derived from wider historical moments and cultures
  e.g. Peter Berger and Thoman Luckmann's *The Social Construction of Reality*, Bob Connell's *Masculinities*
- *Discourse theory*
  Meanings constituted through language systems and power relations
  e.g. Michel Foucault's *Herculine Barbine*
- *Symbolic interactionism*
  Meanings emergent in local contexts and situations through interaction with others
  e.g. Robert Bogdan's *Jane Fry*
- *Hermeneutics*
  Meanings as understanding, 'thinking through' and 'with' others, inter-subjectively
  e.g. Dilthey/Ricoeur
- *Phenomenology*
  Meanings as descriptions of consciousness
  e.g. Lawrence Watson's *Understanding a Life History as a Subjective Document*
- *Semiotics*
  Meanings as sign systems, linked to signification and process through which signs related to each other take on arbitrary meanings
  e.g. Barthes, *Barthes on Barthes*
- *Ethnomethodology*
  Meanings as rule systems to speech and conversation
  e.g. Charlotte Linde's *Life Stories*
- *Psychodynamic*
  Meanings of the life story as unconscious dynamics of body, emotional conflicts, 'family troubles' and conflicts with outer worlds
  e.g. Freud's *The Interpretation of Dreams*

---

between the developments of their own life cycle and the ways in which external crises and situations (wars, political and religious changes, employment and unemployment situations, economic change, the media and so forth) have impinged on this. A life history cannot be told without a constant reference to historical change, and this central focus on change must be seen as one of life history's great values (Thompson, in Bertaux, 1981). Thus life stories can become guides to 'people of their times'.

2 *Ambiguity, processes and change*   Most social science in its quest for generalizability imposes order and rationality upon experiences and worlds that are more ambiguous, more problematic and more chaotic in reality. If we check our own experiences, for example, we know that our lives are often flooded with moments of indecision, turning points, confusions, contradictions and ironies. A lot of social science glosses over this interstitial but central region of life. Questionnaires, experiments, attitude scales and even the perusal of existing social science literature and historical documents can often give a form and order to the world which it frequently does not have. Researchers seek consistency in subjects' responses when subjects' lives are often inconsistent. The life history technique is peculiarly suited to discovering the confusions, ambiguities and contradictions that are played in everyday experiences. When Wladek is giving his story to Thomas and Znaniecki, 'there is little consistency of standpoint. He changes his standpoints during the description, as he changed them during his life; for example, his momentary attitude towards any member of his family is dependent on just the phase of relation with him that he happens to recall' (Thomas and Znaniecki, 1958: 1913). As Howard Becker comments:

> The life history, more than any other technique except perhaps participant observation, can give meaning to the overworked notion of process. Sociologists like to speak of ongoing processes and the like but their methods usually prevent them from seeing the processes they talk about so glibly. (Becker, 1966: xiii)

3 *Perspectives on totalities – the life as a whole*   Most social science is involved in a process of amputation. Psychologists will amputate a 'personality', the 'attitude', the 'intelligence quotient' from the totality of the life experience while sociologists will amputate the 'structure' and the 'culture' from the totality of daily lived experience. All social science invariably has to amputate, select and organize materials from a point of view. The perspective (or point of view) of life history research, however, can be the totality of the biographical experience – a totality that necessarily weaves between biological bodily needs, immediate social groups, personal definitions of the situation, and historical change both in one's own life and in the outside world. It is quite mistaken to see life histories as thoroughly individualistic – lives move persistently through

history and structure. As such more than almost any other method it allows one to grasp a sense of the totality of a life. As Robert Bogdan says:

> The autobiography is unique in allowing us to view an individual in the context of his [sic] whole life, from birth to the point at which we encounter him. Because of this it can lead us to a fuller understanding of the stages and critical periods in the processes of his development. It enables us to look at subjects as if they have a past with successes as well as failures, and a future with hopes and fears. It also allows us to see an individual in relation to the history of his time, and how he is influenced by the various religious, social, psychological and economic currents present in his world. It permits us to view the intersection of the life history of men with the history of their society, thereby enabling us to understand better the choices, contingencies and options open to the individual (1974: 4)

The life story as a topic: towards an action model of life story telling

Life stories may also be seen as topics to be investigated in their own right. Here I would want to know not just what light life stories may throw on meanings, moralities and lives of cultures, but also how the telling of a tale is very much the product of a culture. Here the life story itself comes under scrutiny: just why do people tell the stories of their lives? What makes them tell their stories in particular kinds of ways? Would they tell them differently – or not at all – in different times and places? And are some stories simply not able to be told: the so-called 'silenced voices'? And who is this sociologist, psychologist or anthropologist who thinks they have the right to 'seduce' these stories out of people? And indeed what role do they play in all this – surely they do not just bring out the voice (and maybe when 'it' does not want to speak?), but they can also help fashion the very things that are said? And then, how does this social scientist come to present such a story. Indeed, by this late stage, just who is the author of the life story being told? And more: what happens to the story once it is told – what roles does it play in the social world, and for how long? Is there 'an afterlife of a life story', a life that it takes on of its own with real consequences for those around it – maybe those included in the story, but not the telling of it? These and other linked questions will be addressed at various stages in this book; but the point here is that once life stories are seen as topics, a whole new set of self-conscious questions about the construction, organization and reception of life stories comes into play. To put it complexly, we now confront 'a constructed understanding of the constructed native's constructed point of view' (Crapanzano, 1986: 74). This idea of *reflexive and recursive life stories* (that life stories are composed, invented, made up and that they are complex social processes in which the gatherer and reader of stories are as much implicated as the teller) is currently very much centre stage in social analysis. No life story can really be told or read with innocence these days. It seems to me that what we need to explain is *just why and how people come to tell their stories (or don't), why and how they assume the forms that they do, what happens to them once told, and how they connect to the life being told.*

There are many ways in which the 'life story as topic' can be approached. Here, however, I want to keep it simple, and isolate a number of elements that need thinking about whenever a life story is seen as a topic. Overall, this might be called *an action model of story telling.*

A first major group to think about are the *producers of life stories*: mainly as *story tellers* but also as *coaxers*. Story tellers can turn themselves into social, biographical objects – they can write or speak lengthy auto-biographies exploring their inner natures. They can produce voluminous correspondence or diaries that display the minutiae of their lives. They can become compelled to explain 'who they really are' to their social workers, lawyers, doctors, psychiatrists, counsellors, teachers – and friendly local social scientist. They provide life histories for sociologists, oral histories for oral historians and case studies for psychologists and clinicians. They even, and more complexly, perform their stories – not just in words and scripts but as emotionally charged bodies in action.

Closely allied to these tellers are a second kind of producer: the *coaxers, coachers and coercers*. These folk possess the power, at least momentarily, to provoke stories from people. Their line of activity is to seduce stories: coaxers become listeners and questioners. They probe, interview and interrogate. They send out questionnaires and solicit 'problem letters'. Sometimes they gather in groups to make others tell their stories and sometimes as individual therapists they just simply clasp their hands, smile and listen. They are the oral historians, the life story interviewers, the researchers. They are also the courtroom interrogators, the doctors, the therapists, the chat show hostesses, the tabloid journalists. They coax, coach and coerce people to tell their stories. Coaxers can play a crucial role in shifting the nature of the stories that are told.

A second major group are the *readers of stories*: their line of activity is to consume, to interpret and make sense of all these stories. These are the viewers who 'gaze' at the docusoap, who listen to the life of a star on prime time TV; the bookworms who consume life stories and oral histories, the student who is compelled for her course to read the bio-graphy of Wladek, *The Polish Peasant*. Just how these 'readers' interpret the story is a crucial process in understanding stories. Reading is a social act that depends on time, place, contexts: so readings change with theses. Sometimes people can be brought to outrage and sometimes to better understanding; sometimes such 'consumption' becomes a passionate hobby and sometimes it is all a matter of great indifference; sometimes it is a tool kit and manual for moral guidance and sometimes it is a source where a person can literally find themselves in the text. Sometimes people hear so lightly what others say intensely, and sometimes people heal su intensely what others say so lightly. Stories are brought alive in their reading, and we need to ask how this is done. Who hears and how?

All these people – story tellers, coaxers, readers – are engaged in assembling what we might call *life story actions* around lives, events and happenings. Life story telling is a social process. At the centre of much of this *action* often (but not always) emerges the *story texts*: the objects which harbour the meanings that have to be handled through social interactions. These 'congeal' or 'freeze' already preconstituted moments of a life from the story teller and the coaxer and await the handling of a reader or consumer. The meanings of stories are never fixed but emerge out of a ceaselessly changing stream of historically grounded interactions between producers and readers in shifting *contexts*. They may, of course, become habitualized and stable; but always and everywhere the meaning of stories shifts and sways in the *contexts* to which they are linked. Life stories get told and read in different ways in different contexts. The consuming of a tale centres upon different *interpretive communities* who can hear the story in certain ways (and hence not others) and who may produce their own 'memories'. These communities themselves are part of wider habitual or recurring networks of collective activity Stories do not float around abstractly but are grounded in historically evolving communities, structured through age, class, race, gender. There is often an organized pattern behind many of the tales that are heard (which may help partly explain why some tales become popular and others do not).

So here we have it: life stories, story tellers, coaxers, readers, actions, texts, contexts and interpretive communities. Figure 2.1 puts all this into schematic form and demonstrates the working of 'life stories'. Here we start to see how the telling of life stories is always socially constructed – no story just hangs loose, free of social context – and depends upon a constant flow of joint actions circulating between tellers, coaxers, texts, readers and the contexts in which the stories are told: tellers can only select, coaxers can only sift, texts can only sieve and readers can only interpret. Each of these processes compounds the other till the link between reality and the story become very fragile.

Biographical work and the stories we live by   Once life stories start to be viewed this way, many interesting questions can start to be handled more clearly. We can say that people turn themslves into socially *organized biographical objects*. The 'life' now becomes clusters of stories, about our pasts, presents and futures. We come '*to story*' our lives through the culture we live in, and we use this very culture as a way of 'writing' into ourselves who we are. And we do it all the time. Indeed, as Dan McAdams says in the opening lines of his book *The Stories We Live By*:

> If you want to know me, then you must know my story, for my story defines who I am. And if *I* want to know *myself*, to gain insight into the meaning of my own life, then I too must come to know my own story . . . a story I continue to

revise, and tell myself (and sometimes to others) as I go on living. We are all tellers of tales. We seek to provide our scattered and often confusing experiences with a sense of coherence by arranging the episodes of our lives into stories. (1993: 11)

Elswhere, I have suggested a number of story sources which can play a prominent role in assembling the story of a life (see Plummer, 1995a: ch. 3 – though my examples here are all 'sexual stories'). When hearing a life story, it is often wise to ponder just how these stories are coming to be told in this way, and where they come from. Thus *significant others* – from parents and family to loved ones, teachers and friends – may be the important people in your life who play a part in shaping the stories of that life (and of course as the people change so the stories change). These 'others' often tell you 'the kind of person you are' and remind of what you did in the past. Life story production is not an isolated affair: others help you tell the tale, and who better than those you value most? Sometimes these others are more abstract – they are *'generalized others'*. Here a sense of a life story is constructed from the fragments provided in the wider culture. From great literature to soap operas, from adverts to news, you look for signs of a life though the culture, for clues as to how a life should be lived and for elements of a self identity. Then there are the array of *'personal props'* scattered around a life and which help in its telling: from photograph albums to video diaries, to collections of clothes, books and 'old records', 'props' are deposited in a trail behind a

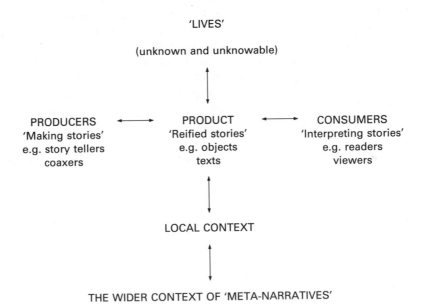

FIGURE 2.1   **Elements of the social action story process (Plummer, 1990a: 37)**

life as it is lived and can be regathered to enable a telling of a life. Just to look at an old photograph album can help create a sense of who you once were and assist in the telling of a life. Then there is *memory work*. As we will see in Chapter 10, memory is much more than a simple psychological attribute, it is also a social event: memories get attached to particular groups and provide group stories of how things are or were. In many ways, memories are our best stories – the ones we come to tell most habitually and most routinely to others. Then there is *self work and creative moments*. Here we turn to the way in which an individual actively works to 'create' their own sense of self through combinations of all the above, creating out of it all a sense of a unique story and a unique being. Many of the elements of stories are collective, communal, shared; but their final assemblage makes them into a unique story. And out of all this, what must never be underestimated, is the *act of telling* itself which turns inarticulated experience into something much more tangibly a *sense* of truth. Jean-Paul Sartre, in *Nausea*, is very insightful on this:

> Nothing happens while you live. The scenery changes, people come in and go out, that's all. There are no beginnings. Days are tacked on to days without rhyme or reason, an interminable, monotonous addition . . . Neither is there any end: you never leave a woman, a friend, a city in one go . . . Shanghai, Moscow, Algiers, everything is the same after two weeks . . .
>
> That's living. But everything starts to change when you tell about a life; it's a change no one notices; the proof is that people talk about true stories. As if there could possibly be true stories; things happen one way and we tell them in the opposite sense . . .
>
> This is what fools people: a man [*sic*] is always a teller of tales, he lives surrounded by his stories and the stories of others, he sees everything that happens to him through them; and he tries to live his own life as if he were telling a story . . . (1938/1965: 56–7, my editing)

I have only started the exploration of 'stories as topic' here. There are many more questions that need addressing – some of them will be developed later in the book. Thus, in Chapters 7 and 8 I will consider how lives get written into narratives; in Chapter 10 I will consider how lives and stories are connected; and in Chapter 11, I will think about the ethical and political consequences of life story telling.

A temporary conclusion . . .

This chapter has made a number of simple distinctions about the kinds of life story available today: the long and the short; the comprehensive, the topical and the edited; and the naturalistic, researched and reflexive. It should be clear that these are not mutually exclusive discrete categories but overlap and feed into each other. It is rare these days to encounter a life story that exists in one of these pure forms. What is also clear is that the broadest tendency in recent writings has been to move from life stories 'out there' as reflecting the life as a 'resource', to accounts that favour a more reflexive understanding of lives as struggling processes in construction – as 'topic'. One thing is clear: the gathering or reading of life stories in social science can never again be as innocent as perhaps it once was. This is a theme which will pervade this book.

Guide to further reading

Introductions to **life stories** in their full diversity include: in sociology, Norman Denzin's *Interpretive Biography* (1989), Charlotte Linde's *Life Stories: The Creation of Coherence* (1993), Robert Atkinson's *The Life Story Interview* (1998), Daniel Bertaux's edited *Biography and Society* (1981), Liz Stanley's *The Auto/Biographical I* (1992) and Prue Chamberlayne et al.'s *The Turn to Biographical Methods in Social Science* (2000). There are also special issues of journals devoted to the topic: see *Literature and History*, Vol. 14, No. 1 (1988); *Gender and History*, Vol. 2, No. 1 (1990); *Sociology*, Vol. 27, No 1 (1993); and *Current Sociology*, Vol. 43, No. 2/3 (1995).

The classic introduction to the whole field is Gordon Allport's *The Use of Personal Documents in Psychological Science* (1942). The core introduction in anthropology is L.L. Langness, *The Life History in Anthropological Science* (1965), updated in L.L. Langness and G. Frank, *Lives: An Anthropological Approach to Biography* (1981). Other guides include L.C. Watson and M.B. Watson-Franke, *Interpreting Life Histories: An Anthropological Inquiry* (1985), and Charlotte Aull Davies's, *Reflexive Ethnography* (1999: chs 8 and 9). The classics for psychology include William McKinley Runyan's *Life Histories and Psychobiography* (1982), Dan McAdams's *Power, Intimacy and the Life Story* (1985) and *The Stories We Live By* (1993) and A.I. Rabin, Robert A. Zucker, Robert A. Emmons and Susan Frank (eds), *Studying Persons and Lives* (1990). The earliest book-length appraisal of the method is John Dollard's *Criteria for the Life History* (1935), which sets out criteria for the appraisal of life histories and applies them to a number of cases. Subsequent overviews and commentaries are those by H.S. Becker in his introduction to C. Shaw's *The Jack Roller* (1966 edition), which is reprinted in his *Sociological Work* (Becker, 1971).

The work in **oral history** is vast and there are many resources to guide the newcomer into it. Paul Thompson's *The Voice of the Past* was originally published in 1978 but is now in its 3rd edition (2000). It remains a comprehensive review. Several other good guides include: Rob Perks, *Oral History: An Annotated Bibliography* (1990); Rob Perks, *Oral History: Talking About the Past* (2nd edn, 1995); D. Ritchie, *Doing Oral History* (1995) and V.R. Yow, *Recording Oral History: A Practical Guide for Social Scientists* (1994). Three useful collections of readings are: S.B. Gluck and D. Patai (eds), *Women's Words: The Feminist Practice of Oral History* (1991); Rob Perks and Alastair Thompson (eds), *The Oral History Reader* (1998);

and David Dunaway and Willa K. Baum, *Oral History: An Interdisciplinary Anthology* (2nd edn, 1996). Three classics which debate theoretical issues are: Elizabeth Tonkin, *Narrating Our Pasts: The Social Construction of Oral History* (1992); J. Vansina, *Oral Tradition: A Study in Historical Methodology* (1965) and Allesandro Portelli, *The Death of Luigi Trastulli and Other Stories: Form and Meaning in Oral History* (1991). For updating and regular information see two major journals: *Oral History Review* (from the Center for Oral History, U-205, 404 Babbidge Road, University of Connecticut, Storrs, CT 06269-1205, USA), and *Oral History* (available from the Department of Sociology, University of Essex, CO4 3SQ, UK). See also *Memory and Narrative* (Vol. 1, 1997), the *International Journal of Oral History* (Vol. 1, 1980), which became the *International Yearbook of Oral History and Life Stories* (1993–1996), as well as journals in New Zealand, Canada, Australia, France, Spain, Germany, Brazil and elsewhere. There is a short but useful guide to world oral history societies and their journals at the end of Rob Perks and Alastair Thompson (eds), *The Oral History Reader* (1998: 465–71). For some web site listings, see Gluck et al., 'Reflections on oral history in the new millennium' (1999: 25–7).

Mass observation is based at the University of Sussex, under the auspices of Dorothy Sheridan, both the earlier archives and the more recent studies (Mass Observation Archive, The Library, University of Sussex, Falmer, BN1 9QL). It also has a web site (see Appendix). On **genealogy**, see Julia Watson's critical 'Ordering the family' (1996) and some of the sources she refers to: the *American Genealogist*, *Genealogical Journal*, *National Genealogical Quarterly*, and Doane and Bell's *Searching for Your Ancestors*.

On the role of **personal experience and auto-ethnography**, see recent works by Pierre Bourdieu, *Homo Academicus* (1988), Rosanna Hertz (ed.), *Reflexivity and Voice* (1997), Deborah E. Reed-Danahay (ed.), *Auto/ Ethnography: Rewriting the Self and the Social* (1997), and Barry Glassner and Rosanna Hertz's edited *Qualitative Sociology as Everyday Life* (1999). See also the works by Carolyn Ellis and Michael Flaherty (eds), *Investigating Subjectvity* (1992b), Carolyn Ellis and Art Bochner, *Composing Ethnography* (1996), and Susan Krieger, *Social Science and the Self* (1991). Three recent studies which draw heavily upon personal experience are Carolyn Ellis's *Final Negotiations* (1995), Susan Krieger's *The Family Silver* (1996) and Laurel Richardson's *Fields of Play* (1998).

There is now a vast literature in 'biographical work'. The term itself, I think, was originally coined in Gubrium and Lyncott's 'Alzheimer's disease as biographical work' (1985). A good introduction to the whole field is in chapter 1 of Gary Kenyon and William Randall's *Restorying Our Lives: Personal Growth Through Autobiographical Reflection* (1997), but the whole book is very readable and full of ideas.

3 Accessories to a Life Story: From Written Diaries to Video Diaries

I have often thought that there has rarely passed a life of which a judicious and faithful narrative would not be useful.

(Samuel Johnson, 1750)

It is perhaps as difficult to write a good life as to live one.

(Lytton Strachey, 1880–1932)

Miss Prism You must put away your diary, Cecily. I really don't see why you should keep a diary at all.
Cecily: I keep a diary in order to enter the wonderful secrets of my life. If I didn't write them all down, I should probably forget all about them.

(Oscar Wilde, 1895, *The Importance of Being Earnest*, Act II)

Every person their own methodologist! Methodologists get to work!

(Mills, 1970: 137)

Having seen something of the standard range of life stories, this chapter goes on a whirlwind tour of ways of adding to them. Although the most standard approach has been to take a life story through an interview, there are many other 'tools' that can be employed – from simple diary keeping to more elaborate video diaries. In this chapter, once again, the the aim is fairly basic: to provide illustrations of these allied methods and hopefully to encourage their use.

Diaries

For Gordon Allport (1942: 95), the diary is the document of life *par excellence*, chronicling as it does the immediately contemporaneous flow of public and private events that are significant to the diarist. The word 'contemporary' is very crucial here, for each diary entry – unlike life histories – is sedimented into a particular moment in time: they do not emerge 'all at once' as reflections on the past, but day by day strive to record an ever-changing present. Every diary entry declares, 'I am here, and it is exactly now' (Fothergill, 1974: 9). Yet whilst this is true it would also be naive to believe that each day's entry is that alone: for at least in sustained diary keeping, the diarist will eventually come to perceive the diary as a whole and to plan a selection of entries according to this plan. Indeed, as Fothergill comments:

> . . . As a diary grows to a certain length and substance, it impresses upon the mind of its writer a conception of the completed book that it might ultimately be, if sustained with sufficient dedication and vitality. If, having written regularly and fully for, let us say, several months, (s)he were to abandon the habit, (s)he would be leaving unwritten a book whose character and conventions had been established and whose final form is the shape of his life. (Fothergill, 1974: 44)

Such an issue is clearly raised by the most famous diaries of all: those of Samuel Pepys. There was little of significance before his daily nine-year venture, which led to 1,250,000 words in some 3,100 pages, and today it is generally deemed to 'fulfil all the conditions of what a diary should be' (Ponsonby, 1923: 82). Yet whilst it is common to believe that Pepys simply 'sat down every night for nine years just scribbling with effortless frankness the little incidents which [he was] honest enough to record as having caught [his] attention at the moment' (Fothergill, 1974: 42), it becomes clear from the new revised Latham–Matthews edition that the diary was not produced daily, but rather evolved: 'a product fashioned with some care, both in its matter and style' (Pepys, 1970: ciii). Diaries, then, are certainly valuable in talking to the subjectivity of a particular moment; but they usually will go beyond this to a conception of some whole.

Whilst there are a good number of literary diaries – see the classic studies by Ponsonby (1923) and Fothergill (1974) – there is little socio-logical usage. Park employed them in his Race Relations Survey in the 1920s (cf. Bogardus, 1926) and Palmer's research text *Field Studies in Sociology* (1928) can cite two other studies – Cavan's (1928) analysis of two suicide diaries and Mowrer's (1927) case study of Miriam Donaven, a young woman whose marriage gradually fell apart. Both these studies involve the use of diaries in only a very limited way, and subsequent reviews have hardly been able to depict any sustained refinement of the method (cf. Allport, 1942: ch. 8; Denzin, 1978a: 223–6), not least perhaps because the diary as a form of writing seems to be going out of fashion. Yet 'diaries' may still be one of the better tools for getting at the day-to-day experiences of a personal life; and some (often feminist) social scientists have tried to resurrect their importance (e.g. Bell, 1998).

Four apparent forms of diary research stand out. (See Allport's dis-cussion of the intimate journal, the log and the memoir (1942) for a slightly different classification.) The first is simply where *informants keep diaries*. The anthropologist Pat Caplan, for instance, asked her key Tanzanian informant Mohammed to keep a diary as well as keeping one herself, and they serve as a core organizing device for the book *African*

Voices, African Lives (1997), organized through themes such as 'marriage', 'puberty rites', 'the land', 'the sea' and 'being an ancestor'. Another study, by Maas and Kuypers (1974) of adjustments to old age in the lives of 142 upper class San Franciscans, asked a number of their respondents to keep diaries for a week. The subjects were given booklets with a day allocated to each page (each page subdivided into morning, afternoon and evening) and were given the following instructions:

> We would like you to keep a daily diary to help us get some idea of how you spend your time during a typical week. We are especially interested in the kinds of things you do, when you do them, for how long and whether you do them with other people. As you write your diary, be sure to include the time of the day when you get up, have your meals, go out of the house, and any other major activity. Also be sure to include whom you met, what you did with them. You may also want to include some of the thoughts and feelings that you had during the day. At the end of the week, look over the diary to see if you have described a pretty typical seven days. Make any comment you want about what you have written . . . (Maas and Kuypers, 1974: 218)

Their study is subsequently richly documented with extracts from these diaries. In their instructions the authors have attempted to get round two central weaknesses – *selectivity* (by indicating what should be included) and *typicality* (by asking their respondents to comment upon this) – but it is essentially a somewhat flat method, for their concern was more with creating ideal types and statistical probabilities than with insights into specific lives.

This method has recently been applied in the pandemic of AIDS to look at men's sexual lives. In what Anthony P.M. Coxon (1996) and his colleagues at Project Sigma call *'the sexual diary'*, men are asked to keep a regular diary of their sexual encounters – usually for a month or so. They are asked to log in – on a daily basis – a record of their partners, activities, days, times and setting in which various sexual activities occurred (from a long and interesting list of various sexual practices!), adding in comments on ejaculations, roles played and the like. Their 'sexual diary analysis' has led to a significant database logging on over 50,000 sexual acts in 25,000 sexual sessions, by 1,035 individuals. In the end, however, this style of research once again does move more and more towards a quantitative study of 'events' rather than an interpretive study of lives. The same can be true of much of the work which adopts time *'logs'* and *'time budgets'*. Sorokin pioneered this method when he asked informants to keep detailed 'time-budget schedules' showing just how they allocated their time during a day (Sorokin and Berger, 1938) and others have used similar approaches in documenting the events of 'One Boy's Day' (Barker and Wright, 1951) (cf. Gershuny and Sullivan, 1998).

Perhaps the most celebrated use is that of Oscar Lewis. Lewis's particular method focused on a few specific families in Mexico, and the analysis of a 'day' in each of their lives. Of course his actual familiarity with each family was in no way limited to a day – nothing of value could possibly be gained from that. He 'spent hundreds of hours with them in their homes, ate with them, joined in their fiestas and dances, listened to their troubles, and discussed with them the history of their lives' (Lewis, 1959: 5). But in the end he decided that it would be analytically more valuable, for both humanistic and scientific purposes, to focus upon 'the day' as a unit of study. Thus each family – Martinez, Gomez, Gutierez, Sanchez and Castro – is first presented as a 'cast of characters' and then followed through one arbitrarily chosen but not untypical day of their life. Lewis believed that a study of a day had at least a threefold value: practically, it was small enough to allow for intensive observation, quantitatively it permitted controlled comparisons across family units, and qualitatively it encouraged a sensitivity to the subtlety, immediacy and wholeness of life.

A third type of diary study has been called *'the diary diary–interview method'*. Here, Don Zimmerman and Laurence Wieder were involved in examining the Californian counter-culture and found considerable difficulties in observing the full daily pattern of activities of their subjects. In place of observation they instituted a method in which respondents were paid a fee of $10 to keep a full diary for seven days. As they comment:

> The diary writer was asked to record in chronological order the activities in which he or she engaged over the course of seven days. We provided the formula: Who/What/When/Where/How? We asked them to report the identity of the participants in the activities described not by name, of course, but by relationship to the writer – e.g. room-mate, lover and so on – using initials to differentiate individuals and noting the sex of those involved. The 'What?' involved a description of the activity or discussion recorded in the diarists' own categories. 'When?' involved reference to the timing of the activity, with special attention to recording the actual sequence of events. 'Where?' involved a designation of the location of the activity, suitably coded to prevent identification of individuals or place. The 'How?' involved a description of what ever logistics were entailed by the activity, e.g. how transport was secured, how marijuana was obtained. (Zimmerman and Wieder, 1977: 486)

Of particular interest in their method is not just the rich documentation they gained about seven days of a person's life, but the fact that the person is subsequently interviewed step by step on each facet of the diary that has been presented.

The above three forms of diary research – the requested, the log and the 'diary diary–interview' – all entail the social scientist soliciting diaries and are comparable to the social scientist soliciting life histories. But there is a fourth type which depends on applying pre-existing diaries. Just as the life historian could also turn to pre-existing biographies to analyse, so the diary researcher could examine the plethora of pre-existing diaries. Many people publish 'diaries', from the lowly to the famous. And they can become a wonderful resource for analysis. But there are also many contemporary examples of this writing – as is seen in the outporing of AIDS diaries, capturing the illness, the stigma and the dying (e.g. Chambers, 1998; Monette, 1992). In each case an original subjective story is told from which the social scientists could start to learn a great deal. Thus, two much discussed and celebrated diaries are those of Arthur Munby and Hannah Cullwick, where a working class 'servant girl' reveals her day-to-day curious relationship with her middle class employer, as he reveals his. It has been the subject of many re-readings and reflections on gender and class in Victorian times (Davidoff, 1979; Stanley, 1984, 1992).

Letters

Letters remain a relatively rare document of life in the social sciences. Without doubt, the most thoroughgoing use of letters is still to be found in Thomas and Znaniecki's *Polish Peasant*, where on discovering that there was extensive correspondence between Poles and Polish emigrés to America, an advertisement was placed in a Chicago journal offering to pay between 10 and 20 cents for each letter received. Through this method they were able to gain many hundreds of letters, 764 of which are printed in the first volume of their study, totalling some 800 pages and arranged in fifty family sequences. Each sequence is prefaced with a commentary that introduces the family members and the main concerns. The letters, highly formal, are designated 'bowing letters' and exist primarily 'to manifest the persistence of familial solidarity in spite of separation' (1958: 303). In addition to this, Thomas and Znaniecki suggest that the letters perform five main functions corresponding to five main types of letters. These are:

1   Ceremonial letters – sent on such familial occurrences as normally require the presence of all the members of the family – weddings, christenings, funerals, Christmas, New Year, Easter. These letters are substitutes for ceremonial speeches.
2   Informing letters – providing a detailed narration of the life of the absent member of the family group.
3   Sentimental letters – which have the task of reviving the feelings in the individual, independently of any ceremonial occasion.
4   Literary letters – which have a central aesthetic function.
5   Business letters (cf. Thomas and Znaniecki, 1958).

The letters are used inductively to arrive at a more general characterization of peasant society, particularly its subjective aspects. It remains to this day the most detailed use of letters, and an example is given below. Since 'The Series' is too long to reproduce, I have selected an extract from a concluding section on 'fragments'. It deals with demoralization of a wife in the absence of her husband. The latter, in spite of his emigration, shows more familial feeling, even with regard to the children, than the wife. The letter tends to establish a relation of solidarity between the husband and the rest of the family as against the wife

'Praised be Jesus Christus.' . . . And now, dear father, what does all this mean that you write me? Why does my wife not wish to come to America, and writes me such stupid things that I am [illegible word] with her? I have sent her a shipticket for all, and she writes me such silly things and is not ashamed of it. When I sent the ticket I sent for all, and not for her alone. Could I leave the children? My heart does not allow me to leave my own children. Then, dear father, if she does not wish to listen it will end badly for her. Dear father, bow to her [ironically] and take the children to yourself, and I will send you directly two hundred roubles for the children, and let her do as she pleases. And if not, then give this shipticket to [sister] Kostka. Let Kostka come with this ticket. She has only to give the name and the age of my wife. Let her come with the children, and when Kostusia [Kostka] comes we will do well together, and my wife, as she was a public woman, so may she remain a public woman. And if the children fear to go, please, father take them to your home; I will send you 200 roubles. Let her not make a fool of me in America, as if I were her servant; this is neither right nor necessary. When someone read me that letter of hers, finally I did not let him finish, because I was ashamed.

If nobody comes with this ticket, I will get the money back and will send it directly to you, father, for the children. And if not, let Kostusia come alone if the children don't want to come. [B. Leszczyc] (Thomas and Znaniecki, 1958: 816–17)

Another vivid use of letters in social science is to be found in Gordon Allport's editing and interpreting of the *Letters from Jenny* (Allport, 1965; Simeoni and Diani, 1995b). These letters were written by an ageing woman to two friends of her son – Isabel and Glenn – between 1926 and her death in 1937. As Jenny is thwarted by everything around her (especially by her son), and totters from one deep despair to another, she takes time out to write it all down and post it to these remote friends. They rarely meet and the whole story unfolds as a dramatic first person narrative. The readers can tease their way into Jenny's obsessive relationship with her son, into her crises, into her changing reconstructions of things written earlier, to an increasingly predictable series of 'resigned' moments, even happy ones, followed by a long slump into what she calls her 'slough of despond'. The vividness of the letters derives from the way they report life as it happens – each dreadful anxiety is shared with the letter's recipient. And all the way through, too, we get glimpses of the wider social world; she works for some time in a children's home and captures in her letters the appalling conditions where she has to be 'a whipper, a common spanker of little children, a beast, a cur for fifty dollars a month' (Allport, 1965: 32); she ends up her days in an old people's home where she initially feels 'wonderfully well' (p. 97), and finally cries how she is 'hungry to death for a little human companionship' (p. 130).

The case of Frank Moore, an institutionalized alcoholic, in *Escape from Custody* (Straus, 1974) differs from both the immigrant's and Jenny's letters in so far as the recipient in this case is the sociologist. For over 25 years Frank Moore corresponded directly with Robert Straus about his experiences of drifting in and out of institutions, in and out of work and on and off alcohol dependency – 'the life of a wharf rat' as he puts it. Sometimes, as when he is treated on 'antabuse' to shake him off alcohol, the letters can carry a sense of optimism – 'this antabuse treatment, to my mind, affords the first real test with regards to any constructive treatment. I hope I shall be worthy of the opportunities this place seems to afford,' he writes on 17 June.

Such writings indicate that many insights can be gained from the study of letters, yet these materials are only rarely to be found in social science. And in good part this may simply be due to the obvious fact that such letters are increasingly hard to come by – letter-writing appears to be a dying art and even when letters are sent they are most commonly thrown away rather than stored and collected. Bundles of 300 or so letters from the same person to the same recipient (like Jenny's described above) must today be seen as relatively rare and exciting finds. And even when one recipient keeps all the letters, it is unlikely that both will so that even with the immigrants' letters only one side of the exchange was typically found (cf. Riley, 1963: 242). When letters are used these days, they tend to be letters that are written to magazines and newspapers or letters that are solicited by the researcher as in, for example, Nancy Friday's volumes on sexual fantasy (Friday, 1976). That said, there are signs of a resurgence of interest in letter writing through 'electronic mail' (although this does seem to take a quite different and more casual mode!). It could be that in the future the analysis of e-mail will take on an increasingly significant role.

Nevertheless, even when such letters are available, social scientists are likely to remain suspicious of their value on a number of scores. First, as Ponsonby remarks, 'letters may be said to have two parents, the writer and the recipient' (Ponsonby, 1923: 2). Consequently, every letter speaks not just of the writer's world, but also of the writer's perceptions of the recipient. The kind of story told shifts with the person who will read it – witness the different letters produced by Robert Burns to his mistress, his friends, his wife on the same day. The social scientist then should view a letter as an interactive product, always enquiring into the recipient's role. In all the studies described above this is largely a mystery; the recipients included unknown family members, a sociologist and two remote friends. What would the stories told look like if the letters had been sent to other recipients: if the Polish peasants wrote to the sociologist, if Frank

Moore wrote to remote friends, and Jenny wrote to her family! They would surely look very different indeed.

A further problem with letters concerns what Webb et al. referred to as the 'dross rate' (1966: 105). Letters are not generally focused enough to be of analytic interest – they contain far too much material that strays from the researcher's concern. Thus Allport acknowledges that he has cut Jenny's letters down by two-thirds (Allport, 1965: vi), presumably because they otherwise would have produced unmanageably boring and repetitive ramblings that would be of little value to social science. Yet, of course, in cutting out this dross rate, Allport may also be engaged in selecting Jenny's ideas to focus upon issues that interest him. A form of hidden censorship and selective screening may be taking place.

'Vox populi' and guerrilla journalism

When many lives are recorded in less depth than life histories, and offered to the reader with little commentary, we can speak of 'guerrilla journalism' – a term coined by one of the leading exponents of this method, Studs Terkel, for himself. Terkel's great skill lies in simply getting people to talk into his recorder: in *Hard Times* they tell of the Depression, in *Division Street: America* they tell of city life in Chicago, in *American Dreams* they talk of aspiration and change in America, and, most celebratedly, in *Working* 130 Americans speak of their jobs, the violence it does to them and their 'search for daily meaning as well as daily bread' (Terkel, 1968, 1970, 1977, 1978, 1981). Characteristically, this style of work – with its affinity to the naturalistic novels of Zola, the voices to be found in Mayhew and the reportage of Agee and Evans in *Let Us Now Praise Famous Men* – shuns any claims to being theoretical or scientific: the search for criteria of adequacy like those given by Dollard are of no concern. Thus, Terkel comments in the opening of his oral documentation of city life in Chicago:

> Being neither sociologist nor a research man, motivational or otherwise, I followed no blueprint or book or set of statistics. I played hunches – in some instances, long shots . . . I was on the prowl for a cross section of urban thought, using no one method or technique . . . I realized quite early in this adventure that interviews, conventionally conducted, were meaningless. (Terkel, 1968: 19–21)

Terkel listens, records, transcribes and then publishes, with the minimum of comment and the maximum of content. Whether what the people say is valid is left to the reader, although Terkel's memoirs *Talking to Myself* provide personal accounts of some of the interviews (Terkel, 1978) and elsewhere he has commented on his method (Grele, 1975; Parker, 1996).

'The literature of fact': faction, the new journalism, and the new auto/biography

One curious breed of life document, largely neglected by the social scientist, is the writing that takes on the form of a fictional novel but which is dealing with true events fully researched by the author (Berger, 1977; Weber, 1981; Zavarzadeh, 1976). Such an approach has a long history – Defoe's *A Journal of the Plague Year*, Dickens's *Sketches by Boz*, or Orwell's *Down and Out in Paris and London* are early examples. More recently, social scientists have been know to fictionalize their fieldwork, often to make it more readable and more accessible as a novel (as in *Return to Laughter*, by Laura Bohana (pseud. Eleanor Smith Bowen), 1954). This can make the line between fact and fiction hard to draw (as in the controversies surrounding the Yacqui Indian tales of Carlos Castaneda, see Chapter 12). The whole idea gained prominence in America in the postwar period, notably with the publication of Truman Capote's *In Cold Blood* (1966). For this 'murder story' Capote researched a notorious slaying of an entire family by two young men, who were subsequently caught, tried and executed. Whilst the story unfolds, the reader is aware that this is fact not fiction. Yet it is produced with the skill of an artist, not that of a scientist.

The boundaries of this life document are 'blurred' here. It incorporates all those studies which are clearly literary and humanistic but which deal with researched fact rather than fiction. Tom Wolfe's name for it is '*The New Journalism*' (the title of a 1973/5 book), which he defines simply as 'journalism that would read like a novel'. It involves detailed research into a real life topic that is then written up in a literate, fiction format, usually jettisoning a grand style for a more down-to-earth approach. Partially such writing sets out to dethrone the novel, achieving a novelistic style but around factual matters.

Sometimes this genre can be made to embrace the tradition of oral interview, such as the works of Studs Terkel (as above) or the journalist and war correspondent John Hersey, whose *Hiroshima* provides six interviews with atomic bomb survivors (1972). Sometimes it is signposted as a highly subjective account by an observing writer – Agee's personal tale of share-croppers in the Mid-West during the Depression is a classic example (Agee and Evans, 1965). Sometimes the social scientist is actually seen to exemplify it – Oscar Lewis's work, for example, is frequently cited. There is clearly no firm boundary to this style of work except that it all manages to weave a literary (and literate!) tale around detailed research and analysis of a real life event.

Although around for some 30 years or so, this 'literature of fact' keeps sprouting new forms and rejuvenating itself: 'style journalism' (Peter York), 'rock journalism' (Tony Parsons), travel writing (Bill Bryson), 'true crime' reporting (for example, Gordon Burns's accounts of Peter Sutcliffe and Fred West, and Blake Morrison's account of the Jamie Bulger case) and 'confessionalism' of all kinds (cf. Denzin, 1997).

Possessions and 'biographical objects'

What a person owns, or fails to own, can serve as a useful 'memory jogger' in research. But it goes deeper than this – indicating a lifestyle and identity. Pierre Bourdieu puts this powerfully:

> Identity is found in all the properties – and property with which individuals and groups surround themselves, houses, furniture, paintings, books, cars, spirits, cigarettes, perfume, clothes, and in the practices with which they manifest their distinction, sports, games, entertainment, because it is the synthetic unity of the habitus, the unifying generative principle of all practices. Taste, the propensity and capacity to appropriate (materially or symbolically) a given class of classified, classifying objects or practices, is the generative formula of a life style. (Bourdieu, 1984: 173)

To grasp the significance of this, conduct a little experiment on yourself. Simply move around your house or room, inspecting each item in it – from clothes to furniture, from photos to books, from CDs to memorabilia. Ponder the circumstances in your life that led to you getting this 'possession' – your interests and friends, where you were at the time, what's happened to it since, your feelings towards it then and now. A bookcase or a record/CD collection is a goldmine of biographical incidents – many items may have been acquired randomly and have little history, but many others will speak hugely complex stories. Ponder too what this says about your lifestyle. Sometimes, this looking over 'the family silver' can provide telling metaphors for a life (cf. Krieger, 1996). Rummaging through attics can be particularly rewarding and, on occasions, dustbins are not without a tale to tell. Indeed, there is a whole specialist interdisciplinary field of 'garbology' studies, which spends its time rummaging through dustbins and rubbish tips to suggest that 'what people have owned – and thrown away – can speak more eloquently, informatively and truthfully about the lives they lead than they themselves ever may (Rathje and Murphy, 1992: 54; cf. Webb et al., 1966: 41).

A classic illustration of this concern is the systematic examination of the possessions of fourteen poor families living in a Mexico City slum, by Oscar Lewis (1969). As he puts it:

> The inquiry opens up a mine of interesting questions. What proportions of their income do poor people spend on furniture, on clothing, on religious objects, on luxury items, on medicines? How much of what they buy is new? How much second hand? To what extent do they depend on gifts or hand me downs? How do families in poverty finance their purchases? Where do they do their shopping? How wide are their choices? What is the physical condition of their possessions? How long do they manage to hold on to them? I was able to obtain rather detailed information on all these matters. (Lewis, 1970: 442)

His analysis considers thirteen categories of possession and does provide a number of interesting insights. For instance, all the poor families had at least one shelf for religious ornaments, but this was the only category of possessions where the poorer families had spent more than the better off.

This interest in how possessions speak about lives has developed into a major part of 'cultural and consumption studies', a newish field of study which focuses especially on 'material cultures' and how objects come to illustrate and play key roles in lives. These studies look at the life choices and decisions that lead people to collect objects like 'clothing, vehicles, homes, foods, drinks, magazines, fragrances, pets, entertainments and alterations to our bodies – all convey information to us and others about who we are' (Belk, 1995: 64). Often such objects are part of a person's 'cultural capital' (cf. Bourdieu, 1984), helping to fashion their position in the hierarchy of the society in which they live.

Although modern western cultures may find meanings to lives in all these consumable possessions, 'biographical objects' can be found in all societies and can assume very different meanings. The anthropologist Janet Hoskins (1998), for example, has studied the Kodinese of Eastern Indonesia and shown that although they may not 'tell their stories' in particularly western modes, they do have 'objects' – drums, betel bags, special cloths with special iconography – which assume enormous significance in the telling of their tales.

My listing of adjuncts to a life story could continue. Some researchers, for example, have made use of the inscriptions on tombstones (Warner, 1963), scrutinized suicide notes (Schwartz and Jacobs, 1979), looked at CVs (Danahay, 1996; Miller and Morgan, 1993), read obituaries (Nardi, 1990), examined photographs and art in people's homes – who is displayed and how (Halle, 1993) – looked at the making of quilts and the stories behind them (including the AIDS quilt) (Lewis and Fraser, 1996), and examined monuments of all kinds. Everywhere, it seems, there are documents of life awaiting the sociological eye.

Life stories and the 'other senses': the case of the world of the visual

Most of the western human sciences are 'verbal' and structured through narratives and the written word: it is comparatively rare to find arguments made through visual images. Words matter, images are suspect. The same is true of life stories. In the main they are organized through the conventions of writing: lives are written. Yet we also inhabit worlds of other senses – of sight and touch, of sound and smell. In some cultures, other senses may be seen to play a much larger role – the Ongee of the Adaman Islands, for example, live in worlds ordered much more by smell, whilst the Trotzil of Mexico find a world where heat and temperature underpin the cosmos (cf. Classen, 1993). By and large, 'a world of other senses' has not been featured in the human sciences. We do not generally document the smells and tastes of lives; though as the new millennium is reached, certain of these senses are playing (belatedly) an increased role. Sound and recordings are becoming more prominent and there are growing numbers of 'sound archives' (the new British Library in London, for instance, houses a wide selection of recordings in the National Sound Archive). Likewise, visual representations have moved from being highly specialist art forms to being accessible to almost everybody – photographs, films, videos and computer graphics are becoming more and more 'democratized' in ever-more sophisticated forms, providing wonderful accessories to the telling of a life. In what follows, I will briefly locate some issues around the visual – but there are many excellent book-length introductions to this important and expanding area (e.g. Chaplin, 1994: see further reading at the end of the chapter).

Photographs

To start thinking about this, three quotes may be helpful:

> It is the advent of the Photograph. . . which divides the history of the world. (Barthes, 1984)

> In no other form of society in history has there been such a concentration of images. Such a density of visual images. (Berger, 1972)

> You could never envisage all the camera has seen, countless images scattered at random in time and space like the fragments of a vast and ancient mosaic, the remnants of a visual holocaust, the ruins of representation . . . colossal . . . a unique map, a phantom topography, coiling the entire globe, an endless collage which in the end forms . . . another world, the true surrealist universe . . . you will never know a limit to all the stories, plots, parables, histories, myths and fictions spawned in this oneiric archive – assuming it can exist – the truths it could tell if only we knew how to read its languages, interpret its codes, translate its evidence . . . (McQuire, 1998: Introduction)

These are startling quotes. They suggest at once the newness, the power and the pervasiveness of the photograph. They suggest that contemporary history is shifted by the photograph. And they hint strikingly at the way in which the camera has entered the modern mind. If diaries and letters became central life documents (as least in the middle classes) during the nineteenth century, then they have now been rapidly overtaken by photography. Born at approximately the same time as sociology, photography has gone on to become many things. In Susan Sontag's early essay *On Photography* (1979), she suggests inter alia that the photograph has become the democratiser of personal documents (in family albums and holidays shots for all), a major new genre of art, the embodiment of individualism (in the rise of photographic portraiture), a mode of refusing experience, a strategy for conveying immortality, and last but not least, a form of surveillance and control. Likewise, John Berger's telling account *About Looking* (1980: 52) suggests how quickly photography came to be used for matters as diverse as 'police filing, military reconnaissance, pornography, encylopedia documentation, family albums, postcards, anthropological records ... sentimental moralizing, inquisitive probing, ... aesthetic effects, news reporting, ... formal portraiture ...'. Others, more recently, have seen it as creating a radical shift in the very ways we live – as generating a new visual technology which becomes a way of life and shaping what Celia Lury has called a 'prosthetic culture' where the naturally given body is transformed into a more experimental and shifting one. A camera can 'frame, freeze and fix its objects', turning how the body and the world is seen into something different from what it once was (1998: 3). In their growing (digitalized) sophistication, photographs can now be taken inside the darkest recesses of the human body, as well as at the farthest reaches of our planet. They can be 'morphed' via computer technologies into photos that bear no resemblance to an actual reality. They can document a life, but they can also invent a life.

Yet despite the billions of photographs being produced by lay person and professional alike each year for a multitude of purposes, many branches of the human sciences, and especially sociology, remain relatively untouched by it. In the 1880s, Lewis W. Hine – trained as a sociologist at Chicago and New York – used photos to express the subjective story, of 'photo-interpretations', especially those that revealed social inequities – of young children in factories, of poor housing, of immigrants arriving at Ellis Island off New York (Hine, 1977). And in the earliest days of the *American Journal of Sociology*, photographs were a regular feature in connection with its muck-raking, reformist articles: between 1896 and 1916 thirty-one articles used 244 photographs (see Stasz, 1979a). Likewise, many of the early Chicago studies – Frederick Thrasher's The Gang, for example – included an array of photographs. Recent studies in this tradition such as Mitch Duneier's *Slim's Table* (1992) and *Sidewalk* (1999), which both include photos – in the former case there seem to have been lots to draw upon from the work of Ovie Carter (Duneier, 1992: 164–8). Still, in the main sociologists have not taken much interest in what should now be viewed both as a major artefact of twentieth-century life and a (potentially) major tool for investigation.

The lead has primarily come from journalistic photographers (such as Jacob A. Riis's visual depiction of impoverished styles in New York City's slums (Riis, 1971), and photojournalists (such as the National Press Photographers Association, 1978). The breakthrough in social science is usually seen to be in the work of anthropologists: particularly the pioneering work of Gregory Bateson and Margaret Mead on *Balinese Character: A Photographic Analysis* (1942). Married, and both working on Balinese culture for nearly a decade prior to this classic study, they sought to capture the *ethos of the culture*; words seemed lacking, and they struck upon the idea of using photographs. Indeed, with Bateson photographing and Mead directing, they took some 25,000 photos over two years. They did not select or get people to pose for photos but took them rapidly and randomly and then used them subsequently (or at least 759 of them!) to inform and illustrate the text which described aspects of the culture of the Balinese. Overall the book's photos are organized into cultural categories: spatial orientation and levels; learning; integration and disintegration of the body; orifices of the body; autocosmic play; parents and children; siblings; stages of child development; and rites of passage. In a chapter on rites of passage, for instance, photos of marriages and funerals are placed opposite a text which describes them (an example is reproduced in Figure 3.1). Recently, some of Malinowski's earlier photographic work has been published for the first time (Young, 1999).

Sociology turned its attention to the photograph more seriously during the 1970s: a small group of American sociologists became concerned about its use, organized exhibitions of their photographic work, and coined the term 'visual sociology'. Howard Becker (1974), for instance, wrote a major review of the state of the field in general (looking at its history, uses, theoretical issues and general problems) for the journal *Studies in the Anthropology of Visual Communication* and a new 'International Visual Sociology Association' came to be established with its own journal and newsletter (Harper, 1994).

There are many ways in which photography can be put to work for sociology. Curry and Clarke (1977) suggest it may serve as an illustration, as visual information or as source material for analysis, whilst Wagner (1979: 16–19) suggests fives modes of photographic research: as interview stimuli, for systematic recordings of social phenomena, for sustained content analysis, for 'native' image-making and for 'narrative visual theory'. Photographic theory – by contrast – tends to champion a more critical approach. Using semiology and psychoanalysis, it has developed a critical analysis of the process of 'signification' how signs and meanings are produced – and the relation between the photographic image and reality (cf. Barthes, 1984; Burgin, 1982; Sontag, 1979). In what follows, I will chart just four strands of use in social science, which hint at this increasing complexity: how photos may be used as *documentation*, as *visual theory*, as *resource* and as *critical representation*.

Perhaps the most obvious use to date is that of the photograph *as documentation* – an essentially descriptive task where the photo is designed simply to illustrate text. Thus, Don Kulick's study of Brazilian *Travesti* (1999) includes a number of photographs of transvestites and transsexuals which bring a richer life to the text: you can see what injecting silicon into the buttocks does to them! Jerry Jacobs's photographs of a retirement community, *Sun City* (1974), captures the cleanliness and desolation revealed in the ethnographic text. On the surface, these are unextraordinary, unremarkable yet surprisingly uncommon ways in which photographs could be used to enhance life stories. This 'documentary tradition' can also be extended to book-length studies. Michael

Plate 43

COCKFIGHTING

Of the large variety of autocosmic toys of childhood, one of the most important of those which persist into adult life is the fighting cock. Cockfighting, in Bali, is a gambling sport which is indulged in by a very large proportion of the male population. There are certain individuals, however, who are particularly addicted to it, who keep many fighting cocks, go constantly to cockfights, and bet more than they can afford. Men whose citizenship is incomplete or who have been disappointed in some way "take to" cockfighting, as men in our civilization take to drink.

The evidence for regarding the fighting cock as a genital symbol comes from the postures of men holding cocks, the sex slang and sex jingles, and from Balinese carvings of men with fighting cocks. The postures imagined by the carver are even more diagnostic than those of the living men.

1. Watching a cockfight. The men in the front rank of the audience, and especially those whose cocks are fighting, usually squat in this way with their arms supported on the knees at a point just above the elbows. The man on the right had lost his citizenship in the village because his only child had been a girl. He was an addict of cockfighting. M. M. observed that when he was excited watching his cock in battle, he moved his hands as if he were identifying with the conflict rather than with his own cock. In his hand movements, it appeared that one hand represented one cock while the other hand represented the other.

Unidentified man in left foreground; I Kari on the right.

Bajoeng Gede. Jan. 21, 1937. 4 Ga 37.

2. Watching a cockfight. The man on the left is squatting in the typical position, and has his fingers extended so that they just touch the ground.

Nang Oera; Nang Salib.

Bajoeng Gede. Feb. 2, 1937. 4 K 20.

3. Matching the cocks and making them angry. First the cocks are tried one against another to find two which will fight. This is done by holding them so that they face each other, while their owners pluck at their combs, flutter their hackle feathers and make the cocks peck at each other (as in this photograph). The first bet is placed by the owners, and this bet is always even. (Later bets are placed by both owners and spectators and various

odds may be given.) Before the fight each man holds the other man's cock, so that he can feel the enemy cock's strength and make sure that it is not much stronger than his own. When the cocks are matched and angry, they are separated and a long steel spur is carefully bound onto the lower surface of each cock's left foot. The cocks are again brought together and after further teasing are freed to fight each other. The rounds are regulated by an umpire with a water-clock.

Batoean. Oct. 5, 1937. 16 R 33.

4. Matching the cocks and making them angry. The man facing the camera is ruffling up the hackle feathers under the cock's neck with quick upward-patting movements (cf. Pl. 38, fig. 2).

Nang Oera facing the camera; Nang Salib behind him.

Bajoeng Gede. Feb. 2, 1937. 4 K 16.

5. Man holding a cock. He is rising from a squatting position. Many men spend hours sitting, playing with their cocks.

Nang Karma.

Bajoeng Gede. Jan. 17, 1937. 4 C 5.

6. Man examining the legs of a cock. Every fighting cock has an elaborate toilet every day including a bath (like that of a baby) with water containing onions and various leaves.

I Lanoes, vagrant worker and habitual clown.

Bajoeng Gede. Oct. 24, 1936. 3 A 22.

FIGURE 3.1   **Cockfighting: from a series of similar plates in Gregory Bateson and Margaret Mead's** *Balinese Character: A Photographic Analysis* **(December, 1942). © New York Academy of Sciences, reproduced with permission)**

Lesy's *Wisconsin Death Trip* (1973) illustrates the approach. Fortuitously, he gained access to some 3,000 glass negatives taken by a small-town photographer between 1890 and 1910 which, while formally posed, nevertheless represented the ordinary 'events these people, or people like them, once experienced'. Small-town life, the Great Depression, massive incipient change, religion, disease, death: the photos capture vividly these and other themes conveying in one complex image what would take thousands of words to capture. Interspersed with the full-page photographs are direct textual quotations – newspapers, novels, madhouse records of the period – which, taken all together, 'recreate a re-vision of a past time so separated from the present by the cunning sleights of the fearful memories of one human lifetime, that to recall, reveal and recreate such a past is as difficult as driving a tunnel through a granite mountain to the sea' (Lesy, 1973). It is a startling work, and, like most mentioned in this study, has to be 'read' for its substance: I cannot start to do it justice. Yet it signposted a new tradition for personal documents, one that Lesy himself followed further, three years later, in his *Real Life: Louisville in the Twenties* (1976), another rich photographic essay. Lesy's books also illustrate the possibility of gaining a much closer relationship between document and theory, for the photos are fully linked in with the text; they do not merely illustrate, they integrate.

The model for this kind of work is revealed in the classic 1930s study of average – and thereby poor – white families of tenant farmers in the Southern States of America: *Let Us Now Praise Famous Men* by James Agee and Walker Evans. Here Agee, no sociologist, spent time absorbed in the lives of the tenant families whilst Evans (later to be famed for his *American Photographs*, 1938) produces the first volume of the study with photographs of places, objects and people. As Agee says, 'The photographs are not illustrative. They, and the text, are co-equal, mutually independent, and fully collaborative (1965: xiii).

A few sociologists have taken this further, through what has been called *'narrative visual theory'*, where the 'implicit elements of social theory are clearly acknowledged' (Wagner, 1979: 18). Here the photos are systematically selected through a tacit theory – Jackson looks at prison life (1977, 1978), and Harper looks at tramps (1978). They come close to being ethnographies, which instead of relying upon the written word become organized through visual imagery. In some cases, photos have been taken as a basis for organizing an autobiography (e.g. Barthes, 1977; Spence, 1986). From this, the task may be to theorize lives through photography.

Photos may also be used as a *resource* for further explanations. Photos may be taken, and then discussed with the subjects in a technique known as 'photo elicitation' (cf. Collier and Collier, 1986). In Banish's work on *City Families* (1976), the technique was to combine interview with photography. This researcher first visited selected families in order to take photographs of them as they wished to see themselves and then returned both to talk about the photographs, to ask which was their favourite and to interview them about their hopes and aspirations in life. The study is composed of the preferred photographs on one page matched with the interviews and oberservations on the opposite page. Of added interest in this study is the range of families studied and the contrasts drawn between the families of two cities: London and Chicago.

From this comes one of the most apparent methods for using photographs in social science: to ask the respondent for *a look at their family albums* (cf. Musello, 1979; Spence and Holland, 1991). In a most striking way, all manner of details about childhood relationships, friendship, family rituals and family history can be highlighted. Jo Spence and Patricia Holland, for example, ponder what is allowed and what is not allowed to go into family photos, and suggest that such photos work at the borders between a personal memory, a personal unconscious, and a social history which bridges wider social conventions of public myth and 'cultural memory' (for more on this see Chapter 10). More widely, in a general study of photography Akeret coins the term 'photoanalysis' and suggests the following useful scheme of questions to be asked:

What is your immediate impression [of the photograph]? Who and what do you see? What is happening in the photo? Is the background against which the photo was taken of any significance, either real or symbolic? What feelings does it evoke in you? What do you notice about physical intimacy or distance? Are people touching physically? How are they touching? How do the people in the photo feel about their bodies? Are they using their bodies to show them off, to hide behind, to be seductive, are they proud of their bodies, ashamed? What do you notice about the emotional state of each person? Is he: shy, compliant, aloof, proud, fearful, mad, suspicious, introspective, superior, confused, happy, anxious, angry, weak, pained, suffering, bright, curious, sexy, distant . . . Can you visualize how those emotions are expressed in facial dynamics and body movement? If there is more than one person in the photo what do you notice about the group mood? Is there harmony or chaos? How do people relate? Are they tense or relaxed? What are their messages towards each other? Who has the power, the grace? Do you see love present? What do you notice about the various parts of each person? Look carefully at the general body posture and then the hands, the legs, the arms, the face, the eyes, the mouth. What does each part tell you? Are the parts harmonious or are there inconsistencies? Pay particular attention to the face, always the most expressive part of the person. Learn to read any photo as you would read a book from left to right then downwards. Go over it again and again, each time trying to pick out something you have missed. Ask yourself more general questions, as many as you can think of. What is obvious and what is subtle? What is the sense of movement or is there any? What memories and experiences does the photo stir in you? How do you identify with the people in the photo? How are you alike, how different? What moves you most about the photo? What do you find distasteful about it? Is there anything that disturbs you? Try to define the social and economic class of the people photographed. What is their cultural background? If it is a family, would you want to be a member of it? Would you want your children to play with theirs? If the photos are personal – of you, your family, friends or associates – try to remember the exact circumstances of the photo session. How have you changed since then? How have you remained the same? (Akeret, 1973: 35–6)

The list, concludes Akeret, could be endless. His questions are primarily geared towards psychological interpretations rather than cultural ones; a sociologist would need to tease family albums and photographs of respondents through a series of sociological problems. In short, there is a major tool here for sociologists but one that remains considerably underused.

Questions such as these, then, hint strongly at another way of approaching photographs in social science: as *critique*. Much – if not most – recent work in photography approaches the image in a highly critical mode. For example, in her very telling analysis of family albums, *Family Frames* (1997), Marianne Hirsch shows through a series of case studies that whilst our habits of seeing family albums are usually routinized, they can be violated and jolted through radical departures from the so-called family norm. She compares, for example, rather traditional images of families found in books like Edward Streicher's *The Family of Man* (1955), with those images found in Meatyard's *Family Album of Lucybelle Crater* (1974) (where family members are photographed with grotesque masked faces); in Sally Mann's *Immediate Family* (1992) (where her children are posed often naked with a kind of 'seductive' childhood innocence); or in the work of Christian Boltanski (where hundreds of anonymous photos, often hung in impersonal ways, radically challenge notions of family unity) (Semin et al., 1997). Photos, we learn, can be used to 'unfix the gaze' (Hirsch, 1997: 141). More and more, we need this critical photographic work to be included with life stories. We need to sense, along with Barthes, that photographs do not simply call up the past or provide routes into memory: they are themselves their own invented images that can be used to invent their stories.

Film and the 'documentary tradition'

Norman Denzin (1995) has called the twentieth century the 'cinematic age', a time when the cinema and its moving visual images have come to assume enormous importance as a means of communication in many people's lives across the globe. Once again, only a few social scientists have ever countenanced the significance of film. It has been left to a whole group of others – the documentary, journalistic and ethnographic film makers – to take seriously its possibilities. Yet the medium should surely be the social scientist's dream: life as it is lived accurately recorded as it happens, and constantly available for playback and analysis! There will be problems, for sure, but it is a most remarkable resource which could have changed the face of much social science out of all recognition during the twentieth century. Somehow, it scarcely touched it.

Initially, it was the 'documentary film makers' who breathed life into an old form. Robert Coles provides a pithy history:

> The noun *document* goes back centuries in time. It is derived from the Latin *docere*, to teach, and was originally, of course, used to describe something that offered clues, or better, proof, a piece of paper with words that attested evidence. In our time, a photograph or a recording or a film have also qualified as documents. In the eighteenth century (1711), the word *document* became more active – a verb whose meaning conveyed the act of furnishing such evidence; and eventually . . . the range of such activity expanded: first one documented with words on paper; later one documented with photographs and a film crew. Interestingly the verb would get used this way, too: 'to construct or produce (as a movie or novel) with authentic situations or events', and 'to portray realistically'. Here the creative or imaginative life is tempered by words such as 'authentic' or 'realistic' . . . In the early nineteenth century (1902) the adjective documentary emerged – a description of evidence, naturally, but also as 'relating to or employing documentation in literature or art' . . . In this century . . . the noun documentary arrived, telling of a product, 'the documentary presentation of a film or novel' . . . (Coles, 1997: 19–20)

At the turn of the nineteenth century, the first motion pictures often focused on recording 'actualities' – like *Record of a Sneeze* (1894) and *Workers Emerging from a Factory* (1895) – usually shot in one take and lasting little more than a few minutes. By 1903, 'editing' was discovered and with it, the possibility of manipulating the images – shooting speeds, time, continuities, space. Soon anthropological ethnographers started to film various tribal peoples engaged in social rituals – Spencer, in 1901, filmed Australian aborigines in kangaroo dances and rain ceremonies, while in 1914 Curtis filmed the Kwakiutl Indians. But the birth of the documentary film is commonly agreed to be Robert Flaherty's (1922) *Nanook of the North*, about Eskimo life. Flaherty, a compassionate romantic appalled by the dehumanization of modern technology (cf. Calder-Marshall, 1963), lived in 'Eskimo country' for eleven years and, under the most adverse conditions, shot his film on the life of one specific individual – Nanook. In this film he reveals the constant struggle for life in a hostile environment. Sensitively, the power of the image is left behind:

> One of Flaherty's most successful visual techniques was to follow an exotic act visually, showing it step by step as it developed, not explaining it in words. In one sequence of *Nanook* we see Nanook tugging on a line leading into a hole in the ice. We are engaged in that act, and think about it. Eventually, the suspense is broken: our questions are answered when Nanook pulls out a seal. Flaherty creates the same visual involvement when Nanook makes the igloo – especially at the end of the sequence, when Nanook cuts a slab of ice for a window, sets it in place, and fixes a snow slab reflector along one side. For a time we are

puzzled and, therefore, involved. But when Nanook steps back, finished, we understand. (Heider, 1976: 24)

But even here, in its founding moment, we can see a critical problem. Just where were Flaherty and his camera to be placed inside the small igloo when Nanook was being filmed? How was it staged – the film cameras were exceedingly large in those days? Where was the author of the film? 'Critical documentary' only emerged later to pose such questions of the apparent authenticity of the materials.

In its original form, Flaherty's film and his others – *Moana, Man of Aran, The Land* and *Louisiana Story* – were silent, and most that followed until the early 1960s lacked synchronous sound. Although a founding classic, it is now seen as a highly 'romantic' text – raising further issues about the narrative organization of such films (see Chapter 9 for a wider discussion of narrative). In contrast, later documentarists offered more 'realist' accounts – especially depicting the lives of great cities – like Walter Ruttman's *Berlin: The Symphony of Great Cities* (1927). In the work of the founder of the 'British School' of documentary – John Grierson – the camera was now focused 'inward on the problems of the "average" person and analyzed the situation of individuals in occupations and the importance of national and local issues and institutions'. This is not the place even to attempt to write a history of the documentary film – there are many good books which do this (e.g. Heider, 1976; Sherman, 1998). But it is important to sense another tool in the making – one which more recently has culminated in all kinds of important developments: from *'cinema vérité'* (e.g. Frederick Wiseman's films discussed below; the controversial *Harlan County, USA* by Barbara Kopples, which looked at the strike of coal miners in Kentucky), *'docu-soaps'* (like those featured on televison which focus on such topics as airports, families, hotels, or small communities), where a 'fly-on-the wall' approach is adopted; and *critical documentaries*, such as Bonnie Klein's *Not a Love Story* (1981), which provides a radical feminist analysis of pornography.

For Karl Heider, *Dead Birds* (1961) about the Dani, marks the watershed of ethnographic film; thereafter synchronic sound enabled people to talk about their lives as well as simply living them on film. Robert Gardener's Ethiopian film *Rivers of Sand* takes a Hamar woman relaxing before the camera and speaking about her life, with shots interspersed to illustrate her commentary. Heider concludes his review by suggesting that since 1963 ethnographic film has become 'institutionalized, bureaucratized and established' (1976: 44), reviews of films being a regular feature of the *American Anthropologist* since 1965, and a special organization, the Society for the Anthropology of Visual Communication, emerging in 1973 with its own journal. Film is now accepted as an integral part of the anthropologist's armoury.

This is far from the case in sociology. There have been a few attempts, such as Morin's work with Rouch on Parisians talking about the summer of 1960 (the Algerian War dominated) in *Chronicles of a Summer*, but in the main sociologists have either ignored the medium or used documentaries created by film makers, like those of Frederick Wiseman (Atkins, 1976).

Frederick Wiseman's films perhaps come closest to embodying sociological concerns: most deal directly with the ways in which individuals throughout their hierarchies cope (or fail to) with the day-to-day pressures of social institutions. As he puts it:

> What I'm aiming at is a series on American institutions, using the word 'institutions' to cover a series of activities that take place in a limited geographical area with a more or less consistent group of people being involved. I want to use film technology to have a look at places like high schools, hospitals, prisons, and police, which seems to be very fresh material for film; I want to get away from the typical documentary where you follow one charming person or one Hollywood star around. I want to make films where the institutions will be the star but will also reflect larger issues in general society. (in Rosenthal, 1971: 69)

Hence his 'documents' treat not 'lives' but 'institutions' – the police in *Law and Order* (1969), hospitals for the criminally insane in *The Titicut Follies* (1969), army life in *Basic Training* (1971) as well as films on *Welfare*, *High School* and *Hospital*. For Wiseman, it is blindingly obvious that all films are 'subjective' documents – how could they be otherwise? Yet they are 'fair': honest, worked at, not driven by ideological commitment, desirous of showing that people are much the same in their daily struggles and 'very suspicious of people who can make . . . glib classifications, whatever that classification may be, and wherever it may fall politically' (Wiseman, 1971: 325).

The rise of video

> In today's world life does seem to be on videotape. Monitors reflect faces as shoppers walk along department store aisles. Videotaping is a common sight at children's soccer and baseball games and at weddings, bar mitz-vahs, and birthday parties. The prevalence of video in our lives has steadily expanded. We can document our own lives as we perceive them, and we can record our vision of events. At the heart of the video explosion is the desire not only to record oneself and one's family but to present that view of the self back to the self after documentation. (Sherman 1998: 257–8)

Generally 'standard cine film' is expensive, requires specialist knowledge, often requires numerous 'takes' and skilful editing, plays to cinema audiences and is almost an 'elite' form when compared to the democratized video recorder and film. For with video, we find a medium that is cheap, accessible, home based and extremely versatile – requiring relatively little skill in the first instance. It differs too from standard

BOX 3.1   SOME DOCUMENTARY FILM LANDMARKS

1895   Louis and Auguste Lumière's Workers Emerging from a Factory –
        one of a number of early 'shorts'
1890s   Newsreels
        Charles Pathé and the Pathé Gazette (1907) 'March of Time' (in the
        US some 20 million watched this at 9,000 cinemas each week), 'This
        Modern Age' (the UK version)
1910   Herbert Ponting, With Scott in the Antarctic
1921/2 Robert Flaherty, Nanook of the North – the life of an Inuit and his
        family, and their hard life on the ice. Shows a strong collaboration
        between Nanook and Flaherty
1926   Alberto Cavalacanti, Rien que les heures (a day in Paris)
1927   Robery Flaherty, Moana – 'a visual account of events in the daily life
        of a Polynesian youth' (Grierson, 1966: 13)
1927   Walter Ruttman, Berlin: The Symphony of a Great City
1929   John Grierson, Drifters – shows the life of herring fishermen as they
        cast their nets and face a storm
1929   Basil Wright and Henry Watt, Night Mail – poetic representation of
        a post train on its journey from London to Glasgow
1936   Pare Lorentz, The Plow that Broke the Plains
1937   Leni Riefenstahl, Triumph of the Will – the famous documentary
        that displayed Nazi Germany
1945   Carol Reed, The True Glory
1954   Lionel Rogosin, On the Bowery
1957   CBS, The Twentieth Century
1960   Jean Rouche initiates cinema verité with Chronicle of a Summer –
        follows a group of Parisians with varying experiences ('unhappy in
        love', a 'concentration camp survivor' etc.), and seen as a real life
        drama. At the end, the film is discussed by everybody
1962   Frank Capra, Why We Fight
1962   Wolfe Koening/Roman Kroita, Lonely Boy
1968   Frederick Wiseman, High School – one of a number of celebrated
        Wiseman films, this one showing a US High School
1976   Barbara Copple, Harlan County
1977   Peter Adair's Word is Out – a range of elderly gays tell their 'coming
        out' stories
1980   The Life and Times of Rosie the Riveter
1981   Bonnie Klein and Linda Lee Tracey, Not a Love Story: A Film About
        Pornography (looks at women's experiences of porn)
1989   Michael Moore, Roger and Me
1990   Jennie Livingstone, Paris is Burning
1993   Tom Joslin's Silverlake Life: The View from Here – a landmark
        autovideo of a couple infected and dying with HIV
1995   Frederick Wiseman, High School 2

television by providing highly individual (or individuated) watching. First used in 1956 (for television production practices) and becoming domestically available in 1969 (with Sony and Akai), only in 1978 did the first reliable systems appear on the market (Sony's now defunct Beta, and JVC's VHS). So for the first edition of this book, video was just emerging as a popular form; but now – 20 years on – it is everywhere a volatile, expansive, proliferating media with a seemingly inexhaustible array of functions: to probe, document, persuade, analyse, archive and play with events. Once again, I can only express surprise at how few sociologists seem to have made much use of it; and indeed a whole new generation of 'video' experts seems to have emerged outside of sociology to do sociology's work! There are now several generations of 'video workers' who have used video as radical means of transforming the orthodox visual image and of providing a whole library of 'alternative video forms'.

Video can be used for a variety of purposes, some of its more colourful roles being 'video petitions, interplanetary cameras, robotics probes, surveillance eyes . . .' (Renov and Suderburg, 1996: xv). In life story research, it has been used more mundanely – for instance, as a permanent *archival record* of key events, as for example in the mass collection of holocaust survivor stories, where the aural/oral tape is supplemented by the visual testimony (cf. Langer, 1991). It has also been used as 'a technology of memory' (a way of jogging the memory or 'thickening it'), as a 'technology of confession' (as in Wendy Clarke's 'Love Tapes' project) (see Moran, 1996).

One of its most telling roles has been in the growth of the *video diary*. Here a teller of a story records a fragment of their own life – most famously as seen in the BBC video series *Video Nation*, shown since 1994 on a regular, nightly slot of BBC. Lasting about two minutes each, the recordings constitute a major new form of 'vox populi' – with the BBC providing assistance in their production. Each tape is logged in detail, cross-referenced and archived in the British Film Institute's national Film and Television Archive. By late 1998, some 7,000 videotapes – adding up to 10,000 hours of recording – had been organized around dozens of subjects. These included such themes as 'On the Job' (work and unemployment), 'State of Play' (how we use our spare time) 'Life, Death, God and Everything' (on the nature of belief). There are also versions of the concept in Hong Kong, Israel and Africa. The series gives camcorders, videotapes and training to over 250 people in Britain and then asks them to make their film on aspects of life in the UK. (There is also an even more 'populist version' of this in various television programmes where people just send in their own video clips – like *America's Best Home Movies*.)

Taking all this further is the development of what may be called *'video autoethnography'*. Here people may be trained or enouraged to make a video about aspects of their life that concern them. Sometimes this may be done individually: Ruth Holliday (1999) provided her 'queer' subjects with camcorders and asked them to record the ways they dressed for different contexts – at home, work and play – and then to provide a commentary on the films as they were edited. As she says, video diaries gave 'respondents the potential for a greater degree of reflexivity than other methods, through the process of watching, re-recording, and

editing their diaries before submission'. Each diarist had at least a month
to make their diary (p. 476). In contrast, Salome Chasnoff, got her group
of African American and West Indian teenage mothers – 'happy, relaxed
young women' (1996: 111) – to make a collective video on their own
motherhood. They became *The Fantastic Moms*, and they established
themselves as the experts. They became the 'authorities on the subject'
through 'researching, planning, storyboarding, enacting, framing and
shooting, reflecting, reviewing, being viewed' (p. 129); through 'running
the tape recorder, writing the script, posing the questions, expressing the
opinions' (p. 115); and finally through being in and making the film. In
the final video film, they established who they were in three key ways:

> (1) as speaking subjects, first person, present tense, I say what I am and what I
> am not; (2) as performing subjects, I speak for myself, for my own design; and
> (3) as subjects of speech, I am the one of whom I speak. They particularised
> and historicised themselves, demystifying the stereotype [of black mother-
> hood] . . . (p. 129)

Within this video, they were able to provide a strong counter-story to the
dominant story one of sad, deprived, desperate young mums.

Thus, video becomes a powerful form of critique. Orthodox media
accounts of lives – ones that use familiar settings, storylines and language – start to be seriously challenged by an 'alternative video media',
where often life stories are told in disturbing and unsettling ways.
Women's stories, 'race' stories, stories of people with AIDS and HIV –
and many others – have become the subjects of these new critical videos
(cf. Juhasz, 1995, 1999; Renov and Suderburg, 1996). Reviewing a number
of such videos focused around HIV and AIDS films, Alexandra Juhasz
(1995) suggest that these video alternatives

> articulate a rebuttal to or a revision of the mainstream media's definitions and
> representations around AIDS, and [help] to form [a] community around a new
> identity forced into existence by the fact of AIDS. Producing alternative AIDS
> media is a political act that allows people who need to scream with pain or
> anger, who want to say, 'I'm here, I count', who have internalized sorrow and
> despair, who have vital information to share about drug protocols, coping
> strategies or government inaction, to make their opinions public and to join
> with others in this act of resistance . . . (Juhasz, 1995: 3)

Modes of video The film theorist Bill Nichols (1991, discussed by
Sherman, 1998: 261) has outlined five major modes of documentary film
and video. To some extent, they mirror the development of life stories,
autobiography and research in general, and this suggests the ways in
which life stories come to be seen. First, there is the *expository* – following
on from Flaherty, where the authority speaks from on high. The author
of the documentary tells the tale. Second, there is the *observational* – here,
real time is followed, and there is a focus on individuals: the camera tries

to empathize with them, tries to 'be in their shoes'. It is the classic ethnographic mode. Third, there is the *interactive* – here, the camera itself becomes a self-conscious presence: the viewer can no longer imagine the film is just there or the story is just being told, because the camera – often shaking or being seen – reminds us that this is humanly produced film through a camera. It is *cinema verité*. But, fourthly, this can be taken further: and a *reflexive* mode suggests a much more critical approach to the problems of representation. Finally, in the *performative*, self-consciousness and reflexivity mixes with multiple narratives (as in *Common Threads, Tongues Untied*).

Critique and the camera: the camera always lies

What should have become very clear during this brief trip to the visual image in life story work is the ways in which the medium is increasingly used as a radical, critical tool. If anybody ever thought that 'the camera never lies' or the 'photo represents reality' this has become firmly challenged. In just the same way as life stories are seen as 'constructions', so too are visual images: the camera always lies and the question becomes: how much does it lie and in what ways? In Woody Allen's film *Zelig*, for example, the hero played by Woody Allen is able to appear as a parade of significant twentieth-century characters against an imported film montage of 'world significant' newsreel clips – making it appear that he is present. Likewise, in Oliver Stone's hugely controversial film *J.F.K.* (based on the assassination of John F. Kennedy) he is able to splice actual news footage with the fictional, conspiratorial narrative that he presents. Actual documentary merges with fiction. And with the arrival of computer photo technology these tricks of playing with the camera have become available to everyone. Through the skills of computer programs, photographs can be completely reorganized: splicing old characters with new, deleting friends and lovers who are no longer friends and lovers; and placing known people against new and unknown backdrops. Photos from the past may be updated; and photos from the present may be rendered old and sepia.

This is just the playful iceberg tip. What is now possible is for subjects themselves to take hold of the (web) camcorder and present the ways in which they view the world, the stories of their lives in ways that may challenge dominant story modes. 'The visual' can be used as a means of social change.

Conclusion

In this chapter I have been deliberately wide ranging: from photography and film through diaries and letters. But I have not aimed to be comprehensive or detailed, merely to suggest a whole battery of research tools, widely ignored and neglected in both research texts and courses. They cry out for more and more use in the social sciences. They have enormous potential for exploring concrete social experience in a humanistic fashion. They are powerful yet still relatively neglected tools. And they harbour potentials for radically transforming the human sciences in the twenty-first century.

Guide to further reading

Diaries have received relatively little discussion, although Allport (1942) and Denzin (1978a) both consider them. V. Palmer's early text *Field Studies in Sociology* (1928) devotes a chapter to them, and they are mentioned in M. Riley's *Sociological Research* (1963). All these treatments, however, are very brief, and only Zimmerman and Wieder's 'The diary diary– interview method' (1977) provides a sustained methodological discussion of its use (but this is related to one specific study). Pat Caplan's study *African Voices, African Lives: Personal Narratives from a Swahili Village* (1997) finds the letters and diaries of Mohammed scattered into the notes of the book's anthropologist author – an important recent use of the diary in a Swahili village. In James D. Sexton's edited *Son of Tecún Umán: A Mayan Indian Tells his Life Story* (1981), Ignacio tells the story of 'his life, his people, his town and his country'. Asked to keep a diary, he agrees and does so from 1970 to 1981. Around 140 pages long, each dated diary entry has a heading such as 'Poverty, Insomnia and Illness', 'My Brother's Murderers Are Shot' and 'The February 4th Earthquake'.

Much debate has been generated around the use of the sexual diary method – see A.P.M. Coxon's *Between the Sheets* (1996). There is also some discussion of diaries in literary studies. The classic here is A. Ponsonby's *English Diaries* (1923), and a more recent study is R.A. Fothergill's *Private Chronicles* (1974). These studies give many illustrations of literary diary writing. More popularly, see also Tristine Rainer (1978) *The New Diary: How to Use a Journal for Self Guidance and Expanded Creativity*.

For a useful and comprehensive listing of diaries see C.S. Handley, *Annotated Bibliography of Diaries*, 4 vols (1997) (also available in CD-Rom).

Letters get even scantier treatment, and so the reader is advised to look at the three studies mentioned in this chapter: W.I. Thomas and F. Znaniecki, *The Polish Peasant* (1958), G. Allport, *Letters from Jenny* (1965) and R. Straus, *Escape from Custody* (1974). In addition, see the letters of William Tanner in J. Spradley, *You Owe Yourself a Drunk* (1970).

On **'guerrilla' journalism** and 'oral testimony', see the interviews and commentaries with practitioners in R. Grele's *Envelopes of Sound* (1975) as well as the brief comments in many of the introductions to the volumes which use the method. The work of both Tony Parker and Studs Terkel comes oddly together in Tony Parker's *Studs Terkel: A Life in Words* (1996), where Parker interviews Terkel. Terkel's key works include *Division Street*

(1968), *Hard Times: An Oral History of the Great Depression* (1970), *Working* (1977), *Talking to Myself* (1978), *American Dreams* (1981), *The Good War* (1984), *Chicago* (1986), *Race* (1992), *Coming of Age* (1995). Tony Parker's work includes *The Courage of His Convictions* (1962), the story of Robert Allerton (tape-recorded over six months) and telling of a violent working class recidivist who, at the age of thirty-three, has nine convictions, has spent twelve and a half years in prison, and espouses high moral principles; the *Unknown Citizen* (1963), which tells the story (partly in the form of an essay) of 'Charlie Smith', who has spent nearly all his life in institutions; *A Man of Good Abilities* (1967), which includes many letters and tells of a middle class criminal, Norman Edwards; *Five Women* (1965), which provides the voice of five female criminals; and *The Twisting Lane* (1969), on sex offenders. His work remained prolific until his death in the 1990s, with studies of lighthousekeepers, unmarried mothers, prison life and so forth, and has often been adapted for television documentaries. A recent compendium may be found in *Criminal Conversations* (1999).

The **literature of fact** or 'non-fiction novel' is an ill-defined and amorphous area, but one that could well be developed by social scientists. Literature students have analysed its form, notably M. Berger's *Real and Imagined Worlds* (1977), M. Zavarzadeh's *The Mythopoeic Reality* (1976), A. Borenstein's *Redeeming the Sin* (1978) and R. Weber's *The Literature of Fact: Literary Non-Fiction in American Writing* (1981). The latter is particularly useful in analysing some examples including the work of Truman Capote, Norman Mailer, Agee, Hersey and Wicker. These – along with Tom Wolfe, Hunter S. Thompson and Joan Didion – are often seen as the founders of '*The New Journalism*', with a book of that title being published in 1973 and edited by Tom Wolfe. More recent reviews of this blossoming area include: Tristine Rainer, *Your Life as Story* (1998) and Blake Morrison, *Too True* (1998).

On '**biographical objects**', material culture and consumption, see Janet Hoskins, *Biographical Objects: How Things Tell the Stories of People's Lives* (1998); William Rathje and Cullen Murphy, *Rubbish! The Archaeology of Garbage* (1992); Daniel Miller, *Acknowledging Consumption: A Review of New Studies* (1995). See also the *Journal of Material Culture* (Sage). The Garbage Project has been based at the University of Arizona since the 1970s and its web site home page http://wacky.ccit.arizona.edu/~bara/gbg-in~1htm

On more **unorthodox methods**, the standard source remains E. Webb et al., *Unobtrusive Measures* (1966; 2nd edn 1999), updated a little in L. Sechrest, *Unobtrusive Measurement Today* (1979). See also T. Bouchard, 'Unobtrusive methods: an inventory of uses' (1976).

On **worlds of sense**, see the book of that name by Constance Classen (1993).

On **sound archives**, see the web site of the British Library National Sound Archive at: http://www.bl.uk/collections/sound-archive and the *Journal of the International Association of Sound and Audio-visual Archives*.

Visual data: a good general introductory textbook on photography in general is Liz Wells (ed.), *Photography: A Critical Introduction* (1997); and a useful overview of visual sources more generally is Michael Emmison and Philip Smith's *Research the Visual* (2000). The link between photography and autobiography is discussed in Linda Haverty Rugg's *Picturing Ourselves* (1999). On the general value and analysis of visual imagery, see Douglas Harper 'On the authority of the image' (1994); Michael Ball and Gregory W.H. Smith's *Analyzing Visual Data* (1992), the Colliers's *Visual Anthropology: Photography as a Research Method* (1986, 2nd edn), which discusses the photographer as participant observer and reviews the history of its use. See also Clarke's *Introducing Visual Sociology* (1977), a short introductory text with a 'workbook' attached and a useful if outdated bibliography; and J. Wagner's (1979) anthology *Images of Information*, again out of date but it provides a wide-ranging and useful set of readings showing many of the problems involved in using photos in research and teaching. Three journals are of particular value in including photographic studies: *Studies in the Anthropology of Visual Communication, Qualitative Sociology* and an *International Journal of Visual Sociology* (Vol. 1, 1984). The journal *Current Sociology* contained a 'Trend report: theory and practice of visual sociology', by Leonard Henny in 1986. There is also an 'International Visual Sociology Association'. The American Sociological Association does now feature a regular programme of films and videos at its annual meetings, showing that the importance of this medium is slowly being recognized outside of anthropology (which has taken it seriously for some time).

On **photography**, the classic, critical accounts are by John Berger, *Ways of Seeing* (1972) (as well as his later (1980) *About Looking*), Susan Sontag's *On Photography* (1979) and Roland Barthes *Camera Lucida* (1984). Two more recent 'histories' of the camera and its changing role in modernity are to be found in Scott McQuire's *Visions of Modernity* (1998) and Celia Lury's *Prosthetic Culture: Photography, Memory and Identity* (1998). There is also an excellent discussion of sociology and visual representation by Elizabeth Chaplin (1994) in a book of that name which organizes itself through discussion of the critical theory of visual representation and the empirical basis of visual work. It discusses copious examples of photographic studies, including the Bateson and Mead text. A major figure in the use of photography in sociology is Howard Becker, whose key article 'Photography and sociology' (1974) discusses issues of sampling and theory while reviewing many studies. A shorter discussion by Becker is 'Do photographs tell the truth?' (1979). For an example of photography at work, see Michael Lesy's *Bearing Witness* (1982). On family albums, see Marianne Hirsch, *Family Frames* (1997).

On **anthropological film**, see Paul Hockings's *Principles of Visual Anthroplogy* (2nd edn, 1995). Useful studies of ethnographic and **documentary film** include Sharon R. Sherman's *Documenting Ourselves: Film, Video and Culture* (1998), Lewis Jacobs's *The Documentary Tradition* (1979),

Jack Ellis, *The Documentary Idea* (1988), Peter Loizos *Innovation in Ethnographic Film* (1993) and a compilation of sources edited by Kevin McDonald and Mark Cousins, *Imagining Reality: The Faber Book of the Documentary* (1996). Karl G. Heider's *Ethnographic Film* (1976) is a classic which provides a brief history, a catalogue of films, a discussion of both making films and using them for teaching, and a long account of the attributes of such film. Karl Heider has also compiled the catalogue *Films for Anthropological Teaching*, through various editions (8th edition, 1995), which is obtainable from the American Anthropological Association, 1703 New Hampshire Avenue NW, Washington, DC 20009. Reviews of films are now commonplace in the *American Anthropologist*. See also the *Historical Journal of Film, Radio and Television* (cited in K. Short, 1981: 36). On Wiseman's work, see Atkins (1976).

On **film in general**, Norman Denzin has discussed how the twentieth century became the 'cinematic society', with film overtaking other media as a major means of communication, and the critical problems with this, in many sources. For a selection, see: *Images of Postmodern Society* (1991), *The Cinematic Society* (1995) and *Interpretive Ethnography* (1997).

On **video**, see Michael Renov and Erika Suderburg (eds), *Resolutions: Contemporary Video Practices* (1996). The wider contexts are discussed in John Hanhardt's *Video Culture: A Critical Investigation* (1986). As an example of critical video work, see Alexandra Juhasz's *AIDS TV: Identity, Community and Alternative Video* (1995), which also contains an excellent 'videography' compiled by Catherine Saalfield. She also reviews six feminist critical videos in 'It's about autonomy, stupid: sexuality in feminist video' (1999).

Finally, for an important overview of documents in general, see John Scott's *A Matter of Record* (1990).

4 The Auto/Biographical Society

Estragon: All the dead voices.
Vladimir: They all speak at once.
Estragon: Each one to itself . . .
Vladimir: What do they say?
Estragon: They talk about their lives.
Vladimir: To have lived life is not enough for them.
Estragon: They have to talk about it.
(Samuel Beckett, *Waiting for Godot*, 1952)

Our society has become a recited society, in three senses: it is defined by *stories*, (*récits*, the fables constituted by our advertising and informational media), by *citations* of stories, and by the interminable *recitation* of stories . . .

(Michel De Certeau, *The Practice of Everyday Life*, 1984: 186)

There is little doubt that fascination for 'life' narratives is a defining feature of Western societies, linking phenomena as disparate as the documentary evidence occasionally collected to enliven quantitative research and the sensational outbursts filling in the intervals between TV commercials on the reality-show catwalk.

(D. Simeoni and D. Diani, 'Biographical research', 1995a: 1)

The telling of a life is a messy business. It comes in many forms, shifting across time and space. Sometimes it is silenced and at other times it speaks volumes. Indeed, right now at the start of a twenty-first century, the telling of life stories has become such a voluminous business that we could even start to talk of something like an 'auto/biographical society': life stories are everywhere. In this chapter, my aim is to sense a little of how the tellings of lives have changed and grown and to capture some of the emerging dilemmas around them. My main task will be to start an analysis of some of the key elements that would be needed for a kind of genealogy of life stories. I will detect a long-term (western) shift from an oral culture stuffed full of folklore handed across the generations, and still to be found in much of the world today, and sense the emergence of a more text based society where written narratives of lives start to appear. And I will move on to more recent developments, where stories have become increasingly told by the powerless, where they have been told more reflectively, and where new modes of a kind of 'cyber-story telling' have entered the popular media and hi-tech worlds. A lesser aim is to start some kind of evaluation of such stories and the role they play in lives, a task continued throughout the book. Here I will just note the paradox: a world of life stories that can surely aid human emancipation and help people understand their lives may also be a world which, if we are not careful, leads to a packaging of stories where they may easily become forms of control, consumption and self-absorption, robbing lives of the very authenticity they thought they were claiming.

Elements for a genealogy of life stories: the rise of the personal tale

From oral to written traditions

Throughout most of human history, telling the stories of lives has largely been an oral tradition – passed down across generations, suitably modified and reconstructed, showing why things got to be the way they were, feeding into the great myths people may later come to live by. The tales of religious figures – of Christ and Buddha, of Mohammed and of ancestors long worshipped – all these lives feed into the cultural brico- lage. Oral traditions have been defined as 'verbal messages which are reported statements from the past beyond the present generation' (Vansina, 1985: 27). It is the story handed down across generations – through performance or poetry, through epic tale or song, through reminiscence and 'memorized speech', through 'historical gossip' and 'eyewitness accounts' (all terms developed and discussed in Vansina's classic text *Oral Tradition as History*, 1985).

Whilst oral traditions are still widespread today (cf. Tonkin, 1992: Introduction), most cultures now either have, or are at least deeply aware of, written traditions. Indeed, a significant shift in the telling of lives comes with their being inscribed into written texts. Once inscribed, they can take on a life of their own across the generations: awaiting inter- pretations. With the earliest depictions of lives in Stone Age drawings on walls through their depictions into more permanent and elaborate elite hieroglyphics of the Pharaohs some 3,000 years BC – preserving records of their lives and riches in the great tombs, temples and pyramids – and on to the scribes of Christian monasteries – we find the tales of a life starting to take on a life of their own. And here indeed are stories that enable the historian, the archaeologist and the narratologist even surer routes than those provided by oral traditions into undertstanding the cultures of the past. Written lives solidify and accumulate more densely than oral ones.

The rise of the individual and the autobiographical form

Just when did the autobiographical form appear? Georg Misch (the son- in-law of the philosopher Wilhelm Dilthey who played an influential

BOX 4.1 SOME 'CLASSIC' AND NOTABLE BIOGRAPHIES

4th century BCE

	Greece	Xenophon	*Memorabilia*
		Plato	*Dialogues*
1st century BCE		Plutarch	*Lives of Noble Greeks and Romans*
		Svetorias	*Lives of Caesars*
		Svetonius	*Lives and Opinions of Eminent Philosophers*
Early 3rd century	Rome	Laertus	
1212–14	England	Eadmer	*Life of St Anselm*
14th century	Italy	Boccaccio	*Life of Dante*
1550		Vasari	*Lives of the Most Excellent Architects, Painters and Sculptors*
mid 16th century	England	William Roper	*Life of St Thomas More*
1605		Francis Bacon	*Advancement of Learning*
1779–1781		Samuel Johnson	*Lives of the English Poets*
1791		James Boswell	*Life of Johnson*
1850		Ralph Emerson	*Representative Men*
1908–33		Gertrude Stein	*Three Lives*
1910		Freud	*Leonardo Da Vinci*
1920s		Virginia Woolf	*The New Biography*
1918		Lytton Strachey	*Eminent Victorians*
1947		Sartre	*Lives of Baudelaire, Genet and Flaubert*
1958		Erikson	*Young Man Luther*

For a much more detailed chronology see Catherine Parke, *Biography: Writing Lives* (1996).

part in providing a philosphical base for life histories) in his classic history of autobiography devotes some 2,724 pages (out of a total of 3,881 pages) to the story of autobiography during the Middle Ages, but takes the form back as far as the ancient Egyptian tomb inscriptions (Misch, 1951). Likewise, Paul Thompson, in his much more modest book on oral history, remarks: 'Oral history is as old as history itself. It was the first kind of history. And it is only quite recently that skill in handling oral evidence has ceased to be one of the marks of the great historian'

(Thompson, 1978: 19) Rather mischievously, one of the key contemporary writers on autobiography, James Olney, has written:

> The first autobiography was written by a gentleman named W.P. Scargill; it was published in 1834, and was called the The Autobiography of a Dissenting Minister. Or perhaps the first autobiography was written by Jean Jacques Rousseau in the 1760s (but he called it his Confessions); or by Michel de Montaigne in the latter half of the sixteenth century (but he called it Essays); or by St Augustine at the turn of the fourth–fifth century (but he called it his Confessions); or by Plato in the fourth century BC (but he wrote it as a letter, which we know as the seventh epistle); or . . . and so on . . . (Olney, 1980: 5)

Whatever may be the case, it would be wrong to suggest that these testaments of personal lives which have existed throughout history would have the same meanings then as they do now. To read Augustine, for example, is to enter a world dominated by a concern with reflective, religious submission, whilst to read modern accounts is often to enter a secular world where reflection is minimal and individual self-absorbtion is maximized! The roots of this individualism (and humanism) as major forms may be traced back at least to the medieval period – the religious confession transcending the penance, the sensitive human portraiture becoming distinguished from the hierarchically observed picture, romantic and courtly love rising from instrumental marriage; through the era of Thomism, with its gradual separation of reason and revelation, the secular and the religious – and on to the Renaissance period. But it is surely with industrialization that the modern so-called 'Possessive Individual' is announced. A new kind of individual with a new kind of 'self' seems to emerge (cf. Taylor, 1989). As the influential literary critic Lionel Trilling once put it: 'At a certain point in history men became individuals' (Trilling, 1972: 24). It is probably at this moment that people, overwhelmingly from the west, start to develop fully a sense of themselves as objects of introspection, of interest, of value; when the individual begins to brood and reflect over his or her inner nature; a time when the individual starts to retreat from the public life into the realms of privacy – the inner thought, the private home, the real self. There are many cultures in time and space where such an individual self is not to be found – many African cultures, and many countries in South East Asia for instance, and often linked to their religions, do not sense such an individuated or private self as does the modern west (for an account of selves in other cultures, see Brian Morris, 1994).

In the latter part of the twentieth century, much sociological writing has testified to this change. A wide range of terms have appeared which all attempt to capture varying aspects of this: 'the self' or 'identity' has been variously described as in crisis (Erikson), impulsive (Turner), fragmented (James), mutable (Zurcher), saturated (Gergen), protean (Lifton), other-looking (Riesman), narcissistic (Lasch), actualizing (Maslow),

BOX 4.2   TRADITIONAL, MODERN AND POSTMODERN IDENTITIES

TRADITIONAL IDENTITIES ARE
more likely to be tied to:
place
kinship
community
hierarchy
religion . . .

And hence more likely to be:
stable
static – little change over long periods of time . . .
unified
fixed
given
taken for granted and hence unquestioned

MODERN IDENTITIES ARE
'To make it new'

are more open to:
rationalization (science, technology)
capitalization (production, markets)
bureaucratization (rules, hierarchy)
secularization (death of God)
urbanization (big city life)
individualization (ideology of self)
democratization (aims of equality and freedom . . .)

which often means a less strong sense of place and
loss of meaning . . .
homelessness

likely to become more:
fragmented
pluralized
individualized
impulsive
destabilized
'in crisis' but also 'empowering'

POST-LATE MODERN IDENTITIES
'The end of the meta-narrative'

Accelerating changes means
identities become linked to:

hi-tech and hi-media
changes in time and space . . .
globalization and glocalization . . .
fragmentations and differences . . .
loss of one big story
tribalisms

and become more
self-reflexive, self-conscious and
ironic
relational and relating
saturated
cyberlinked and simulated
prone to anxiety

For further reading on all this, see Kenneth Gergen, *The Saturated Self*
(1991); Anthony Giddens, *Modernity and Self-Identity* (1991); Roy
Baumeister, *Identity: Cultural Change and the Struggle for Self* (1986).

situated (Benhabib), postmodern (Sarup), and self-reflexive (Giddens).
The list goes on; and what lies at the heart of this enormous outpouring
of writing about 'the modern human being' is the idea that a highly
individuated, self-conscious and unstable identity is replacing the old,
stable, unitary self of traditional communities. These new selves are
'constructed' through shifts and changes in the modern world, and
partly create a new sense of permanent identity crisis. The search for
'understanding' and making sense of the self has become a key feature of
the modern world.

Diane Bjorklund (1999) has reviewed two hundred years of North
American autobiography to capture how such written accounts can be
seen to provide different and shifting visions of a self. Not suggesting
that everything can be neatly slotted into her characterization, she
nevertheless suggests four 'ideal type' models. The earliest model takes
autobiography to be a kind of 'morality play' – the life story may see
human nature as essentially corrupt, and the life as contingent upon
religious searching and conversion. This is followed by what she calls
'masters of fate', whereby the stories of self envision people gaining
control over their own destinies – where there is both 'character' and

'will power'. Next comes 'the uncertain self' where psychological models – such as those provided by Erik Erikson – come to play a crucial role, and instinct, feelings, drives become the key to understanding human life. And finally, once again, she ends by suggesting that the contemporary self at the end of the twentieth century has become 'beleaguered': a sociological view that sees the impact of society on self-conception. For her, the 'autobiographical self' may be seen as a 'dialogue with history' (1999: 18). What is grasped in this account is the way 'the human being' changes, even in very recent times, bringing new languages and metaphors of the self with it. 'Writing the story of your life' becomes central to this sense-making. As Dan McAdams says: 'if you want to know me, then you must know my story, for my story defines who I am'. In short, 'Identity is a Life Story' (McAdams, 1985; 1993: 11).

There are optimists, pessimists and agnostics on these recent trends. Some suggest this individuality has now gone so far as to create a narcissistic culture of self-absorbed individuals with no sense of public life, shared morality or outer control (cf. Lasch, 1979). The preoccupation with individualism, choice and changing identities is seen to be part of a wider social and moral breakdown. Others have suggested too that this brooding introspection – embodied in the 'confessional' – is part of a more general shift in control: from the outer constraints on the *body* to the inner constraints on the *soul*. Through *the technologies of the self* power circulates, regulates and embodies surveillance (cf. Foucault, 1977, 1978). By contrast, optimists sense that we are discovering a broader, more available cultured individuality. A growing control over our lives, an increased sense of choice, the democratization of personhood: these are the features that accompany the rise in individualism. This virtue of the 'autobiographical society' is well stated by the liberal historian Karl Weintraub in this more agnostic, cautious, closing paragraph of his major 'essay' on autobiographical study, *The Value of the Individual*. He writes:

> When understood in the best terms, a view of life resting on a loving admiration for the diversity and the manifold richness of life is a magnificent one. It embodies the deepest respect for the formative powers of man. Even if we can know nothing about ultimate human purpose and the end objectives of this mysterious process of life, we can derive gratification and hope from a conception of cosmic order where creative individuality adds forever to the growing richness of the world. There is nobility in our willingness to understand men [sic] on their own terms and to complicate our judgment by giving each man [sic] his due. There is a refinement of knowledge in a perspectivist understanding of reality. All matters of great value exact their price. We pay for our commitment to individuality by incurring the dangers of lives floundering in capricious subjectivism, the pursuit of arbitrary whims, the loss of real selves in unrealistic dreams, and by cutting mistakenly the life giving interaction between self-formation and responsible cultivation of our given social and cultural world. Only the future can show whether the price is too

high and whether we can live responsibly with the ideal of the self. Perhaps those are right who say that history has no lessons. But historical contemplation may, at least? help us to be wiser. The only admonition that the historian gives us that is worth repeating may well be that, whatever else we do, we ought to live our lives as responsible heirs. (Weintraub, 1978: 379)

Until the dawn of the Enlightenment, documents of lives were primarily documents of memorable events (*memoirs*), of great deeds done (*res gestae*), or philosophers' lives; there were few instances in which there were ponderings about the nature of one's inner self. Saint Augustine's *Confessions* (around AD 400) is a notable exception – it is always cited as the foundational text of 'autobiography', and it is seen as setting the major pattern of coherence for the next fourteen centuries: admitting sins in order to be saved, in search of the spiritual core. For most scholars of the autobiographical form it is precisely this *search for a self* which is its hallmark; and the very word autobiography, suggests Karl Weintraub, did not appear until 1796 (cf. Olney, 1998). As Georges Gusdorf writes in 'Conditions and Limits of Autobiography' (1956), 'autobiography is not possible in a cultural landscape where consciousness of self does not, properly speaking, exist' (Olney, 1980: 30).

There are some key figures who signpost the modern personal document. Thus, when on 1 January 1660 Samuel Pepys sat down to record the first entry in his famous diaries – a task he was to regularly perform for the following nine years – we find the symbolic emergence of the modern diary as a distinctive form. When at the end of the eighteenth century Rousseau published his *Confessions* (1782) and Goethe his *Dichtung und Wahrheit* we have the emergence of the distinctive autobiography, a form 'inspired by a reverence for the self, tender yet severe, [seeing] the self not as a property but as trust' (Pascal, 1960: 181); it is motivated by '*Selbstbestimmung*' – a search for one's inner understanding – and is a search not a clear answer. Throughout it 'holds the balance between the self and the world, the subjective and the objective' (Pascal, 1960: 180), casting light upon both.

These concerns of the humanities – of understanding the inner world, the pursuit of self, of linking self with an outer world, of grasping the outer world via the inner world, of capturing the 'real life' – all start to be reflected in the emerging social science around the middle part of the nineteenth century. In England, Henry Mayhew's studies begin to give voice to the ordinary people of mid-Victorian England; in France, Frederic Le Play started the painstaking task of documenting family budgets as indicators of family life; a little later, in Vienna, Sigmund Freud was to begin his famous explorations into dreaming, autobiography, biography and the inner mind. And in America, notably in the work of the Chicago School of Sociology, life stories were to have a symbolic sociological birth, first in William Thomas and Florian Znaniecki's *The Polish Peasant* and Clifford Shaw's *The Jack Roller*.

Puzzling the auto/biography

All this is, of course, too simple, though it surely makes clear that self/ life stories have a shifting history. Attempting a full genealogy of auto/ biography is as hard a task as doing it for any other form of writing, like 'the novel', and is well beyond the scope of this book. The term is unclear, multiple and contested – and so are the routes to understanding the pathways to its contemporary manifestations. Some useful starts are to be found in books like Karl Weintraub's *The Value of the Individual* (1978) (though its male bias is very much in evidence); and the more recent feminist-inspired accounts by Liz Stanley (1992) of auto/ biography and Laura Marcus (1994) of auto/biographical discourses. Such studies clearly show that the literature is consistently haunted by a number of troublesome questions – what we might in effect see as issues around 'The Philosophy of Auto/Biography and the Self'. The debates have a repetitive refrain and some we have already met (and we will continue to meet them throughout this book). They are very grand: *What is a life? How indeed can we know a life? What is the link between telling a life and living a life? What are the ways of telling a life? How does 'writing a life' differ from a telling? How does a life's telling link to a culture and its history? How does the reading of a life link to the telling of a life? And to truth? Are all lives to be told equally or are some better to tell?* Or to put it all another way, we are concerned with understanding the three components harboured in the word: *autos* (what do we mean by the self?), *bios* (what do we mean by the life?) and *graphe* (what do we presume in the act of writing?). Finding answers to such questions is not easy and they have been the basis of philosophical reflections for centuries. Yet they are returned to over and over again in the musings over telling a life. So let me at least try to be clear what I think the issues are.

First, is the problematic nature of the very lived life or the life experi- ence. Whatever this may be (and it is hotly debated), it cannot be the same thing as the telling of a life. The flow of existential experience, of phenomenological consciousness, of movement and brute being, of self and identity – all these are key concerns and we all know them as the stuff of everyday life. Certainly auto/biography and life stories set out to engage with such issues, but they remain elusive. Getting at this bedrock of experience remains an honourable goal for many, but critics suggest that these very terms imply humanity as capable of existing free from social constraints and discourse and are hence suspect (cf. Scott, 1998). Can there really be a realm of experiences which can exist independently of the telling of them? Maybe without the telling of a life, the flow of a life – 'experience' – would have no meaning, no referent. Indeed, is it possible to live a life without in some way telling it? Can a life be imagined without some sense of the person accumulating traces of their experiences into some form of coherence through a narrative form – as they live through it? Some sense of time, of place, of family and friends, of wider connections? So it may be that the very lived life itself is bound up with versions of speaking and telling about it.

In any event, part of the auto/biographical quest must be a concern with the kinds of tellings given of the life. Certainly, as I suggested above, the life is not told in the same way across all cultures. Western ways have come to be orchestrated by particularly individualistic notions that are driven in part by the quest to understand the self – and to move inwards towards self-knowledge. Autobiographical theory often suggests that a deep understanding of a life is a high intellectual and spiritual goal for an individual's life – maybe the highest of all goals. Indeed, classically: 'In autobiography we encounter the highest and most instructive form of the undertanding of life' (cf. Marcus, 1994: 137 et seq.). Often, the life story in its various forms is seen as a journey towards an ultimate, truer understanding of a unique inner being, an inner quest for self: the injunction to know yourself.

Autobiographical writing aims to capture this self-reflexive process, to know it through consciousness, to ultimately understand the flow of this particular life. Part of the philosophy of autobiography, then, concerns this self-reflective debate and the streams of consciousness it provokes. Whether in St Augustine's spiritual soul-searching quest in the fifth century or in Rousseau's late eighteenth-century soul-searching, there is often a tension within the telling: reflections on time, memory, coherence and truth jostle with an attempt to 'confess' the life. As Dilthey (a key student of autobiography) says, whilst agreeing with Augustine:

> The starting point is always the same here: it lies in *discovering the reality in one's own interior life*. 'You who wish to know yourself, do you know that you exist?' 'I know it.' 'How so?' 'I don't know.' 'Do you feel yourself to be simple or complex?' 'I don't know.' 'Do you know that you move yourself?' 'I don't know that.' 'Do you know that you think?' 'I know that.' 'Then it's true that you think?' 'Yes, it is true.' (Dilthey, 1923/1988: 234; emphasis in original)

And this links to a third issue: from these reflections is it possible to detect a deep – even essential or core – self? The goal may be to get at the essential life, its underlying design (Pascal, 1960), and the pathways into this come through the reflective life and the reflections. The challenge is to find the 'real' or 'authentic' self in the telling. Liz Stanley's probing account provides two strong images to capture this problem. What she sees as a conventional model can be likened to using a microscope – 'the more information about the subject you collect, the closer to "the truth" – the "whole truth" – you get' (Stanley, 1992: 158). This is a strong 'realist' perspective and it pervades much auto/biographical work. The life can ultimately, with another focus, be grasped! It suggests that auto/biography can hold out the hope of a true, real essential self, awaiting discovery. Yet Liz Stanley does not think this is possible. In critical contrast, she sees auto/biographical work as more akin to a 'kaleidoscope':

'Each time you look you see something rather different, composed mainly of the same elements but in a new configuration' (Stanley, 1992: 158). It all depends on how you look. She uses her own work on Hannah Cullwick and A.J. Mumby (see Chapter 3), as well as research she has conducted on serial killer Peter Sutcliffe to make it very clear that the researcher's changing position in all this must be included. There is no 'fixed' core story for her. And so this leads to a sense of all the elements in the kaleidoscope that need attending to – and there are many of them.

Not least are the issues of 'writing' and 'reading' a life. Whilst people may have always told the stories of their lives throughout history, the writing/reading of lives becomes something newer (mass writing after all is a relatively recent development). We can start to sense that 'acts of writing' help us see that lives are always 'composed' and that it may the very act of composition itself which lies at the heart of the auto/biographical mode. It is not the real life, but the composed life. The emphasis on being able to gain access to the real, essential self is greatly diminished, if non-existent. And the life story is seen to be an artefact, a creation depending upon time, space, audience and a multitude of 'rhetorical tricks' that allow a person to write a life. It may indeed be constrained by the laws of genre – the writing conventions which dictate the form of auto/biography. Again, feminist sociologist Liz Stanley puts it well when she says:

> the notion of the 'reconstruction' of a biographical subject is an intellectual non-starter. It proposes we can somehow recover the past, understand it as it was experienced and understood by the people who actually lived it. Good history eschews such a belief and so too should good biography. In contrast, within a feminist and cultural political approach, questions like 'the past from *whose* viewpoint?', 'why *this* viewpoint and not another?', and 'what would be the effect of working from a *contrary* viewpoint?' should be asked. The past, like the present, is the result of competing negotiated *versions* of what happened, why it happened, and with what consequences'. (Stanley, 1992: 7)

The leading psychologist Jerome Bruner also puts it forcefully:

> an autobiography is not and never can be a way of simply signifying or referring to a 'life as lived'. I take the view that there is no such thing as 'life as lived' to refer to. On this view, a life is created or constructed by an act of autobiography. It is a way of construing experience – and reconstruing and reconstruing till our breath or our pen fails us . . . (1993: 38)

Once this is accepted, the conventions of telling a life become of great interest. We become more and more concerned with the arts of writing and presenting the life. And the classic distinction of biography, auto-biography and fiction become altogether less clear. (Stanley hence uses the term auto/biography, a convention that I will largely follow to high-light this problematic relation.) Thus, for example, an almost standard requirement of classic auto/biography is to start telling the life at the beginning or birth, move through various linear stages of a life, and go as close to death as you can by the end with the assumption that the 'true' life is being followed in the narrative! Yet we do not have to follow these linear narratives – this is just a convention. We can instead adopt 'more experimental' forms. And this is just what can be found in a number of great modern 'auto/biographies' where the nature of autobiographical writing is itself under challenge, often being spliced with fictional tricks and devices. Gertrude Stein's *The Autobiography of Alice B. Toklas* (1933) is actually the autobiography of Stein (and see also her *Everybody's Autobiography*, 1938/1985); Virginia Woolf's work as a whole contains a complex fusion of fiction and auto/biographies in works as diverse as *Orlando: A Biography* (1928), *A Room of Her Own* (1929) and *Moments of Being* (1978); Roland Barthes's work threatens to abolish the very genre with its self conscious trickery (see *Roland Barthes by Roland Barthes*) (1975). Indeed, almost all modernist writers play with the form – from Nietzsche's *Ecce Homo* to Sartre's *Words* – recognizing the story of a life can never be the life as lived. Indeed, it may be possible to detect an abrupt rise in experimentalism at the end of the twentieth century, with the spread of postmodern thought. The distinctions between author and subject, autobiography and biography, fiction and fact become more and more blurred.

And all this now has to be linked to the layers of theorizing placed over the life story. All the great intellectual strands of the twentieth century have been used to shape autobiographical writing. Freud's theory of the unconscious seeps into more and more accounts (and Freud himself uses it to great effect in his study of Leonardo (*Leonardo da Vinci and a Memory of his Childhood*, 1910). Sartre's existentialism is clearly present in his own autobiographical works. Barthes's own book *Roland Barthes by Roland Barthes* (1975) is self-consciously deconstructive and playful (it actually being quite hard to learn much about his life from the curious melange of fragments that he throws up in seemingly chaotic fashion!). In all of this there is a serious questioning of author and authorship – enough for some to deny the very existence of the auto-biographical mode – collapsing it into power, discourse, language. Here we ask with Foucault 'What is an author?' (Foucault, 1979a), and declare with Barthes 'The death of the author' (Barthes, 1977).

A final puzzle is, on the surface, more simple: whose life can be told? In much of the classical writing the answer is clearly that of the 'exemplary' life. Here the story is taken to be that of 'great men', great leaders, or else 'men of letters', the 'genius' producing 'great auto-biographies' (which usually can be taken to tell us significant things about an important culture!). Here are great leaders, literary figures, usually western men, where the 'public life' is stressed over the 'private life'. They often come to be seen as exemplars of the historical moment. As Dilthey writes of this – 'a man looks at his now existence from the standpoint of universal history', 'man knows himself only in history, never through introspection', 'the totality of human nature exists only in history', 'only history tells a man what he is' (Dilthey, 1923/1988: 15). These are grand claims. They exclude many writings of women and other classes, for example. Yet, even at the end of the twentieth century, with auto/biography everywhere, a distinction still runs right through it: some lives are really worth reading about, others much less so. Once again, as Liz Stanley trenchantly saw as she was reviewing a number of telling biographies, even within feminism the most discussed are usually those of the intellectuals – Gertrude Stein, Simone de Beauvoir, Audre Lorde, Virginia Woolf, Djuna Barnes, etc. – rather than more popular figures – Shirley Maclaine, Martina Navratilova, Dora Preven (Stanley, 1992: 100). The minor tales, the confessionals, the stock journalist stories are bypassed in favour of the great literary characters.

Making new voices: collective stories 'up from below'

Yet a change is in the air. It is not that 'ordinary voices', 'hidden voices' and 'voices from below' could not tell their stories at all. They could – but with difficulty, and rarely in the public sphere (cf. Habermas, 1989; Lara, 1998). The dominant forms of auto/biography that appeared in the public domain were those of the wealthy and powerful, which usually meant white, western, middle and upper class men. But what we start to see more and more with the slow 'democratization of society' (whereby some principles of choice, equality and individuality become a little more widespread) is the emergence of 'other' kinds of stories being told – stories from the margins, writings which start to work at the borders of boundaries and differences. The working class challenging the middle class, women challenging men, slaves challenging oppression, the young challenging elders. Gradually, more marginal voices speak – indeed have to speak; and as they do, they speak not just of themselves but of and for 'others' in the world. The autobiographies 'from below' hence work to create a different sense of autobiographical form, one where consciousness of self becomes more of a collective exploration than just a private one. The author is somehow located as a member of a class, a gendered group, a generational group, an outcast group. Indeed, these stories can transcend the traditional isolated 'individual' of classic autobiography – the St Augustine or Rousseau – to create a more collective awareness of others. This is the start of what might be called 'collective autobiography' (Hazlett, 1998). Thus, in the famous biography of a Guatemalan woman – already introduced in Chapter 2 – we read a now almost classic remark in the opening of the book. She says:

> My name is Rigoberta Menchú. I am twenty-three years old. This is my testimony. I didn't learn it from a book and I didn't learn it alone. I'd like to

stress that it's not only my life, it's also the testimony of my people. It's hard for me to remember everything that's happened to me in my life since there have been very many bad times but, yes, moments of joy as well. The important thing is that what has happened to me has happened to many other people too: *My story is the story of all poor Guatemalans. My personal experience is the reality of a whole people.* (Menchú, 1984: 1; emphasis added)

A personal tale is now a story of a whole people.

Thus any geneaology of an auto/biographical society must now start to detect the moments when various tales of the outcast, the marginal and the silenced begin to appear and how they come to take a hold in the imagination of a wider society. Tentatively, I would date such shifts from the late eighteenth/early nineteenth century when there appears to have been a growth in writings that move into the margins and help redefine fields. Some of the earliest of these stories are to be found in tales of the outcast poor, 'common lives', and delinquents (cf. Bennett, 1981; Stanley, 1992: 12). We can also detect a growth of interest in the hitherto ignored 'women's autobiographies'. 'Slave narratives' of North American blacks become noticed and start to play a prominent role in the anti-slavery movement. Spaces, then, are opened up which, by the mid-twentieth century, allow for more and more 'voices' to enter: holocaust survivor stories, lesbian and gay coming out stories, the tales of different age generations, health stories and narratives of HIV/AIDS, stories from indigenous peoples who have been 'colonized'.

Consider, for instance, women's auto/biographies and personal narratives on which much has been written recently. It has been argued that they often bring with them a different voice and a distinctive form: that they are more likely to be understated; have less concern with their own achievements; focus more on the private and the personal and less on the public; and have more 'embeddedness' and connectedness to others. Liz Stanley's impressive review of this field is careful, however, not to overstate this – some of these characteristics can easily be found in male auto/biographies too (Stanley, 1992: 132). At the same time, she does argue for a distinctive feminist auto/biographical method which should inevitably be rooted in women's ontology or experience of the world (men therefore cannot write such an auto/biography) and which would stress contingency, an 'anti-spotlight' stance, anti-realism and a self-awareness of textual practices (Stanley, 1992: 253).

Apart from a burgeoning field of women's autobiography – often blended with class (Steedman, 1986) and ethnicity (hooks, 1992) – within modern feminism, there has been a remarkably strong concern with 'telling the personal tales', often as a way of bringing to voice a private worry that then becomes a public problem. Thus, Susan Griffin begins her famous study of rape – *Rape: The Power of Consciousness* (1979) – with the line: 'I have never been free of the fear of rape . . .'. Nancy Friday starts her study of mothers, *My Mother, My Self* (1977) with the lines: 'I

BOX 4.3   A SELECTION OF WOMEN'S AUTO/BIOGRAPHIES

Maya Angelou	*I Know Why the Caged Bird Sings* (1969)
	The Heart of a Woman (1981)
Gloria Anzaldúa	*Borderlands/La Frontera* (1987)
Domitila Barrios de Chungra	*Let Me Speak!* (1978)
Simone de Beauvoir	*The Prime of Life* (1962)
Vera Brittain	*Testament of Youth* (1985)
Marie Cardinal	*The Words to Say It* (1983)
Jung Chang	*Wild Swans: Three Daughters of China* (1991)
Angela Davis	*With My Mind on Freedom* (1975)
Isak Dinesen	*Out of Africa* (1937)
Anne Frank	*The Diary of a Young Girl* (1952)
Lillian Hellman	*Pentimento* (1976)
Helen Keller	*The Story of My Life* (1902)
Doris Lessing	*The Memoirs of a Survivor* (1974)
Audre Lorde	*The Cancer Journals* (1980)
	Zami: A New Spelling of My Name (1982)
Harriet Martineau	*Harriet Martineau's Autobiography* (1877)
Mary McCarthy	*Memories of a Catholic Girlhood* (1957)
Margaret Mead	*Blackberry Winter* (1972)
Kate Millett	*Flying* (1974)
	The Loony Bin Trip (1990)
	Sita (1977)
Ann Oakley	*Taking it Like a Woman* (1984)
Sylvia Plath	*The Journal of Sylvia Plath* (1982)
Margaret Sanger	*An Autobiography* (1938)
Jo Spence	*Putting Myself in the Picture* (1988)
Carolyn Steedman	*Landscape for a Good Woman* (1986)
Gertrude Stein	*Autobiography of Alice B. Toklas* (1933)
	Everybody's Autobiography (1937)
Beatrice Webb	*My Apprenticeship* (1926)
Virginia Woolf	*Moments of Being* (1976)

have always lied to my mother. And she to me . . .'. Adrienne Rich starts her study of mothering (*Of Woman Born*, 1976) with the line: 'My children cause me the most exquisite suffering of which I have any experience. It is the suffering of ambivalence: the murderous alternation between bitter resentment and raw edged nerves, and blissful gratification and tenderness.' Whilst Betty Friedan starts her pathbreaking *The Feminine Mystique* (1963) with: 'The problem lay buried, unspoken for many years in the minds of American women. It was a strange stirring, a sense of dissatisfaction, a yearning that women suffered in the middle of the twentieth century in the United States. Each suburban wife struggled with it alone

. . . "Is this all?"'. And much earlier, in a classic remark, Sojourner Truth asks: 'Ain't I a woman?'

> That man over there says women need to be helped into carriages, and lifted over ditches, and to have the best place everywhere. Nobody ever helps me into carriages, or over mud-puddles, or gives me any best place! And ain't I a woman? Look at me! Look at my arm! I have ploughed an' planted, and gathered into barns, and no man could head me! And ain't I a woman? I could work as much and eat as much as a man – when I could get it – and bear the lash as well. And ain't I a woman? I have born thirteen children and seen them most all sold off to slavery, and when I cried out with my mother's grief, none but Jesus heard me! And ain't I a woman? (From 1851 speech by Sojourner Truth, cited by Collins, 1990: 14)

Many classics of feminism, then, start with a personal narrative and many women's lives have been told. But increasingly they highlight not an essential woman's experience but a range of differences – cutting across ethnicities, class, disabilities, ages, health and sexualities. (For a critique and evaluation of some of this, see Marcus, 1994; Smith and Watson, 1998; Stanley, 1992.) The collective stories start to get fractured into a proliferation of what might be called 'difference stories'.

From slave narratives to a Black Public Sphere Another interesting example must be the stories of 'blacks' in the United States. Indeed, black autobiography with its roots in slave narratives serves as something of a paradigm for this kind of work. Certainly, as black studies of different kinds grew in the 1970s onwards, the autobiographical mode was usually at its heart because, as James Olney remarks:

> black history was preserved in autobiographies rather than standard histories, and because black writers entered into the house of literature through the door of autobiography. From Frederick Douglass to Malcolm X, from Olaudah Equiano to Maya Angelou, the mode specific to the black experience has been autobiography . . . In black autobiography and criticism of it, we have something akin to a paradigm of the situation of autobiography in general . . . (1980: 15)

Many of the earliest slave accounts were actually told through conditions of slavery, documenting the lives of some men and women as they lived the lives of slaves. The story of Frederick Douglass is usually seen as the most famous (it warrants a place in the Penguin Classics series). Although he suffered the many indignities and horrors of slavery, one of his captors did at least afford him the opportunity to learn to read and write; and shortly after he escaped from slavery in 1838, he turned his hand to writing the narrative of his life. Published in the spring of 1845, priced at 50 cents, and 125 pages long, it immediately became a best-seller (cf. Douglass, 1982: 19). The tone and style is to be found in many slave narratives, exemplified by the following:

> If at any one time of my life more than another, I was made to drink the bitterest dregs of slavery, that time was during the first six months of my stay with Mr. Covey. We were worked in all weathers. It was never too hot or too cold; it could never rain, blow, hail or snow, too hard for us to work in the field. Work, work, work was scarcely more the order of the day than of the night. The longest days were too short for him and the shortest nights too long for him. I was somewhat unmanageable when I first went there, but a few months of this discipline tamed me. I was broken in body, soul and spirit. My natural elasticity was crushed, my intellect languished, the disposition to read departed, the cheerful spark that lingered about my eye died: the dark night of slavery closed in upon me; and behold a man transformed into a brute. (Douglass, 1845/1982: 105)

The writing on slavery is colossal. Much has been gathered through what might now be called 'oral history' projects, the most famous being the New Deal's Federal Writing Project in the 1930s which gathered stories from former slaves asking 'What does it mean to be a slave? What does it mean to be free? And, even more, how does it feel?' They are published in forty-one volumes as *The American Slave: A Composite Autobiography* (Rawick, 1971–9), with a more popular (now paperback) version in *Lay My Burden Down: A Folk History of Slaves* (Botkin, 1945/ 1994): a history in which 'the people are the historians as well as the history, telling their own story in their own words' (p. xii).

These narratives then are often seen to be the wellsprings out of which African American literature has evolved in the United States: they set patterns, genres, sensitivities and feelings for how such work could be done; and they have helped shape what has been called a 'Black Public Sphere' (Black Public Sphere Collective, 1995).

'Coming out' through life stories: gay and lesbian lives   One of the clearest of situations where voices have appeared telling their life stories where once there was silence is in the case of gay and lesbian stories. Until roughly the 1970s, if any life stories were to be told of 'homosexuality' they were usually to be told by doctors and moralists, and were couched in the most negative terms – since homosexuality was seen as a sickness, a pathology and a crime. There were a few 'confessional' biographies – like Peter Wildeblood's *Against the Law*, and a few semi-autobiographical novels – like Radclyffe Hall's *The Well of Loneliness*, for example; but in the main there was a stigmatizing silence. Yet in tandem with the arrival of 'gay liberation' an unceasing number of life stories started to be told – sometimes as autobiography, sometimes as biography, sometimes in film and video, and often in collections of 'coming out' stories – where large numbers of gays and lesbians spoke of their own experiences of being silenced, of being in the closet, of learning about gayness, of coming out,

of settling down. Books such as *Gay Voices from East Germany, Growing Up Before Stonewall, Walking After Midnight: Gay Men's Life Stories; Quiet Fire: Memoirs of Older Gay Men, The Coming Out Stories, Lesbians Talk Transgender*. And with them, as with women, the working class and 'blacks', major archiving projects start to appear to house these testimonies.

Living with AIDS   As a sign of just how pervasive such life stories have begun to be, AIDS stories started to appear almost simultaneously with the announcement of the disease itself. Not only did the human interest story start to appear within the gay press within weeks, researchers were gathering compilations of stories and 'victims/survivors' and their relatives were publishing full-length autobiographies. Thus, Lon Nungesser's *Epidemic of Courage* was published in 1986 and gathers thirteen life stories of men and their relatives (under such titles as 'Speaking for Ourselves' by Bobby Reynolds and 'A Mother's Love' by Gertrude Cook), published more or less as interviews with Nungesser's questions incorporated. (Nungesser talks about his own illness as shaping the book – 'to reveal the reality of AIDS as one is living through it is the contribution I have to offer', Nungesser, 1986: xiii.) Such 'academic' stories have continued to this day, but in addition there has been an enormous outpouring of life stories – ways of dealing with death, ways of coping with the illness, ways of dealing with rage, ways of just getting down what was happening – now a huge chronicle awaits the twenty-first century reader: it is probably chronicled as no other disease has been in history, though there are now many illness narratives for all kinds of illnesses (see for instance Cook, 1991; and Mathiesen and Stam, 1995 on cancer narratives). We have: *The Screaming Room: A Mother's Journal* (Barbara Peabody, 1986); *The Walking Wounded: A Mother's True Story* (Beverly Barbo, 1987); *Thanksgiving: An Aids Journal* (Elizabeth Cox, 1990); *Surviving and Thriving with AIDS* (Michael Callen, 1987/1990); *The Absence of Angels* (Elizabeth Glaser and Laura Palmer, 1991); *Mark: How a Boy's Courage in Facing AIDS Inspired a Town* (Jay Hoyle, 1991); *Reports from the Holocaust* (Larry Kramer, 1989); *Borrowed Time* (Paul Monette, 1992); *Ryan White: My Own Story* (1991); *To All the Girls I Loved Before: An AIDS Diary* (J.W. Money, 1987); *Goodbye I Love You* (Carol Pearson, 1988); and John Preston's edited collection *Personal Dispatches* (1989), amongst many, many others. It also led to thousands of mini biographies on the AIDS Quilt (see Chapter 10; and Ruskin, 1988), which in turn inspired a film of some of these stories).

The Warholian moment   It would seem that by the start of the twenty-first century, everyone in the minority world has a potential story to be told, and many others in the third or majority world are starting to claim rights to tell them too. No longer is the life story the privilege of the intellectual, the rich, or the elite – although it is clearly still their dominant form. But now auto/biography has spread across the globe and become a sign of self- and group awareness, and of a kind of equality of life: we can all speak the life. In all these instances there is a marked autobiographical turn from tales of an elite to tales previously not told. The genealogy of voices from below leads to seeing the task of these stories as being much more engaged in a political practice . . . at the end of the twentieth century, more and more diversity in human lives appears in the life story form. On the surface, there has been a shift from 'dominant stories', dominant genres', 'dominant memories' to a language of resistance, the popular, alternatives, difference.

Yet caution is needed. Starting to think about how voices come to recognize themselves and get their audience (cf. Chapter 2) soon leads to more questions about whether a voice takes on a particular form or not; whether indeed the voice gets changed in this process of speaking. This is what much post-colonial theory would argue: that ironically, marginal voices can often be co-opted into dominant ones through the very processes of telling their stories. And likewise, many women's autobiographies get co-opted into the canon of middle class male autobiography, using their theories and conventions. More generally, Patricia Hill Collins says:

> Oppressed groups are frequently placed in a situation of being listened to only if we frame our ideas in the language that is familiar to and comfortable for a dominant group. This requirement often changes the meaning of our ideas and works to elevate the ideas of dominant groups. (1990: xiii)

Pulp confessionals, cyberdocuments and hi-tech lives

Autobiography and 'confession' may have had a long history in thought – from St Augustine to the newer Marginal Voices located above – but it is during the latter part of the twentieth century that it starts to appear in new forms of media, often giving it new features. We should not be surprised to find that just as the 'new information technologies are transforming the way we produce, consume, manage, live and die . . .' (Castells, 1998), so they are starting to change the very way we tell the story of our lives.

As a quick opening example of a shifting form, consider what might be called the 'paperbacking of confessions'. This is often linked to self-help worlds, where the personal tale is turned into an international best-seller – books like Nancy Friday's *My Mother, My Self* (1977), Rosemary Daniell's *Sleeping with Soldiers* (1984), Robin Norwood's collections of *Letters from Women who Love Too Much* (1987), studies of *The Soap Opera Syndrome* (Davidson, 1988). As one writer puts it, it is 'the self on the shelf' (Greenberg, 1994; Irvine, 1999). Since the 1960s, such 'confessional' books have rarely been out of the best-selling book lists. And as I write, it has culminated at century's end in a form of television confessional talk show: at its best perhaps in the now defunct *Donahue* and *Oprah*, at its worst maybe in *The Jerry Springer Show*. These are modern day 'freak shows' (Gamson, 1998), with the life on full media display, backed up with therapeutic suggestions – *The Talking Cure* (Shattuc, 1997). These are the many programmes which encourage people to go on screen and announce their lives, usually the most tragic parts of them, to a very wide audience. Incest, abuse, transgender, violence, wives who kill, men who abuse – these are the daily fodder of such shows. They are mass produced confessional tales. The new auto/biography has now moved into the new talk show auto/biography.

Life stories in an age of mechanical reproduction: from Benjamin to Baudrillard One of the first and most influential writers to start noticing how the shifts in technology were shaping 'art' forms was Walter Benjamin (1892–1940). He argued, in a very influential paper, that art forms were changing dramatically in the new modern world. They were becoming increasingly reproducible – in everything from books and cheap art prints, to photos and postcards. (We can take this on further to electronic forms such as computers and videos.) The original authenticity of art – and in our case, the story of a life – was being broken down. Originally full of 'aura' – authenticity, uniqueness, spontaneity – art becomes detached from its source and turned into 'a plurality of copies' (Benjamin, 1990: 30). Once this happens 'art' (and 'life stories') can become a mass form. More, people expect art to be reproduced and the very acts of creation become clouded with the potential of reproduction and its reception by a mass audience.

But if Walter Benjamin gave us the age of mechanical reproduction – one where the unique life story can become the paperbacked best-seller, where the story told of a life round the fire becomes the industry of 'confessional telling' exemplified in self-help books – then Jean Baudrillard (1929–) has given us the age of the simulacrum, where the actual lived life can become entrapped in a hi-tech whirl of media simulations, of chat shows, of computerized imagery. Now the lived life is no longer embodied and bounded as it was in the past; rather it swirls into a curious simulated form of its own apart from its author and apart from its authentic being. Go, for instance, into a web site, search for 'autobiography' and you will come up with millions of entries of all kinds: from thousands of school children telling their lives in simple formats for a classroom project to CD-Roms that help you format your family tree; from the most personal sexual autobiography in a 'chat room' to the published life stories on line of Thomas Jefferson, or Alex Haley's *Roots*. And when we watch films like *The Truman Show*, *Pleasantville* or *The Matrix* we find lives entrapped within media forms. In the much acclaimed *The Truman Show*, for example, 'Truman' – the lead character – is born on television and lives the story of his life entirely encapsulated through a television village (though somehow escaping at the end). In all this, the boundaries between life, media and the story of a life are seriously changing. Reproductions, then, are everywhere; and we start to sense that 'life stories' in the twenty-first century harbour so many changes that it may seem we have entered the age when science fiction becomes the new 'reality'.

Indeed, it is as if some of the utopian and dystopian tales written by the science fiction writers over the past century or so are starting to come true. From Mary Shelley's *Frankenstein* 'cyborg' – half science/half person – to George Orwell's *1984* stuffed full of surveillance strategies and monitoring the personal life in a myriad of ways, it would seem new forms of being may well be in the making, which connects to the telling of life stories in new forms. Utopian images sense a new human being in the making who will be more autonomous, liberated, free, and who is confronting more and more choices – especially around who they are to be: what has been called the postmodernization of intimacy. Here life stories start to be told in more and more fluid ways. In contrast, dystopian images sense a new human being turned into a mechanical robot or lost in a dehumanized cyberspace – efficient yet clichéd. Here we find what could be called – after George Ritzer's (1995) work – *The McDonaldization of Society*. Life stories become controlling, calculable, predictable, efficient (perhaps most apparent in the standardization of the 'Curriculum Vitaes' – the marketed story of a life for job persuasion) (Danahay, 1996). For still others, the story is more mixed: here the (post-) modern human being becomes a pastiche (Gergen, 1991). And all this is present in the popular imagination of films like *Terminator*, *Aliens*, *Lawnmower Man* etc. where the 'morphing of the body' (best known from *Terminator 2* and *The Abyss*) suggests that objects and humans melt seamlessly into one another.

New trends in life documents

The backdrop to all this is the rise of a new series of technologies that are implicated in postmodern life. The old low-tech is being shifted into the new hi-tech. From print and sound recordings, through film and video, on to new digital forms – personal computing, web sites, CD-Roms, e-mail etc.; and ultimately towards lands only dimly sensed – cyberspace, virtual realities, medical scanning, the new genetics. A new world of holography, satellites, cybernetics, fibre-optics, digitalism, and virtuality may start to re-order the forms in which our lives are assembled, displayed and stored.

We have already seen some of the changes in the processes through which our lives get told (cf. Chapter 3): the sound recording in oral history, the visual record in the photograph, the documentary film, the rise of video diaries and video/ethnography. Just one hundred years ago, few lives could be told through any of these media: now they are quite widespread and even global. But all these are about to change. For example, as photographs move from the *analogic* mode they have previously displayed since their inception to a *digital* mode, so – it has been argued – we are moving into a 'post-photographic era' where we will reach 'the end of photography as we know it' (Mitchell, 1992; Ritchin, 1990). For analogic photography simply allowed copying; digital photography allows for a complete remixing and splicing of digitalized images. Likewise, as oral history confronts the new technologies, not only do massive databases become instantly accessible across the world, but voice recognition techniques make direct transcription of tapes possible. Combined with developments in video and hypertext, oral histories of everyone may soon be available! We now also have the accessing of lives in and through e-mail, CD-Roms, web sites and qualitative data packages. Not only are these increasingly common in the more formal 'auto/biographical worlds' of social sciences, there are also many popularly available programs for 'writing your own family geneaology', 'writing your own life', 'writing your own web page', or going into life story web sites that encourage the free exchange of life stories – not all of them sexual! Life stories may be put in digital form and made accessible with hypertext allowing the reader access to an electronic document where each page has many buttons which can lead you to further pages: you can access a life story and then find sounds, film clips, images, archives that are linked to the life. This life is not fixed, but one assembled through the reader. We are just at the start of what may be called 'virtual life story documents' – existing in computer memories, but having no tangible form in print. And, of course, through a global information highway, much of this can move across vast spaces in rapid time. If any of this was to become widespread (and surely much of it will?) life story telling will have undergone a major change. And yet even more: we can find many other new modes of encoding lives – from finger printing, eye scanning and bar codes, on to the new mechanisms visually invading the personal body – *mammography* (usually for breast cancer), *ultrasonography* (where sound waves help build up a portait of the self), and the *CAT scan* (computerized axial tomography) which can go deep, right into the bones (injected fluids making cancers in the bone visible). Finally, we can detect the very *DNA* encoded in our body (Cook in Smith and Watson, 1996: 63–85). The so-called stories of our life are starting to penetrate our very 'souls'.

Once upon a time there was a dispute between so called 'ancients' and 'moderns'. The 'ancients' would dig around in the past but find so little documentation to go on that they had to 'wring the last ounce of information out of them'. The 'moderns' by contrast 'drown in documents' (Vansina, 1985: 158). To this we may now add the 'post-moderns': at the dawn of the Information Age, we have reached new levels of 'saturation'. We can now be overwhelmed with the numbers of lives and tellings. Almost everyone can have their Warholian 15 minutes of fame.

The problem may now be to devise the best ways to simplify, sift and select from such a cornucopia.

The dark side of life stories

I have written this chapter in a fairly optimistic mood. From St Augustine's deep explorations of his inner self to the recovery of oppressed and marginal voices in slave narratives or HIV stories and on to the rise of personal web sites in cyberspace, we may trace the rise of auto/biography as a positive force for understanding and social change. But as I hinted at in the opening sections, all is not necessarily well with such life story work at the start of a new century. Indeed, it has many critics who sense something less than benign in this life story telling that seems to be everywhere. There is, then, a dark side.

Three main problems are coming to the fore. First, as we started to see with Benjamin above, there is a copying and commodification effect. Mimesis. Cliché. We start to live our lives through the stories of others, repeating and rehearsing others' stories as if they were our own, turning them along the way into commodities – literally stories that may be exchanged or sold. Many auto/biographical stories thus start to get a tired, passé feel about them: we have heard it all before. Rather than the story being a clue to authenticity as Weintraub and others claimed, it has become a cliché, endlessly recycled, repeated, replayed.

Closely linked, such repetitions can easily become extensions of control. Indeed, in a broad sense this is Foucault's concern in his critique of the confessional society. The life story telling becomes a 'technology of the self': one of the means through which power is dispersed and lives are constituted and regulated. Sidonie Smith and Julia Watson's *Getting a Life* (1996) charts the many new ways in which 'autobiography' is becoming ubiquitous in everyday life – taking on new forms and extending its reach. It can be found in film, electronic mail, video, TV talk shows, newspaper 'personal' ads; in CVs, medical investigations, therapies of all kinds, as well as records kept in all kinds of institutions. This is not Rousseau's *Confession*: it is a million little theatres of confession in which everyday lives are acted out. It is everywhere.

And finally, there is the fear of an excessive individualization and personalization – what Smith and Watson have called 'the paradox of radical individualism [which] haunts late twentieth century "America"'. As they tellingly ask:

> What does the right to privacy mean in a world of fragmented and dispersed subjects?
> What does it mean to insist on a culture of individuals whose very individuality must be authenticated again and again?

What kind of autobiographical subjects are produced and verified in a culture that commodifies self-authentication?
How does commodification operate at a time when the bases of authentication seem unstable?
How do we account for the simultaneous promise and corrosion of identity and identity politics? For the promise of subject formation and the disillusion of deformation?
How can we account for the obsessive desire to find a 'true' self in the midst of a culture that fetishizes what we might call tourist identities, throwaways . . .?
(1996: 7)

In conclusion

We are living in the auto/biographical society. Worlds of life story telling have been in the making for the past millennium, but they are more and more taking on new forms. This chapter has tried to sense a bit of this evolving form. It is a long journey from St Augustine's *Confessions* to cyberspace and television confessionals.

Guide to further reading

Helpful discussions on the **history and development of biography and autobiography** include Laura Marcus's *Auto/Biographical Discourses: Theory, Criticism, Practice* (1994) (which looks at nineteenth- and twentieth century 'western' developments), Liz Stanley's *The Auto/ Biographical I* (1992), which takes a strong feminist stand and seeks to politicize the field, and Diane Bjorklund's *Interpreting the Self* (1999), which looks sociologically at 'two hundred years of American autobiography'. In literary theory, the work of James Olney is central, and three main books can be cited: *Memory and Narrative: The Weave of Life-Writing* (1998); *Autobiography: Essays Theoretical and Critical* (ed., 1980) and *Metaphors of Self: The Meanings of Autobiography* (1972). See also Robert Folkenflik (ed.), *The Culture of Autobiography: Constructions of Self Representation* (1993); Karl Weintraub, *The Value of the Individual* (1978), and Roy Pascal, *Design and Truth in Autobiography* (1960). On **biography**, very useful is Catherine Parke, *Biography: Writing Lives* (1996). See also A. Shelston's *Biography* (1977), and R. Gittings's *The Nature of Biography* (1978). On the **oral tradition**, the classic source is Jan Vansina's (1985) *Oral Tradition as History*, which is itself a second edition of an earlier 1965 book *Oral Tradition*. Two important supplements to this are Ruth Finnegan's *Oral Tradition and the Verbal Arts* (1992) and Elizabeth Tonkin's *Narrating Our Pasts: The Social Construction of Oral History* (1992).

On **individualism and the self**, see Lukes's *Individualism* (1973), which provides a critical inventory of the uses of the term. On the rise of individualism, see Nicholas Abercrombie et al.'s *Sovereign Individuals of Capitalism* (1986). The changing nature of the individual and the self under industrialization and postmodernity is discussed in many places: for a selection see Richard Sennett, *The Fall of Public Man* (1974); Ken Gergen, *The Saturated Self* (1991); Antony Giddens, *Modernity and Self Identity* (1991); James Holstein and Jaber Gubrium, *The Self We Live By* (2000); and Manuel Castell, *The Power of Identity* (1998), which is Volume 2 of his *The Information Age*.

On specific **kinds of voices**, there are now numerous commentaries. A number are cited in the text. For some general commentaries, see: on delinquency, James Bennett, *Oral History and Delinquency: The Rhetoric of Criminology* (1981); on class, see John Burnett et al., *The Autobiography of the Working Class: An Annotated, Critical Bibliography* (1984); on women, see Liz Stanley, *The Auto/Biographical I* (1992); Sherna Gluck and Daphne Patai, *Women's Words: The Feminist Practice of Oral History* (1991); Sidonie Smith and Julia Watson, *Women, Autobiography, Theory* (1998). A valuable guide to black feminist studies is Patricia Hill Collins, *Black Feminist Thought: Knowledge, Consciousness and the Politics of Empowerment* (1990). On slave narratives, see Sidonie Smith, *Where I'm Bound: Patterns of Slavery and Freedom in Black American Autobiography* (1974); Stephen Butterfield, *Black Autobiography in America* (1974); and Charles Davis and Henry Louis Gates Jr, *The Slave's Narrative* (1985). On postcolonial and indigenous peoples, see Linda Tuhiwai Smith, *Decolonizing Methodologies: Research and Indigenous Peoples* (1999). On lesbian, gay and other sexual stories, see the general discussions in Ken Plummer's *Telling Sexual Stories* (1995). For examples, see Peter Nardi et al. *Growing up before Stonewall: Life Stories of Some Gay Men* (1994), Kevin Porter and Jeffrey Weeks' *Between the Acts: Lives of Homosexual Men 1885–1967* (1994) and the work of Gary Dowsett, *Practicing Desire* (1996).

On the **new information age technologies**, some key sources are: Manuel Castells, *The Information Age* (1998, 3 vols); Donna Haraway, *Simians, Cyborgs, and Women: The Reinvention of Nature* (1991); Mark Poster, *The Mode of Information* (1990); Christopher Dandekker, *Surveillance, Power and Modernity Polity* (1990); Michio Kaku, *Visions: How Science Will Revolutionize the Twenty First Century* (1998). *Resisting the Virtual Life* (1995), edited by James Brook and Iain A. Boal, provides a critique of much of these new developments. A lively series of discussions around (post-) modern uses of biography is to be found in Sidonie Smith and Julia Watson's *Getting a Life* (1996).

Ethnographies of the new technologies include: Annette H. Markham, *Life Online: Researching Real Experience in Virtual Space* (1999) and Sherry Turkle, *Life on the Screen* (1996).

5 'Chicago' and the Making of a Sociological Method

It seems no exaggeration to say that for roughly twenty years, from the First World War to the mid-1930s, the history of sociology in America can largely be written as the history of the Department of Sociology at the University of Chicago.

(Lewis A. Coser, 1978: 311)

If one reflects on it, I think the fundamental premise in the case of Park and Thomas and the associates there at Chicago is just that of recognizing that a human group consists of people who are *living*. Oddly enough this is not the picture which underlies the dominant imagery in the field of sociology today. They think of a society or group as something that is there in the form of a regularized *structure* in which people are placed. And they act on the basis of the influence of the structure on *them*. This is a complete inversion of what is involved and I would say the antithesis of the premise that underlay the work of Park and Thomas with their recognition that there are people, wherever you find them constituting a group – a small group or a huge society or an institution or what not – there are people who are engaged in living, in having to cope with situations that arise in their experience, organizing their behavior and conduct in the light of those situations which they encounter, coming to develop all kinds of collective arrangements which are ongoing affairs. And this, it seems to me, is the thing that particularly marks the position of the so-called Chicago School . . .

(Herbert Blumer, in Lofland, 1980 (reprinted in Plummer, 1997: vol. 4, p. 189); emphasis in original)

The last chapter surveyed a number of strands in the making of an auto/biographical society: it is a very messy genealogy with many pathways, dilemmas, shifts in fortune and trajectories hinted at. A comprehensive study must be awaited, though there are some good specialist starts (e.g. Bennett, 1981; Marcus, 1994). In this chapter, my task will be more straightforward. I want to focus on one thin line of development – one that suggests a foundation for the sociological tradition of life story telling. (We could write similar histories for anthropology, psychology, psychoanalysis, history, literature, folklore, feminism, postcolonialism, the world of the margins and marginality, journalism, video, documentary!) My claim is that the life history method in sociology gathered a distinctive momentum within the tradition of Chicago sociology during the 1920s and 1930s. But of course, even this – connecting as it does to the history of 'sociological research' (cf. Platt, 1996), the nature of Chicago sociology (Plummer, 1997), and the development of symbolic interactionism (Plummer, 2000) – have all been contested in recent times. And in practice, it all starts further back in time anyway – with the nineteenth-century researchers and reformers (like Mayhew, Booth, Adams and the Webbs), who took a great interest in personal documents; and it moves on to the current day, with newer developments in auto/ethnography. But as a specific history, I am suggesting there was an important *symbolic shaping moment* in the development of a sociology of life stories. And it is exemplified in the work of two 'canonical' studies in the early twentieth century: the publication of the massive Chicago project *The Polish Peasant in Europe and America*, by William Isaac Thomas and Florian Znaniecki, and the multiple 'delinquent' life histories gathered by Clifford Shaw throughout much of the 1920s and 1930s and embodied most clearly in the story of Stanley, the 'Jack Roller'.

Enter a Polish peasant . . . and a delinquent boy

Sociology was scarcely thirty years old in America when the Thomas and Znaniecki work was published, and as Blumer remarks 'there is no doubt that in the 1920s and 1930s *The Polish Peasant* was viewed extensively in sociological circles as the finest exhibit of advanced sociological research and theoretical analysis' (1979: vi). It has indeed variously been called a 'monumental work', 'a classic', 'a milestone' and a 'turning point' (e.g. Allport, 1942: 18; Bruyn, 1966: 9). Today it is rarely read, rarely even mentioned, but it is not too difficult to see how these early superlatives came to be applied to it. In sheer size, it must rank as one of the largest of sociological products; it was originally issued in five volumes and contained no less than 2,200 pages. Its manifest problematic was a central 'public issue' of the time: migration and cultural change. Between 1899 and 1910, Poles had accounted for one-quarter of all immigrants to the United States and indeed by 1914 Chicago (with its 360,000 Poles) ranked as the third largest Polish centre in the world – after Warsaw and Lodz. But, like any adequate sociological study, its concern lay not just with a specific social problem but with wider issues of social theory. Considered in its pages are the problems of individualization (what are the forms of social organization that allow for the greatest amount of individualism?); of community (what happens to the community and the family under conditions of rapid social change?); of abnormality (how far is abnormality the unavoidable manifestation of inborn tendencies of the individual and how far is it due to social conditions?); of the relations between the sexes (how is the general social efficiency of a group affected by the various systems of relations between man and woman?); and, a problem still much neglected to this day, the issue of social happiness (see Thomas and Znaniecki, 1958: 78–86 especially).

Of equal importance was their methodological position, most of which is found in the introductory 'Methodological notes', written largely by Znaniecki, after their empirical work was completed (see Znaniecki, 1934). They notably took a middle position on the two debates which have dominated sociology since its inception. The first concerns the relationship between the individual and the social: unlike Durkheim's famous dictum to treat social facts as things, Thomas and Znaniecki advocated a position in which both individual and social factors must always be taken into account in any social study. Their dictum, now largely forgotten, states that 'the cause of a social or individual phenomenon is never another social or individual phenomenon alone, but always a combination of a social and an individual phenomenon' (Thomas and Znaniecki, vol. 1, 1958: 44). In the text they illustrate this with reference to two brothers who have a tyrannical father; a good son who tends to be submissive to the father and a bad son who tends to revolt against the father. The response here is a combination of two different factors: the tyranny of the father remains constant, but the interpretation that the boys have towards him varies. Thus for one boy there is a sense of family solidarity while for the other boy there is a tendency to self-assertion. This leads them to the important distinction (which now runs right through sociology) between the objective factors of the situation and the subjective interpretation of that situation. For them, both issues must always be taken into account.

These features, amplified as they are in considerable detail, should be enough to provide interest in the study. But it is a combination of all of this with an intensive use of human documents that is its major claim to fame, for throughout the volume there is sustained the most thoroughgoing use of personal documents to be found in the social sciences. These personal documents fall roughly into five main groups.

- The use of letters – the greater part of one volume consists of 764 separate letters arranged into fifty series.
- A major life history statement by one Polish peasant, Wladek, which, while it runs into 300 pages, is abridged from a larger version, and may be only one of a number of similar life histories.
- A set of newspaper materials coming from the archives of a Polish peasant newspaper.
- A series of documents collected primarily through social agencies – both those in Poland where people wished to emigrate to America and those in America where people had arrived.
- Third person reports gleaned from social work agencies and court records.

Whilst the last three sets of records are of interest, it is primarily for the letters and the life history that the study is famed. Undoubtedly, then, *The Polish Peasant* is a classic and makes many central contributions to sociological debate. Yet, shamefully, it has fallen into obscurity. Indeed, even by 1948 Shils could note its neglect with alarm:

> The neglect of *The Polish Peasant in Europe and America* is another witness to the American sociologist's tendency to disregard and then re-do what was done before because of the slipshodness of the education of students and the failure of their teachers to assimilate and extend the best that has preceded them. (Shils, 1948: 26)

Shils's comment highlights the position that existed in America after the Second World War and has remained the same since then. But before it was to fall into decline, life history research was to enjoy a brief flowering period: indeed, there is much evidence that during the 1920s and 1930s it was an important approach for sociologists in America, and was gathering momentum in Europe.

Enter Stanley and the delinquent boys . . .

In his important study of *Oral History and Delinquency*, James Bennett has traced the evolution of delinquent 'oral histories' from the earliest work of Henry Mayhew in his 'startling investigations around 1850 of London workers and street people' through to a much more recent 'autobiography of a girl drug addict' (Bennett, 1981: xi). But in my view, pride of place has to be given to Clifford Shaw's life history of the delinquent Stanley – the 'Jack Roller' or 'mugger' as we may call him today. I think it is the most famous case study in criminology, and one of the most frequently discussed in sociology. It has – rightly or wrongly – an almost 'canonical' status amongst life histories (second only, perhaps, to Wladek above). The Jack Roller's story was one of a number of life stories of delinquents collected by Clifford Shaw at the Institute for Juvenile Research in Chicago during the 1930s as part of a much wider analysis of delinquency which included fieldwork studies, statistical spot mapping, reform policies and theorizing delinquency.

Stanley met Clifford Shaw – his 'co-author' – in 1921 when he was 14. And all the signs are that they established a very close and mutual affection for each other, one that lasted throughout their lives (see Chapter 11). The story is built up from a number of means: listing of delinquencies and institutionalizations; followed by instructions from Shaw to give a 'detailed description for each event, the situation in which it occurred, and his personal reaction to the experience' (Shaw: 1966: 23); then amplified and written further. Shaw is clear that 'the story is presented precisely as it was written by the boy' (Shaw, 1966: 47).

Born 1 October 1907 of Polish background, when Stanley is four years old his mother dies and a step-mother, whom Stanley dislikes enormously, brings her own children to make a family of fifteen children. Living in a slum section of Chicago, in a four-room basement, Stanley's life soon turns to trouble: as one reviewer of the book commented at the time:

Chronic runaway at six and a half; beggar before seven; school truant before eight; shoplifter at eight; . . . in custody twenty-six times before the age of ten; thirty-eight times by the age of seventeen, including three terms in the St Charles School for incorrigible boys and one year each in the Reformatory at Pontica and the Chicago House of Correction . . . (Bain, 1930: 285)

From a number of sources, it is possible to see that this life story – more perhaps than many others – was clearly a positive relationship between two people. On a number of occasions, Stanley talks glowingly of Shaw and it is clear too that Shaw and his wife invited Stanley into their home and kept in close contact. Whatever may have constituted the text of Stanley, there is clearly a great deal more going on all around it. Retrospectively, Stanley talks of

the natural and simple charm of Shaw's great and humane personality proved over the ensuing years to be genuine . . . I had many visits with Shaw and his family which I enjoyed greatly . . . it certainly would not be far fetched to state that the Shaws were my real parents . . . Now if anyone ever had influence over me it was Shaw . . . (Snodgrass, 1982: 26, 33, 171)

and he recalls on the occasion of Shaw's death in 1955, through a condolence note to his wife, the occasion of their first meeting where 'instinctively I knew him as a friend' (Snodgrass, 1982: 3). When Stanley writes the second account of his life in the 1970s, the warmth he still feels for the Shaw family is also clear.

Most accounts of *The Jack Roller* see the story as illustrating, clarifying and developing theories around crime. Indeed, Clifford Shaw can in part be seen as assembling the story so that it speaks to such things as learning crime (differential association theory), the impact of the city (ecological theory), the power of stigma and segregation (labelling theory) as well as many psychological theories. The book became a landmark criminology study, reprinted in 1996 (with a fine introduction from Howard S. Becker) and still in print in 1999.

The hey-day of the human document

The Polish Peasant and *The Jack Roller* were both met with much critical acclaim, and sparked off a series of methodological disputes over the relative merits of clinical and statistical techniques. Although Thomas left Chicago in 1918 (at the age of 55), Shaw continued to work at the allied Institute for Juvenile Research for many years; and the new leaders of the Sociology Department, Robert Park and Ernest Burgess (under the chairmanship of Albion Small initially), were highly instrumental in encouraging the use of such an approach. Park, especially as director of the Pacific Coast Race Relations Survey (1923–5), produced a number of life history questionnaires and encouraged their use, along with that of diaries and letters. Emory S. Bogardus's research text of 1926, *The New Social Research*, not only reviews these documents, and Park's role in them, but shows just how significantly they were regarded. While a quarter of the book is explicitly devoted to their discussion (Bogardus, 1926: 131–89), much of the remaining analysis is focused upon the interviewing styles for such work. Likewise, Burgess believed that the case study was to sociology what the microscope was to biology (cf. Burgess, 1945). Both in his work on delinquency and on the family, he placed enormous value on the personal document case study, and saw no conflict with the supposedly rival statistical approach. In 1927, he remarked that 'if statistics and case study are to yield their full contribution as tools of sociological research, they should be granted equal recognition and full opportunity for each to perfect its own technique' (Burgess, in Cottrell et al., 1973: 287). He was to hold this view for a long time, exploring both approaches fully in his study of the adjustment of 1,000 engaged couples (cf. Burgess, 1941, 1945)!

It is of little surprise, then, that under their inspiration – and in line with the general Chicago injunction to 'get off your seats and do research' – this period produced a number of central studies. In the field of criminology especially, the reforming Clifford Shaw gathered numerous life histories (with Burgess), of which *The Jack Roller* was only the most famous: *The Natural History of a Delinquent Career* (1931), and *Brothers in Crime* (1938) were others. Edwin Sutherland, the dean of American criminology, who was at Chicago until the mid-1930s, detailed the craft of Chic Conwell, *The Professional Thief* (1937, 1967). Many of the Chicago monographs of this period drew upon personal documents of some form – Cavan's *Suicide* diaries (Cavan, 1928), Thrasher's photographs of *The Gang* (1926), Zorbaugh's observers' reports on *The Gold Coast and the Slum* (1965), Mowrer's (1927) cases of family breakdown, and Blumer's student letters on their experiences of going to the movies (1933). Everywhere, it appears, case studies were encouraged: A.S. Stephan, one of Burgess's students, remarks:

> You would have to write a paper on why you were interested in the family. In fact, every course that Burgess taught you could be sure that the first paper you write [would be] why are you interested in criminology, why are you interested in the family. Then you would write a paper on 'A Day in the Life of the Family' . . . Yes, you'd remember your own family. (Carey, 1975: 179)

And Burgess himself remarks on some comments he made to Nels Anderson during his study of 'The Hobo':

> I recall Nels Anderson telling me he was greatly bored by his land-lady, in the rooming-house district where he was studying the homeless man, telling him her life history. I told him, 'Why it's invaluable, you must get it down on paper' . . . Out of this one document you get more insight into how life moves in a rooming-house area, and especially from the stand-point of the rooming-house keeper, than you do from a mountain of statistics that might be gathered. So what we get from the life history, of course, also enables us to pose more questions to the statistician, to get to the other answers. (Cottrell et al., 1973: 13)

The 'case study' and the 'statistical method' generally appear to have been the two major approaches to research during the 1920s, and most sociologists – like Park, Burgess, Shaw (cf. Shaw and McKay, 1969) and Faris (1937: 102–3) – appear to have accepted their mutual benefits. Yet Martin Bulmer (1984), Jennifer Platt (1996) and others have recently made it very clear that it is wrong to identify Chicago solely or even mainly with so-called 'qualitative research' – it has a long tradition of survey methods and quantitative work (and in recent years this has become dominant (Fine, 1995). Some, like Samuel A. Stouffer (in his 1930 PhD) drew out 'experimental comparisons' between the two methods to show that both were valid, that an investigation could get at the same material accurately through either method. In so doing, however, he hinted that case study material was much more arduous to collect and analyse, and hence by implication suggested that quantitative research was preferable (cf. Stouffer, 1930; Cavan et al., 1930). Others were less compromising and more acidic in their view of case studies, the most outspoken being the positivist George Lundberg who waged war on 'cases' for nearly two decades. For him, the case study was not and could not be scientific: it was always 'the tail to the statistical kite'. It could be used as a 'first step', but for any scientific work the cases then had to be 'classified and summarised in such form as to reveal uniformities, types and patterns of behaviour' (Lundberg, 1926: 61; Lundberg, 1941). Likewise, prediction, so necessary for science, was only possible if a sufficient number of cases had been observed (a debate much more fully discussed in 1951 by Paul Meehl).

Despite these criticisms, case histories remained connected to the sociological stage during this period. Perhaps the major indication of the importance that American sociology was beginning to place on the role of human documents was the interest taken in it by the newly formed Social Science Research Council. Fifteen years after its inauguration in 1923, it set up a committee on the appraisal of research whose aim was to look at studies that had made 'the most significant contributions to knowledge in their particular discipline'. Six such studies were selected, the representative for sociology being, not surprisingly, *The Polish Peasant*.

The ensuing appraisal by Herbert Blumer must still stand not only as the most thorough review of Thomas and Znaniecki's work but also of the more general use of personal documents. Blumer's background as a Chicago sociologist and the mantle-bearer of George Herbert Mead's philosophy led him to be highly sympathetic to the report whilst nevertheless subjecting it to stringent criteria of assessment. Indeed, so stringent were his criteria that in general he found the report to be a scientific failure. He argued, for instance, that the *representativeness* of each document was not established; that the *adequacy* of each document for the purposes for which they were employed was not proved; that their *reliability* was not checked by independent sources; and, finally, that the *validity* of the interpretation drawn from any single document was not demonstrated. As we shall see later, these may not be the best criteria for evaluating such documents (cf. Chapter 7). Still, and paradoxically, despite Blumer sensing these severe failings, he went on to claim that the report was a success and listed eight 'important contributions which have made *The Polish Peasant* meritorious and which explain the profound influence which it has had on sociology and social psychology'! He lists these as:

(1) A demonstration of the need of studying the subjective factor in social life.
(2) The proposing of human documents as source material, particularly the life record, thus introducing what is known as the life history technique.
(3) A statement of social theory which outlines the framework of a social psychology and the features of a sociology. The view of social psychology, its subjective aspects of culture is particularly influenced.
(4) A statement of scientific methods which have stimulated and reinforced the interest in making sociology a scientific discipline.
(5) A number of important theories, such as that of personality and social control, and disorganization.
(6) A variety of concepts which have gained wide acceptance, such as attitude, value, life organization, definition of situation and four wishes.
(7) A rich content of insights, evocative generalizations and shrewd observations.
(8) An illuminating and telling characterization of Polish peasant society.

What is perhaps of chief importance is the marked stimulation which it has given to actual social research (Blumer, 1939; and reprinted in 1979: 81–2; see also Plummer, 1990a).

Following on Blumer's appraisal, a one-day conference was organized by the Social Science Research Council on 10 December 1938, to consider the value of *The Polish Peasant* study and personal documents, of which the full proceedings were published (Blumer, 1939/1979). Again, this indicates something of the importance that American sociology was attributing to this method, an importance that was to be further extended when the conference decided that four of its disciplines (sociology, history, psychology and anthropology) should set up their own appraisal of the personal document method for submission to the Council. This heralded the publication of two significant volumes extending the debates further during the early 1940s. The most prominent of these reports was written by Gordon Allport (1942), prominent because, although it was the psychology submission, he discussed in a 200-page document the general use, forms and value of the life history approach, and prominent too because Gordon Allport was to go on during his lifetime to advocate, more strongly than anybody else, the use of the idiographic case study method in psychology. His major illustrative example of this approach, *Letters from Jenny* (described in Chapter 3), was not to be published until 1965, but from the 1940s until his death in 1967, he remained the most ardent champion of the individual case study in psychology. He argued that every life was unique and needed to be carefully studied for its own generalizable patterns: most psychology went in pursuit of general laws about traits abstracted from concrete individuals (the intelligence quotient, the attitude) and ignored the unique constellation of these traits in one individual. Prediction about individual behaviour was never possible on the basis of theories about universal traits which ignored unique constellations. As he put it, rather strikingly,

> Suppose we take John, a lad of 12 years, and suppose his family background is poor; his father was a criminal; his mother rejected him; his neighbourhood is marginal. Suppose that 70 per cent of the boys having a similar background become criminals. Does this mean that John has a 70 per cent chance of delinquency? Not at all. John is a unique being with a genetic inheritance of his own; his life-experience is his own. His unique world contains influences unknown to the statistician: perhaps an affectionate relation with a certain teacher . . . such factors . . . may offset all average probabilities. There is no 70 per cent chance about John. He either will or will not become delinquent. Only a complete understanding of his personality, of his present and future circumstances, will give us a basis for sure prediction. (Allport, 1962: 411–12)

The second major report to emanate from the SSRC enquiry drew together what was known about personal documents in history, anthropology and sociology. The historical survey by Louis Gottschalk focused mainly on criticisms of the approach; the anthropological review by Clyde Kluckhohn focused mainly on the types of documents available and the means of gathering and analysing them; while the sociological survey of Robert C. Angell (Cooley's nephew) reviewed some twenty-two studies produced between 1920 and 1940 and examined their bearings upon research into historical sequences, sociological theory and sociological method. This was an important review because it located the 'state of play' of such research by the early 1940s very thoroughly, concluding that 'there has been real advance, although the gains are not startling' (Gottschalk et al., 1942: ix). Whatever 'advance' was made by this time was to be largely ignored during the next forty years – certainly no comparable review has ever been made. These two major SSRC reports probably only signpost the iceberg tip of concern about personal documents: 'statistics' vs 'case studies' seems to have been a central sociological debate of the period.

As an adjunct to the Council's work, John Dollard had been asked to review some life history research which was subsequently published in 1935 (before the two major reports) as *Criteria for the Life History*. This neglected but central study sought to establish broad principles for assessing the value of any social science life history – criteria that would set it apart from literary biography or the commonsense tales of everyman. 'The material', claims Dollard, 'must be worked up and mastered from some systematic viewpoint' (1935: xx).

Such a viewpoint entailed seven principles, which are spelt out in some detail. In summary, Dollard argued that any life needed to be analysed through its various contexts and stages, and then adequately conceptualized. Four criteria were elaborated which analysed the life in its various contexts: (i) the organic, (ii) the familial, (iii) the situational and (iv) the historical-cultural. Thus, for Dollard, life history research is interdisciplinary – we need to draw from biology, psychology, psychiatry, history and sociology in order to see how lives are embedded in four shaping and shaped contexts. But these contexts then need to be viewed developmentally – (v) 'the continuous related character of experience from childhood through adulthood must be stressed' (p. 26) – and interactionally, to show (vi) how 'the organic materials' get elaborated into social behaviour. Finally Dollard argued that the social scientist must arrange and systematize the material: he must (vii) 'play an active role over against his material; he must do the critical work of fashioning the necessary concepts, of making the required connections, and of piecing the whole life history together' (1935: 34).

Dollard encouraged the use of these seven criteria both in the construction of future life histories, and in the teaching and appraisal of existing ones. Indeed, his own study then proceeds to assess six studies (seven, if the passing consideration of Radin's *Crashing Thunder* is included) which represent different approaches and disciplines. Allport has usefully summarized this data in a table (see Table 5.1).

The discussion by Dollard has been largely ignored, perhaps because the criteria are regarded by some as merely reflecting Dollard's own 'personal' preferencs (especially for psychodynamic theory), but more probably simply because the publication came at the end of the hey-day of life history research. For between the early 1940s and the 1970s there was a steep decline in interest and discussion around the kind of research that Dollard favoured (cf. Bertaux and Kohli, 1984; Zetterberg, 1956).

The Chicago voice

Elsewhere, and in much detail, I have discussed the history and themes of the so-called 'Chicago School of Sociology' in which life documents were seen to play an important role (I say 'so-called' because the 'school' is constantly being 'contested'!) (Plummer, 1997). Likewise, elsewhere I have suggested a strong affinity with the wider theory of symbolic interactionism (Plummer, 1991, 2000). Intellectual arguments were developing that could lend weight to its strategies. For the documentary approach to become academically acceptable, it required institutional and intellectual legitimation; and this is what 'Chicago' accomplished. From the mid 1930s onwards, the arguments subsequently tottered as the more 'scientific', less subjective approaches of Lazarsfeld and Parsons came into the ascendancy. The life story approach remained but the legitimations got lost; and hence it was slowly relegated to the subterranean margins of 'proper' research. Chicago sociology was an amalgam of philosophies – pragmatism, formalism, humanism, romanticism – and although it surely embodied a number of contradictions and fostered dissenting traditions (it was also renowned via Ogburn for its

TABLE 5.1 Dollard's evaluation of six cases

Criterion	Adler	Taft	Freud	Thomas	Shaw	Wells
(i) Subject viewed as specimen in cultural studies	–	–	+	++	++	++
(ii) Organic motivation must be socially relevant	–	+	+	+	––	+
(iii) Role of family group in transmitting culture must be recognized	–	–	+	o	+	o
(iv) Elaboration of organic materials into social behaviour must be shown	o	–	++	–	–	–
(v) Continuous related character of experience from childhood through adulthood must be stressed	++	+	++	o	+	+
(vi) 'Social situation' must be continuously and carefully specified	o	–	+	–	++	–
(vii) Life history material must be organized and conceptualized	+	+	++	o	o	–

+ Indicates fulfilment of the criterion.
o Indicates the criterion is not fully met.
– Indicates the criterion is not met.

See A. Adler, 1929; J. Taft, 1933; S. Freud, 1925; W.I. Thomas and F. Znaniecki, 1958; C. Shaw, 1966; H.G. Wells, 1934.

Source: Allport, 1942: 27

quantitative work and its Community Fact Book), it assembled arguments that made it lastingly clear just how important 'human
documents' should be for social science.

In the first place, it urged the researcher to shun abstractions and to go
instead in pursuit of the detailed, the particular and the experiential. Life
documents were always manifestations of such concerns; and within
them, the researcher would find the multiple dichotomies that philosophers debate to be only so much intellectual nicety. The organic com-
pound revealed in the human document blends mind with body,
individual with group, subjective with objective, freedom with con-
straint. Philosophers have spent millennia debating such ideas, and
whilst small advances have been made, the actual debates still exist.
Look at lived life, said the Chicagoans, and there you will find the
contradictory antimonies being worked out. A naturalistic fidelity to the
world was thus encouraged – a naturalism which invariably shows that
concrete humans cannot be grasped in abstraction (cf. Blumer, 1979;
Matza, 1969).

A second strong claim to emerge from Chicago highlighted the need
for a dual concern with the subjective and the objective: 'values' and
'attitudes', 'subjective and objective definitions of the situation', 'natural
and cultural sciences', 'humanistic coefficients' – throughout all the
writing, the necessity to look at how people grasp their own worlds was
persistently stressed as one crucial component of the account. It is hard
to imagine a single better tool for getting at this than the human
document.

Another claim to emerge from this tradition was the inevitability of
perspective: all tales, even scientific ones, are told from a point of view. A
modesty, a scepticism and a disdain for the Grand Absolute followed in
its wake, leaving, once again, the life document as the exemplary case of
the more tentative perspective. They could never be the whole truth,
since that was inaccessible anyway; but used carefully, they could throw
out a limited truth and challenge that 'certain blindness' common to
most people.

And, finally, its stake was with the marginal and the underdog.
Spawned on romanticism and libertarianism, it believed humans were
equal but mutilated by power. Its politics were naive, and its practice
straightforward: make no grand claims, just repeatedly show little
groups of humans what they do to each other – especially 'give voice' to
those who may not be heard – and then trust for a quiet catharsis
of comprehension with a re-alignment of action. All wider dreams of
change are utopian.

None of the claims of Chicagoans are grand ones: by the logic of their
thought they cannot be. Nor, today, are they popular views: they could
be dubbed with some justification 'anti-intellectual', 'liberal' and
'reformist'. And yet, as I suggested in Chapter 1, there is an affinity
between some of these ideas – perspective, marginality, experience and

pragmatism especially – and the contemporary move towards a post-modern sensibility.

A cautionary conclusion: a postmodern sensibility, again

Some readers may have noticed along the way that each chapter of the book so far has drifted towards a sort of a caution about the changing ways in which life stories are being told. Indeed, a common theme to emerge is that *life stories are not as straightforward now as they might have been in the past.* They are 'constructed'; they are topics of investigation; they bring self-consciousness and the author and subject together in the text; they have had to engage with the new technologies; they have become 'auto/biographic ' and 'autoethnographic'. The same might now be said of the Chicago history. What was once seen as Wladek or Stanley's life, can now be viewed as a textual production. To take a quick look at Stanley as a 'topic' or as a 'narrative textual construction' leads us to see that ' the empirical subject merges with the social scientist and becomes a first order analytic textual construction' (Denzin, 1992: 40). Dramatically, Norman Denzin suggests:

> Shaw and Burgess conflated the flesh and blood subject (the real Stanley) with the empirical subject (the youth who was interviewed) and turned him into an analytic, ideal type, the classic inner city delinquent. He then became a complex first and second order textual production. Stanley and Clifford Shaw became one in *The Jack Roller*. They cannot be uncoupled, for to take Shaw (and Burgess) out of the picture is to leave only an empty story of Stanley. There is no Stanley without the investigative tale told by these two sociological experts. The natural history, life history method permitted the illusion to be sustained: that the real Stanley, and the real Stanley's experiences, had been captured. Once these illusions were in place, the interactionist experts could then write their objective, analytic, interpretative accounts of Stanley's life. And then he could lead that life . . . (1992: 41)

Denzin suggests that there is a severe ignorance of the 'pervasive grey areas that join . . . life histories with narrative fictions', making them little more than romantic tales comparable to the film tales of the time found in classic gangster crime stories like *Dead End Kids, Boy's Town* and *Knock on any Door*. Stanley is little more than 'a sociological version of a screen hero' (Denzin, 1992: 41).

And so, whilst we can continue to see the Chicago School as providing the major social entrée to the personal document approach, we may also have to start recognizing at the start of the twenty-first century, that its approach was important but in the end untenably naive. It started to make the bridge to pragmatic, experientialized, localized knowledges, but it could not, and did not, go far enough. Much of the rest of this book will be pushing at these newer visions.

Guide for further reading

For a major **historical review of research traditions**, see Jennifer Platt, *A History of Sociological Research Methods in America, 1920–1960* (1996); and for a clear account of the history of qualitative method, see various contributions in Denzin and Lincoln's *The Handbook of Qualitative Research* (1994). A classic is Marie Jahoda et al., *Marienthal* (1972; appendix). A helpful discussion of American documentary research in the 1930s may be found in W. Stott, *Documentary Experience and Thirties America* (1977).

The Polish Peasant in Europe and America was first published between 1918 and 1920 in five volumes but republished in a two-volume edition in 1927. I have been using the 1958 Dover reprint. Since it is a very long study, a clear introduction to it is C. Madge's excellent *The Origin of Scientific Sociology* (1963, ch. 3). (The abridged 100 page version edited by Eli Zaretsky seems to me an oddity to be avoided.) The most helpful general appraisal is H. Blumer's *Critiques of Research*, originally presented to the SSRC in 1939 but reprinted in 1979 with a new introduction and re-appraisal by Blumer. I offer a revaluation of it in 'Herbert Blumer and the life history tradition' (Plummer, 1990a).

Stanley and *The Jack Roller* are discussed in Read Bain 'Review of the Jack Roller' (1930), Jon Snodgrass and The Jack Roller, *The Jack Roller at Seventy* (1982), and Norman Denzin, *Symbolic Interactionism and Cultural Studies: The Politics of Interpretation* (1992).

An early commentary on life history research is R.S. Cavan (1929), 'Topical summaries of current literature', but the key texts of the 'hey-day' period which are absolutely central reading for anyone interested in this area are J. Dollard's *Criteria for the Life History* (1935), L. Gottschalk et al., *The Use of Personal Documents in History, Anthropology and Sociology* (1942) and G. Allport's *The Use of Personal Documents in Psychological Science* (1942).

The **history of Chicago sociology** is well documented. The stages leading to its hey-day in the 1920s and 1930s are detailed in R.C. Hinkle's *Founding Theory of American Sociology* (1980); its core programme is analysed in Martin Bulmer, *The Chicago School of Sociology* (1984), I have provided a comprehensive collection of analyses and readings in Ken Plummer (ed.), *The Chicago School* (1997) (4 vols). The wider tradition of Chicago and pragmatism is spelt out in D. Rucker, *The Chicago Pragmatists* (1969). Biographies of Robert Park are provided by Fred Matthews, *Quest for an American Sociology* (1977) and W. Raushenbush, *Robert E. Park* (1979), the former giving a great deal of background Chicago history through the personal details of Park's life. All the key sociologists at Chicago are to be found in the *Heritage of Sociology* series (published by the University of Chicago Press). These studies include W.I. Thomas (by M. Janowitz, 1966), F. Znaniecki (by R. Bierstedt, 1969), R. Park (by R. Turner, 1967), E. Burgess (by L.S. Cottrell et al., 1973) and G.H. Mead (by

A. Strauss, 1964). The influential G. Simmel is also considered in this series (by D. Levine, 1971).

Some of the philosophical inspirations to the personal document tradition and symbolic interactionism may be found in the work of Dilthey (1833–1911) (for an introduction to his work see M. Ermarth, *Wilhelm Dilthey*, 1978), and the pragmatists (see I. Scheffler, *Four Pragmatists* (1974) for an introduction). Paul Rock's study, *The Making of Symbolic Interactionism* (1979) traces symbolic interactionism back to Hegel and Kant and provides a sturdy epistemological defence of it in the wake of critiques from 'realist' theoreticians.

The theory of symbolic interactionism is outlined in Herbert Blumer's *Symbolic Interactionism* (1969), given a textbook treatment in J.P. Hewitt's *Self and Society* (6th edn, 1994), and a reader in N. Herman and Larry Reynolds, *Symbolic Interaction* (1994). Its position in relation to method is most helpfully discussed in Norman K. Denzin's *The Research Act* (1978, 2nd edn). An up-to-date appraisal of the work of Blumer may be found in Rob Stones's *Key Sociological Thinkers* (ch. 6, 1998). Major readings on this whole intellectual tradition may be found in Ken Plummer, *Symbolic Interactionism* (2 vols, 1991). There is a Society for the Study of Symbolic Interactionism which produces its own journal, *Symbolic Interaction*, and has an annual volume of *Studies in Symbolic Interaction* (vol. I, 1978), edited by Norman K. Denzin.

6 Getting and Doing Life Stories

He advised me to keep a journal of my life, fair and undisguised. He said it would be a very good exercise, and would yield me infinite satisfaction when the ideas were faded from remembrance. I told him that I had done so ever since I left Scotland. He said he was very happy that I pursued so good a plan. And now, O my journal! Art thou not highly dignified! Shalt thou not flourish tenfold? Nor former solicitations or censures could tempt me to lay thee aside; and now is there any argument which can outweigh the sanction of Mr. Samuel Johnson? He said indeed that I should keep it private, and that I might surely have a friend who would burn it in case of my death. For my own part, I have at present such an affection for this my journal that it shocks me to think of burning it. I rather encourage the idea of having it carefully laid up among the archives of Auchinleck. However, I cannot judge fairly of it now. Some years hence I may. I told Mr. Johnson that I put down all sorts of little incidents in it. 'Sir', said he, 'there is nothing too little for so little a creature as man. It is by studying little things that we attain the great knowledge of having as little misery and as much happiness as possible . . .'

(entry in Boswell's *London Journey* diary, of a coffee shop
meeting with Samuel Johnson, 16 July 1763)

We have travelled a long way since the journals of James Boswell in the mid-eighteenth century. Slowly, the painstaking craft of solitary journal writing has turned, at the start of the twenty-first century, into a rather big business. As Chapter 4 suggested, we have become 'the auto/biographical society'. Part of this entails manuals galore on how to keep diaries, write journals, trace family genealogies, understand yourself (e.g. Rainer, 1978, 1998; Steel, 1980). But part of this has also been the growth of life story as a social science research method, accompanied by a proliferation of 'how to' texts and guidelines. Indeed, this is part of the significant growth of books on every aspect of methodology and 'how to do research': there is a publishing boom in methods, of which the second edition of this book is but a part! And yet, for quite a while people just did research – there were no protocols, courses, readers, manuals, 'how to' packages, CD-Roms and computer programs to structure and organize the work. Looking at the old Chicago fieldwork studies, it is clear that for most of these researchers, it was a baptism in fire: just go out there, and do it! 'Write down only what you see, hear and know like a newspaper reporter' (Johnson, 1990: 13). Likewise, until very recently, anthropologists were rarely trained in 'how to do it' fieldwork – it was a matter of just going into the field. Even today many anthropologists express surprise at courses in methods, or methodology textbooks. For them, the charm of research lies in the doing, not the talking. As the anthropologist Krober once said: 'some can and some can't' (and cited in Johnson, 1990: 12).

And at the same moment as a proliferation of books appears to tell you 'how to do it', another set of books appears which tells you this is all wrong, and in any event social science cannot be done. Here is the strong critique by postmodernists of contemporary social research which suggests that it has failed to address both the *representational crisis* – that all research is a narrative production, and the *legitimization crisis* – that the authority of social science 'experts' needs a much better epistemological, political and moral warrant for the 'authoritative' claims they make (Denzin, 1997: ch. 1). So much huge funding is given to research in the social sciences, whilst the meticulous problems of *what it all means* remain at bay. As someone who has researched and studied in sociology for many years, I have to agree: over and over again I read articles and say, so what? Over and over again, students do projects and dissertations because they have to; not because I sense any profound anxiety over what it represents or what it can legitimately say. Over and over again, people are troubled by social science (Agger, 2000).

So I have a problem. On the one hand, I wish to march into the land of 'research texts' – prescribing how to do life stories and make sense of them. On the other hand, I wish to join the land of (optimistic) 'post-modern doubters' – attacking the state of social science from all sides. And yet, this is just what I do plan to do. I wish first of all to suggest – admittedly with a fair degree of doubt – just how to go about 'doing life stories'. But then, at the end of the discussion, I will suggest that there really are rather major problems with all this. The remaining chapters of the book will hence turn to the broader issues. However, I do this not with a view to making the work of life stories redundant: but rather as ways of sharpening them up and giving them more – if also more problematic – meaning. A self-consciousness about method is the way ahead for me.

So this chapter and those that follow, which deal broadly with 'how to do life stories', must come with apologies and health warnings. Reading them could be bad for your intellectual health! Whilst I aim to set out some of the issues for the actual doing of a life story – starting with the planning and going through to the interviewing and the writing up – in the end this is no substitute for a critically self-aware consciousness of what it is you are doing. There are really no short cuts. Still, there are bits of accumulated wisdoms, skills and tips – what Howard S. Becker has deliciously called 'the tricks of the trade' (Becker, 1996) – which could help a novice. And there are stacks of postmodern doubts to add to these.

In this chapter I think a little about how to gather life stories, and in the next chapter how to analyse and theorize them. Problems will be raised; and in later chapters I look at ways of narrating such stories, the myriad practical and ethical problems such research raises, and the crisis of legitimation it brings – how to appraise their 'truth' and 'value'. It will help if you keep in mind the model of 'story telling production' which I outlined in Chapter 2: for here, you are about to become the coaxers, seducers and producers of such stories and self-reflexivity is a key part of this.

Thinking ahead: five kinds of research questions and seven phases of research!

To start with, and to get the broadest of orientations, it may help to see all research as raising five basic sets of problems which have to be confronted at every stage of work. The five problems, which I have previously called – perhaps a bit pretentiously – 'a paradigm of methodological problems', are:

1   The Substantive Questions. This deals with the concrete, empirical area you are looking at and focusing on establishing just what it is you want to know. For instance, you may want to investigate the life stories of Egyptian Bedouin women (Abu-Lughod, 1993). These are the fairly straightforward 'What?' questions of the research. What, indeed, do you want to know?

2   The Social Science Questions. This deals with the kind of knowledge you want to produce – largely matters of epistemology or knowledge foundations are raised here. For instance, do you want to produce 'hard, 'objective' data – or more 'soft, subjective' data: and why? Are you in search of 'the real life' or in search of 'interpretive under-standing' – issues we have discussed in the earlier part of this book. We deal largely with the intellectual justification for the kind of 'data', knowledge, understanding to be achieved: essentially with the 'Why?' questions of social research.

3   The Technical Questions. This concerns the nitty-gritty, nuts and bolts questions of actually doing the research – of getting the samples, doing the interviews in the best way possible, making the analysis. This question deals with the 'How?' of social research. It is the stuff of most 'hands on' research textbooks.

4   The Ethical and Political Questions. This concerns the so-called 'extra-technical' and 'extra-scientific' research questions – with such matters as the political justification for this study and the ethical implications involved in it. It sees research as a human and social activity and asks questions around this. Does this research exploit anyone? Does it play some useful positive social role for a marginalized/oppressed group?

5   The Personal Questions. This concerns the dual impact of the
    research on the researcher's life and the researched person's life. It
    asks about the ways in which research is always a personal process,
    impinging in many ways on lives both of the researched and the
    researcher. It is in this sense always reflexive.

Each of these five problems should be conceived dynamically: at the
beginning of the research, *during* it, and *after* it they will constantly have
to be confronted. Any full account of the methodology of any project
should hence involve an analysis which, simply tabulated, looks as in
Figure 6.1.

A sequence of research?   Many suggest that research is most usefully
conceived as a series of stages. Thus the anthropologist James Spradley
(1979) suggests 'some tasks are best accomplished before other tasks', and
outlines a series of steps as a twelve-point Developmental Research
Sequence (DRS)) from 'Step One: Locating an Informant' to a final 'Step
12: Writing an Ethnography'. More recently, David Fetterman titles his
book: *Ethnography: Step by Step*, suggesting a path, and the need to move
'step by step through the ethnographic terrain' (1989: 23). And most texts
suggest a basic sequence: Nigel Gilbert's widely used British text (1993)
for example is organized around 'beginnings', 'into the field', 'back home'
and 'endings' – all of which sounds reasonable enough. For me, there are
possibly seven stages to ponder:

Kind of problem	Time phases of research		
	Prior to the 'interview'	During the 'interview'	After the 'interview'*
1 Substantive			
2 Social scientific			
3 Technical/practical			
4 Ethical/political			
5 Personal			

* A caution is in order. In these chapters, I will be dealing mainly with life story
interview research: the work involved in the use of letters, photographs, diaries or
video-making may be similar but the content would certainly be different. They often
raise different issues, and for convenience, therefore, this chapter is restricted to only
one personal document form, the 'created' life history.

FIGURE 6.1   **A paradigm for the analysis of methodological problems**

1   Getting problems – crucial in deciding which 'methods' to use.
2   Planning – deciding the 'who, how, where, when and what' of the study.
3   Doing – the actual fieldwork, interview or gathering of stories.
4   Managing – being organized through files, transcriptions and/or 'coding'.
5   Analysing and interpreting – thinking through (even theorizing) your data.
6   Presenting – which usually means 'writing', but could mean film etc.
7   Archiving – getting it all together, to perhaps leave for posterity?

And yet I go cautiously. This should not be mistaken as an inevitable, chronological progression, what has been called the 'lie of chronological research' by Stanley Cohen and Laurie Taylor (1976/1992). Indeed, one of the first understandings of research conducted in the real world – as opposed to the textbook – is that it is a messy, human affair: if it is not, then it is time to worry. For nothing goes as planned, all rules have to be broken, all stages merge with each other. Expect this, and you will not be disappointed! But expect to follow a rigid sequence of phases, and all will not be well: the lack of flexibility will lead to trouble. Although difficult, each of these processes blur and blend with the others. For example, 'analysing and interpreting' should *always* accompany the research interviewing since accumulated 'data' will give insights into new research problems; 'presenting ' should not all be done at the end but during the course of the research as it can sharpen the analysis and alert you to changing issues; and planning – and preparations – will inevitably be taking place constantly. Even archiving, which looks like it will be the last thing you would do, is usefully planned from the outset – so the 'data' you collect comes in an appropriate form!

    In what follows, I deal with 'phases' one to seven. Chapters 7 and 8 look more closely at issues of writing. And a note on 'archiving' is to be found in the Appendix.

Posing some problems – getting some questions

The most important thing to ask of any research is a beguilingly simple question. It is: '*So what is the problem? What is it that is bugging you? What do you want to know?*' Everything else flows from this (cf. Flick, 1998: ch. 5). Perhaps this will start as a broad theme – 'I want to look at life in an African village', 'I want to see how the Green Movement impacts environmental policies', 'I want to understand the stages a life goes through'. But this has to be narrowed, focused and turned into a clearer and manageable problem. The people you study, the methods you use will all follow on from this: questions should shape methods and not the other way around. Only some problems and questions will lead to life story research; it is not suitable for all.

For the moment, assume you are interested in asking questions that are to be linked to the story of a particular life: you want to know as much as you can, in the person's own voice, about how they see their life unfolding. And maybe you want to focus on a particular kind of theme – their health, their family life, their 'criminal career'. In a now classic opening strategy, you may ask them to see their life as a book and to simply suggest chapter titles. These chapters could be the key stages of their life, or maybe the central turning points and epiphanies – the big changes that they see. Or they may be divided by some of the key themes seen within their life. In any event, such a question allows them to provide their own mini-plan to help guide you into the key issues or time periods.

You will probably want to consider some or all of the following (see also Box 6.1):

- A sketch of the 'stages' or 'phases' of your life.
- A sense of the pivotal events in your life – crises, turning points, epiphanies, major things (and then explore what happens all around).
- Key themes around 'work, love and play'.
- Areas where you have experienced conflicts.
- Key people at key moments – lovers and friends, 'villains, heroes and fools' – significant others; and think about the parts they played.
- The 'artefacts of your life' – like photos, diaries, calendars, collections, newspapers/letters – that may serve as memory joggers.
- Your changing body and the places it's been – its environments.
- Any spiritual quests – birth, life, illness, death and the universe!
- Ways in which there may be elements of coherence, and conversely contradiction, in your life.
- A chart of how you have seen yourself (identities, self-image, self-esteem) at different stages of your life: who are you, and how have you changed?
- 'Life secrets' you cannot tell (sex, money, etc.)

Getting the life story into context: 'life course research'

One way of generating questions about lives comes through the inter-disciplinary branch of social science analysis known as 'the life course paradigm'. This directs us to think about four key elements: the location of lives in time and space, the linking of different lives, the importance of human agency, meanings and individual goals, and the timing of lives (Giele and Elder, 1998). Life course research adds to the 'auto/biographical' tradition (the focus of this book) a range of other research traditions (many of which are quantitative), such as lifespan developmental psychology, historical demography, longitudinal research,

BOX 6.1   SOME GUIDELINES FOR LIFE STORY QUESTIONS

Drawing from a number of sources, below are some questions that it would be worth thinking about in the design of your own life history study.

- **An opening instruction** from Dan P. McAdams

  I would like you to begin by thinking about your life as if it were a book. Each part of your life composes a chapter in the book. Certainly the book is unfinished at this point; still, it probably contains a few interesting and well defined chapters. Please divide your life into its major chapters, and briefly describe each chapter. You may have as many or as few chapters as you like, but I would suggest dividing it into at least two or three chapters, and at most seven or eight. Think of this as a general table of contents for your book. Give each chapter a name and describe the overall contents of each chapter. Discuss briefly what makes for a transition from one chapter to the next . . . Looking back over your entire life story with chapters, episodes and characters, can you discern a central theme, message or idea that runs throughout the text? What is the major theme of your life . . .

Source: D.P. McAdams, *The Stories We Live By* (1993: 256–64)

- **Living a life like a book . . .**

Imagine your life is being written down as a book: what do you think would be the main chapter headings for it? The following are illustrative examples of the first headings, around which discussions could then take place:

Chapter 1   Being born the eighth daughter of a Durham coal miner
Chapter 2   A poor childhood
Chapter 3   Moving away: sleeping under the stairs in London
Chapter 4   Meeting a husband
Chapter 5   The war years – from Rosie the riveter to evacuation
Chapter 6   You've never had it so good: Two children in an era of
                     rationing
Chapter 7   Working whilst the boys grow up
Chapter 8   A few years together: the death of a good husband
Chapter 9   Making new friends
Chapter 10   Ill and alone
Chapter 11   A strange way to go

- **A short agenda of key items to cover in writing a life story**

Birth and family of origin
Cultural setting and traditions
Social factors
Education
Love and work

Historical events
Retirement
Inner life and spiritual awareness
Major life themes
Visions of the future
Closure

Source: Robert Atkinson, *The Life Story Interview* (1998). In his book Atkinson provided guidance on a full list of questions under each of these headings.

- **Sample life narrative questionnaire**

Life in general

1 Everyone has a life story. Tell me about your life, in about twenty minutes or so if you can. Begin wherever you like and include whatever you wish.
2 What were the most important turning points in your life?
3 Tell me about the happiest moments in your life.
4 What about the saddest points?
5 Who've been the most important in your life?
6 Who are you closest to now?
7 What does your life look like from where you are at now?
8 If you could live your life over, what would you do differently?
9 How do you explain what's happened to you over your life?
10 If you had the opportunity to write the story of your life, what would the chapters be about? Chapter 1? Chapter 2? . . . What about the last chapter?

Self

How would you describe yourself when you were younger?
How would you describe yourself now?
Have you changed much over the years? How?
What is your philosophy of life? Overall, what is the meaning of life to you?

Source: extracted from Jaber F. Gubrium, *Speaking of Life: Horizons of Meaning for Nursing Home Residents* (1993: 189–90)

cohort-sequence studies, the sociology of age and ageing, panel studies and 'event histories'. In all of this, it helps to see that 'Changing lives . . . are in continuing interplay with changes in society and its structures' (Riley, 1998: 29). All these issues come together in the different trajectories of the life course.

'Life course' research makes a number of conceptual distinctions which are useful in thinking about 'lives'. It may help if you read the next section with a pen and paper in hand and try to sketch out the position of your own life through these terms. Figure 6.2 starts to show how this might be done.

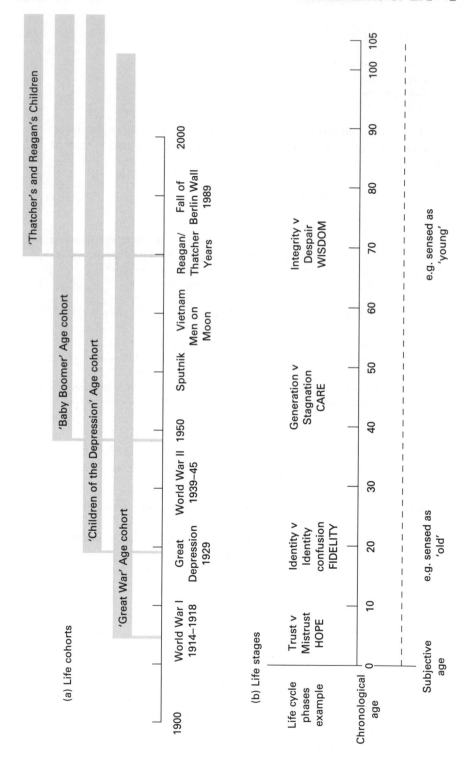

(a) Life cohorts

(b) Life stages

Chart 2   Psychosocial crises

	1	2	3	4	5	6	7	8
Old Age VIII								Integrity vs. Despair, disgust. WISDOM
Adulthood VII							Generativity vs. Stagnation. CARE	
Young Adulthood VI						Intimacy vs. Isolation. LOVE		
Adolescence V					Identity vs. Identity confusion. FIDELITY			
School Age IV				Industry vs. Inferiority. COMPETENCE				
Play Age III			Initiative vs. Guilt. PURPOSE					
Early Childhood II		Autonomy vs. Shame, doubt. WILL						
Infancy I	Basic trust vs. Basic mistrust. HOPE							

FIGURE 6.2 Mapping a life: life cohorts and life stages. (a) Life cohorts; (b) life stages; (c) Erikson's (1982) Eight Stages of Man

A first broad set of concepts are historical and demographic. Lives need to be located on a *'historical time line'* and through their demographic features. A life occurs within a definite historical time span. A line of key world events can be drawn which 'situates' a life firmly within its specific cultural history. South African lives, Australian lives and Peruvian lives will have a differing sense of key dates and experiences within their cultures. I have listed here just a few Anglo-American themes: clearly a life that has been through two world wars (those born before 1914) has a different historical matrix to one that has not (those born after 1946). From this, and very simply, we can locate *birth cohorts*: people born in the same year, or in a cluster of named years. Closely linked is their *'age cohort generation'*: a group of people – a collective – born in a specified period of years, and who are hence tied together through a particular shared historical time period. Most obvious examples of this would include 'the Children of 1914', 'the Children of the Great Depression' (cf. Elder, 1974), the 'Baby Boomers' (cf. Light, 1988), the 'Hippy Generation' (Hazlett, 1998) and on to 'Thatcher's Children' and the 'Millennial Generation'. This is a most important way of locating a group of people – akin to locating them in class and gender, especially when it is tied to what we might call a *'generation cohort perspective'*. This is the more subjective sense that people acquire of belonging to a particular age reference group through which they may make sense of their 'memories' and 'identities' (they share a common perspective and say things like: 'We all lived through the war together', 'In our days, feminism was more active', 'I was part of the Peace Movement in Vietnam', 'I am an older gay – part of the Stonewall Generation'). The former category is structural – it locates a person in the society overall; the latter is more subjective – it shows who people identify with over time. Both nevertheless take the researcher into an important awareness of historical time – and how different lives are shaped throughout by different historical baselines and different historical roots. To put it bluntly: a child of the Thatcher or Reagan Generation cannot have experienced the Second World War at first hand as their grandparents inevitably would have; and such factors need to be located in looking at a life. Often these critical locations are to be found in a person's 'youth' period. Shared generational and historical experiences come to play a key role in a life *history* approach.

Next, and linked to these historical features, is the changing sequencing and phasing of a life course. A basic starting point here is *chronological age* – being a baby or a child for instance. A very common sequencing here is that of the passage from babyhood, though childhood, youth, middle age, old age and so on. These have commonly been called the 'seasons of a life' (Kotre and Hall, 1999; Levinson et al., 1978; Levinson et al., 1996). But these categories are themselves a problem – ageing for example is now quite frequently broken into a 'third age' (65–74) and a fourth age (74+), or into the younger elderly (65–75), the 'older elderly' (75–85) and the very old (cf. Macionis and Plummer, 1998: 386). Indeed, as we find more and more people living longer, the category of 'centenarian' will become increasingly common. Age phase categories shift across different cultures: 'childhood', 'middle age' and 'youth' are now seen to be recent historical inventions – they are certainly not found in all societies (e.g. Shweder, 1998). We understand now that 'life phases' themselves change across history. More than this: they are also sub-jectively experienced categories. Thus, it often helps to distinguish between the obvious *chronological age* (the most straightforward ques-tion: how old are you?), and linked concerns such as *subjective age* (how old a person feels – the 'ages of me': Kastenbaum et al., 1972), *inter-personal age* (how old others think you are) and *social age* (the age roles you play – so you can 'act much younger – or older – than your age'). Chronological age can be a poor predictor of each of the latter.

All this is closely linked to mapping lives as a *'life trajectory'* or as a *'life course'* – 'a pathway defined by the ageing process or by movement across the age structure' (Elder, 1985). It is common here to see a tripartite life course – characterized by an early period of preparation, a middle part of work (including domestic work), and a final part for 'retirement' (Kohli and Meyer, 1986). We used to be able to think very straightforwardly of this – long periods of work were followed by retirement, punctuated by raising children, maturation and growth, followed by disengagement and decline. For men the emphasis was mostly on work; for women, on raising children. But nowadays the shape of lives is changing: heterogeneity, fragmentation, discontinuities have happened for many and the sequencing is no longer quite so clear. Not all cultures have the same 'shape' to this life course; again, it can change historically. And some contemporary writers are talking about the postmodernization of the life course – how the formal patterns found in the past are breaking down, with people 'dipping in and out' of phases in a much less regularized and institutionalized fashion.

Within a life trajectory, we can then go on to identify *'critical life events'* (from major events like death and divorce to less significant ones), the working through of *central life themes* – like love, work and play (Freud) or attachments and autonomy (Kegan, 1982) – and linked to this *life cycle crises*. There is a very substantial amount of writing and analysis of these themes – spearheaded by Erik Erikson's classic work on the Eight Stages of Man (1982), but now developed in many directions (I consider this a little more in Chapter 8). Again, though, we must distinguish between scientific accounts that try to capture some sense of an 'objective' series of phases lying so to speak within a life, and the more subjective aware-ness of subjects of their own sense of crises, their subjective identification with age, and the process of subjective reminiscences. Often much of this is caught in what has come to be called the 'life review' or 'reminiscence projects'. Key questions here could include: 'What do you see as import-ant or significant in your life?' 'Describe three memories that you have been thinking about lately. Tell something about your past that is most important to you – that is, something that has had the most influence on your life' (Settersten and Mayer, 1997: 250).

The quest for life stories in research

Allied to all this is the problem of just when life stories will be most useful in research. I think they will be at their most helpful when what you want to understand are people's direct understandings of the social worlds in which they live (see Chapter 2). In research, life stories can be particularly useful for generating new ideas – often as a tool for exploring a new field; as a method used to complement other research strategies; as a way of ending a project – by drawing all the strands of a project together; and as a case history standing in its own right.

Generating ideas and sensitizing concepts   Life stories, perhaps more than any other method, can sensitize a researcher to key issues. Life stories can help generate miniature *sensitizing concepts*, built up through listening closely to what people have to say about their lives. As Angell and Freedman remarked a long time ago:

> Expressive documents [life histories] have generally been used in the exploratory rather than the final stages of the research process. Their greatest value perhaps has been in giving investigators a feel for the data and thus producing hunches with respect to the most fruitful ways of conceptualizing the problem . . . (Angell and Freedman, 1953: 305)

Listening to a life enables us to 'take the role of the actor and see the world from that standpoint' (Blumer, 1969: 73). Out of the words and languages used comes a sensitivity to developing lines of enquiry and creating slightly broader concepts to deal with this. Out of this comes a sensitizing concept – nothing formal, fixed or grand, but a concept which 'gives the user a general sense of reference and guidance in approaching empirical instances . . . and merely suggest[ing] directions along which to look' (Blumer, 1969: 148; cf. van den Hoonaard, 1997).

Complementing research   Life stories may complement other methods and 'balance the objectivism of the experiment, the survey and participant observation with the internal, covert and reflective elements of social behavior and experience' (Denzin, 1978a: 252). This can be clearly seen in some of the early Chicago studies: during the 1930s, for example, a great deal of research was conducted on delinquency – everything from large statistical surveys to fieldwork studies of gangs. Clifford Shaw, a leader in the field, produced a great many life stories of delinquents of which three major books were published. These three life history books produced by Shaw on delinquents should be located within the overall analysis by Chicago sociologists of delinquency. Indeed, his colleague Edward Burgess was very keen to combine life history documents of delinquents with a full-scale statistical survey treatment at a later stage (cf. Bogue, 1974; Burgess, 1945; and see the introduction to Shaw, 1966). As Becker says in the introduction to *The Jack Roller*:

> Much of the background any single study would either have to provide in itself, or even worse, about which it would have to make unchecked assumptions, was already at hand for the reader of *The Jack Roller*. When Stanley speaks of the boyish games of stealing he and his pals engaged in, we know that we can find an extensive and penetrating description of that phenomena [*sic*] in Thrasher's *The Gang* [a participant observation study] and when he speaks of a time he spent on West Madison Street, we know we can turn to Nels Anderson's *The Hobo* [another life history] for the understanding of the milieu Stanley then found himself in. If we are concerned about the representativeness of Stanley's case, we have only to turn to the ecological studies carried on by Shaw and McKay to see the same story told on a grand scale in mass statistics. And similarly, if one wanted to understand the maps and correlations contained in ecological studies of delinquency, one could then turn to *The Jack Roller* and similar documents for that understanding. (Becker, 1966: ix–x)

Rounding it off: a consolidating, clarifying and concluding role? Much social science can appear to be very heavy going: a lot of theory often seems to deny a sense of the rich empirical world. Life stories can be wonderful at overcoming the theoretical fog which obfuscates so many studies: its rich detail exemplifies the theory. An excellent example of such a benefit can be found in Glaser and Strauss's 'classic' case history of a 54-year-old dying cancer patient, Mrs Abel. It represents the culmination of a five-year research project which examined the organization of dying in contrasting hospital wards, focusing particularly on the temporal ordering of the dying process (the stages through which patient and medical personnel moved in confronting pain and finally death), and the structuring of knowledge surrounding death (the awareness and non-awareness, suspicions and pretences by participants and patients of incipient death). A number of reports resulted from this research, but the two major contributions produce substantive (or grounded) theories of 'awareness contexts' and 'status passages' connected with dying cancer patients (Glaser and Strauss, 1968, 1967b). In these studies, many different forms of 'awareness' and 'dying trajectories' are discussed, illustrated from fieldwork, and theoretically clarified into broader issues such as 'status passages'.

But something is missing. Death is the omnipresent, overwhelming experience of the human condition; extreme emotions of grief, despair, fear and anguish become entrapped with it. All of us who have experienced the death of loved ones know the emotional upheavals it generates. And somehow to talk of this in terms of 'dying trajectories' and 'awareness contexts' invites us to be appalled at sociological aridity. The case of Mrs Abel stops all this, for here is the unfolding story of two research nurses recording the lingering death of an increasingly isolated and rejected woman experiencing ever growing pain from terminal cancer, whose last words before an operation from which she never recovered were 'I hope I die' (Strauss and Glaser, 1977: 21). Charting her pain, her last days and her final ill-prepared and lonely death over 150 pages leaves no room for insensitivity. Yet at the same time the authors draw us back to their more theoretical volumes – a bridge is made between experience and general theory. They show 'how well a theory or theories may usefully and relevantly explain and interpret a single case history from a sociological perspective . . . [and] in showing how well the theory works, the sociologist shows how well it can be used on other simple cases for understanding and possibly controlling them' (Strauss and Glaser, 1977: 177).

The role of a case study or a case history?   From this, another distinction worth making at the outset is that between writing a *case history* or a *case study* (Strauss and Glaser, 1977; Ragin and Becker, 1992). Some personal documents may be used for the value they have in themselves (they tell 'a good story'), having something interesting to say in depth about a certain social phenomenon, be it a village community (Bell, 1994) or a disastrous flood (Erikson, 1976) or a particular life. This is the case *history*. In contrast, a case *study* uses the personal document for some wider theoretical purpose. The documents of a life are not of particular interest *sui generis*, in themselves, but only as they relate to some wider goal. Jack Douglas, for example, uses a number of 'suicide accounts' in his book *The Social Meanings of Suicide*, but he is not interested in the stories as such but rather in using them as a means to give credence to his phenomenological account of suicide definitions (see Douglas, 1967, ch. 17). As Strauss and Glaser put it:

> The research goal in a case history is to get the fullest possible story for *its own sake*. In contrast, the case study is based on analytic abstractions and constructions for purposes of description, or verification and/or generation of theory. There is no attempt at obtaining the fullest possible story for its own sake . . .

In sum, the case history gives prominence to the unique story and story line – whereas in the case study the story is eventually subordinated to a more abstract purpose (Strauss and Glaser, 1977: 183).

Planning the research

Living with ambiguity is a central feature of life history research and there is no easy way to plan it. But in this section, I think a little about some of the questions that need to be asked once it starts to become clear what question and problems the research will be looking at.

Selecting lives: who shall be studied?

Long ago, the psycho-life-historian Erik Erikson tellingly remarked that 'Sampling is the strategy of persons who work with vast universes of data; it is a strategy of plenty' (Erikson, 1973: 15). Conversely, life history research is the strategy of the poor – of the researcher who had little hope of gaining a large, representative sample from which bold generalizations could be made. The issue of traditional sampling strategies is hence not usually at stake; rather, the problem is a different one. Who from the teeming millions of world population is to be selected for such intensive study and social science immortality? Why Stanley, Jane Fry and Rigoberta Menchú? Qualitative researchers only really seek samples that are 'information rich' – they are much less concerned with representativeness. So life stories may provide 'intensity sampling' where key informants provide great insight into a particualr area; or 'critical case sampling' where stories are selected on the basis of providing detailed information on key, critical experiences (cf. Morse, 1994: 228; see also Johnson, 1990; Miller, 2000). At base, though, there are two ways researchers have approached this problem – through luck, chance and being pragmatic; or through 'selective sampling' based on clear, usually conceptual, criteria. The first depends on serendipity – nobody is chosen, they are just 'stumbled upon'; the latter is more formal, and linked explicitly to some theoretical or methodological criteria.

A chance encounter   Many life history studies do not appear to have been planned; a chance encounter, a subject of interest emerging from a wider study, an interesting volunteer – these seem common ways of finding a subject. Most famously (and apocryphally), W.I. Thomas initially discovered some of his letters when some garbage was thrown out of a window down a Chicago alley and landed at his feet! (cf. Janowitz, 1966: xxiv). But it is everywhere: Bob Bogdan met Jane Fry in a chance encounter when she was a speaker for a gay group at a social problems seminar (Bogdan, 1974: 6); Sutherland met Chic Conwell in 1932 through Reitman – 'The King of the Hoboes' – who was both literary and keen 'to learn an honest, useful life' (Snodgrass, 1973: 7 and cf. Blumer and Hughes, 1980); and Joan Ablon met a group of 'little people of America' (i.e. dwarfs) 'through the luck of meeting a family with a dwarf child'. As she says: 'I am a great believer in chance happenings. These often lead us to important subjects for study – subjects we had never thought about before' (Ablon, 1985: 196).

Sometimes, a subject is found by chance as part of a wider project. Thus, Frank Moore was the 'thirteenth of two hundred and three' men interviewed by Straus in 1945 for a study of alcohol and homeless men

(Straus, 1974: viii); Cheryl was 'one of many informants in a study of youth culture from 1964 to 1969 in four urban communities' (Schwartz et al., 1980); Stanley was one of 'a series of two hundred similar studies' of delinquent boys (cf. Shaw, 1966: 1; Snodgrass, 1978: 4); and more recently, Leon Pettiway's group of 'gay, drug-using, transgendered' life stories are drawn from a wider research project of similar people (Pettiway, 1996: xxii). In all these studies there is little sense of a sustained search for a suitable subject through explicit criteria; rather the feel is that the sociologist scooped 'finds' – people who they got along with, had a good story to tell and who could say it well. But 'chance' is by its very nature a risky affair, and often a more formal search is required.

Looking for the right person   Although luck can happen, it will not guarantee a subject for research. More often, the search is on for the 'right' subject. Usually this will mean adopting a conceptual issue and searching out people who exemplify it. Thus in a now classic study of artisan workers in France, Daniel Bertaux sought out life stories of people who had continued to work in small, private bakeries – when most industrialized countries had gone in for large-scale production. 'French bakers' became his topic (Bertaux and Bertaux-Wiame, 1981).

Another feature of this 'selective sampling' is between three kinds of person: the marginal person, the great person and the common person.

'Strangers', 'Outsiders and 'Marginal People'   have probably been the most frequent and most fruitful choice of subject. The marginal person is one 'who fate has condemned to live in two societies, and in two, not merely different but antagonistic cultures' (Stonequist, 1937/1961). It is Georg Simmel's (1908/1950) 'Stranger' – a person who may be in society but not of it and who comes to develop a special sensitivity to being 'in and out'. It is Harold Garfinkel's (1967) 'Practical Methodologist' who becomes aware of the fragility of reality construction by being placed in unsettling situations. All of these lives are lived at a cultural crossroads. Experiencing contrasting expectations as to how he or she should live, the subject becomes aware of the essentially artificial and socially con-structed nature of social life – how potentially fragile are the realities that people make for themselves. In this awareness the subject throws a much broader light on the cultural, order, the 'OK world' that is routinely taken for granted by most (cf. Jansen, 1980).

Thus, Don Talayesba, the Sun Chief, lies on the edge of Indian and American culture (Simmons, 1942), James Sewid experiences the culture conflict of a Kwakiutl Indian facing modernizing Canada (Spradley, 1969), Wladek leaves Poland for Chicago, Victor – the Wild Boy of Aveyron – lives halfway between humanity and 'beasthood' (Lane, 1977); Jane Fry and 'Agnes' travel from male worlds to female worlds (Garfinkel, 1967) and Frank Moore, an institutionalized alcoholic, lives on the margins of social respectability (Straus, 1974): all of these reveal the value of choosing a subject between two worlds. Agnes the hermaphrodite is perhaps the most explicit use of a case study in this fashion. Garfinkel, working with the psychiatrist Stoller, focused intensively upon the cultural productions of a hermaphrodite – of being born an ambiguous boy and later becoming self defined as a girl and woman. Out of this highly atypical case, Garfinkel is able to clarify the artfully worked nature of gender meanings, showing how Agnes comes to sense a social, but taken-for-granted, world of gender expectations, and how she has to work hard to fit herself into them. Through this documentary study of one case, Garfinkel is able to produce a list of standardized expectations about gender as a social product in this society. Most people assume gender, but it is through the atypical case who finds such an assumption problematic that such a listing becomes possible. For most people gender is commonsensical and taken for granted, and the marginal case can highlight this (cf. Garfinkel, 1967; Kessler and McKenna, 1978).

The traditions of 'Great Men'   Marginality can be fairly readily identified, greatness cannot. But it is this criterion which some historians use in order to throw light on *Kultur* – socially significant events rather than routinely accepted ones. 'Great Men' – Goethe, Luther, Napoleon, Gandhi, Hitler – are selected because in them, uniquely, are to be found certain values and crises which have a much wider bearing on the age in which they live than those of the common man. In this view, 'the average man is to Goethe as a lump of coal is to the Kohinoor diamond' (Mandelbaum, 1967: 124). The classic tradition of autobiography writing has more often than not shown this interest in Great Men. Likewise, in 'psychohistory' the Great Man approach is often followed, as in Erik Erikson's celebrated case histories of Luther, Ghandi and Hitler (e.g. Erikson, 1959). Erikson has a particular fascination with 'greatness', suggesting that the identity crises of great people mirror the identity crises of their time; such people have unusually powerful childhood consciences reflecting their periods (thereby commonly appearing old in their early years; cf. Roazen, 1979: 75).

In search of 'ordinary people'   This concern with Great Men is one that has been severely challenged in recent times (cf. Chapter 4; Stanley, 1992), and the sociological approach rarely espouses it, preferring instead to seek out the marginal or the commonplace. *The ordinary person* seems to come closest to providing a source for generalizations to a wider population, but in effect it is notoriously difficult to locate such a person. Almost everyone stands 'out of the ordinary' on some dimension or the other. That is the essence of an intensive, ideographic approach. Nevertheless, with due caution, researchers have often focused upon samples of 'ordinary people' as a source (this is particularly true of oral history), or have sought a few people about whom initially there appeared little that was extraordinary – not too marginal, not too great. White's *Lives in Progress* (1975) is a good example perhaps of this latter approach, where volunteer students were the basis of selection.

Some other concerns

It helps if your informant meets certain more practical criteria too. An obvious one is accessibility of place and time. Since meetings may take place over several years, and meetings may last for two to three hours each week someone who is extraordinarily busy is unlikely to make a good informant. Likewise the subject should live within easy distance – a subject who lives many miles away will create problems! Then there are certain 'qualities' that are advisable in the subject – the anthropologist James Spradley (1979: 45–54) suggested that a good informant should be thoroughly enculturalized (hence fully aware, deeply involved and informed in their particular cultural world), currently involved (their account is hence not simply a reinterpretation of past experiences but a statement of current practices) and non-analytic (informants who are overly intellectual and overly abstract are of less value than those who talk about their experience in the raw). I think that subjects should also be fairly articulate, able to verbalize and have a 'a good story to tell' – although, under the right conditions, all people will meet this criteria.

In addition to this, a good relationship between the researcher and the subject is important. Life history research, perhaps more than any other, involves establishing and maintaining a close and intimate relationship with the subject, often for a number of years meeting regularly each week. Where there is an underlying dislike, lack of respect or hostility between the two people, this is hard to do. Indeed, I sometimes wonder just how many life history studies may have been started which have subsequently come to a sticky end because of hostilities developing in this highly intimate relationship. (I discuss this in more detail later.)

A number of other issues should be considered at this early stage. First, think about the *motivations* of all involved: yours and your subjects. Just what are you both up to in this? The subject may be curious as to why you, the researcher, are interested in him or her and you should be ready with a response – a response that may well include career and professional advantage side by side with some tangible political and/or moral concern for a social problem. At the outset it is necessary to come fairly clean with the subject, who will very likely sense a whiff of exploitation unless you do. At the same time, try to grasp the motivation of the subject: why on earth should anybody be willing to let a social scientist into his/her life to hear all their intimate details? Long ago, Gordon Allport suggested some thirteen reasons why people might be willing to disclose themselves (and there have been longer lists: see

Rainer, 1998: 12–13). Amongst these were a kind of 'special pleading' (providing a self-justification), exhibitionism, a desire for order, literary delight, securing an 'own personal perspective', a relief from tension, simple monetary gain, filling in one's life, a therapeutic encounter, redemption and social reincorporation (a confession), a desire to help science or to further public service, a desire for immortality or simply as a course work assignment (Allport, 1942: ch. 5).

Some life history subjects get paid (small) fees. At times this may be the prime incentive, especially with marginal subjects, so that the whole enterprise may be based on a cash transaction. Frank Moore, for instance, the institutionalized alcoholic, received between one and five dollars for almost every letter that he wrote to Straus (Straus, 1974: 20, 306) and often the researcher 'sent tobacco, clothing, writing materials, books, candy, copies of articles on alcohol or other subjects of mutual interest, and copies of my own publications on descriptions of other professional activities' (p. 21). Frank Moore wrote a lot of letters and clearly got a lot of rewards; but helpful as this was to Frank Moore, he strongly implies that this money was a debt that he built up to his researcher, not something that was rightfully and contractually his. Thus, Straus, had to reassure him: 'You have no financial obligations whatsoever to me' (p. 305). Money does not seem anything like as important as the intrinsic satisfaction derived from one's own self-reflection. Consider Frank Moore again:

> Methinks I have received far more than I have contributed. My own evaluation of this correspondence is that it has been to me what the confessional box is to the Catholic, what the wailing wall is to the Hebrew, what the psychiatric couch is to the woman in menopause . . . with the added advantage you answer every time . . . Whatever this correspondence might have meant to you, it prevented me from laughing myself to death or murder. The correspondence was like the touchstone of alcohol to a man who had reached his particular peak of mental pain. (Straus, 1974: 371)

Financial rewards, whilst present, do not seem to be as important as the emotional rewards. In general, life stories are quite satisfying in their own right. To know that somebody is sufficiently interested in one's life to be willing and bothered enough to take it down in great detail is rewarding; it is gratifying to clarify one's own view of one's life; and it is satisfying to finally obtain a document about oneself. Frequently, of course, these accounts will be little more than justificatory apologies. Motivations, therefore, need to be carefully reflected upon. The researcher needs to ask: what does the interviewee hope to gain from this?

A second area to consider in advance is *anonymity*. Whilst it is a commonplace in most social science research to guarantee the anonymity of the subjects, in the life story pure and proper so much intimate detail is likely to be revealed that it will not be too difficult for anybody dedicated to finding out who the subject is, actually to do so. I will discuss this issue further in the chapter on ethics, but the extent to which names, places and life events might need changing should always be discussed with the subject (and reflected upon in his or her own mind). For instance, the selection of a subject who performs significant historic-ally unique acts in his or her life might raise very serious problems as to the suitability of that subject. If only one person had played such a prominent role in their community, written a particular sort of book, been employed in a unique occupation, organized a particularly famous television programme, undergone a famous operation, then the inclusion of such a story in their life history may make them instantly recog-nizable. So it may not be a matter simply of changing names or even places, but also sometimes changing the life history events. This, of course, could make a travesty of the issue of truth. The opening of Pat Caplan's life story of Mohammed produces verbatim her discussion with him on some of these issues (Caplan, 1997).

Thirdly, ponder the *kind of life story you want to obtain*. Very often tellers will find it hard to grasp just what you want to do – they have no training in life story analysis, after all, and their experiences of inter-viewing may be limited to what they have seen in market research or on television. Making the method sound too elaborate and complex can confuse the respondent. Often the best way is simply to give them some existing life story – maybe in a book – to look over. This should give them a good idea of what you will be doing. You will need to clarify with the subject whether the life history research is simply going to depend upon transcriptions of an interview situation or whether it will be com-bined with participant observation, talking to their friends, the reading of their letters and discussion of their photographs. Indeed, if the latter techniques are going to be brought in, much more of the subject's time may be needed – along with a sense of involvement and commitment: the researcher will almost be trying to become a close friend of the subject and in doing this the life history goals may lead to a potential tension between friendship and professionalism.

Fourthly, think about the *logistics of the interviewing situation* (see below too). Frequently this is left to chance. Once clear that a life history study is being embarked upon, time should be taken with the subject to discuss in detail many matters. These include such things as when and where you will meet, whether they want to see transcripts of their interviews and have the chance to chat about them, the kinds of questions you will be asking, and whether these questions will be given in advance or not.

You may also want to discuss what *the final product* might actually look like and the degree of control that the subject will have over the contents; and whether the final product will be published under the subject's pseudonym or the researcher's name. Of course many of these issues may change along the route, but some preliminary meeting to clarify these things, while making the research a little bit formal, will help to establish it as research and will give both the researcher and the subject a clearer sense of where the enterprise is leading. One useful checklist for thinking about the interview has been provided by Gorden (1969: 165–73). He suggests eight questions that should be asked:

> How should I introduce myself? How should I explain the purpose of the interview? How should I explain the sponsorship? Should I explain why he [*sic*] was selected? How to discuss anonymity? Should any extrinsic reward be mentioned? How should the interview be recorded? How open are we going to be?

One final feature to worry you! How are you going to *record the interview*? (cf. Thompson, 2000; Yow, 1994). The two major ways include either taking handwritten notes, as in many of the earlier Chicago studies and in *The Professional Fence* (Klockars, 1975), or tape-recording. Each has its pros and cons but, on balance, provided you can work technical gadgets well – and many can't! – taping is probably best. Nowadays CD-Rom mini-discs can provide a 'state of the art' recording, complete with facilities for your own tracking the interviews into organized themes. (At the time of writing (1999), such machines have just gone onto the popular market: but they are not cheap.) With tape or disc in hand, some role play rehearsals will be needed before entering the field. For a machine that breaks down, a battery that runs out, a tape that overruns, a microphone not switched on, an unclean mini-disc, an outside noise that drowns the talk, and an overused tape can all cause havoc. These days, too, the use of video recording seems more and more plausible (it is quite cheap) and useful (it is better at capturing the wider 'feel' of what is happening because it shows facial gestures etc.). Nevertheless, video is still seen as quite threatening and has not yet become that widespread as a recording technique, except in special fields like conversational analysis. (As I write I suspect it will be rapidly replaced with the digital video disc, which is much better quality and much more manageable.)

Doing the research: getting a life/performing interviews

Studs Terkel is one of the leading vox populi oral historians – recording hundreds of voices and editing them into many books. In a series of discussions, he captures something of the method:

> The first thing I'd say to any interviewer is . . . 'Listen.' It's the second thing I'd say too, and the third and the fourth . . . 'Listen . . . listen . . . listen . . . listen.' And if you do, people will talk. They'll *always* talk. Why? Because no one has ever listened to them before in all their lives . . .

'Do you work to a framework?' they sometimes ask me. And sometimes I answer yes, and sometimes I answer no. What I am trying to put over is that there aren't any rules, each time's a new beginning. That's what's exciting about it'

Listening, and keeping a curiosity is the key . . . I am curious about all of it, all the time. 'Curiousity never killed this cat' – that's what I'd like as my epitaph.

In the one-to-one interview you start level in the unconfidence, in not knowing where you are going . . . You're Columbus, you're starting out onto the unknown sea. There are no maps because no one's been there before. You're an explorer, a discoverer. It's exciting – and it's scary, it frightens you. Remember that . . . There aren't any rules. You do it your own way. You experiment. You try this, you try that. With one person one way's the best, with another person, another. Stay loose, stay flexible . . . (Studs Terkel, 1996: 163–6)

As we have seen (Chapters 2 and 3), life stories can be gathered in a number of ways. Through writing, interviewing, videoing, recording, observation and the collection of archive materials – diaries, photos, artefacts. In this section my prime focus will be the life story interview – mainly because it is by far the most common tool. Indeed, it has been said that we now live in the 'Interview Society' (Silverman, 1993). Almost everybody has experienced or even conducted some kind of interview – from interviews for employment, college, or social security to interviews with doctors, police, customs officials, or market researchers. Likewise, our media is inundated with interviews, from news commentators and talk shows. 'Interviews' have become part of most people's everyday lives.

The branch of interviewing that concerns us here is the 'social science interview', which itself comes in many forms – standardized or flexible, focused or open, directive or non-directive, 'formative' or 'mass', survey or ethnographic, individual or group, structured or unstructured, long or short, active or passive. Many of these differences may be loosely clustered along a continuum that runs somewhat along the lines shown in Table 6.1.

At one end lies a fairly formal approach to interviewing; at the other a much more 'open' and flexible approach. They are suited to different kinds of research. Many life story interviews approximate to the positivist mode, such as those found in panel or longitudinal studies like the British Household Panel Study, the German Socio-Economic Panel and the Study of American Families (SAF). (For a review of these projects see, Scott and Alwin, 1998.) The research style that I am discussing in this book, however, moves towards the interpretive. This 'life story method' tends to favour conducting open and in-depth interviews in a highly active and interactive fashion using only the most general of guides in order to help the subject construct a sense of their cultural world. Positivists tend to want to produce answers to *why* questions that can

TABLE 6.1 **Two ends of a continuum of interview forms**

Positivist pole	Interpretive pole
Interviews 'collect' data	Interviews 'construct' data
Standardized through questionnaire	Flexible – shaped by checklists
Mass – can be used for many	Idiographic – used for fewer people
Focused – planned answers	Open – follow hunches
Structured and hence easy to administer	Unstructured and hence requiring more personal skills and sensitivities
More predictable	Less predictable
Survey research	Ethnographic research
'Objective' – best for facts	Phenomenological/'subjective' – best for moods, feelings, emotions subjectivities
Sees interviewee as passive	Sees interviewee as active
Less prominent role for interviewer	More central role for interviewer
Less reflexive/reflective	More reflexive/reflective

ultimately be counted; phenomenologists seek to understand *how* a person lives a life in a culture. (It is a similar distinction to the one we have encountered at many stages in this book.)

Interviewing: some common practices

The most common methods of gathering life stories have been threefold: through writing, recording and a combination of observation and interviewing.

The first practice was much used in the past. It simply encouraged people to *write their life history down following a guideline*. This was true of many of the early pioneering studies, such as *The London Survey of the Poor* which asked Bermondsey housewives to write down their experiences (Smith, 1935) and the mass observation research of the 1930s and 1940s (Sheridan, 1993). It is also to be found in the classic Chicago studies of Shaw (1931), Thomas and Znaniecki (1958) and Sutherland (1937), as well as the anthropological studies of Simmons (1942) and Radin (1926), all of which were founded upon the simple expedient, at least initially, of getting the subjects to write their 'own story'.

But with the gradual arrival of the tape recorder, the approach shifted. Bob Bogdan, in the early 1970s, described this newer (second) approach well for his study with Jane Fry:

A few weeks elapsed between our first discussion of the project and the start of our work. Most of our meetings were held during the months of April, May and June of 1972 at my office, and consisted of unstructured interviews which were tape-recorded. We started with informal conversations, pursuing various topics and discussing different phases of her life as they came up. If Jane brought up topics during a taping session which she was unable to finish, I would mention them the next day. We did not attempt to record her life story chronologically, but skipped around from day to day. There was an advantage in this method: it allowed a relationship to develop between us so that the experiences that were difficult for her to talk about were dealt with at later sessions. I replayed certain tapes and at later taping sessions asked Jane questions regarding the chronology of events and so on. Early in the interviewing I asked her to list the main events in her life chronologically, and this listing was used as a guide in organizing the material as well as in directing later taping sessions. During the three months period the material was recorded, we met from one to five times a week, and our meetings lasted from one to five hours. I did not keep an accurate account of the number of hours we spent recording our sessions; an estimate is about a hundred. Over 750 pages of transcribed material was the result of our effort. (Bogdan, 1974: 8)

Bogdan's account highlights both the dependency on a tape recorder and the use of an interviewing style that is highly unstructured. A structured interview is a crutch: it pushes the researcher into a well-defined role (sitting there with a questionnaire in one's lap) and permits the relative security of knowing both what to ask and what is likely to be heard in reply. Without minimizing the many difficulties to which researchers and research books testify, it is a comparatively technical exercise. This is far from true of the more 'open' life history interview. This often simply is not what most people expect of an interview so that it makes the task difficult at the outset; there are no clear prescriptions as to how the subject is expected to behave. Often the subject is expected to take the lead rather than merely responding to a series of cues given by the questionnaire. Furthermore, it is not like a simple conversation, an analogy that is sometimes made, for the researcher has to be too passive for that. The image which perhaps captures this interview method most clearly is that of the non-directive, phenomenologically aware counsellor. All the rules of non-directive counselling, espoused for example by Sullivan and Rogers, could come into play here! Central to this view is the uniqueness of the person and the situation, the importance of empathy and the embodiment of 'non-possessive warmth' in the interviewer! The aim is 'to grasp the native's point of view, his [sic] relation to life, to realize his vision of the world' (Malinowski, 1922: 25). This phenomenological (Lifton) or ethnographic (Spradley) form of interviewing may not always be what is required; sometimes a more structured form of life history may be taken in which the researcher works out a series of general guides at the outset.

A third strategy is even less formal: it involves triangulation (Webb et al., 1966), a mixture of participant observation and almost casual chatting with notes taken. Klockars describes in detail his 'interview routine' with Vincent Swaggi, the professional fence:

Between January of 1972 and April of 1973 I interviewed Vincent once and occasionally twice a week. With the exception of the first few meetings, my weekly visits began in the late afternoon when I arrived at Vincent's store. I would watch him do business for an hour or so, and after he closed, we would go to dinner at a modest Italian restaurant. During dinner Vincent would recount the events and deals he had participated in since I last saw him. As we got to know one another better, Vincent would, in a relaxed fashion, review with me his options on pending deals and ask for my opinion on how he ought to proceed . . . From the restaurant we would drive to Vincent's home; there, in Vincent's consideration the 'real' interviewing would begin. This was signaled by my opening my briefcase and taking out my notebook and pencils. Vincent's part in the ritual was to settle in his large recliner chair and light a cigar. Quite often the topic we would begin with was carried over from our conversation at dinner.

By ten thirty Vincent would usually grow tired; he started his day at five thirty every morning except Sunday. Occasionally an especially productive interview would keep us going to midnight, but usually I would leave by eleven. As I drove home I would dictate my comments, recollections and impressions into a small battery operated tape-recorder. The lateness of the hour, the amount I had drunk during the interview and at dinner, and my attention to driving all took their toll on the quality of these comments. I was usually home in a few hours and always too tired to review my interviewing notes. This task was postponed until the following morning . . . Once or twice we ate at Vincent's home where he prepared dinner with my assistance; once or twice his daughter made a special Italian dinner for us. But for fifteen months the pattern remained virtually the same; an hour at the store, two hours at dinner, three to four hours of real interviewing, an hour of variable quality dictation. In sum I spent roughly four hundred hours, watching, listening to and talking to Vincent over a period of fifteen months. (Klockars, 1975: 218–19)

A few issues on interviewing

Whilst there are many published guides to interviewing, interviews are not really something to read about: they are something to practise and do. Improving interview skills can only really happen through experience. Yet a few comments may be in order.

Getting prepared I have usually found conducting interviews to be, perhaps surprisingly, a nerve-wracking experience – especially at the beginning. I have found it quite easy to become self-absorbed – worrying more and more that it is an ordeal for yourself, and almost starting to forget about the person you are interviewing! So it is important to think through the interview and feel comfortable and well prepared in advance, so you do not arrive with too many worries. Amongst the things to think about are:

- Where the interview should take place. In classic terms in 'the grass hut' or the 'white room', i.e. close to the natural setting of the interviewee, or in the interviewer's own space (Werner and Schoepfle,

1987: 315)? In general, the more interpretive the interview, the better it may be to see the subject on their own 'turf' – not only will it give them, greater ease, it will give you more insight into their social world. There can, however, be problems here – it is worth thinking about some of the potential risks that could happen anytime you enter a 'stranger's home' that you do not know well. (In my early days of interviewing in the field of 'sexualities', I had to make a quick exit from the subject's home on more than one occasion!)

- Potential practical difficulties. Ensure these are sorted out well in advance of the interview. This could include being clear about the questions you plan to ask and your method of recording (with batteries in the tape recorder if that is what you plan to use); that practical arrangements have been sorted out (i.e. where to go and when); and that the interviewee knows what to expect – often usefully done through a short letter or note to them in advance about the interview, which you then run through on arrival. (This can be particularly important if your interview technique is going to be unorthodox!)
- How you will conduct the interview. Perhaps do a dress rehearsal or role play of the interview – with friends, or else yourself – anticipating problems and thinking about such things as dress, body language, eye contact and the like. Think through important but simple matters like the clothes most appropriate to wear, and the kind of seating arrangements that would work best.
- Being well organized on the day. Leave plenty of time to get to the interview (arriving late can throw everything off), and be aware of 'relaxation techniques' such as breathing exercises before arrival. Be clear about opening 'patters', and be aware that a lot of interesting 'material' often happens just when the tape recorder is switched off and you are about to leave. Plan for this.

Being empathetic and a good listener   Always think a great deal about your 'interviewee' – both before you arrive, during the interview, and indeed after it! So much research sees 'interviewees' as merely passive means to your ends, but good (ethical) life story research sees the subject as *an active end in themselves* and your task is to think and feel your way into that subject. Always remember that 'they're doing you a favour' (Parker, 1996: 164). Far too often conventional interview subjects are seen as 'passive vessels of answers' – they sit there and blurt out their response (Holstein and Gubrium, 1995: 8)! But James Holstein and Jaber Gubrium – longstanding craftspeople in this field – have suggested that the interview is best approached as being 'active':

What happens if we enliven the image of the subject behind the respondent? Construed as active, the subject behind the respondent not only holds facts and details of experience, but in the very process of offering them up for response, constructively adds to, takes away from and transforms the facts and details. The respondent can hardly 'spoil' what he or she is actively creating. (Holstein and Gubrium, 1995: 8)

I suggest that you ponder the struggles that lead people to say the things they do in the interview. Ponder what it would be like if you were asked these two simple questions:

Q: What have been the most painful experiences of your life?
Q: Describe your life as the chapters in a book.

Could you do it? How would you respond? Often, first, there is a shock. There is no immediate answer and there is no correct answer either. What you say in response to this question may have to be 'composed', and this composition may lead you to say more – but down a path you may never have anticipated at all. Answers to questions are actively constructed on the spot, and it is worth thinking through just what this 'active interview' means.

Throughout all of this, of course, the ability to listen is crucial. I have been interviewed by people who are quite clearly not interested in what I have to say: their eyes look vacant, their body language is cold, and they rush from question to question not bothering to follow anything up. It is as if they think that once they have turned the tape recorder on, they need not bother to listen. But looking bored and rushing on will not produce good interview results (cf. Rubin, 1997).

Practising techniques Techniques are the specific skills that can be learned in conducting interviews. Textbooks are full of these, and so I will not detail many here. There are a few to stress though. First is *funnelling*. This means having your questions, and linked probes, sorted in a way that will really keep the interview going, opening up issues in the order that emerges as best. Often this takes the form of beginning with *'grand-tours and mini-tours'*. The former sets a wide, broad agenda and often senses the language of the respondents – key words and ideas that the interviewer can then adopt and follow up later; a grand tour might involve no more than five or six big, general questions. This can then be followed by more intensive interviewing (mini-tours) around specific areas (Werner and Schoepfle, 1987: 318; Spradley, 1979: 86).

Second is *attentiveness and responsiveness*. You need to facilitate the respondent's ease and willingness to talk. Hence an emphasis should be given to stimulating the subject's motivation through the expression of interest; to reducing any form of threat to the subject by providing support and giving confidence; to preventing any form of falsification by the subject by mildly probing for further clarification which may reveal discrepancies; and to stimulating the memory of the respondent by providing minor probes which take them back further and further.

Third is the issue of *language*. A basic familiarity with the subject's argot and idiosyncratic linguistic forms is a prerequisite of a good interviewer – although that basic familiarity should not result in the researcher 'showing off' this inside knowledge and making the subject ponder, just who is this 'wiseguy'? Sometimes the 'right vocabulary' could sound fake and pretentious; being unjudgemental may make you come across as too goody-goody!

Fourth is dealing with *resistances*: these are tactics that enable the researcher to explore the resistances found in respondents. When a respondent for example says, 'I don't know anything about that at all', 'I'm too busy now', or 'What do you mean?' the researcher may be awakened to an area that the subject is having difficulty talking about. Strategies need to be pondered as to ways to dig out such information – and of course the great advantage of the life history technique is that these areas need not be immediately followed through but can be re-raised at a later interview. One of the great advantages of life history research is that it usually is a process – never quite finished – so you can return, and ask more. There is no need to get it all at one moment (as with much survey research); certain issues can simply be shelved until a more appropriate time is arrived at.

Formal texts on interviewing – and even testaments by interviewers (cf. Converse and Schuman, 1974) – can alert the researcher to many issues of interview skill. So too can the replaying of video tapes of one's own interviewing. But, like so many of these tasks, I suspect they can only really be learned through a lifetime of mistakes! I have found, for example, that despite all that the books say, when I commence a life history interview so much is dependent upon my mood and whether the interviewee and I get along or not – personal factors that books cannot really describe adequately. As Lofland (1995: 90) notes: 'successful interviewing is not unlike carrying on unthreatening, self-controlled, supportive, polite and cordial interaction in everyday life'. Unfortunately, he concludes, such skills may be a little rare!

Guide to further reading

There are many good books to introduce **the practice of qualitative research**, though fewer on life history practice. A recent, basic but very readable guide is David Silverman's *Doing Qualitative Research: A Practical Handbook* (2000), though there is little on life stories in it. John and Lyn Lofland's work *Analyzing Social Settings* has now been through three editions (1971, 1984, 1995) and remains for me one of the most practical of sources. Lofland's *Doing Social Life* (1976) is also significant for its attempt to bring rigour and a systematic approach to qualitative fieldwork, as is the work by Robert Prus *Symbolic Interaction and Ethnographic Research* (1996). The late Anselm Strauss's work remains seminal in this field (although I find some of it a little too formalistic). Thus, Leonard Schatzman and Anselm Strauss's *Social Research in the Field* (1973) examines the stages of field research – entering, organizing, watching, listening, recording, analysing and communicating; Anselm Strauss and Judith Corbin's *Basics of Qualitative Research* (1998, 2nd edn) provides a general beginner's guide; and Anselm Strauss's *Qualitative Analysis for Social Scientists* (1987) constitutes a more advanced set of suggestions. All give particular prominence to 'coding' and analysis, and much of it is translatable to personal document research. Of considerable practical value, too, is the Chicago manual *Field Work* by B.H. Junker (1960), which also contains an excellent bibliography (still well worth examining, even if a little outdated), and the methodological appendices in S.T. Bruyn's classic but excellent *The Human Perspective in Sociology* (1966). In the UK, the Webbs's (1932) *Methods of Social Study* was a founding text, and more recent classics are to be found in Martyn Hammersley and Paul Atkinson's *Ethnography: Principles in Practice* (3rd edn, 1995) and Robert Burgess's *In the Field* (1984).

Several studies by the anthropologist James P. Spradley provide systematic coverage of **the research process**, from selecting informants through to analysis and writing. See his *The Ethnographic Interview* (1979) and *Participant Observation* (1980). Much of his material has direct relevance to 'doing life histories', and indeed some of his studies – *You Owe Yourself a Drunk* (1970) and *Guests Never Leave Hungry* (1969) – are examples of the method.

In contrast to qualitative field studies, there are relatively few books that provide **guidelines on 'doing life stories'**. Short and helpful are both Robert Atkinson's *The Life Story Interview* (1998) and Robert Miller's *Researching Life Stories and Family Histories* (2000); Paul Thompson's guide in *The Voice of the Past* (2000, 3rd edn) remains a very useful source; Charlotte Linde's *Life Stories* (1993) provides practical help, from an angle that is decidedly based in conversational analysis; and my own earlier account can be found in Ken Plummer 'Life story research', in Jonathan Smith, Rom Harré and Luke Van Langhove (eds), *Rethinking Methods in Psychology* (1995b). For anthropologists – who may use wider definitions encompassing folklore, there is an extremely valuable study by Ruth Finnegan on *Oral Traditions and the Verbal Arts* (1992), which contains a great deal of both conceptual and practical information. There is also much of value in Norman K. Denzin, *Interpretive Biography* (1989). Although written for a more 'popular' audience than this book, I think Tristine Rainer's *Your Life As Story* (1998) provides a wealth of interesting ideas for formulating questions and digging around in people's lives! Some qualitative textbooks provide 'introductions' – see, for instance, Bruce Berg's *Qualitative Research Methods for the Social Sciences* (1988, 3rd edn: ch. 10) and Robert Bogdan and Steve Taylor's *Introduction to Quali-tative Research* (1988, 3rd edn).

The key text on **doing life course research** is Janet Z. Giele and Glen H. Elder (eds), *Methods of Life Course Research: Qualitative and Quantitative Approaches* (1988). See also Richard Settersten Jr and Karl Ulrich Mayer, 'The measurement of age, age structuring and the life course', in *Annual Review of Sociology*, 1997, 23: 233–61. The *Murray Research Center* at Radcliffe College, Harvard, formed in 1976, provides a valuable US archive of longitudinal data sets, as does *The Data Archive* and *Qualidata* based at the University of Essex for the UK. (See the web site listings in the Appendix.)

There are many books on **interviewing**. An original and lively account is James Holstein and Jaber Gubrium's *The Active Interview* (1995). On life story interviewing itself, see Robert Atkinson's *The Life Story Interview* (1998) and Robert Miller's *Researching Life Stories and Family Histories* (2000). For more general accounts, see Steinner Kvale *InterViews* (1996); Andrea Fontana and James H. Frey 'Interviewing', in Denzin and Lincoln's *Handbook of Qualitative Research* (1994); James Spradley, *The Ethnographic Interview* (1979); O. Werner and G. Mark Schoepfle, *Systematic Fieldwork*, vol. 1: *Foundations of Ethnography and Interviewing* (1987) and R.L. Gorden, *Interviewing: Strategy, Techniques and Tactics* (1969). Gorden's classic has been through several editions (4th edn).

7 Thinking about Life History 'Data'

> I have never been impressed by the argument that, as complete objectivity is impossible in these matters (as, of course, it is), one might as well let one's sentiments run loose . . . That is like saying that as perfect aseptic environment is impossible, one might as well conduct surgery in a sewer. (Clifford Geertz, 1973: 30)

Collecting life stories can produce masses and masses of 'data'. By the time it comes to be 'written' as a book or thesis and ultimately 'read' by others, it will have been pared down, edited, truncated, streamlined. Only in the work of a Proust – who famously takes thirty pages describing his tossing and turnings before falling asleep – do we find the minutiae of a life recorded: most life stories are the victims of major amputations. This chapter turns to some of the methods of this amputation.

Put more bluntly: how to handle all this data? How to turn a testimony of a teller into a public record (tape, CD-Rom, video, photo)? How to organize that record to find what you want? And how to start to make some kind sense of it all? Broadly, you will have to turn a mass of inchoate, unstructured impressions and talk (i) through a process of transcription and editing into (ii) a series of files (on paper, on CD-Rom, on disc, on video?) which are in turn (iii) organized through indexing, coding and sorting. And in this very process of managing the data, a new 'story' might start to appear. As the late sociologist Elliot Liebow has eloquently written about his 'lives' of homeless women:

> To make sense of my notes was, in effect, to write the book. This was far and away the most difficult part of the study. For me, to make sense of my notes meant to organize them and order them, along with my own ideas about them, into a more or less coherent whole that told a story. A true story, I hoped. (Liebow, 1993: 323)

Managing the data: from 'fieldnotes' to 'filenotes'

Transcription

A first major task after interviewing for most life story researchers is transcription (and possibly editing too). This is a hugely time-consuming – and often boring – process. For every hour of tape, it can take up to ten hours to transcribe – especially if you are to engage in analysis at the same time. The transcription will usually take place directly onto a disk with a good word processing system – or a qualitative computer assisted program (QCAP), where, with luck, lines can be numbered. When doing printouts as much space as possible should be left round the text (double spacing, wide margins) to allow for scribblings of all kinds of comments. If using paper copies, five or six copies will make it very easy for the final analysis to be done with scissors cutting up the transcripts into appropriate files. More commonly these days, everything will be done on disk files – with a package like NUD.IST or The Ethnograph, analysis and coding can be done on screen, and the files sorted through the program. All this work should be done as soon as possible after the interview so that the process of analysis and data collection can proceed side by side. Consider the extent to which a *literal* translation is required – for example, whether all the faltering, mumbling and confusions of everyday talk should be included, whether the text should be smoothed and rounded out in the transcription, and whether issues of mood and feeling should be commented upon. All this will depend on the purpose. Standardly, the aim has been to make the transcript as readable as possible – without losing it meanings. A little editing may be required along the way, but in general serious editing should be left to a later stage – when fashioning the story into a finished product (see Bob Blauner on this: 1987). Ruth Finnegan, reviewing a number of studies, suggests that the following edits are quite usual:

1   Leave out 'uh's and other hesitations . . . like 'you know' or 'I mean'
2   Repair false starts and corrections
3   Omit interviewer responses like 'I see' or 'yeah'
4   Use standard spellings, not dialect
5   Do not use 'eye spellings' ('enuff' for 'enough')
6   Use punctuation as for normal written prose
7   Subject to the provisos above, do not correct or interpret . . .'
    (Finnegan, 1992: 196–7)

But to list such conventions, useful as they are, is also to realize how problematic transcription can be. For instance, in some branches of social science, like conversational analysis, the prime aim is to get the speech patterns down as accurately and as exactly as possible – attention even being paid to such things as the milliseconds of a pause between speakers. Here a very detailed mode of transcription is required (for an example of how this is done and applied to life stories, see Charlotte Linde's *Life Stories* (1993: xii–xiv)). Others may be much more concerned with the way things are said physically and emotionally: that is they want the transcript to say things about their passions in the interview (when they cry or laugh, smile or 'go cold'), of the emotional work involved (Kleinman and Copp, 1993). And for still others, there may also be a visual record that is required – perhaps to capture aspects of body language. Ideally, this would involve videoing the interview (Lomax and Casey, 1998). However, the data is finally 'transcribed', it is usual then to show it back to the 'subject', so that their feedback can be given. Sometimes they do not want to see it; but sometimes they then refuse permission for you to use it (cf. Liebow, 1993: xvii).

A linked issue may be the problem of *translation*. This might sound like a problem that would concern only a special kind of transcript: how, for instance, to translate the story of a Guatemalan peasant woman (Rigoberta Menchú, 1984) into readable English? But these days this is a much wider issue. For all life stories are embedded in particular cultures, and the act of translation is an attempt to 'transplant' the language from one culture so it can make sense in another without losing its original meanings. Thus it is not just a matter of translating Spanish to English – itself a task fraught with difficulties of interpretation. It is also a matter of noting Afro-American patter and Rap Speak, of being sensitive to the languages of gays, lesbians or transgender speak, of knowing the nuances of disability worlds. Literal translation may contain many biases that lose the feel of the life and the talk (see Finnegan, 1992: ch. 9).

Indexing, coding and filing

With the 'life' in a manageable form on paper or disc, files need to be developed which will make key themes and issues rapidly available for analysis and archiving. The latest hi-tech digital technologies are likely to make this a very streamlined process in the future – CD mini-discs already exist which allow you to carve a recording up into locatable files. More mundanely, John Lofland has discussed such processes in the important *Analyzing Social Settings* (1995), and from this I can suggest three basic forms that are likely to be needed: *core files, analytic files* and *personal log*.

Core files should contain all data in its pure and richest unedited form, arranged and catalogued in strict chronological order, and an index file which lists all the documents, their file names and other notable features. This main file should (like all files) be doubly backed up, and rendered as permanent. This is the ongoing and complete record of all the materials that are gathered.

In addition to this, however, there must also be a series of constantly changing *analytic files*: here the newly gained data are read with an eye to particular theoretical themes and concepts that have evolved in the research thus far or are found pristine and new in the transcript. Key themes are highlighted in the text (maybe by key words, maybe by a specialist computer package that searches for named words and themes) so that eventually all relevant sections can be cut, referenced and placed in the appropriate analytic or thematic file. They will constantly have to be jiggled around and then be 'cut and pasted' (literally or on the computer) into themed theory or analytic files. You can cut and paste as much as you like, as long as you keep the main files intact. Hopefully, these analytic themes will slowly develop into the overarching structure of the life history book.

A third set of files that can usefully be kept comprises *a personal log*. These are designed to convey the researcher's changing personal impressions of the interviewee, of the situation, of their own personal worries and anxieties about the research. These should be a necessary part of any research process. Ideally these would also be kept in master files so there is a chronology – a diary if you like (cf. Palmer, 1928) – of the personal research experience; but they could also be arranged into analytic files, perhaps to help clarify the ethical and personal problems of the research enterprise as they occur. (Other files may need to be kept: many of these are discussed in Judith Fiedler's *Field Research*, 1978.)

Now all this talk of filing may sound very boring – a long way from the humanistic concerns this book champions! But the fact is that filing – as C. Wright Mills once observed – is indeed an 'intellectual production'. It is the record of the work that you are doing and without it the final 'product' will be that much worse. As he says, files are 'a continuously growing store of facts and ideas, from the most vague to the most finished . . . all projects with me begin and end with them, and books are simply organized releases from the continuous work that goes into them' (Mills, 1959/1970: 199–200). In doing life history research, a good filing system harbours your intellectual life.

Analysing and 'theorizing' the stories

Getting the story can be fun, but making sense of it takes much longer and requires a lot of work. Indeed, the analysis is likely to take at least two or three times as long as the interview took. In many ways this is the truly creative part of the work – it entails brooding and reflecting upon mounds of data for long periods of time until it 'makes sense' and 'feels right', and key ideas and themes flow from it. It is also the hardest process to describe: the standard technique is to read and make notes, leave and ponder, re-read without notes, make new notes, match notes up, ponder, re-read and so on. Here my concern is with all this work that goes on around the collected data. It involves first the problems of making sense of the 'data' (or 'evaluation', which classic-ally could mean representativeness, validity and reliability though I will argue that these may well not be appropriate criteria for life story work); and secondly, the logics of analysis and the theorization into the life: how to move beyond the life, the story, to something maybe a little more general?

The 'so-called classic problems' of 'representativeness, validity and reliability'

Every standard textbook on research will tell you that the tools for evaluating research entail *reliability, validity and representativeness*. And life stories can indeed be assessed in this way. But, as Robert Atkinson (1998: 59) notes: 'reliability and validity are not necessarily the appropriate evaluative standards for a life story interview'. For others, working in a more postmodern mood, such as Norman Denzin (1997), they have become utterly inappropriate – leading only to a spurious 'scientism'. I also agree that such conventional modes of evaluation may well not be at all suitable in many instances: that, indeed, different goals and different kinds of data require different modes of evaluation. Indeed, in the final chapter I will be suggesting more appropriate tools – that link to matters of pragmatics, aesthetics and morality. But for the time being, I want to look at some of the more orthodox lines.

The problem of representativeness　One of the most apparent attacks on life history research is that it fails to provide representative cases and thus hurls the reader into the eccentric world of the atypical – a story in itself, but no more. This completely misunderstands the nature of such research – where insights, understandings, appreciation, intimate familiarity are the goals and not 'facts', explanations or generalizations. It may, however, be useful here to think of *a continuum of 'representativeness'* (the observant reader may note I am rather prone to continuums!). At one extreme, we get a fairly clear idea of how typical the life stories are. In a study of the elderly by Paul Thompson and his colleagues, for instance, he tells us that they at least used an 'earlier sample survey as our starting list', and although he recognizes that there is no claim to 'statistical representativeness' he does proceed to check how his sample of life histories matches the general population (and shows that two important minorities – the 'never married' and 'couples with no children' were missing). Hence, in this instance there is quite a clear sense of what kinds of people are speaking in the book (Thompson et al., 1990: 14). Another good example of this end of the continuum is Stanley, the 'Jack Roller', who is firmly located as being both typical and not typical of juvenile delinquency in Chicago in the 1920s. In clarifying his typicality, Burgess can show how the characteristics of Stanley 'match' the feature of their wider samples: he 'grew up in a delinquency area', 'lived in a broken home', 'began his delinquent career even before he started school', 'had institutional experiences in rapid succession', and became a 'jack roller' (cf. Shaw, 1966: 184–5). In these cases, then, we can indeed use life stories and make some sense of representativeness. We might see this as a bonus.

But at another extreme, *generalization really does not matter*. The case history may explicitly be viewed as a unique and necessary story to be told: the aim is to grasp a unique experience for what it tells us about just that. Of course, there are insights and lessons to be learned. But there is no necessary superiority in the ability to generalize – indeed, many think of it is as a failing. Many historians and most 'writers' have little anxiety in dealing with a unique case and shunning the general: neither, on occasions, should social scientists. Thus, for instance, when we hear the tale of one Ignacio Bizzaro Ujpán, a Tzutuhil Mayan Indian, who recorded his life for eight years in a diary and told his story to James D. Sexton, we soon realize that we are in the land of a unique and original tale from which we may learn unique and original things (Sexton, 1981). True such studies will legitimately get into trouble if they naively push their claims too far (though they can of course *speculate* on wider implications).

But midway between these extremes is a possibility advocated by Blumer of seeking out key informants who have a profound and central grasping of a particular cultural world. As he says in commenting on *The Polish Peasant*:

> A half dozen individuals with such knowledge constitute a far better 'representative sample' than a thousand individuals who may be involved in the action that is being formed but who are not knowledgeable about that formation. I put the matter in this startling way to call attention to the fact that the use of human documents sets a markedly new and unsolved methodological problem of representativeness. A problem which sociologists across the board do not recognize, much less address. (Blumer, [1939] 1979: xxxiii)

This leads us to see that the problem of representativeness need not always be discussed in the same terms as statisticians might do. Some sixty years after Blumer first uttered the above comments, it remains the case that the idea of representativeness has been dominated by a statistical conception. And it may be that the renewed interest in life story work should bring with it a reconsideration of this debate. The question here may be quite simply put: what does the 'story' actually *represent*?

The problem of reliability and validity   The other major problems that it is usually argued should be addressed concern reliability and validity – two central issues of all research methods which have a curious relationship to each other. Reliability is primarily concerned with technique and consistency – with ensuring that if the study was conducted by someone else, similar findings would be obtained. Validity is primarily concerned with making sure that the technique is actually studying what it is supposed to. A clock that was consistently ten minutes fast would hence be reliable but invalid since it did not tell the correct time. In general, reliability is the preoccupation of 'hard' methodologists (getting the attitude scale or the questionnaire design as technically replicable as possible through standardization, measurement and control); while validity receives relatively short shrift. 'Attitude scales' may thus frequently be consistent but bear a highly tentative relationship to 'attitudes'. Indeed, as Frazier (1976: 129) remarks, 'it is probably safe to say that validity is more likely to decrease as the ease with which reliability is tested increases'. The closer I am to the phenomenon I want to understand, the nearer I am to validity.

In life history research these two issues have been rarely discussed, perhaps because the problem of reliability is very hard to tap. Given that usually the virtue of life histories lies in the relatively free flowing babble of talk, to attempt standardization of questionnaires is to invite invalidity. But without such standardization and cross-checking, attacks become very easy for the conventional methodologist to make. Herbert Blumer, once again, comments:

> Many critics charge that the authors of personal accounts can easily give free play to their imagination, choose what they want to say, hold back what they do not want to say, slant what they wish, say only what they happen to recall at the moment, in short to engage in both deliberate and unwilling deception. They argue, accordingly, that accounts yielded by human documents are not trustworthy. (Blumer, 1979: xxxiv)

The problem, however, is really being tackled from the wrong end: validity should come first, reliability second. There is no point in being very precise about nothing! If the subjective story is what the researcher is after, the life history approach becomes the most valid method – for reasons signposted at many points in this book. It simply will not do to classify, catalogue and standardize everything in advance, for this would be a distorted and hence invalid story. And yet I have my doubts that even validity is the issue here.

In what follows I want to go in search of validity in the life story – my main concern will lie with examining the possible sources of bias that inhibit the life history document from being valid. And yet in following this task, I want to show that a 'decontextualized' knowledge like this is very hard to support. In the end, this raises quite serious doubts about the so-called objectivity of much social science.

The sources of bias in life stories: a critical analysis

In social science research generally three domains of bias are traditionally recognized; those arising from the subject being interviewed, those arising from the researcher and those arising from the subject–researcher interaction. In the first domain, the *subject* may lie, cheat, present a false front or try to impress the interviewer in some way. Of particular importance may be the way in which the subject attempts to create a consistent and coherent story for the interviewer's benefit –

even going to the extent of rehearsing it prior to the interview. It is indeed odd how, sometimes, respondents are able to repeat more or less in the same words a story told two months earlier – as if they had rehearsed and learnt a script. Of relevance here are all those features which psychologists have designated 'demand characteristics' (Orne, 1962) whereby the respondent enters the situation, tries to work out what the interviewer is getting at, and proceeds to answer in accord with this. And, most centrally, the subject may desire to please the researcher and gain positive evaluation (cf. Phillips, 1973: esp. ch. 3). The second domain is concerned with the *interviewer*. Most blatantly, the researcher may hold prejudices and assumptions which structure the questioning: a 'non-directive' interviewer might be accused of harbouring the desire to encourage a person to tell the more outrageous and problematic things in his or her life, thereby encouraging a distortion of the more sensational episodes. The researcher may also bring biases into the situation by virtue of his or her age, class, gender and general background – not to mention pre-existing theoretical orientation. Sometimes, too, issues of mood may influence the researcher, as Webb et al. say:

> Just as a spring scale becomes fatigued with use, reading 'heavier' a second time, an interviewer may also measure differently at different times. His [*sic*] skill may increase. He [*sic*] may be better able to establish rapport. He may have learned necessary vocabulary. He may loaf or become bored. He may have increasingly strong expectations of what a respondent 'means' and code differently with practice. Some errors relate to recording accuracy, while others are linked to the nature of the interviewer's interpretation of what transpired. Either way, there is always the risk that the interviewer will be a variable filter over time and experience. (Webb et al., 1966: 22)

Finally, of course, bias may creep in through the very interactional encounter itself: the setting may be too formal to encourage intimacy or too informal to encourage an adequate response. All the interactional strategies discussed by writers like Goffman (e.g. 1959) may well come into play here, and sometimes the life history interview may be seen as an elaborate dramaturgical presentation (cf. Denzin, 1978a: 123–33).

I have charted these three sources of bias in Box 7.1. They lead, I think, to a very important observation. A close examination of all bias in research could only be possible if researcher and informant were mechanical robots. To purge research of all these 'sources of bias' is to purge research of human life. It presumes a 'real' truth may be obtained once all these biases have been removed. Yet to do this, the ideal situation would involve a researcher without a face to give off feelings, a subject with clear and total knowledge unshaped by the situation, a neutral setting, and so forth. Any 'truth' found in such a disembodied, neutralized context would be a very odd one indeed. It is precisely through

BOX 7.1   A BRIEF CHECKLIST OF SOME DIMENSIONS OF 'BIAS'

Source One: The Life History Informant
Is misinformation (unintended) given?
Has there been evasion?
Is there evidence of direct lying and deception?
Is a 'front' being presented?
What may the informant 'take for granted' and hence not reveal?
How far is the informant 'pleasing you'?
How much has been forgotten?
How much may be self-deception?

Source Two: The Social Scientist–Researcher
Could any of the following be shaping the outcome?
(a)   Attributes of researcher: age, gender, class, race etc.
(b)   Demeanour of researcher: dress, speech, body language, etc.
(c)   Personality of researcher: anxiety, need for approval, hostility, warmth etc.
(d)   Attitudes of researcher: religion, politics, tolerance, general assumptions
(e)   Scientific role of researcher: theory held etc. (researcher expectancy)

Source Three: The Interaction
The joint act needs to be examined. Is bias coming from:
(a)   The physical setting – 'social space'?
(b)   The prior interaction?
(c)   Non-verbal communication?
(d)   Vocal behaviour?

these 'sources of bias' that a 'truth' comes to be assembled. The task of the researcher, therefore, is not to nullify these variables, but to be aware of, describe, publicly and suggest how these have assembled a specific 'truth'. It is just such accounting which lies at the heart of much ethnomethodology and allied critical work (cf. Ashmore, 1989; Cicourel, 1964; Silverman, 1973).

Validity checks   This said, I am certainly not arguing for an 'anything goes' perspective: quite the reverse. Knowing the constructed nature of social knowedge makes for a much greater caution in its interpretation and for much greater sensitivity to the kinds of checks that are possible. It may help to suggest some of these checks.

First, ask your subject to read the entire product and present an autocritique of it. Sometimes a comparison may be made with similar written sources. Reading biographies of other criminals, for instance, can throw up points of major divergence or similarity. Sutherland thoroughly documents his account of a thief with other 'biographies of thieves' and no noticeable discrepancies were found. (Though at least one commentator is suspicious of this – see Snodgrass, 1973: 15.)

Compare your story with official records. If the subject provides 'factual data' that are likely to have been recorded somewhere – births, deaths, marriages, divorces, imprisonment, operations, schools and so forth – it is possible to check up on the accuracy of the story. Shaw's delinquent boys were all matched up to the official records and where there were any inconsistencies they were pointed out to the boys. Nevertheless, official records are often unreliable (cf. Douglas, 1967). Indeed, in the case of Jane Fry, her transsexual case records were directly at odds with her own perspective (Bogdan, 1974). On the records Jane is sick and disordered; in her account she is not. Who is to be believed? This becomes an issue in the 'politics of perspective' – those at the bottom of the heap being less likely to have their voice heard or believed, those nearer the top, like psychiatrists, being more readily legitimated (cf. Becker, 1971). Cross-checking with physical data, therefore, is not always as straightforward as it may seem at first glance (cf. Frazier, 1976: 233–4).

Make comparisons with other informants, either interviewing those in similar roles or else those who knew the subject well. Thus the stories of Frazier's black youth (Frazier, 1967) were checked through interviews with parents, and Jackson writes of Sam the Thief:

> Most of what he says is true. I have checked out what I could by talking with other thieves who knew him on the streets and with convicts who knew him in prison, and by spending considerable time with him in both prison and the free world. [It] was read by a number of consultants . . . a Texas warder, lawyers . . . (Jackson, 1972: 16)

The overarching problem in all this is to know what the goals of the research are. In oral history the aim may be to gain information about the past; in a psychological life story, to gain information about a person's development; and in a sociological life history, to find insights into the workings of a culture. The goal of the life history analysis will dramatically affect issues of validity. For instance, the oral historian's goal – of recapturing the past – is altogether more ambitious than the sociologist's goal, who is in a sense merely concerned with getting at the way a person sees his or her life history at the moment of the interview. For the oral historian the task is to dig up the truth of fifty or sixty years ago, and the validity checks required here are enormous since all kinds of more objective materials for that historical era need to be gathered for corroboration. In contrast, for the sociologist the account becomes 'a vocabulary of motive' – a set of linguistic devices drawn from the existing wider culture which can be used both to re-interpret the past, to fashion the present and to anticipate the future (cf. Mills, 1940). The linguistic constructs that people make about their lives at a given point in time are of interest sociologically in themselves. They can throw light on wider issues of ideology, context and language and they have become much studied by both sociologists of knowledge, motivational theorists and deviancy sociologists (cf. Marshall, 1981). However, these 'accounts' are no more than that. This indeed is precisely what Thomas recognized when challenged with the criticism that Wladek's story was not true; what is of interest, he remarked, was that it was true for him at that moment. It captured that person's subjective reality, his definition of the situation; this area should be a legitimate part of sociological investigation, and the personal document is the best tool for getting at it.

Reading the story: logic and theory in life story work

Many life stories – probably most – can stand on their own as 'good stories': we can learn from understanding the voice of a life. The social scientist may choose to 'frame' the story a little with a few observations and comments, but attempts to link this up to systematic theorizing or methodological logics are rare. 'Stanley', 'Wladek', 'Jane Fry' and 'Rigoberta Menchú' all just 'tell their story'.

Nevertheless, social science probably proceeds best through some sense of cumulative, if partial, generalization – building up ideas and concepts into layers of theory and understanding. An optimistic view of postmodern theory might shun the global and the grand, but it certainly does not shun the notion of theory. Theories are simply ways of piecing the world together; though they can come in many forms (grand, middle range, grounded; inductive, deductive, abductive; operational, propositional, systematic, formal) and have many purposes (explanatory, sensitizing, connecting). But always they work to provide a link between the very specific and particular and the more abstract and general. Life stories are nearly always geared to the more specific and particular and theory gives them a bridge to wider concerns. It can help the story find a place in the wider world.

Theoretically, we can use life stories in at least three ways:

1   to take a story to challenge some overly general theory;
2   to take a story to illustrate or illuminate some wider theory;
3   to take a story as a way of building up some wider sense of theory.

1 Challenging theory through the negative case   Life histories and personal documents provide rich data which can be used to cast doubt on received theories and to throw light on future directions for theoretical research. As Becker comments, 'it can be a negative case that forces us to decide a proposed theory is inadequate' (Becker, 1966: xi). Dukes goes so far as to suggest that while individual case studies are very limited in establishing generalizations, 'an N of 1 when the evidence is "negative", is as useful as an N of 1,000 in rejecting an asserted or assumed universal relationship' (1965: 77). If the search is on for falsification, then a case study may be just as good as a massive survey, although in practice it would be only an extremist who would reject a theory on the basis of one refuting case. It is much more likely that it would lead to either a revision of the theory (as in analytic induction) or a return to larger samples for probabilistic statements.

Charles Frazier's (1976) study *Theoretical Approaches to Deviance* puts this approach to use. He starts his study by outlining three of the dominant approaches to deviance – socialization theories, labelling theories and control theories – which are then teased through fifty 'self-perceived life histories' gathered through interviews with inmates from state prisons in Florida and Illinois. In some ways, Frazier comes closer to large-scale interviewing than providing deep life histories: but the numbers are in a sense immaterial here – what matters is the matching of a life with a theory. For the study is primarily concerned with showing the fit, lack of fit and mixture that the theories displayed when matched against concrete lives – Hubert, Don, Albert, Ken. The interviewees were not directed into theories but were allowed to free float around six broad topics – memorable events, relations with others, self-conceptions, deviant acts, perceptions and reactions of others and appraisals of life circumstances – and the 'story' of the emergent 'deviance', its patterning and change is then analysed through the contrasting theories. As Frazier comments:

> The procedure involves looking at the life-history case not only to see that it is consistent with hypotheses derived from the theory under consideration, but also to see whether anything else that is important in the case fits the theory or not. In other words, the life history researcher should inquire as to whether what is supposed to be present and operating in the cases is there in fact, and whether all that is present and operating causally in the development of behaviour patterns can be explained by the theory. If something is at work in the development of criminal or delinquent behaviour patterns that is outside the explanatory range of the test theory, or is not consistent with it, the theory is less than completely reliable and must be considered generally less credible. (Frazier, 1976: 136)

He sees his approach as following in the tradition of Lindesmith who, after Znaniecki, championed the use of analytic induction in his study *Opiate Addiction* (1947) (later to be emulated in the more famous study of marijuana use by Howard Becker, *Outsiders*, 1963). This basic logic of qualitative research will be discussed later: it sees the need to scrutinize a case in detail to modify the general theory to fit it, and then for a rigorous pursuit of further cases to be examined and subsequently to generate theoretical modification. Hence it both generates and tests theory. Out of such an approach it is possible for life history research to return to the search for universals and not simply to examine the negative, falsifying case. (For a critique of this approach, though, see Turner, 1953, in Denzin, 1970.)

2 Illustrating theory 'It would', says Allport, 'be a pedant indeed who would prefer the collections of facts and strings of abstractions that psychology offers to the vivid portraits presented by gifted writers' (Allport, 1965: 158), and amongst these gifted writers he includes Mrs Jenny Masterson, whose letters have been introduced in Chapter 3. These letters, and many other personal documents, certainly tell a rich and rewarding story to the reader but left in their original 'raw' state they demand interpretive work from the social scientist. Thus (and this is probably the most frequent function of theory in life documents) when the story is told, the social scientist sets forth with his or her theories, speculating on their relevance, comparing rival accounts, filtering the data through concepts and hypotheses that science has constructed. Jenny's letters, for example, are sifted through three psychological approaches; the existential which takes seriously her own worldview – 'its major motifs and themes' – the structural dynamic, which looks behind this to identify 'the traits and dispositions that motivate her', and the depth analysis which focuses upon the unconscious source of motivation in childhood and family. The reader is then led to 'consider the arguments, weigh them and render his [*sic*] own verdict' (1965: 211). Maybe, speculates Allport, from such eclecticism 'a true synthesis of theories' may be derived. A similar goal is to be found in Rettig's commentary upon *Manny: a Criminal Addict* (Rettig et al., 1977). This rich first person account shows us a Puerto Rican lad's entry into his 'ganging days' in the Bronx, the graduation into more organized hustling and crime ('In my head I thought I was a big time gangster'), the drift to heroin mainlining and onwards through Sing Sing Prison, Synanon and the California Rehabilitation Center: a life of crime, hustling, dope and 'connections'. The story is told, and the reader is taken on a lightning tour of deviancy theorization: Merton is evoked to explain Manny's 'socially obstructed goal attainments' (1977: 207); 'Manny's self-report data supports the central assumption of Sutherland and Cressey's theory' (p. 208); and the structural-functional and sequential development accounts of prison life are compared through Manny's experience, with the latter being found to be more adequate (p. 216). Hence, the story comes to serve as a prop in illustrating the relevance of a wide range of deviancy theorizing and to make steps towards 'an integrated theoretical perspective in the final chapter'. The authors conclude:

We will advance the notion that the broad, general run of street criminal careers similar to his can best be understood by referring to theories of social strain, differential opportunity, and institutional labelling processes rather than by casting them within a pathological frame of reference. (Rettig et al., 1977: 239)

Here, then, as so frequently, theory plays a multiple role: illustrative purposes are pushed to a more general theory.

3 Building theory from life stories: classical logics of research   Life stories may be seen as embodying ideas for later-to-be-formulated theories. The life history here provides a whiff of theory: it provokes, suggests, anticipates – but it does not formulate. Reading the following quote from Stanley, a delinquent (Shaw, 1966) in the late 1920s, anticipates the subsequent more formal development of 'the labelling theory of deviance':

> The cell was bare, hard and drab. As I sat on my bunk thinking, a great wave of feeling shook me, which I shall always remember because of the great impression it made on me. There, *for the first time in my life, I realized that I was a criminal.* Before, I had been just a mischievous lad, a poor city waif, a petty thief, a habitual runaway; but now, as I sat in my cell of stone and iron, dressed in a grey uniform, with my head shaved, small skull cap, like all the other hardened criminals around me, some strange feeling came over me. *Never before had I realized that I was a criminal. I really became one as I sat there and brooded. At first I was almost afraid of myself, ebbing like a stranger to my own self.* (Shaw, 1966: emphasis added)

It was only a few years after this that the first explicit formulation of labelling theory was made by Tannenbaum in his *Crime and the Community* (1938) and some forty years later it was something of an orthodoxy (cf. Plummer, 1979). Now I am obviously not suggesting that Stanley 'generated' labelling theory – only that life histories can often provoke, suggest and anticipate later theorizations.

Sutherland's work on *The Professional Thief* (1937) provides another illustration. Quite early in his career Sutherland gathered the case materials from Chic Conwell, certainly well before he had developed the theories with which he later became identified – differential association, social disorganization and 'white collar crime'. Now although these *concepts* are nowhere to be found in Conwell's story, a close reading will show the ideas to be firmly present. At base, crime is an ordinary, learned phenomenon. It could well be that the story of Chic Conwell was instrumental in later generating the more full-blown theoretical accounts (cf. Schuessler, 1973; Snodgrass, 1973; Vasoli and Terzola, 1974).

These are very general and unsystematic ways of building theories. But there have been attempts to make this process much more rigorous by developing explicit logics to deal with it. The three most frequently discussed are (a) Znaniecki's analytic induction, (b) Glaser and Strauss's grounded theory and (c) Sartre's 'progressive–regressive method'. While each one could be used with life history research, in practice this has been rare. I will simply suggest the value of each briefly.

Analytic induction was introduced to sociology by Florian Znaniecki (although not used by him; 1934: ch. VI), in contrast to enumerative induction (whereby statistical generalizations are made from a limited, but known, sample of cases). In most respects analytic induction is the logic most suited to case studies and life histories because it is quite happy, initially, not to have pre-existing formulations or large samples. Rather, it proceeds from scrutiny of one case to produce a low-level generalization, which then starts to define and characterize a given phenomenon. As Znaniecki says, 'In analytic induction certain particular objects are determined by intensive study, and the problem is to define the logical classes which they represent . . . [it] abstracts from the given concrete case characters that are essential to it, and generalizes them, presuming that in so far as they are essential, they must be similar in many cases' (1934: 249–51).

The method has been defined by Peter Manning as 'a non-experimental, qualitative sociological method which employs an exhaustive examination of cases in order to prove universal, causal generalizations' (Manning, 1982). From such a definition, the affinity between analytic induction and case study methods should be apparent. Typical examples are Lindesmith's work on opiate addiction (Lindesmith, 1947), Becker's work on marijuana smokers (Becker, 1963) and Cressey's work on embezzlement (Cressey, 1953). Yet none of these deals with one case alone; they all deal with many. Nevertheless, the method proceeds by the intensive inspection of one case out of which a definition of the field to be investigated and a tentative explanation of it is derived; from this the procedure is to examine another case in great detail, and this may involve a possible reformulation of both definition and explanation to create a new generalization which holds for both cases; a third case will then be inspected and likewise modified so that the statements made about it also hold for the preceding two cases. Slowly a statement is built up which is applicable to a number of cases and which constitutes a generalization. More specifically, Cressey describes the research procedures as follows:

> The complete methodological procedure, then, has essentially the following steps. First, a rough definition of the phenomenon to be explained is formulated. Second, a hypothetical explanation of that phenomenon is formulated. Third, one case is studied in the light of the hypothesis with the object of determining whether the hypothesis fits the facts in that case. Fourth, if the hypothesis does not fit the facts, either the hypothesis is reformulated or the phenomenon to be explained is redefined so that the case is excluded. This definition must be more precise than the first one. Fifth, practical certainty

may be obtained after a small number of cases have been examined, but the discovery by the investigator or any other investigator of a single negative case disproves the explanation and requires a reformulation. Sixth, this procedure of examining cases, re-defining the phenomena and reformulating the hypothesis is continued until a universal relationship is established, each negative case calling for a redefinition or a reformulation. Seventh, for purposes of proof, cases outside the area circumscribed by the definition are examined to determine whether or not the final hypothesis applies to them. This step is in keeping with the observation that scientific generalizations consist of descriptions of conditions which are always present when the phenomenon is present but which are never present when the phenomenon [is] absent. (Cressey, 1953: 16)

Grounded theory was introduced by Glaser and Strauss in 1967 in their book *The Discovery of Grounded Theory* (Glaser and Strauss, 1967b). It is by far the most popular strategy and has been developed enormously over the past thirty years by many practitioners. Its concern is to move around a chosen empirical field sampling items that emerge as theoretically relevant until 'a dense' analysis is completed. The goal is to produce theories out of the data rather than from some *ad hoc* prior conceptualization; it involves an intimate, first hand acquaintance with the empirical world. Such a familiarity, however, is nevertheless rigorously ordered: the researcher moves from one particular sampling source to another according to theoretically relevant criteria that have evolved in the previous source. It hence involves both 'theoretical sampling' and 'constant comparison' and such strategies may not always be feasible in the execution of life history research. Thus, where a life history means a long examination of one case, it would not usually permit making comparisons or to sample adequately (except, perhaps, within the one life). On the other hand, if an examination occurred of personal documents such as letters, photographs, diaries, then the strategy may work very well. Nevertheless, although the grounded theory strategy does not of itself immediately facilitate life history research, Glaser and Strauss do believe that the case history study may be of value in bringing out constant comparisons: at the end of their study of Mrs Abel, a dying cancer patient mentioned in Chapter 4, they write:

> To achieve . . . theoretical integration he [the researcher] can sample theoretically for his case histories. This means that if he has a case history, and a theory to explain and interpret it then he can decide – on theoretical grounds – about other possible case histories that would provide good contrasts and comparisons. For example, our case history of Mrs. Abel, a hospital dying trajectory, might well be compared to a recovering trajectory in a tuberculosis hospital: thus we will be comparing two kinds of hospital careers. The resulting comparative analysis is different from that used in case studies for description, verification or generation. In the case studies, one analyses similarities and differences to establish empirical generalizations and variations and to verify and generate theory. (Strauss and Glaser, 1977: 184)

The progressive–regressive method. A third 'logic' has been introduced by Jean-Paul Sartre (1905–80). In his three-volume work *The Family Idiot* (1981, 1987, 1989), he poses a problem (with which we became familiar in Chapter 1), of how to reconcile universal and singular within social science method. He asks:

> What . . . can we know about man? For a man is never an individual: it would be more fitting to call him a universal singular. Summed up and for this reason universalized by his epoch, he in turn resumes it by reproducing himself in its singularity. Universal by the singular universality of human history, singular by the universalising singularity of his projects, he requires simultaneously examination from both ends. We must find an appropriate method.

What could such a method be that traverses this singularity and universality? In his *Search for a Method* (1963), he develops the idea of the 'progressive–regressive method'. Put quite simply (something Sartre was never famed for doing!), this method is a way of reading a life through moving both backwards (to sources and conditions in class, race, gender, emotion etc.) and forwards (to pragmatics and consequences) from a key event in a person's life – linking all this to wider issues of history and culture throughout. It is a method of 'totalization', trying to see ways through the whole life by moving through it and connecting to wider issues.

R.W. Connell's study of *Masculinities* (1995) attempts to use Sartre's method of life history analysis, and is very concerned to rebut the notion that studying lives is necessarily an individualistic preoccupation. On the contrary, he suggests that 'life history method always concerns the making of social life through time. It is literally history' and for him it can bridge the personal and the cultural/historical, seeing the life story as a set of bridging practices. In this study he selects four clusters of (Australian) men (numbering 36), whom he senses as being situated in society at key 'crisis tendencies' around being a man. Thus he looks at small groups of young working class men who are without jobs, at small groups of gay men who are concerned with their gay/male identity, at others who are part of a 'green' environmental movement – heterosexual but 'soft' men; and a fourth group of men who could be seen as part of the new middle class. All these men are potentially experiencing some worries over the construction of their 'masculinities'. And Connell is involved with taking their life stories (through focused interviews and strategic sampling), and then moving through them to grasp their lives and how they are handling the crisis of masculinities. He tries to get 'the narrative sequence of events', a structural analysis of gender relations; and a systematic analysis 'tracing the making and unmaking of masculinity' (Connell, 1995: 89–91). After this, the groups as a whole were reanalysed – taking on board the singular narrative with the more collective and historical experiences. What this study tries to show is the use of life histories placed within a broader historical and theoretical frame of gender relations being enacted and worked through at a major point of crisis. Here, life story, social structure, narrative and theory are all at work together. It is the 'progressive–regressive method' at work.

Conclusion: the myth and reality of research

The gathering of personal documents in social science is usually a long and complicated process, and only a few of the issues involved have been raised in the past two chapters – preparing, gathering, storing, analysing and theorizing. Curiously, very few researchers have ever written about the 'doing' of life histories – probably because to do so is to give an order and a protocol to work that is thoroughly disorderly! I may therefore have performed a disservice to the method in this chapter.

Indeed, although I have tried over the past two chapters to raise many important 'strategies' around 'life document' research, at many places the reader may have sensed my doubts. I have been trying to lay it all out in some order – yet I talk of the 'lie of chronological research'. I have been suggesting protocols for interviews – yet I quote Studs Terkel saying 'there are no rules'. I talk about representativeness, but run sharply away from the conventional meanings of that term and argue to return it to the idea of what it 'represents'. I discuss validity, only to produce 'a continuum of constructions' which tells me that validity is more or less impossible. All in all, I do not think I have been very persuasive.

In the chapters that follow I hope you will see why. Many of the problems with the life story approach, in its simpler forms anyway, are about to be raised. I plan to look at narrative issues, ethical and moral issues, personal issues as well as issues of truth. At the start of the twenty-first century, doing this kind of social science research must be seen as involving a great deal of reflexivity, and avoiding overly sharp protocols. I am not even convinced that much research needs huge amounts of funding – other than to keep people in jobs. What is required is more thinking about research – what it represents and means. And it is along this path that the rest of the book now moves.

Guide to further reading

Practical tips on **organizing and managing data** abound in C. Wright Mills's classic 'On intellectual craftsmanship', an appendix in his *The Sociological Imagination* (originally published in 1959). On this see also Anselm Strauss, *Qualitative Analysis for Social Scientists* (1987), a formal approach by A. Michael Huberman and Matthew Miles, 'Data managament and analysis methods' (1994) in Denzin and Lincoln's edited

Handbook of Qualitative Research (1994: 428–44), as well as their fuller account in *Qualitative Data Analysis* (2nd edn, 1994). Charlotte Aull Davies in *Reflexive Ethnography* (1999: ch. 10), also includes a discussion on 'using computers' for analysis (see pp. 203–12). For fuller discussions of software and the new qualitative computing analysis, one of the earliest discussions was Nigel Fielding and Raymond Lee's *Using Computers in Qualitative Research* (1991), and now the literature on this is both specialist and vast. Some discussions of CD-Roms can be found in Peter Read, 'Presenting voices in different media: print, radio and CD Rom' (1994), reproduced in Perks and Thompson's *The Oral History Reader* (1998: 414–20). The journal *Computers and Humanities* (Kluwer Academic), which was established in 1966, regularly discusses computer applications to the humanities, including the CD-Rom formatting of literary texts. See also Mann and Stewart's *Internet Communication and Qualitative Research: A Handbook for Researching Online* (2000).

On keeping **records and fieldnotes**, see John and Lyn Lofland's *Analyzing Social Settings* (3rd edn, 1995), Robert Emerson et al.'s *Writing Ethnographic Fieldnotes* (1995) and Roger Sanjek's edited *Fieldnotes: the Making of Anthropology* (1990). This last volume contains many discussions of the experience of keeping fieldnotes and the problems inherent in this.

On **problems of analysis**, the idea of a sensitizing concept is fully discussed in Will C. van den Hoonaard's *Working with Sensitizing Concepts: Analytical Field Research* (1997). On the logic of analytic induction, see W.S. Robinson 'The logical structure of analytic induction', *American Sociological Review*, 16: 812–18 (1951), and Peter Manning, 'Analytic induction', in R. Smith and P. Manning, *Qualitative Methods* (1982) and reproduced in Ken Plummer's *Symbolic Interactionism*, Volume 2 (1991: 401–30. For a useful more recent discussion of grounded theory, see Anselm Strauss and Juliet Corbin's 'Grounded Theory Methodology: An Overview' (1994), as well as their book *Basics of Qualitative Research* (2nd edn, 1998).

Standard discussions of 'validity and reliability' are featured in Alan Bryman and Robert G. Burgess (eds), *Analyzing Qualitative Data* (1994), Ian Dey, *Qualitative Data Analysis: A User Friendly Guide for Social Scientists* (1993), David Silverman's *Interpreting Qualitative Data: Methods for Analyzing Talk, Text and Interaction* (1993) and his *Doing Qualitative Research* (2000); as well as the influential work of Anselm Strauss – in *Qualitative Analysis for Social Scientists* (1987) and (with Juliet Corbin) *Basics of Qualitative Research* (2nd edn, 1998). See also David L. Altheide, *Qualitative Media Analysis* (1996), and Amanda Coffey and Paul Atkinson, *Making Sense of Qualitative Data: Complementary Research Strategies* (1996).

8   Writing Life Stories

The Children of Sanchez is not a literary work, but it renders a mass of literary works redundant. Why write a novel on its characters or their milieu? They tell us much more by themselves, with a much greater self-understanding and eloquence.

(Jean-Paul Sartre, 1970)

The fully mature ethnography requires a reflexive awareness of its own writing, the possibilities and limits of its own language, and a principled exploration of its own modes of representation. Not only do we need to cultivate a self-conscious construction of ethnographic texts, but also a readiness to read texts from a more 'literary critical' perspective. Sociologists and their students must cultivate the discipline of reading their own and others' arguments for their stylistic and rhetorical properties.

(Atkinson, 1990: 180)

How to present a life? Most of the time it seems to be through writing, and this is what the next two chapters look at: the writing of a life story and its link to narrative. Later, I will suggest that there are many other ways of 'presenting a life' that do not necessarily stay with the written word – from drama to video diaries – and will raise again the idea that a changing social science might render itself more accessible, even populist, if it would think wisely about a wider array of ways of 'presenting itself' to different audiences. But I will start with the classic case: of writing.

The problem of writing

Writing is the dark secret of social science. A blank page, so full of possibilities, so rarely discussed – at least until recently. While many research manuals pile up their instructions on how to do research – to interview, to experiment, to sample, to data analyse – typically very little is said about how 'findings' get communicated to an audience. It is assumed. Yet communication lies at the heart of all social science: it is something which every social scientist has to do. From fledgling undergraduates writing a term paper or 'doing a project' to doctoral candidates writing up their thesis; from the conference paper to the formal scholarly journal article; from the 'scientific text' to the myriad of writings that appear in books: every social scientist has to write! It is the *sine qua non* of social science. And yet it is also a mystery: just how does the text, and in this case the life story as text, appear?

In the world of objectivist, positivist social science, writing generally parodies the style of the physical sciences; the tables, the findings, the tested hypotheses, simply speak for themselves and the exercise is simply one of *presenting* not *writing* 'the findings'. The style here is largely that of the external privileged reporter merely reporting what has been found. It is seen to be the vehicle which 'traps' the findings or the arguments of the study: writing displays reality. It is a means to an end. Any discussions about 'how to do it' can hence be relegated to mere technical problems of technique – syntax, grammar and of 'house style': what are the rules for presenting a thesis in a particular university, the 'house rules' that guide selection for a particular journal or book publishing company? Writing here is a technical matter which enables the writing to mirror or reflect reality.

Joseph Gusfield was one of the first to suggest that 'scientific writing' is itself a form of rhetorical work – stuffed full of artifice, convention and literary devices that seek to persuade the reader. Referring to a wide range of scientific papers on the 'drinking–driving' problem, he shows how a seemingly neutral and dispassionate language may indeed be able to evoke a 'whole bucketful of emotions – comic, tragic, pathetic' (Gusfield, 1976: 30). Even the scientific conventions can have implicit persuasive consequences. Yet such writing must be seen to adopt these conventions, for without them, readers will hardly start to take them seriously as science. For that is what science has to look like to persuade! And a consequence of this mode of writing is to render most such texts 'unreadable' to all but the smallest of like-minded *cognoscenti*. Thus a central characteristic of science writing (but also social science) is that it is illiterate, ugly and stark – not to mention heavily overburdened with jargon and pretentious language! It is not really meant to be read at all. Because so little concern is given to 'writing social science', the style of much of it readily becomes the butt of many attacks and jokes. Indeed, one of the leading British ethnographers, Paul Atkinson, has claimed, in an important review of the writing behind a large number of ethnographic fieldwork studies, that atrociously dull writing characterizes much social science: texts appear that are 'by any criteria, inept and unreadable'. Talking of sociologists overall, he hints that many seem 'almost to revel in producing repellent texts' (Atkinson, 1990: 11). Their writing is distant, undecipherable and dull. As the writer Edmund Wilson said long ago:

> As for my experience with articles by experts in anthropology and sociology, it has led me to conclude that the requirement in my ideal university, of having the papers in every department passed by a professor of English, might result

in revolutionizing these subjects – if indeed the second of them survived at all.
(Wilson, 1956: 164)

There are many exceptions to this, of course. A number of scientists –
from Richard Dawkins to Stephen Jay Gould – write very elegantly for a
broader audience and their works sometimes become best-sellers.
Likewise, many of the classics of social science are just that because their
authors knew how to write: Freud's work, for instance, is viewed by
some as primarily 'literature'. And Sartre can say of Oscar Lewis's *The
Children of Sanchez* that whilst it 'is not a literary work, . . . it renders a
mass of literary works redundant. Why write a novel on its characters or
their milieu? They tell us much more by themselves, with a much greater
self-understanding and eloquence' (1970: 23). But in the main, these are
the exceptions. Little premium has been placed on 'good writing' in the
social sciences. Look at almost any academic journal to verify this!
    There are some signs this is changing. A number of books have started
to appear which aim to give the student or social scientist some sense of
what is involved in good writing – amongst them Howard Becker's
Writing for Social Scientists (1986), Harry F. Wolcott's *Writing Up
Qualitative Research* (1990), and Karen Golden-Biddle and Karen Locke's
Composing Qualitative Research (1997). They discuss the experiences of
people writing, the problems they face and provide concrete tips on how
to improve writing style. Often the suggestions are unremarkable – they
suggest such things as practising to write regularly; seeing writing not
simply as a means to an end but as an integral part of communication
work, redrafting. They suggest the need for regular daily writing,
revising and re-writing. And they recommend starting to write the day
you start your research – not leaving it all to the end. At the heart of
writing is an activity with a purpose, not something that is a mere
medium. As Harry Wolcott says:

> You have your purpose well in mind when you can draft a critical, clear and
> concise sentence that begins '*The purpose of this study is* . . .'. Although
> structurally this is a most uninteresting beginning, I know of no better way to
> help academic writers find, declare and maintain a focus than to have this
> sentence up front not only in their minds but in their manuscripts. (Wolcott,
> 1990: 16)

Of course, you do not have to keep this opening line – indeed in your
final revisions it should almost certainly go and a more interesting 'catch'
as an opener be introduced. But this will keep you on track whilst you
are writing. Indeed, pin it up over your desk and keep going back to it . . .
if you cannot do this, maybe you do not know what you're doing!
    Now this new 'practical literature' can be very helpful for the novice in
writing up life stories and humanistsic research: at the very least it makes
people think about writing skills. But during the 1980s there was another

development which took Gusfield's issues further and brought a concern with 'writing strategies' to the fore – a move identified especially with the work of anthropologists George Marcus and Clifford Geertz as well as some sociologists like Laurel Richardson, Susan Krieger and Norman Denzin. These new writers have a lot to say that will help in the writing of lives.

Writing strategies, writing cultures, writing lives

This recent turn to self-conscious concern about *the social acts of writing* has led to a clear demarcation between writing as a *reflection* of research to writing as *formative* – as shaping the very knowledge (or life narrative) we are trying to present. Writing no longer 'merely' captures reality, it helps 'construct' it. From many different theoretical persuasions – the sociology of knowledge, constructivist psychology, discourse theory, narratology and the like – social science writings come to be seen as discourses open to their own investigations. There is a 'crisis of representation' and language can no longer be assumed as a simple transparent display of meaning. Instead, all writing may be seen as a 'gloss' (in ethnomethods), as a speech act, as a discourse, as rhetoric, as narrative, as a social construction. Furthermore, such writing is bound up with self, power and values. As Laurel Richardson remarks: 'No textual staging is ever innocent. We are always inscribing values in our writing. It is unavoidable' (Richardson, 1990: 12). There is a turn to understand the very act of writing: to grasping the ways in which lives and realities are assembled through the texts which present them. And with this comes a strong awareness of the *conditions that shape textuality*. We can see whether texts are 'readerly' (allowing the reader to make easy sense of the text) or 'writerly (allowing the writer a much freer play in the construction of his or her text (cf. Atkinson, 1992, after Barthes). In a major summary of this growing concern, James Clifford comments about the writing of one major social science form: ethnography.

> Ethnographic writing is determined in at least six ways: (1) contextually (it draws from and creates meaningful social milieux); (2) rhetorically (it uses and is used by expressive conventions); (3) institutionally (one writes within, and against, specific traditions, disciplines, audiences); (4) generically (an ethnography is usually distinguishable from a novel or a travel account); (5) politically (the authority to present cultural realities is uniquely shared and at times contested); (6) historically (all the above conventions and constraints are changing). These determinations govern the inscription of coherent ethnographic fictions. (Clifford and Marcus, 1986: 6)

This is not true only of ethnographic enquiry, but all enquiry. The simplest way of grasping this is to take any finished 'text' like a book, essay or life story, hold it in your hands, look at it, and *ponder: just how did this writing come to get there with those words in that form. What were the social conditions that enabled this text to be organized in this way? How might a self and a voice have entered/composed this text?* Once asked like this, I find a string of questions can be sensed which help guide the social acts of writing. Amongst these are:

1   Questions of audience: *Who are to be the readers of these writings? Who is to become the significant other of the text and how might they read it?* Whenever writing takes place, somebody is an implied reader: be it a teacher, a colleague, a public or the self. *Who* it is written for will shape *what* is written.

2   Questions of intent: *What is the purpose behind this writing? Why write? What is your point in putting the word on paper?* There are many motivations for writing: gaining good grades for an essay, getting publications for academic tenure or promotion, seeking to educate and inform, to 'change the world', to make money and achieve 'glittering prizes', to attain posterity.

3   Questions of genre: *What social science conventions are to be drawn upon in writing the text? What helps it to be recognised as one mode of writing rather than another?* Thus an article for a psychology journal may bring different conventions of presentation from one for economics, history, cultural studies or mass marketing. Language, referencing, length, 'evidence', presentational styles will all differ.

4   Questions of intrusion, interpretation and voice: *How much of the 'data', 'argument', or 'theory' belongs to you – and how much of it belongs to others? Just how much does the voice of the author intrude upon the voice of the speaker, subjects, researched? How does the writer present – or not present – themselves as an authority? How does the 'self' of the author enter – or not enter – the text? What can or should be edited out and are there guides for selection?* This raises issue about the links between a writer and the subject, and in particular about how much voice is to be given to the subject.

5   Questions of intertextuality: *How does this text use other texts? Indeed, what other texts help shape the texts being created? What traditions, titles, references, quotations, styles are borrowed in the assembling of a new text? What other 'texts' get into your text?* Most texts borrow from others. If it goes too far, it is called plagiarism. But pure texts that reference nobody else and make allusions to no other traditions are usually not taken seriously academically. Social scientists are 'textual poachers'. But what are the rules for this poaching?

6   Questions of narrative: *What narrative conventions are drawn upon? Who is telling, what is the plot, where does it happen, when does it happen, and why does it happen?* All writing may be seen to assume a narrative form, and it may fit into well identifed patterns. There may be basic social science narrative structures that need to be located. One analyst, for instance, has been able to reduce all of Freud's work to

two basic narrative structures: the child as beast needing taming, and the mind working as a machine with delicate checks and balances (Schafer, 1981 in Mitchell, 1992: 27–8).

7 Questions of rhetoric, stylistics and poetics: *What strategies are used to 'persuade' the reader of arguments? How might writing style shift understanding? What is the aesthetic dimension of writing?* Poetics in social science writing is not a frill or a luxury. More and more it is recognized that social science writing is itself a rhetoric, which displays argumentation (Billig, 1987; Brown, 1977; Willard, 1983).

8 Questions of mechanics: *Just how does one write? How does one get down to the praticalities of writing etc.?* These are the sorts of questions I was posing earlier through the work of Becker and Wolcott.

9 Questions of domain assumptions: *What is 'taken for granted' before writing? What is smuggled into the text unwittingly from the wider culture? Do such assumptions need to be rethought at all?* For behind all writing is a structure of logics and coherence, and to be clear what this is can add greatly to a sharper argument and a more critical approach. Dominant traditions of western writing – patriarchal writing, colonizing writing, heterosexist writing – are made apparent and alternatives sought (cf. Said, 1985; Sedgwick, 1990).

10 Questions of medium: *In what media will the work be presented, and what rules might regulate the production of knowledge within such media? What basic form will the writing take?* There are, for instance, different rules for essays, reports, journal articles, books: often there are house rules which prescribe modes of presentation, even guidelines on how to write. But more than this, maybe media other than writing are to be used – the visual or the performative, for instance. And if so, *what are these other presentational technologies and what are the rules which guide how work should be produced for them?*

For the rest of this chapter and the next, my broad concern is to sense ways of writing life histories (and by implication this may also say something about ways of 'reading' such stories). What follows is a short glimpsing of some of the new issues of communication emerging in the social sciences, all of which start to make for a very different looking social science. My interest does not lie in the fact that many people are now writing like this: generally they are not, though I hope more will do so in the future. Rather my concern is to highlight these new modes of writing in order to throw light upon what is conventionally assumed in writing practices. Understanding these 'new worlds of writing' helps us to critically rethink some of our older and tired academic practices. As Laurel Richardson says: 'Deconstructing traditional writing practices is a way of making writers more conscious of writing conventions' (Richardson, 1998: 93). In turn, this may not only sharpen our writing: it may also deepen our understanding of what we are trying to know. Robert Atkinson comments:

The fully mature ethnography requires a reflexive awareness of its own writing, the possibilities and limits of its own language, and a principled exploration of its own modes of representation. Not only do we need to cultivate a self-conscious construction of ethnographic texts, but also a readiness to read texts from a more 'literary critical' perspective. Sociologists and their students must cultivate the discipline of reading their own and others' arguments for their stylistic and rhetorical properties. (1998: 180)

In search of an audience

One of the first issues in this task is to ask: *For whom do we write?* Audience matters, because it starts to shape the way we write. The same message would probably be written differently if it was written for a lecturer giving grades, for a newspaper column, for a close but 'non-social science' friend, or for an academic publication. Writing a life history for a Master's degree, or for a 'family tree' album will lead to very different styles. (And all this is closely linked to genre – for example whether to make the life history more like fiction, or a scholarly biography.) In academic work, by and large, there is a known audience for the writing: and to write in the wrong genre, use the wrong jargon, even using the wrong theories, is to be without an audience – or worse, to be with a very angry audience! Scholars charmed by Foucault would not get a good reception at a conference organized by sociobiologists or rational-choice theorists! The rules of the game are framed through and with your audience, and 'writing' must always be wary of this. Once this is clear, it becomes apparent that a deep irony of much social science writing is that it rarely writes for the people of whom it speaks! As one commentator on Bedouin women's stories remarks: 'In a sad way the women whose stories I retell here are not the audience of this book. For the most part, the words I have fixed here are not the kinds of words they consider worthy of being written down' (Abu-Lughod, 1993: 36). And it is but a short step from this to the problem of exploitation that I address in Chapter 11.

More broadly, the audience of most social science writing is a special kind of academic, mainly western, middle class audience. Very little of the human sciences are really written with a popular audience in mind. Indeed, 'popularizers' are generally looked down upon as people who trivialize, oversimplify, and deal in clichés. There would almost seem to be a reward for not being 'popular': for avoiding the mass media, for using obscure language, for rendering the world even more complex than perhaps it is. Phrases like 'dumbing down', 'popularizers', or trivializers are often given to those who seek a wider audience, and a kind of academic elitism works to privilege the distanced academic. A system of informal control works to stop writers being accessible: they will be called 'mindless', 'journalists' and lacking in 'theoretical sophistication'. Such 'popular works' will not usually be taken seriously in matters of career promotion or evaluations, and will often work against the academic (The English Research Assessment Exercise – amongst its very many follies – does not even countenance 'popular writing' or 'textbooks'. There are no prizes for such work.) There is even a major strain of radical academic thought which prizes obscurity over clarity – 'clarity is a means of subjection, a quality of both official, taught language and of correct writing, two old mates of power: together they flow, together they flower, vertically to impose an order' (Trinh, 1989: 16–17). Yet all this really has to be very odd: for the human sciences concern humans – it speaks to their concerns, issues, worries. Why should it be written just for academics hiding in ivory towers? As George Ritzer (himself the author of several text books and the popularizer of the idea of *The McDonaldization of Society* (1995) wryly notes: 'Given the intrinsic interest of [sociology's] subject matters, it can only be assumed that sociologists have laboured long and hard to avoid attracting larger interest in their work' (in Wilson et al., 1998: 446).

Yet 'life stories' and 'documents of life' are usually, by their very nature, the very forms of knowledge that are more accessible, that can inform, stimulate and even – dare it be said – entertain! Television and press consistently recognize this – they know that a good place to start almost any news item is with a 'human interest' story – the real life story of a refugee, a person with AIDS (which gained its human face when actor Rock Hudson died), an earthquake tragedy is best analysed through the plights of particular 'victims/survivors'. Academics very rarely provide such material, or help in their analysis. Yet they could not only provide them: they could bring more critical, radically questioning positions to them. Why, I am often led to ask, do so many social scientists run away from the popular – and render so much of their work hidden, obscure, relatively 'useless' and often destined for the dustbins of history? All that work, all that publication, all those conferences: and all with so little pay-off!

Maybe there is now a strong case for courses, training and books which will address the need for a *popularization of social science*. Amongst the concerns to be discussed in a 'crash course' on such matters would be:

1 the ways of getting across a discipline's logic and approach – a way of thinking – to a wider audience;
2 the ways of reducing jargon and unnecessary words whilst still making a valid point;
3 the ways of getting across the complex nature of data and ideas whilst still being able to say something;
4 the ways of presenting material in sound bites for the media without rendering them trivial;
5 the ways of developing strategies for a much more assertive mode of presenting sociology to a public world;

6   the ways of understanding more about public culture and speaking
    and explaining the insecurity of disciplines that run away from the
    media and popular forms;
7   getting across insights into the complex natures of descriptions and
    writing within social science so that 'readers' are better able to
    critically assess the multifarious 'texts' they are confronting all the
    time.

Students of life stories and documents of life could play a major role in
this since such stories nearly always exhibit more accessible and popular
forms. They can easily become part of a more popular culture (cf. Allen,
1994).

Author intrusion, editing and interpretation

Another issue concerns how far the researcher-cum-writer should
'intrude' upon the gathered stories? Issues of editing and interpretation
are raised here. We have already seen (Chapter 6) that editing already
raises itself as an issue in transcribing tapes. Now we have the problem
of editing a text for the final writing. This is a big problem and a big
decision. Many life stories are so long that it is impossible to present
them in full detail. Often, many life stories have been gathered – too
many to publish in full. And often life stories are convoluted, rambling
affairs where there is a great deal of meandering chatter and stumbling.
Such stories couldn't really interest many 'readers'. So what to do?

   Some kind of editing will be needed. Staying close to the original
voice, words and texture, editors of life stories will probably first have to
eliminate any excess verbiage, change the names of all the individuals
appearing in the narrative, for purposes of confidentiality, and generally
'tidy up the text'. But it could go much further: the late North American
psychiatrist Robert J. Stoller, in the introduction to *Splitting*, which looks
at transgendered and fetishist lives, suggests some rules that have
governed his own editing:

> First, if there are multiple discussions of the same material usually only one is
> used. Second, stumbling and broken speech is eliminated where it adds no
> substance. Third, to make the material more readable remarks made perhaps
> minutes apart and with other sentences intervening are at times run together
> as if spoken that way . . . Fourth, almost invariably the quotations in each
> chapter are in chronological order . . . [Fifth, where a large proportion of an
> hour is presented my remarks have usually been foreshortened for the focus is
> on the subject . . .] Sixth, details such as names and places have been disguised,
> and – as an unfortunate necessity – data have been left out for the sake of
> confidentiality. Finally, because there are more themes than any one book
> could encompass, huge chunks have been removed *en masse* simply to reduce
> its size. (Stoller, 1974: xiv)

Something like these guidelines are fairly widely in use amongst personal document researchers (cf. Blauner, 1987 for an account of his 'editing process'). Sometimes the editing can involve more extensive 'cutting'. Thus, *The Polish Peasant* story was twice as long in its original form (1918–1921), the *Letters from Jenny* were abridged to approximately one-third of their original length (Allport, 1965) and Don the Sun Chief's 8,000 page diary was reduced (for publication purposes) to one-fifth of its original length (Simmons, 1942). It may well be tedious to have an 8,000 page set of personal notes but, once edited, it still leaves the reader wondering just what has been left out?

It is interesting to look at these studies and consider the kind and degree of editing in mind, though often it is far from clear what has happened. Edwin Sutherland's 'Professional Thief', for instance, says he himself wrote 'two-thirds of it' as a direct response to questions while the rest was gleaned verbatim from joint discussions, and the whole was then 'organized' by Sutherland. But just how much organization did Sutherland do? People have speculated that Sutherland's characteristic style is embodied throughout the book. Did he, perhaps, write it all? Jon Snodgrass, reviewing Sutherland's private papers much later, came across letters from 'The Thief' which certainly seem to indicate Sutherland's overriding role. Thus 'The Thief' writes to Sutherland:

> Many thanks for the copy of *The Thief*. I read it with a great amount of interest and a great amount of confusion too. Sometime I am going to ask you to take a copy and underline in red that which the thief wrote and in blue that which you wrote. You have accepted the philosophy of the thief so completely that it is impossible to identify yours from his. If you had not done so it would be easy to isolate sentences and say that the thief did not say or write that . . . I shall read the book again in an effort to identify something familiar. Even though he did not write certain things, I am sure the thief felt that way and wished that he had. (Snodgrass, 1973: 8)

Here perhaps is the most common strategy for writing up life document research: get your subject's own words, really come to grasp them from the inside, and then yourself turn it into a structured and coherent statement that uses the subject's words in places and the social scientist's in others but does not lose their authentic meaning. But if you do this, you start to be left with a new issue: whose story is it now? When you have so modified it, surely in part it has become yours?

And in addition to editing, there is always the problem of *interpreting*. How much interpretation should be done? Some personal documents are left without any interpretation: the interviews of Tony Parker and Studs Terkel leave the voices in unedited form for the reader to ponder. Other documents are 'framed' by the interpretation: this is the technique of *The Polish Peasant*, where Thomas and Znaniecki surround their letters and their life histories with commentary, in the introductions, in the footnotes and in the conclusions. A third way of treating the interpretation is to place it in a commentary at the end of the documents: this is the standard technique in nearly all the limited life history studies, such as *Box Man* (Chambliss, 1972), *Being Different* (Bogdan, 1974) and *The Fantastic Lodge* (Hughes, 1961). A variant of this is in *Anguish* (Strauss and Glaser, 1977), where in each chapter there is the document (the account of Mrs Abel's dying) followed by a theoretical interpretation.

Finally, there is the more marginal case where the life history subjects do not 'speak for themselves' at all but are to be found within the story of the social scientist. The books are devoted to interpretations of their lives, rather than displaying the original documents from the interviews. Much of the work of the sociologist/therapist Lilian Rubin is like this, where in a series of highly acclaimed and readable books she tends to place her detailed interview material into her own words. These are commonly seen as very elegant studies – of class wounds (*Worlds of Pain*, 1972), of love, sex and marriage (*Intimate Strangers*, 1983; *Erotic Wars*, 1990) and of transcending troubled childhood backgrounds (*The Transcendent Child*, 1997). But Rubin distils her subjects' voices, quotes them judiciously and finally presents her account, not their first person voice. This is a common enough mode – a great deal of social science exists in this hinterland. In sociology, for example, there are the major case histories of David Riesman and his associates in the early 1950s on mass society and the individual (*The Lonely Crowd* and *Faces in the Crowd*), the detailed interpretations of the experiences of class by Richard Sennett and Richard Cobb in *The Hidden Injuries of Class* (1972), the responses to community and individualism which can be found in Robert Bellah et al.'s *Habits of the Heart* (1985) or the edited interpretations of young sex offenders (Messerschmidt, 2000). It is also found in psychology: the work of Robert Coles on deprived children (*Children of Crisis*, 1968) and black women (*Women of Crisis*, Coles and Coles, 1978) are perhaps most central. Likewise, in anthropology, Oscar Lewis often loses the original statements in favour of his commentary. And, of course, in the domain of psychiatry, the standard approach, from Freud onwards, is to lose the first person account in favour of the third person interpretation (Stoller's *Splitting* (1974) being a good exception to this rule). Many of these interpreted documents rank amongst the classics of social science; but, important as they are, they are not truly personal documents in the sense used in this book. For they lack that central ingredient of disclosing the subject's own viewpoint, perspective and expression: this now has to be inferred from the researcher's comments alone. Often this is more insightful and more intellectually cogent than the subject's view, and often too it is an accurate presentation of the subject's world. The people speak from time, to time, but in the main it is interpretation. The reader doesn't have access to the original documents, the person's own story. By the time we reach this style of work the voice of the subject has often been 'written over' by the expert. A very marginal zone has been entered.

I must be careful. One set of life stories of Bedouin women positively validates the above approach of 'writing others' voices' over the study organized around the original voice of one life because the latter tends too much 'to contribute to a sense of the person at its centre as an isolated individual' (Abu-Lughod, 1993: 31). Rather than do this, this author takes a number of critical anthropological themes for each of the chapters of the book – patrilinearity, polygyny, reproduction, patrilateral parallel-cousin marriage, and honour and shame – and then weaves a narrative around the lives of women interviewed. As she says, 'I have taken a variety of Bedouin women's talk – stories of everyday life, arguments, reminiscences, folktales, poems, songs and even a written letter and an essay with oral commentary – and made them into five different narratives' (Abu-Lughood, 1993: 32–3). Within each of these narratives she saw her task as one of making such stories 'readable': cutting the uninteresting, avoiding the repetitive, deleting irrelevancies, giving translations, providing intelligibility and simplicity where it was needed. The words of the women go missing in favour of a coherent social narrative.

A continuum of constructions   To dissect this problem of editing and interpretation, a continuum can be depicted which locates the two major interpreters in any sociological life story: the subject and the social scientist. Both of these bring into any situation their own sets of assumptions. The sociologist is likely to use 'scientific' theories and concepts; the subject, on the other hand, is likely to use his or her 'world taken for granted views'. The problem of analysis is hence the extent to which the sociologist progressively imposes his or her 'theory' upon the understandings of the subject, or the extent to which the subject's own rational construction of the world is grasped and apprehended in its purest form. The 'ideal types' of a subject's interpretation and the sociologist's interpretation may be placed on a continuum of construction, as in Box 8.1.

This continuum locates the extent to which sociologists impose their own analytic devices upon the subject, or the extent to which the subject's own world is allowed to stand 'uncontaminated'. Moving from right to left, the extreme point of the continuum is armchair theory, where sociologists may construct their accounts independently of the subject. This is an extreme form which – by defintion – cannot be encountered in life story analysis (since presumably the material derived from the life story subject would always be incorporated at some point). It is, of course, very common, being generally what social scientists mean by theory (i.e. 'people-go-missing' abstractions).

Moving a little further along the continuum, a common practice is for sociologists to impose (or – more kindly – generate) their own scheme upon the gathered data. Here subjects are hardly being allowed to talk for themselves. I call this 'verification by anecdote' (others call it

BOX 8.1   A CONTINUUM OF 'CONSTRUCTION'

I	II	III	IV	V
The subject's 'pure construction (raw) e.g. original diaries, unsolicited letters, autobiographies, self-written books, sociologist's own personal experience	Edited personal documents	Systematic thematic analysis	Verification by anecdote (exampling)	The sociologist's 'pure construction' e.g. sociological theories

'exampling'), whereby the sociologist's own story is given support by the selection of good examples (whilst providing little justification for selecting these quotes over others). Further along the continuum, there comes a point when the subjects are allowed to speak for themselves but where their voices get organized around themes (with the subject's account usually linked to sociological theory). If I wanted to be pretentious, I might call this 'systematic thematic analysis'(!). One step on, there is the life history document where the sociologist tries to intervene as little as possible. Some intervention, however, is usually necessary, if only to delete the (boring) repetition and stammering found in all people's verbal accounts. And finally, at the most extreme end of the continuum, there is the simple publication of the subject's own accounts with no analysis attached. The most obvious examples of these would be the publication of their own autobiographies, diaries and unsolicited letters.

A question of self and voice: authority and subject in a text

But all this can go much further. Most social science somehow comes to be written as if the author is not there. Words glide across the page, but the composers of such words count as little. Indeed, much critical deconstruction theory actually encourages such a stance – with its 'death of the author'. But thankfully, a small group of social scientists – usually feminist-inspired, are gathering strength and fighting back against this dominant tendency. They are reasserting the importance of *the self in the text*. And they are concerned with the boundaries of the relationship between the researcher who writes the text and the researched who may reside in the text but who is 'written on' or 'inscribed' by the authorial researcher. Whose voices are to be heard within a text has increasingly become a key issue for social research. Susan Krieger has written – in many places (1991, 1996) – most eloquently of this problem:

> Some of us have become increasingly dissatisfied with the tone of remote authority commonly used in the writing of social science and with the way the personality of an author gets lost in social science texts . . . Social science is premised on minimizing the self, viewing it as a contaminant, transcending it, denying it, protecting its vulnerability . . . we paint pictures in which we hope not to exist; or if we exist, . . . are subordinate or nearly invisible (1991: 47, 116) . . . Usually academics speak in a more abstract or explicitly theoretical language, use a technical vocabulary, and refer often to work by other scholars. The academic style is designed to produce distance and to exclude emotion – to speak from above and outside an experience, rather than from within it. (1996: 3)

Curiously, many social science writers – and most students – are told *not* to use the first person 'I'. They are instructed indeed to conceal it, and to write in a third person's voice – as a neutral authority from outside the text. Authoritative modes of writing – given to us from on high by the men in black frocks and white coats – have been the dominant modes of social science writing in the past: a mode of writing characterized by distance, objectivity, neutrality etc. Here the main textual voice is that of the 'expert' whose expertise allows him or her to frame – or erase – the voices of others. 'They' – the subjects – can only speak in the text through the authority of the expert author. Others' voices are trapped in the author(ity)'s concealed voice. In most psychology reports, the only voice to emerge is that of the psychologist – who stands outside the text as a presence who is simply recording the truth. The scientist's voice is clearly the voice at work but it is not made explicit. Such authority prevents the free flowing moving around of multiple voices within the text, and prevents many voices from even being heard. 'Exemplary voices' – often in the form of judiciously selected 'quotes' – are usually firmly under the control of the dominant voice.

In a now classic discussion of sociological voices, Richard Brown (1977: 58) – drawing from Jean Pouillon's *Time and the Novel* – makes some of the issues clear by suggesting three positions that the author may assume in relation to the subject: as superior, as equal and as inferior. (Of course this can be rendered more complex.) 'Grand Theorist' Talcott Parsons is cited as an example of the superior, anthropologist Oscar Lewis as the equal, and (the now largely discredited – see Chapter 11) Carlos Castaneda as an example of an inferior. The distinguishing mark is the extent to which the author permits the narrative of the life subject to dominate the text. For Parsons clearly it is the sociological view that matters; for Lewis there is probably equal measurement between his perspectives on the Mexican family and the Mexican family's own perspective; for Castaneda his perspective is almost entirely subordinate to that of the Indian Brujo. Another distinction that Brown makes concerns the relative 'firmness of the boundaries between' the reported speech and the author's context. Thus, at one extreme there is the study in which the boundaries are very lax indeed; subject and author's comments huddle together. At the other extreme the boundaries can be very tight; the author makes a clear demarcation between sections devoted to the subject's speech and those devoted to his analysis.

Postcolonial theory and feminist theories have been very much concerned with the issue of voice and author, for this is a field of knowledge that is oh-so-very-aware of the ways in which the voices of hidden or subjugated/subaltern peoples can have their voices 'liberated' but also rendered distorted through western 'translators' or researchers. As we have seen (Chapter 4), the autobiographical mode may well be a distinctly 'western' form, and so to trap the voices of other cultures within this mode may well sustain their marginality. But not all writers agree: bell hooks, a leading black US feminist, for example can suggest that the very form of confessional narrative is indeed a form that has a privileged place in African American literary practice. 'More than any other genre of writing, the production of honest confessional narratives by black women who are struggling to be self-actualized and to become radical subjects are needed as guides, as texts which affirm our fellowship with one another . . . Even as the number of novels by black women increase, this writing cannot be a substitute for theory or for autobiographical narratives. (We) radical black women need to tell our stories: we cannot document our experience enough' (hooks, 1992). Such stories may well provide new voices as *resistance texts*.

The problems of authors, voices and self, then, are complex. But they could lead us to consider the possibilities for creating relatively open and *democratic texts* when they contain a fluidity between subjects, researchers and selves. A good illustration of this can be found in Pat Caplan's wonderful book-length life story of Mohammed, a villager in the Tanzanian Mafia Island. It opens with an explicit discussion between Mohammed and the anthropologist author as to how the story should be written, how it will be told and who will read it. It establishes right from the outset a dialogue between subject and author – although Mohammed is clear to the author that: 'You write your name [only] and you alone will know who is the man behind you' (Caplan, 1997: 4). With this is mind, Pat Caplan divides the book into four sections. The first provides 'Mohammed's Story' and takes the form of a transcript between Caplan and Mohammed. The story appears in a question and answer form, and largely takes the form of a monologue – a record of someone looking back over his life. The second part – 'Mohammed as Ethnographer' – is a series of extracts from a diary that Mohammed kept, organized through themes by Caplan – who also writes a commentary. This reads more like a dialogue between author and reader. The third part, 'Three Encounters', is a record of three visits: it is written largely in Caplan's voice, though through her a number of conversations with three main characters – Mohammed, Mwahadia, Subira – emerge. A final section – 'The Search for Knowledge' – draws together diary and further encounters looking at possession by ancestral spirits. Prologue and conclusions appear in the form of dialogues between Mohammed and Caplan. All in all, this book provides an excellent illustration of the problems of moving between voices: neither monologue, nor dialogue, the voices are self-consciously chosen to be different at different places in the text. In so far as 'democratic' and 'open' 'polyvocal' texts are possible, this would seem to be a good example of trying to create such a form (Caplan, 1997).

An interim conclusion

This chapter has started to suggest that the ways in which life stories, and other forms of social science, are written is an interesting and important topic to study. The very modes of writing may indeed shape the life – or the 'findings'. Indeed, in the next chapter I will take this one stage further by suggesting that 'narrative' is the key organizing feature of a life story. It is to the process of narrativization that I now turn.

Guide to further reading

Good **practical writing advice** is to be found in Howard S. Becker's *Writing for Social Scientists* (1986) (he is a sociologist who is generally considered a good writer), Harry Wolcott's *Writing Up Qualitative Research* (1990), and Karen Golden-Biddle and Karen D. Locke's *Composing Qualitative Research* (1997). On the editing of first person accounts, see Bob Blauner's 'Problems of editing first person sociology' (1987).

For discussions of the '**new narrative and writing turn**' in social science, see Paul Atkinson, *The Ethnographic Imagination: Textual Constructions of Reality* (1990); James Clifford and G.E. Marcus, *Writing Culture: The Poetics and Politics of Ethnography* (1986); Clifford Geertz, *The Interpretation of Cultures* (1973); Clifford Geertz, *Works and Lives: The Anthropologist as Author* (1988); Laurel Richardson, *Writing Strategies* (1990); Patricia Ticineto Clough, *The Ends of Ethnography* (1992); and John Van Maanen, *Tales of the Field* (1988). The classical backgrounds to all this can be found in Roland Barthes's, *Writing Degree Zero* (1967) and Jacques Derrida's *Of Grammatology* (1976). I also found the introduction to Lila Abu-Lughod's *Writing Women's Worlds: Bedouin Stories* (1993: 1–45), of value in thinking about writing lives. Finally, a scathing attack on the conventions of sociological academic writing has been provided recently by Ben Agger in his *Public Sociology* (2000). It should be required reading for every formalist academic!

On **popularization**, there is an interesting symposium in the journal *Contemporary Sociology*, 1998, 27 (5): 435–53 called 'Engaging Publics in Sociological Dialogue', with contributions from three leading North American 'popularizers': William Julius Wilson, Pepper Schwartz and George Ritzer (Wilson et al., 1998). See also, the collections of papers in Jeremy MacClancy and Chris McDonagh (eds), *Popularizing Anthropology* (1996); Cheryl Haslam and Alan Bryman (eds), *Social Scientists Meet the Media* (1994) and Susan Allen, *Media Anthropology: Informing Global Citizens* (1994) and William Julius Wilson (ed.), *Sociology and the Public Agenda* (1993). Gesa Kirsch in *Ethical Dilemmas in Feminist Research* (1999) discusses the question 'Who is going to read this?' (ch. 4).

9 Life Stories and the Narrative Turn

We have each of us, a life story, an inner narrative – whose continuity, whose sense, *is* our lives. It might be said that each of us constructs and lives 'a narrative', and that this narrative *is* our identities.

If we wish to know about a man, we ask 'what is his story, his real inmost story?' – for each of us *is* a biography, a story. Each of us *is* a singular narrative, which is constructed, continually, unconsciously, by, through, and in us – through our perceptions, our feelings, our thoughts, our actions; and not least, our discourse, our spoken narrations. Biologically, physiologically, we are not different from each other; historically, as narratives, we are each of us unique.

To be ourselves we must have ourselves – possess, if need be re-possess, our life stories. We must 'recollect' ourselves, recollect the inner drama, the narrative of ourselves. A man needs such a narrative, a continuous inner narrative to maintain his identity . . .

(Oliver Sacks, *The Man who Mistook his Wife for a Hat*, 1986: 105–6)

This chapter continues the discussion of writing life stories started in Chapter 8 through a look at 'narrative'. Narrative may be seen as a most basic way humans have of apprehending the world: 'we grasp our lives in a *narrative*' (Taylor, 1989: 47), and sense that 'narrative is the fundamental scheme for linking individual human actions and events into interrelated aspects of an understandable composite' (Polkinghorne, 1988: 13). Indeed, without it we might just be left with the amorphous jumble of inchoate experience that knows no rhyme or reason, no coherence or patterns. Thus narrative has to be present in every life document and life story, raising issues we have already touched upon at many points so far in this book – of how stories, and a process of 'narrativization', serve to provide some kind of intelligibility and coherence to a life. Narrative structures enable us to speak, and the multitude of fragmenting experiences that constitute our lives come to be patterned into some seeming sense of order. Indeed, without such a narrative thrust within life, chaos may rule. So what is narrative and how does it bring this order?

As we could well expect, there is really little detailed agreement as to what narratives are. Some cast them as a wide net through which all of life is lived (like Barthes quoted earlier: Chapter 3), whilst others (like the linguist Labov) give them a much more precise focus on specific events and causal chains, as an answer to the question: 'and then what happened?' (Riessman, 1993: 17). There is no consensus on the term's meaning. Yet what is clear is that the narrative of a life is not *the* life; and life narratives conform much less to the contours of the life as lived than they do to the conventions and practices of narrative writing. Even unself-conscious tales that seem to be just simply, naturally 'told' are likely to be immersed in the narrative conventions of a culture. Indeed, if life stories do not draw from those narrative conventions, most readers or listeners will find them hard – even impossible – to understand. There may even be rules to govern narratives which would hence govern the telling of lives. In any event, life story research must be closely linked to narrative analysis, which takes the very narrative of the life itself as the topic of investigation

Some basic elements of narrative

A new discipline, narratology (the term was coined by Todorov in 1969) has slowly emerged which takes as its central task the analysis of stories and narratives. Its prime concern is with literary theory, but it nevertheless recognizes an interdisciplinary goal and that a number of disciplines have established their own different approaches to the study of narrative. Thus, in the main literary theory directs us to formal and structural matters of genre, plot, character, trope. Linguistics, by contrast, has developed an approach which highlights narratives as speech acts and conversation – often through intensive analysis of the organization of speech in conversation analysis (Linde, 1993). Psychology, drawing from both 'cognitive' and discourse analysis, has started to develop its own 'narrative psychology' to see 'how people make sense of their lives' (Edwards, 1997: 268), to grasp the means by which 'people organize their experience in, knowledge of, and transactions with the social world' (Bruner, 1990: 35). For Theodore Sarbin it may even be a root metaphor to reconstruct psychology (Sarbin, 1986). Philosophy has long had an interest in narrative. It is there in the early writings of Aristotle and can be found in the recent work of philosophers like Hannah Arendt, Paul Ricoueur and Alastair MacIntyre, whose concerns with story, hermeneutics, texts and narratives have led us to see important ways of linking personal experiences to moral debate. Sociology has directed its attention less to narrative, but its task has usually been to broaden the social context: whilst not denying the value of any of the above, it claims that a fuller picture would need to take on board the historical emergence of narratives, their 'tellability' in specific interactional moments, and their social impact (Plummer, 1995b).

In a short chapter, I cannot go into the wide range of theories that we now have of narrative. I can detect dialogical, hermeneutic, critical, neo-Aristotelian, psychoanalytic, feminist, deconstructive, reader-response, Marxist, formalist, semiotic, structuralist, post-structuralist theories of narrative – to name but thirteen! (cf. Edwards, 1997; Hillis Miller, 1990; Selden and Widdowson, 1993). Yet, combining several strands of thought, it might help to see life story narratives as usually being comprised of several key elements that need attention. A useful start is to think about *story*, *plot*, *characters*, *themes*, *poetics*, *genres* and *points of view*. Any life story could be located on such dimensions.

- *Story* is the most basic element – and usually implies as Kenyon and Randall (1997: 65) aptly put it, 'someone telling someone about somebody doing something'. Stories 'are about someone trying to do something, and what happens to her and to others as a result' (Mattingly, 1998: 7). Who all these people are and what they are all doing becomes the feature of the story. Usually it will imply some kind of 'mere' sequence of events with some kind of moral point ('and the moral of the story is. ..'). Whilst narrative is a wide generic term (like discourse) for recounting and relating, the term story is but one version of narrative. Its importance has been increasingly recognized as the guiding unit of a life story. For

  > Our life is essentially a set of stories we tell ourselves about our past, present and future. These stories are far from fixed, direct accounts of what happens in our lives but products of the inveterate fictionalizing of our memory and imagination. That is, we 'story' our lives. Moreover, we *re*-story them too. In fact, restorying continually goes on within us. (Kenyon and Randall, 1997: 2)

- Plots are more complex: they are the dynamos of stories, they turn them on. In formal (Russian) theory, a 'story' (*fabula*) is raw material awaiting organization by the author, whilst a 'plot' (*sjuzet*) is the literary device. Following Aristotle, it is the 'arrangements of the incidents'. More clearly, we could say that the life story must usually have a dynamic tension which adds momentum, gives a coherence and makes the story interesting: we speak of the plot 'thickening' to indicate events that grab the reader's interest. And in life stories these become important too. As Kenyon and Randall again pithily say: 'no trouble, no tale; no ill, no thrill; no agony, no adventure'. 'Plot carries us from initial calm through ensuing conflict to eventual climax, conclusion and (once more) calm' (1997: 67). Usually plots take on a sequence – a beginning, middle and end (though in some experimental modernist and all post-modern plots, linear time is dissolved or seriously weakened). All the classic life stories have linear time that organizes their plots. And part of the life story is usually organized around a major tension or crisis – what Denzin calls an 'epiphany'. Often 'nuclear episodes' can be identified which detailed 'specific autobiographical events which have been reinterpreted over time to assume a privileged status in the story' (McAdams, 1985: 63). And detours from the main plot give rise to sub-plots.

- *Characters.* Next, the narratives of life stories will be peopled by recognizable 'characters', what McAdams has called 'imagoes'. We write, read or hear life stories being tuned in to look for 'villains, heroes and fools', and seeking a whole array of what has been called 'storytypes' – not far indeed from stereotypes. Usually there will be a protagonist, an antagonist, and a witness of some kind. For some they can feed into a Jungian concern with 'archetypes' – with prototypes such as the Great Mother, the Wise Old Man, Gods and Daemons which are presumed to have some unconscious significance in history. There could be a vast array of such 'personifications' to appear in our stories, but often they are reduced to a small clustering of basic types: fathers and mothers, parents and children, the good and the bad. Listening to life stories may mean listening to the stories of the personifcations that people a life.

- *Themes and story-lines.* Closely linked to plots are the key themes that start to organize a life. Dan McAdams, for instance, suggests that thematic lines are 'recurrent content clusters in stories' (McAdams, 1985: 62), which he sees as always being linked to 'power' and 'intimacy'; others have suggested the importance of agency and communion. Often these become very specific. Looking at the life story of Sara – interviewed by Amia Lieblich – we find she teases the life into four major themes: (a) belonging and separateness (b) closeness, remoteness and the experience of moving, (c) the meaning of teaching as care, and (d) the theme of 'men and the threat of remaining single' (Lieblich et al., 1998: ch. 4).

- *Genres and structures.* Clustering plots into imagoes and thematic lines can lead to narratives eventually become recognizable as falling into definite patterns, types and structures, often performing definite functions. For Hayden White, plots may be tragic, comic, romantic or satirical (White, 1973). For Northrop Frye, they can be ironic, mythical, romantic, tragic or comic (Frye, 1988: 54). For Levi-Strauss, they can be analysed through binary oppositions such as subject/object and sender/receiver. Literature can ultimately be classified into a few major forms – an idea put forward most clearly by the Russian folklorist Vladamir Propp in his analysis of fairy tales and folk stories, where an array of story forms with basic plots, characters and functions were discovered and classified into 37 types. More simply, Langdon Elsbree in his *The Rituals of Life: Patterns in Narratives* has argued that there are a relatively few 'archetypal actions' – 'elementary ritual modes affecting the way we apprehend a story' (p. 14). He suggests these are: '1) Establishing, consecrating a home; 2) Engaging in a contest, fighting a battle; 3) Taking a journey; 4) Enduring suffering; 5) Pursuing consummation' . . . Each is a dramatizing of the self's achievements and failures in a fundamental category of human experience' (Elsbree, 1982: 15).

These 'genres' can be applied to social science writing. Thus, John Van Maanen (1988) has provided an account of *fieldwork genres*, suggesting three major types of tale to be found in ethnography: the 'realist' initiated in the fieldwork of Malinowski, the 'confessional' often embodied in confessional texts where researchers tell all (e.g. Bell and Newby, 1977) and the 'impressionist' such as Clifford Geertz's Balinese Cockfight. (He also hints at 'critical tales', such as Willis's *Learning to Labour* (1978), the 'formal tales' of a Garfinkel or Barthes, the more 'literary tales' of writers such as Tom Wolfe, and the 'jointly told tales' of Klockars and others). Likewise, Laurel Richardson (1990) has suggested five kinds of broad narrative that may be found in sociology: everyday life narratives, autobiographical narratives, biographical narratives, cultural narratives, and collective stories. In looking seriously at the narrative forms of social science writing, a much greater sensitivity to matters of aesthetics, argumentation, genre and metaphor is generated (cf. Atkinson, 1990). Life stories have their own genres too.

All this is very formal and abstract. With genres frequently it is possible to locate a very specific concrete form of writing at work which makes a genre immediately visible. For example, James Olney (a literary specialist on biography) writing about 'slave narratives' (see Chapter 4, pp. 93–4) has found a very clear set of conventions that most follow: it is almost like a 'master plan for slave narratives (irony intended)' (Olney, 1985: 152–3). He suggests this includes:

(A)   An engraved portrait, signed by the narrator.
(B)   A title page that includes the claim, as an integral part of the title, 'Written by Himself' . . .
(C)   A handful of testimonials and/or one or more prefaces or introductions written either by a white abolitionist friend of the narrator [or someone similar during which] the reader is told that the narrative is a 'plain, unvarnished tale' and that 'naught has been set in malice, nothing exaggerated, nothing drawn from the imagination' – indeed, the tale, it is claimed, understates the horrors of slavery.
(D)   A poetic epigraph.
(E)   The actual narrative [which will usually include:]
    1   a first sentence beginning 'I was born . . .', then specifying a place but no date of birth.
    2   a sketchy account of parentage, often involving a white father.
    3   description of a cruel master, mistress or overseers, details of first observed whipping and numerous subsequent whippings . . .
    4   an account of one extraordinary strong and hardworking slave . . . who refused to be whipped.
    5   records of the barriers raised against slave literacy.
    6   description of a 'Christian' slaveholder [and the claim they are invariably worse]
    7   description of food and clothing, work required on a day to day pattern.

      8   account of slave auction . . .

      9   description of patrols, of failed attempt to escape . . .

   10   description of successful attempt(s) to escape, lying by during the day, travelling by night guided by the North Star, reception in a free state by Quakers who offer a lavish breakfast and much genial thee/thou conversation.

   11   taking a new last name . . . with identity as free man.

   12   reflections on slavery.

(F)   an appendix, which provides documentary material – bills of sale, details of purchase for slavery, newspaper items etc. . . . (Olney, 1985: 152–3, edited slightly)

- *Speech acts and the conversational unit*   Narratives may also be seen as 'linguistic units' governed by language rules: such as rules for narrative sequences (giving the speech a sense of time) and rules for coherence. Charlotte Linde has written intensively about life histories in this mode: indeed, she sees, 'a life story [as] an oral unit that is told over many occasions. Conventionally, it includes certain kinds of landmark events . . . both in its content (the items that it includes and excludes) and in its form (the structures that are used to make it coherent), it is the product of the members of a particular culture. Other cultures may include different items and use different forms. Indeed, the notion of a 'life story' itself is not universal, but is the product of a particular culture' (Linde, 1993).
- *Tropes*. Hayden White in his *Tropics of Discourse* (1978) has argued that even history cannot avoid its 'textuality' – it is never just a factual record but depends on imagery, metaphors and ironies. And drawing from Kenneth Burke's 'Four master tropes' – metaphor, metonymy, synedoche and irony – he shows how all historical narrative is infused with this.

T.S. Bruyn, in a wonderful account of participant observation, has suggested eight combinations of imageries that lead to different styles: the romantic, the realistic, the poetic, the factual, the analytic, the satiric, the journalistic and the existential (see Bruyn, 1966). The romantic style is exemplified in the writings of Redfield on Tepoztlan. As Bruyn comments,

Redfield's choice of metaphors leads the reader away from the realities of 'poverty' and the 'hardships' placed upon people who lack technical progress to a vaulted image of 'the culture'. He speaks of *time* in the village as not being determined by the 'clock in the tower or the placio municipal which strikes the hours'; rather, 'the metronome of human interests (Time)' is measured by the season and the 'waxing and waning of the moon'. It is through the 'cadence of nature' and the 'chronometers of sunset and sunrise' that the 'simpler peoples are more directly dependent'.

He contrasts this with the realistic approach of Oscar Lewis studying the same area. For Lewis, the language highlights 'the dire effects of political and economic changes upon the lives of individuals by allowing the people to speak for themselves' (Bruyn, 1966: 246–7).

Qualitative research differs not only in its literary style, but also in the nature of its conceptual analysis. John Lofland, in a review of 'several hundred unpublished articles and book-length reports of qualitative field research over a two-year period', extracts a number of dimensions. He suggests there is a 'generic style' looked for in most qualitative research, a style which 'delineates types of social structures and processes, their internal dynamics and their causes and consequences' (1974: 102). Most qualitative research will be concerned with an issue wider than the subject in hand – the frame ('a basic structural unit onto which or into which other constituents of a whole are fitted, with which they attach or with which they are integrated') (p. 103). In this view specific instances of life stories will always be located in some wider 'frame'. The frame may be conceptual or substantive: thus the life history of Stanley, while of value in itself, will be located in the overall 'frame' of delinquency – and Mrs Abel's trajectory, whilst again interesting in itself, will also be located within the 'frame' of status passages. All individual life histories, therefore, are finally located in some overarching problem.

But whilst this is a central dimension, Lofland can go on to outline eleven variants of this, four of which are crucial. Thus he suggests that reports may differ along the dimensions of 'novelty, elaboration, eventfulness and interpenetration'. The first one highlights the need for the researcher to bring out new, novel, and maybe even exotic frames, ones that have not been hacked to death through earlier research. 'Elaboration' is concerned with the extent the researcher fills out the frame in considerable detail, rather than merely using it as an analytic device for two or three pages and then ignoring it. 'Eventfulness' is concerned with the extent the empirical material is amply and ably provided; too many qualitative researchers engage in abstracted conceptualism by which the concepts become all important and the empirical material is lost in the text (or at the other extreme, where there was nothing but empirical material and the conceptualizations become far too thin). The final dimension Lofland describes as an 'interpenetrated' frame. This is concerned with the way in which the conceptual text blends in with the empirical materials, the crucial distinction being between this and the segregated style (where the first and last chapters are given over to theory and the bulk in the middle is given over to empirical data, made to fit some pre-existing conceptualization). Life histories can be arranged on all these different dimensions.

The narratives of 'life patterns'

A key cluster of narratives for thinking about a life are those linked to 'life development, 'life change', 'life span', or 'life course': it is a sense of how the life moves along, changes, flows. Such narratives tacitly provide answers to questions such as: how has my life unfolded? What patterns does it take? Where might I be heading? Is change possible? Why has my life taken these routes and not others? And ultimately: so what is the story of my life?

Within psychology there is a huge body of work ('life span developmental psychology') which aims to guide us through answers to these questions – from Piaget, Freud and Erikson to Kohlberg, Kegan and Kogan. These are the 'objective' or 'scientific' accounts of life stages which track early childhood through phases of Oedipal traumas, mirror stages, attachment etc. and on to the adult stages – of loss, despair, trust, hope, wisdom etc. Common imagery here involves the 'eras', 'stages', or 'seasons' of a life. This work is well documented and will not be my concern here (but see Chapter 6 where I discuss the stages of a life).

In contrast to this, I am more interested in tapping into some broad metaphorical images through which people come to develop their own sense of how their lives develop – 'the narratives of life patterns'. I have only a little space to identify some of these narratives, but they would make for an interesting full-length study – partially already achieved in Jaber Gubrium and David Buckholdt's *Toward Maturity* (1977). As these authors comment:

> The important questions are not how people respond to life change or proceed through stages, but how they negotiate and generate the reality and meaning of change, stages, and development; how they come to have a sense of them as things separate from themselves; and how they subsequently respond to them as real things. (1977: 8–9)

As was seen in Chapter 6, at the simplest level what may seem to us to be the most basic developmental stages of life – 'childhood', 'youth', 'mid-life' and 'old age' – can all be shown to be contemporary western cultural 'fictions'. The term 'fiction' here does not have negative or false connotations – it simply suggests a cultural reality that has been 'humanly produced' and 'culturally organized' (as cultures invariably must be!) and that is hence not the same in all cultures. Many studies have indeed shown that the meanings attributed to childhood differ across cultures, that 'youth' is a nineteenth-century 'invention', and that the 'mid-life' idea is very recent indeed; having arisen in the west, it may now be going global – exported across the world like Coca-Cola! (cf. Shweder, 1998: x). Further, the idea of 'old age' is open to many meanings: our culture may have invented a 'pernicious master narrative of decline' to engulf the experience of ageing, whereas other cultures invent meanings that are much more positive. There are then 'narratives of childhood', 'middle age' or 'old age' which need to be seen as frames through which we organize our lives.

But there are also accounts of just how our lives come to assume certain patterns. A major divide here rests on just how much the narrative suggests a life is determined by factors outside of itself and how much a life may be open to will and agency.

There are a host of the former tales: people building narratives which see their lives as more or less determined. The *'Selfish Gene' Narrative* is currently one of the most popular ways of thinking about a life which comes from the continuing interest in a neo-Darwinian evolutionism. It is an imagery that ultimately links the human life to the animal life, and sees the outcomes of human behaviour as residing in a long-term survival strategy often linked to human genes. The kinds of people we become are hence to be seen as evolutionary outcomes. Lives can be read off from a strand of DNA.

Equally 'determined' is what we could call the *'Childhood Fix' Narrative*, a story overwhelmingly shaped by early childhood experiences – 'the child is father to the man'. In telling the tale of this life, a great deal of emphasis has to be placed on early life – especially family life, and it usually has to be told in a linear, sequential fashion which implies the life is a cumulative sequence of causes. Freud's work is perhaps the most significant variant of this in modern times – his work is often seen as causing a radical rupture in approaches to biographical study. Here early causal family dynamics, centring around the Oedipus complex, serves to structure psychic life and shape adult personalities. Other 'personality theories' also stress the importance of childhood. Yet there are well known problems with this narrative: Lillian Rubin's *The Transcendent Child* (1997), for instance, tells the stories of eight people whose lives were in some way severely damaged as a child, but who seem to rise above this and achieve some form of success and happiness in their adult life. They become 'transcendent children', and the book tells the 'tales of triumph over the past'.

> The idea that what happens to a child in those early years in the family *determines* the future is much too simple. It assumes, first, that the child is a passive receptacle; second that the experiences of early childhood inevitably dwarf everything that happens afterwards. In reality, however, how the child handles those early experiences makes a difference in the outcome. As does what happens in the years ahead . . . too much intervenes between infancy and adulthood for the experience in the family alone to govern how a life will be lived . . . (Rubin, 1997: 3)

Another form of determinist narrative is what may be called the *Obstacle Race Narrative*. This is perhaps a more balanced view than the childhood determination models as it highlights the stages across the life from birth to death. Here a life is laid out as a grand sequence of stages and possible crises: 'one damn crisis after another'. Again, this is hardly a new image: it is strongly represented for example in Shakespeare's classic tale of players and stages, and in contemporary social science, Erik Erikson has probably been seen as the guru of such models, when he suggests eight critical psychosocial crises – ones that are universal, biologically grounded (or 'epigenetic') but historically shaped; and which work cumulatively – the resolution of one stage leads on to another (with its own new set of crises). Such a model has more recent variants in looking at the 'passages' of 'seasons' of lives – a tradition academically linked with the work of Daniel Levinson and his associates (1978, 1996). For Levinson, the life cycles of men and women can be likened to the stages in seasons – and like the seasons, they do not arrive abruptly but have phases themselves. More popularly, this idea is associated with the work of Gail Sheehey (1995, 1998), who has suggested most recently that a major change is taking place in the life cycles of people today in North America:

> Puberty arrives earlier by several years than it did at the turn of the (twentieth) century. Adolescence is now prolonged for the middle class until the end of the 20s, and for the (working class) until the mid 20s, as more young adults live at home longer. True adulthood doesn't begin till 30 . . . fifty is now what 40 used to be; sixty is now what 50 used to be. (Sheehey, 1995: 35)

Allied to the above, but less ambitious, is an imagery which sees limited stages happening across different moments of the life cycle. It is the '*Career*' or '*Status Passage Narrative*'. Here the core narrative suggests that at particular moments lives face critical 'turning points' or major life events around which a lot of activity happens. This may be some of the most standard life events – having a baby, getting married or divorced, dying. But there are many other paths to significant life events and changes – transitions across work, travel to or living in new countries, shifts into major new roles. Goffman's (1961) account of becoming mentally ill is of this order: in his classic study *Asylums* he argues people suffer not so much from 'madness' but from the contingencies of madness careers. It is not just what one *is*, but the whole panoply of responses from defining self and others who help shape the life cycle and the shifting sense of who one *becomes*. For Norman Denzin the core to all this is an epiphany: 'Epiphanies are interactional moments and experiences which leave marks on people's lives' (1989: 70).

A next story suggests metaphors of '*contingencies, tacit choices, and drift*', where the flow of a life is captured as ceaseless series of microscopic fateful moments, little turning points, and tacit choices taken that are hardly articulated and only dimly noticed that push a life along a certain but always changing pathway. This narrative is caught vividly in the opening quote from Simone de Beauvoir at the start of this book, when she ponders: 'what stroke of chance has brought this about? . . . a thousand different futures have stemmed from every single moment of my past'. This narrative highlights the flow of lives in fateful moments. It suggests we are always making minor decisions and choices in situations where we are only partially aware of the possible outcomes, and where small decisions push us down one pathway rather than many other possible ones. Slowly, our commitments and attachments emerge. In this story, lives are always in drift and ceaselessly 'becoming'. Many of these changes are so mundane they can hardly be noticed at the time they happen, but over longer periods we come to sense more significant change: paths taken that foreclosed others; identities established at the cost of other possibilities; attachments made that took one further along particular journeys and not others (cf. Strauss, 1969). As people tell the stories of their lives, they create a history and project a future.

The summary of a life   Much of this can be put together in the task of finding an underlying motif or pattern of a life. It is something people often do themselves – 'I have had a blessed life', 'My life has been one long worry'. Some researchers have also taken this interest: they read and re-read life stories in order to extract 'master motifs' which seem to underpin a life. Ruth and Oberg, for example, sensed six ideal types of life stories that appeared from their study, which involved 37 respondents and 2,200 pages of text which was reduced to a summary for each person and through which key themes emerged. As they say:

> There proved to be two linear stories, one of misery and one of happiness. According to the dominant qualities of the stories, these ways of life were labeled *'the bitter life'* and *'the sweet life'*. Analyzing further stories, the typology was then supplemented with two discontinuous accounts of life: *'life as a trapping pit'* and *'life as a hurdle race'*. At the end of the analysis, the typology was completed with two gender specific ways of life – *'the devoted, silenced life'* and *'life as a career'*. (Ruth and Oberg, in Birren et al., 1996: 169–70)

Moving beyond the classic narrative texts of life

All writing acts impose an order upon inchoate worlds. Hence an important task in understanding writing is to grasp the rules and logics which facilitate its organization. Indeed, once this is attempted, a common thread is found behind much social science writing: it is the presence of a string of dominant cultural conventions and assumptions which are built into narrative structures; and which shape the very acts of writing, giving the text both its substance and shape. In conventional social science writing, stability and coherence are achieved. When writing a life story, for instance, there is often a sense being conveyed that behind the text there is indeed some kind of unitary life. The text assumes a 'core life', a 'presence', a real and 'whole' person behind it; and this core self brings with it an essential meaning to the life. And often, this core meaning unfolds through a series of stages or images of the life cycle such as I have described above. We have encountered this problem at many times in this book, and narrative theory brings it to the fore.

The problem of narrative workability

What I have tried to show above, then, is a number of elements that help bring a narrative 'to life' – stories and plots, characters and story lines, genres and tropes, life patterns. As in fiction, so in life. The more these elements work well in a narrative, the more we can grasp and understand the story of a life. And to the extent that they are ignored or minimized, so 'a life story' may become harder and harder to understand. Thus the influential literary critic Kenneth Burke suggested some time back that a well-formed story should answer the following question: *'What was done (act). When or where was it done (scene)? Who did it (agent), how he [sic] did it (agency) and why (purpose)?'* (Burke, 1945: xv). When such questions are answered we have the makings of a good story. Taking this further, and drawing from a number of authors (Bruner, 1990; Edwards, 1997; Gergen, 1991, 1999), I would suggest that life narratives – to work well – will usually need most of the following:

- A sense of ordering – usually linear – of events. Even with flash-backs etc. they come in a recognizable form. We cannot comprehend 'timelessness'.
- A sense of a person behind the text – a kind of stability of identity and continuity. We cannot cope very well with people who are all fragments and lack any sense of predictability.
- A sense of voice and perspective belonging to a narrator: someone has to tell the story and that someone should be identifiable. We cannot much bear voices floating around unidentifiably.
- A sense of causality: if this, then that. Plots matter. People are motivated to do things, there are reasons things happen – even if sometime the reason becomes 'chance'.

And yet, recently, all this ordering and 'presence' behind the story has been starkly challenged by 'deconstructionist' writers. This desire for a central coherence has been critically labelled 'logocentrism' (Derrida), 'foundationalism' (Rorty), 'phonocentrism' (which privileges speech over writing and assumes a voice behind the text) and 'phallocentrism' (which assumes a male voice as prime). Looking at cultural conventions, Edward Said's celebrated *Orientalism* reveals how much western writing on the orient constructs myths around the laziness and irrationality of orientals – fixing a meaning both for the orient and the west (Said, 1978/1985). Likewise, in the work of Carol Gilligan on the (presumed) male voice of moral development theories a critique has emerged which seeks a different narrative and voice (Gilligan, 1982, 1990). In another instance, Eve Kasofsky Sedgwick's 'Queer analysis' sees the western narrative of self as organized through a tacit heterosexism (Sedgwick, 1990). There are, in other words, a series of western assumptions that help organize our narratives into quite deep patterns. Life stories and personal documents have these patterns too.

Through displaying the ways in which writing comes to be assembled and to harbour crucial assumptions, new writing often attempts to reassemble texts with a different focus: the logics of speech and writing are fractured and rendered both 'unstable' and less coherent. New modes of writing fracture into difference and multiplicity. There may no longer be a coherent, unified, gendered, stable presence behind the story and its text. So once the dominant assumptions behind writing are sensed, it becomes possible to re-think – and re-write – anew. Dominant genres cease, realist readings end, and a multiplicity of ironic, parodic, pastiched, self-conscious (and hence often unintelligible) voices start being heard.

Examples of variants of this new writing are growing. Much feminism has sensed the need for new assumptions in writing as 'gynocritics': analyses which 'begin at the point when we free ourselves from the linear absolutes of male literary history, stop trying to fit women between the lines of the male tradition, and focus instead on the newly visible world of female culture' (Showalter, 1979). Likewise, there has been the growing discovery of 'black voices' and 'colonized voices' – where western knowledge is seen to have positioned itself as superior to other knowledges, and has hence required serious challenging from new voices, even as it works to exclude other knowledges (cf. Collins, 1990; Smith, 1999). Much of the recent developments of 'Queer Theory' seeks to re-read (and re-write) texts without the presumed core of hetero-sexuality as an organizing principle. In the work of Judith Butler, Teresa De Lauretis and Eve Sedgwick and others, an entire rewriting of sexualities and genders occurs.

New texts and new modes

Thus, in writing the life stories of the future, there may well be an increasing sense of moving beyond these conventional narratives. There may be several hallmarks of this new writing style. One critical writer, Patti Lather, stops right in the middle of her text to ponder some deep questions about what it is she is doing and how she could write it better:

> How do we address questions of narrative authority raised by poststructuralism in our empirical work?

- How do we *frame* meaning possibilities rather than close them in working with empirical data?
- How do we create multi-voiced, multi-centered texts from such data?
- How do we deconstruct the way our own desires as emancipatory inquirers shape the texts we create?
- Why do we do our research? To use our privileges as academics to give voice to what Foucault terms 'subjugated knowledges'? As another version of writing the self?

- What are the race, class and gender relations that produce the research itself? (Lather, 1991)

Another writer, David Jackson, trying to write an autobiography, prefaces it by refusing the dominant modes of such writing. Instead he says he wants to try:

> *Refusing the search for the true self:* . . . transparent recall to reveal a neutral, fixed, absolutely truthful past does not exist. *Rethinking the relationship between past and present:* . . . the significance of past events isn't immutably set for all time, but is constantly being selectively edited and re-focused in terms of my present-day world-view . . . *Challenging chronological, linear sequence:* . . . narrative time 'springs forth in the plural unity of future, past and present' . . . *Recognizing different voices:* . . . rejecting the strong temptation to present the text as a smooth, seamless flow, the product of a unified, consistent, single, voice . . . Refusing a split between the personal and the social: to attack critically the dichotomies, divisions, separate categories that split the personal and the social . . . *Seeing political agency, and acknowledging the structural* . . .
> (Jackson, 1990: 5–13; emphasis added)

Jackson's autobiography actually runs the risk of creating a new genre of writing a life – many of the writing strategies of the past are now self-consciously refused and erased in favour of experiment (see: Nietzsche, Barthes, Stein, Derrida, Sartre and many other less well-known writers, cf. Chapter 4). Yet it is this difficult theme which haunts emerging writing as one century closes and another begins. As both the Patti Lather and David Jackson extracts demonstrate, the writing process is becoming more and more self-conscious and reflective. Social science is no longer a straightforward description of reality out there; instead, the terms used become discussed, elaborated upon and contested. The author is no longer afraid to use the first person: to say 'I' (Krieger, 1991). New ways of writing may bring new ways of thinking.

But it goes further than this. As we move into the twenty-first century, social science may be on the brink not just of new ways of speaking and writing, but also of new ways of *presenting and performing*. The standard social science text has its introduction, literature review, findings, discussion, conclusion, notes and bibliography. It is written for a highly specialized audience, with no concern that any one away from that audience could possibly read it. It comes with all the accoutrements of 'academia'. And to suggest doing it any other way is often to be seen as frivolous, non-academic, indulgent. But why should there be only the one approved way to present social science material? And why, indeed, is this always an elitist and non-populist mode? It seems to me that increasingly the human sciences should face the daunting task of learning how to communicate in more popular and accessible ways.

A major challenge for the twenty-first century has to be to find and develop new and experimental modes of presenting lives and data.

Chapter 3 has suggested that even this may not actually be that new: there are many experiments in photography, recording, film, photographs, video, diaries and letters that have been taking place throughout the twentieth century. But recently, and from a number of stances, there have been clusters of intellectuals and academics who have been experimenting with new ways of presenting their 'data'. There has been a narrowness in the way we think about producing our work, and new forms should be experimented with and – where they work well – they should be added on to the sociological imagination at work: taught, studied, debated, used. The core concerns are to recognize ourselves in and around our research; to see that the presentation of it really matters; and to jolt both author and reader (in almost Brechtian ways) to rethink, and rethink again, just what it is they are doing. For instance, I find exciting the possibilities of:

- Developing a much more extensive use of *photographs, video and visual form*. In Chapter 3, I mentioned some of the excitement around new visual forms – from digital photography to video diaries. As more and more people gain access to these new visual media and become skilled at it, sociologists will just start to look silly and irrelevant if they go on clinging to the written text. New forms of visual literacy are likely to become more and more important in sensing what is going on in lives and society.
- Using active *audience participation*. Why should the presentation of a life or a work require a monologic lecture style format? Some 'experimenters' have brought their audiences into active dialogues with their texts. One writer presents her paper by entreating the audience to chant at regular intervals some of the core concerns of her paper, and in so doing she helps create a collective story and a sense of belonging to the story. It excludes the standard 'work at a distance' approach (Richardson, 1992).
- Presenting findings and lives as *poetry*. Many feminist theorists – notably Adrienne Rich – have experimented with poetry as a way of communicating their ideas. The psychotherapist Miller Mair (1989) has turned much of his work into a poetic mode; the sociologist Carole Satyamurti (1998) has encapsulated her work in poems and stories; and the interactionist Richard Travisano found it much more telling and rewarding to write about his personal depression through poetry (Travisano, 1999). Such work may not be very 'populist', but it certainly helps to reorientate social science away from the linear line and eye.
- Exploring the use of *personal narrative, auto/ethnography, experimental ethnography*. This has certainly taken off in social science (prompted I think by feminism, black and gay studies), and so it is not uncommon to find the personal merged with the academic in more and more writing. But we have also seen some newer and more extreme forms

emerging during this book. I think of Carolyn Ellis's *Final Negotiations* (1995), Susan Krieger's *The Family Silver* (1991) or Richard Quinney's 'Once My Father Traveled West to California' (1996) . . . Here the borderlines between academic work and a personal life story become broken; and intense self-analysis mixes with academic analysis. In a brief extract from a telling passage, Quinney writes:

> You should know that what I tell – what can be said and what can be put on paper – is hard wrought. Once writing came easily; accounts minimally related to my life poured forth. [Note: Quinney was a prominent criminologist of the 1970s, with many books to his name.] Articles and books accumulated. But as I turned to the experiences of my own life for inspiration, the pace slowed. As I became more aware of the living of my own life, journal notes became my primary obsession. My solace and my salvation. A way of making sense of the daily ebb and flow, of the past's hold on the present. Occasionally I would write an essay – conceived as personal essay rather than abstract file . . . Now, the living of a life – my life in connection to all life – is my field of work . . . (Quinney, 1996: 257)

- *Dramatizing* the text. Sometimes this can literally mean turning the research study and the life story into a form of play which can be enacted and which captures the multiple voices found in the research. Thus Carolyn Ellis and Art Bochner turn their research on abortion into a drama. Key scenes – the pregnancy test, the decision, dealing with the decision, the abortion – are enacted by key players: 'the text was written with the express purpose of being performed so that nuances of feeling, expression, and interpretation could be communicated more clearly' (Ellis and Bochner, 1996: 80). But it can also mean more closely studying the performativities of life: Anne Davis Basting studied 'old age' through eight different theatrical productions where older people actually set about constructing their own unique meanings of old age (Basting, 1998).
- Developing *experimental writing styles*. The linear text starts to become challenged and new modes of writing start to appear. Thus, Margery Wolf takes a series of people and events which she studied in Taiwan, but writes them up in three radically different ways: as fiction, as fieldnotes and as a social science article! This is a *Thrice Told Tale* (1992). Carol Rambo Ronai – in studies of stripping and 'mental retardation' – produces *layered accounts* which allow different aspects of the researcher's self to 'roam around the text': she intersperses different voices and selves in the text, commenting back on her thoughts and hence enabling a great deal of reflexivity (Ronai, 1992, 1996). But there are now more and more experiments in writing taking place.
- Writing social science as *fiction* and the use of fiction in social science. We have seen the mode of the 'new journalism' when journalists turn their investigative journalism into a novel; but what we are now

starting to see are social scientists who turn their studies into fiction. They tell the story as a story – drawing it is true upon their research, but making a major concern rest with its readability, its ability to enter a more popular imagination. Is it possible in social science to write fiction? To turn the field research or the life story into a fictional account? It has certainly been done. Classically, the anthropologist Laura Bohanan (who wrote under the name Eleanor Smith Bowen initially) caused a sensation when she wrote her study of an African tribe. She claimed her work as fiction:

> All the characters in this book, except myself, are fictions in the fullest meaning of that word. I knew people of the type I have described here: the incidents of the book are of the genre that I myself experienced in Africa. Nevertheless, so much is fiction. I am an anthropologist. The tribe I describe here does exist. The book is the story of the way I did fieldwork with them. The ethnographic background given here is accurate, but it is neither complete nor technical. Here I write simply as a human being . . . (cf. Bowen, 1954 cited in Edgerton and Langness, 1974: 78)

• Exploring the new technologies – from hypertext CD-Rom to virtual reality – as new ways of presenting the new social science. The skills required here may be quite different from those demanded by writing: 'videoliteracy' and 'computer literacy' becomes essential to their use. Social science seems to be just at the beginning of these new modes of communication. At the most extreme edge, a wholly new way of telling stories based upon 'virtual reality' may be in the making: encased in computer technology, our bodies enter three-dimensional fictional worlds where we can invent our own social science worlds and live them out in real life fantasy!

Conclusion: narrativity and the problem of narrative

The past two chapters have raised problems of writing, presentation, narrative. I have travelled quite a distance from the concern with simply studying the lives. Indeed, whereas in Chapter 1 I pondered a little what would have happened to the social sciences if they had taken as their model the humanities and not the sciences, if they followed Austen or Auden rather than physics and evolutionism, I seem now to have followed the 'humanities' road into a much more theoretical and technical mode. Many of the new trends in literary theory – via 'narratology' and 'deconstruction' – have made such work much more difficult. This is a little ironic, but nevertheless I think there are many things that life story analysis can usefully learn from it.

But care must be taken eventually lest we lose sight of the very documents in their richness and humanity which we wanted to learn from, replacing them with heuristic protocols and 'narratological frames'. To put, for instance, the life document of a holocaust survivor to the scrutiny of narratolgical structural analysis – to detect its story, plot, imagoes, genres, or tropes, and then to 'write' it in new ways – all this raises distinctive issues of ethics and truth. It is to these that we now turn.

Guide to further reading

The **literature on narrative** overflows, and so it is really a question of knowing what aspect of narrative study you are looking for. General, literary introductions include: Selden and Widdowson's *A Reader's Guide to Contemporary Literary Theory* (3rd edn, 1993) and Frank Lentricchia and Thomas McLaughlin, *Critical Terms for Literary Study* (1990). In sociology, James Holstein and Jaber Gubrium's *The Self We Live By* (2000) provides concrete examples of how people make narratives. In psychology, the classic is T.R. Sarbin's *Narrative Psychology: The Storied Nature of Human Conduct* (1986); Derek Edwards has a very useful chapter – 'Narrative and Rememberings' – in his *Discourse and Cognition* (1997). See also Jerome S. Bruner, *Acts of Meaning* (1990). More generally, see Catherine Kohler Riessman, *Narrative Analysis* (1993) and Mia Lieblich, Riva Tuval-Mashiach and Tamar Zilber, *Narrative Research: Reading, Analysis and Interpretation* (1998) – which outlines four kinds of narrative readings; and the series of books edited by Ruth Josselson and A. Lieblich, *The Narrative Study of Lives* (1993–). There are several journals too: see the *Journal of Narrative and Life History*. Within mainly literary theory, there is also a journal called *Narrative* edited from Ohio State University, which is the journal of the Society for the Study of Narrative Literature (www. english.ohio-state. edu/journals/narrative/). There is also *Resources for Narrative Psychology* at http://maple.lemoyne.edu/Ehevern/nrmaster.html

For instances of **narrative at work in social science research**, see Ken Plummer, *Telling Sexual Stories: Power, Change and Social Worlds* (1995); Cheryl Mattingly, *Healing Dramas and Clinical Plots: The Narrative Structure of Experience* (1998); on legal storytelling see a special issue of the *Michigan Law Review*, 1989: 87 (8).

On **genre and life story**, see Mary Chamberlain and Paul Thompson's *Narrative and Genre* (1998).

On **life pattern narratives**, see Jaber Gubrium and David Buckholdt's *Toward Maturity* (1977). A useful discussion of 'Personal Narratives and the Life Course' is by Bertram J. Cohler (1982). Richard Shweder's edited collection *Welcome to Middle Age! (and Other Cultural Fictions)* (1998) provides much anthropological and historical evidence on the lack of universal 'age' stages.

On **new modes of telling**, a number of examples are provided in the chapter. Worth following up more generally are Carolyn Ellis and Michael Flaherty, *Investigating Subjectivity: Research on Lived Experience*

(1992), Carolyn Ellis and Arthur Bochner, *Composing Ethnography* (1996); Norman Denzin, *Interpretive Ethnography* (1997) which reviews a range of these studies in Part 2. There is a special symposium 'Defending Ways of Knowing: Expanding Forms of Presentation' (1996), which is largely expanded and developed in Rosanna Hertz, *Reflexivity and Voice* (1997).

10 The Moral and Human Face of Life Stories: Reflexivity, Power and Ethics

It seems to me curious, not to say obscene and thoroughly terrifying, that it could occur to an association of human beings drawn together through need and chance and for profit into a company, an organ of journalism, to pry intimately into the lives of an undefended and appallingly damaged group of human beings, an ignorant and helpless rural family, for the purpose of parading the nakedness, disadvantage and humiliation of these lives before another group of human beings, in the name of science, of 'honest journalism' (whatever that paradox may mean), of humanity, of social fearlessness, for money, and for a reputation for crusading and for unbias which, when skilfully enough qualified, is exchangeable at any bank for money (and in politics, for votes, job patronage, abe-lincolnism, etc.); and that these people could be capable of meditating this prospect without the slightest doubt of their qualification to do an 'honest' piece of work, and with a conscience better than clear and in the virtual certitude of almost unanimous public approval. It seems curious, further, that the assignment of this work should have fallen to persons having so extremely different a form of respect for the subject, and responsibility toward it, that from the first and inevitably they counted their employers, and that Government likewise to which one of them was bonded, among their most danger- ous enemies, acted as spies, guardians, and cheats, and trusted no judgement, however authoritative it claimed to be, save their own: which in many aspects of the task before them was untrained and uninformed. It seems further curious that realizing the extreme corrupt- ness and difficulty of the circumstances and the unlikelihood of achieving in any untainted form what they wished to achieve, they accepted the work in the first place. And it seems curious still further that, with all their suspicion of and contempt for every person and thing to do with the situation, save only for the tenants and for themselves, and their own intentions, and with all their realization of the seriousness and mystery of the subject, and of the human responsibility they undertook, they so little questioned or doubted their own qualifications for this work.

(Agee and Evans, 1965: 7–8)

Thus speaks the much pained North American journalist James Agee during the course of his celebrated study *In Praise of Famous Men* – a study of poor crop workers in 1930s depression America. He is agonizing over his right to research these people; to tell their stories for a vehicle of journalism. And he brings us straight to the heart of the concerns of this chapter: the personal experience of conducting such research, and the ethical and moral dilemmas it poses. Fifty years on, another journalist posed the same concerns when she wrote:

> Every journalist who is not too stupid or too full of himself [sic] to notice what is going on knows that what he does is morally indefensible . . . The catastrophe suffered by the subject is no simple matter of an unflattering likeness or a misrepresentation of his [sic] views; what pains him, what ranks and some-times drives him to extremes of vengefulness, is the deception that has been practiced on him. On reading the article or book in question, he has to face the fact that the journalist – who seemed so friendly and sympathetic, so keen to understand him so fully, so remarkably attuned to his vision of things – never had the slightest intention of collaborating with him on his story but always intended to write a story of his own. The disparity between what seems to be the intention of an interview as it is taking place and what it actually turns out to have been in aid of always comes as a shock. (Janet Malcolm, 1990. 3)

Although social scientists usually see themselves as way above the plights of 'journalists', I think there are lessons that can be learned. Indeed, one of the dreadful features of so much social science is that it masks and poses as so much objectivity. Studies have often been written as if they had been executed by machines: not a hint of the ethical, political and personal problems which routinely confront the human researcher and the researched subject can be found. Indeed this was originally the claim of social science – to be neutral, cut off, objective. Researchers took their 'subjects' as 'objects' – probing and prodding, poking and peeking, testing and measuring as if they were studying molecules or mice rather than ethically engaged human beings. The point was wrongly but pointedly put by George Homans: 'People who write about methodology often forget it is a matter of strategy not of morals' (Homans, 1949: 330).

Yet the so-called 'value debate' has always been on the agenda, since the earliest days of social science: to be revisited again and again. Most recently, and largely due to the rise of feminism, multiculturalism and postmodernism, the case for a much more committed, reflexive, politi-cally aware, personally grounded style of research has been given a new lease of life (e.g. Denzin, 1997; Ellis and Bochner, 1996; Lather, 1991; Reinharz, 1992; Smith, 1999; Stanley and Wise, 1993). Many studies now take it as a matter of course to depict not just the formal research strategies (like those outlined earlier) but to consider as well the more personal issues of actually doing research – with all the ethical and practical angst this entails. Much research has become increasingly self-reflexive and reflective. Such a change may be decried by some as a narcissistic preoccupation – an introspective navel gazing that deflects from *what* is being argued to *who* is arguing it. Indeed, in its most extreme and potentially dangerous form, research comes to be seen as little more than the elaborate projections of the researcher's own unconscious needs! (cf. Devereux, 1967). But it can perhaps be viewed more modestly and fruitfully as part of a wider growth in pluralism and 'people-based power', since the ethnocentric absolutism of the nine-teenth century. As John Barnes said in the late 1970s:

> The recent increase in concern about what topics shall be investigated, where support for the inquiry shall come from, how the data shall be collected and aggregated, and how the results of the inquiry shall be published has not come about accidentally. It springs from an historical shift in the balance of power between the four parties to the research process [sponsor, gatekeeper, scientist and subject], and from the institutionalization of social inquiry in the ambient culture of industrialized societies. It is one outcome of a movement away from positivism towards a hermeneutic view of knowledge and from an evaluation of knowledge as a source of enlightenment to an evaluation in terms of power and property. (Barnes, 1979: 22)

The social researcher is not a mere medium through which knowledge is discovered; he or she can also be seen as a 'constructor' of 'knowl-edge'. We need to look at how the researcher's personal and social worlds lead to these constructions, and how such constructions are subsequently used in the social world. This is not to deny that there may be some independent truth content in such research; it is merely to recognize that issues of personal experience, social morality and public politics are an ever-present feature of research and need to be firmly confronted. Agee's observation about journalism at the start of this chapter surely poses similar questions for the social scientist using personal documents: by what right can an academic enter the subjective worlds of other human beings and report back to the wider world on them? In this chapter, I propose to examine a few of these more personal and ethical issues.

Entering personal worlds: towards self-reflexivity in research

In a famously candid set of private observations about his life, post-humously published, the pioneer anthropologist Bronislaw Malinowski charted his own personal angst in conducting fieldwork amongst the Trobriand Islanders. Whatever 'knowledge' is to be found in his *Sexual Life of Savages in North Western Melanesia* (1929), there is another tale to be told. And this can be gleaned from his personal diaries – which were never intended for publication. Thus on 26 November 1917, Malinowski can write:

> Yesterday I had what is usually called an attack of feverishness, a touch of fever. Physical and mental sluggishness. Yesterday, for instance, I felt no desire and was not strong enough to take a walk, not even around the Island. Nor had I the energy to get to work, not even write letters to ERM, or even look

over my ethnographic notes. Moreover, I am extremely irritable and the yells of the boys and other noises get horribly on my nerves. The moral tonus is also considerably lower. Emotional bluntness – I think of ERM less intensely than usual. Resistance to lecherous thought weaker. Clarity of metaphysical conception of the world completely dimmed: I cannot endure being with myself, my thoughts pull me down to the surface of the world. I am unable to control things or be creative in relation to the world. Tendency to read *rubbish* . . . (Malinowski, 1967: 131)

All this – and more – from the great social anthropologist who challenged the universality of Freud's Oedipus complex? It seems that the great researcher was human after all. And he is not alone in all this personal angst: all researchers have their trials and tribulations as more and more biographies of 'scientists' and 'researchers' display. Paul Roazen (1979), for example, interviewed over a hundred people who knew Freud and managed to convey something of the way his personal life bore upon his intellectual discoveries; whilst Watson (1968) – the co-discoverer of DNA – has described his own frailties in *The Double Helix*. There are now many 'sociological biographies' which tell the tales of sociologists' personal lives – 'warts and all' (e.g. Berger, 1990; Powdermaker, 1967; Wax, 1971). For some researchers, there actually seems a quite strong need to make their own research selves a presence in the text. Rather famously, Margaret Mead sought visibility:

. . . when Mead was about to give birth to her daughter Catherine, 'The delivery was delayed for ten minutes, until the arrival of the photographer' (Howard, 1984: 208). A movie cameraman was already in position. Others in attendance included 'the obstetrician, several nurses (all of whom at Mead's request had seen the Bateson–Mead film "First days in the life of a New Guinea baby"), a child development psychologist . . . and the paediatrician Dr Benjamin Spock'. (Plath in Sanjek, 1990: 380)

A sense of the personal record is clearly here! And going further still, some have even turned the telling of these personal research 'confessionals' into their own social science art form: a kind of 'auto/ ethnography' and 'self story' (e.g. Ellis, 1995; Reed-Danahay, 1997; Richardson, 1998; and see Chapter 2). What we start to sense in this developing literature is the importance of 'reflexivity'. This is a difficult and even controversial term, with some seeing it negatively as a term to justify excessive self-indulgence in academic work; and others seeing it as a key precondition for good academic work. I have found a number of usages of the term.

Some use it rather sloppily simply to mean self-introspection, but this is not what I think it should mean (that way self-indulgence can lie). It should incorporate this, but go much beyond it. Alvin Gouldner uses it in his magisterial *The Coming Crisis of Western Sociology* (1971) to suggest that sociologists should analyse their own work through the same tools and methods as they analyse society, in effect a sociology of sociology. Pierre Bourdieu, in his *An Invitation to Reflexive Sociology* (Bourdieu and Wacquant, 1992), insists on reflexivity but goes beyond Gouldner: for he identifies three types of bias which may 'blur the sociological gaze' – the social biases (e.g. class), the academic biases (the limits of academic rules), and the intellectualizing bias – which need to be got at through reflexivity. I find it interesting that Bourdieu makes such an issue of the trappings of both academia and intellectual life as ways that censor and impede knowledge, and that it is these that have to be broken down and brought to awareness in specific social spaces. But Bourdieu, on the other hand, is not in favour of deep introspective brooding, or the 'diary disease' of keeping intense analyses of oneself. This is not what reflexivity means to him. A third approach has been suggested by Helen Callaway:

> Often condemned as a political activity, reflexivity, on the contrary can be seen as opening the way to a more radical consciousness of self in facing the political dimensions of fieldwork and constructing knowledge. . . . Reflexivity becomes a continuing mode of self analysis and political awareness. (Callaway, cited in Hertz, 1997: viii)

What reflexivity ultimately means to me is a much greater social and self-awareness/consciousness of the whole intellectual/research process: of (a) the subject of the research along with (b) the social spaces in which the research knowledge is produced, as well as (c) a much fuller sense of the spaces/locations – personal, cultural, academic, intellectual, historical – of the researcher in actually building the research knowledge. There has to be an attentiveness to time – what people take into research situations and take out of them; as well as feeling, identity, body. In the past – as in the case of Malinowski above – this reflexivity has only been tacit and implicit: the actual studies are presented without much personal reflection which is saved for a confessional narrative somewhere else. But what has happened recently is a concern that 'research knowledge' only makes sense if we can acquire understanding about the active processes through which such knowledge becomes produced. If we wish to understand a life story, then, we need also to know where both the researcher and the teller of that life are coming from, what kind of relationship they are having together, and how this fits into the wider social order.

The researcher and the researched: their friends, their enemies and their lovers

A slightly formal way of starting to examine these relations is to return to two classic papers on 'fieldwork roles'. The first, by Raymond Gold (1958), suggested four 'ideal' type researcher roles, ranged along a continuum from *complete observer* through *observer as participant* and *participant as observer* to *complete participant*. The continuum captures nicely the delicate balance needed between the relatively distanced, unattached, objective observer and the relatively involved, subjective participant: in life document research the latter, more subjective, view is stressed – and to gain this, intensive involvement between researcher and subject is a must. Simply getting respondents to write 'raw' letters or simply flicking on a tape recorder for a subject to 'tell their story' will certainly provide a subjective tale, but it will lack the depth and detail that could be gleaned if the researcher was immersed in the subject's world for a long time and tried to build up an in-depth description from the inside.

A second paper, by Patricia and Peter Adler (1987, 1994), suggests that the world of research has changed since Gold's model was first put forward, in that there has been a general shift towards researchers becoming more and more involved. What is hence also needed is a sense of different *membership roles* in fieldwork. They suggest three as prominent: the *complete member* researcher, the *active member* researcher, and the *peripheral member* researcher (Adler, 1987, 1994). Redesigning both Gold's and the Adlers' continuums for life stories and personal documents, I simply suggest a continuum of involvement from the very passive 'Stranger Role', through the 'Acquaintance Role' and on to the most active 'Friendship Role'. I will also add another – rare and controversial – 'lover' role!

The stranger role   At the most passive end of this continuum, then, is the life historian who gathers personal documents from subjects (living and non-living) with nil intrusion or involvement, and who uses these to assemble the subject's own life account. I think this has to be quite rare – and maybe has to depend upon 'dead' documents: Allport's *Letters from Jenny* (1965) provides an account of Jenny's problems entirely from the correspondence she addressed to two people (see Chapter 3), there is no hint of personal interaction. And obviously, when Eric Erikson studied Luther (1959), there was again no chance of communicating with the dead! Likewise, Foucault's *I, Pierre Rivière* (1978) gathers materials from interrogation transcripts in the early nineteenth century. In such accounts there is nil direct involvement of the researcher with the life (although this need not stop the process of self-reflexivity, none of the above make it visible).

Acquaintance role   A little further along the continuum is the life historian, who enters a person's life for a brief interview and then departs, the relationship being defined entirely as a professional interview. Maybe many of the interviews conducted by Studs Terkel for his many oral history-based books – like *Working* (1974/1977), *The Good War* (1984), *Race* (1992) and *Coming of Age* (1995) – must be of this form; he has interviewed so very many people that it is hard to see how he could really get to know many of them well. At the same time, accounts of his work – in *Talking to Myself* (1978) and *Studs Terkel: A Life in Words* (Parker, 1996) – show the man behind the text revealing quite a close attachment to many of his respondents and interviewees. It is actually hard to be a 'stranger' when doing a life story. This is the kind of relationship so characteristic of 'living in the city', where cordiality is extended without intensive intimacies. A casual working relationship is very easy – the researcher possibly having a drink or a meal with their 'subjects'. This is probably the most common role for life story research – where the story will be gathered in a few interview sessions and hence the subject will be seen probably for no more than ten hours in all. This is possibly also the case with Tony Parker's original studies into American murderers and English sex offenders (Parker, 1969, 1995).

Friendship role   At the most extreme, this can result in the individual becoming a close and intimate friend over the period of time. This can create an enormous tension between the professional role of the researcher and the personal commitments of friendship. Oscar Lewis's work on Mexican families captures this last mood very clearly:

> What began as a professional interest in their lives turned into warm and lasting friendships. I became deeply involved in their problems and often felt as though I had two families to look after, the Sanchez family and my own. I have spent hundreds of hours with members of the family; I have eaten in their homes, attended their dances and festive occasions, have accompanied them to their places of work, have met their relatives and friends, have gone with them on pilgrimages to church, to the movies, and to sports events. The Sanchez family learned to trust and confide in me. They would call upon me and my wife in times of need or crisis and we helped them through illness, drunkenness, trouble with the police, unemployment and family quarrels. I did not follow the common anthropological practice of paying them as informants (nor informers) and I was struck by the absence of monetary motivation in their relationship with me. Basically it was their sense of friendship that led them to tell me their life stories. (Lewis, 1961: xx)

Likewise, the criminologist Edwin Sutherland (1937), for example, knew his thief for five years and maintained a friendship afterwards, while Robert Straus (1974) first met Frank Moore, 'the alcoholic', in 1948 and continued to know him until his death in 1972.

During the 1970s Jon Snodgrass revisited the materials for two of the most famous sociological personal documents – Clifford Shaw's *The Jack Roller* and Edwin Sutherland's *The Professional Thief* (Snodgrass, 1973, 1978, 1982). In both cases, it is clear that the researcher had a fairly lengthy and complex relationship with the subject. Thus, Sutherland and Broadway Jones (his real name, though he was known in the text through the anonymized pseudonym of Chic Conwell) became lifetime friends and corresponded and visited one another long after Sutherland left the University of Chicago for Indiana University in 1935. Jones stayed in Sutherland's home at times and Sutherland took him to class to entertain and educate his students. Some people thought that in subsequent years Jones 'hustled' or continued to 'hustle' 'The Doctor', as Sutherland was affectionately called by Jones. Their relationship seems much more substantial than this:

> If they had this 'relationship' all kinds of questions need asking of it. Did Sutherland's personal sympathies toward a friend bias his theoretical interpretations? How did Sutherland relate with Jones when with his personal friends and family? What reciprocal obligations were built up between the two men? What tensions existed? Was a divide between public work and private involvements sustained? How did their relationship develop and end? Little is known about this and yet surely much light could be thrown on personal documents by being able to answer such questions. (Snodgrass, 1973: 9)

Likewise with Clifford Shaw, who seemed to have met Stanley (the Jack Roller) in 1921, as 'a graduate student and resident settlement worker in a Polish neighbourhood' (Snodgrass, 1978: 5). On a number of occasions, Stanley talks glowingly of Shaw, and it is clear too that Shaw and his wife invited Stanley into their home and kept in close contact. Whatever may have constituted the text of Stanley, there is clearly a great deal more going on all around it. Retrospectively, Stanley talks of 'the natural and simple charm of Shaw's great and humane personality proved over the ensuing years to be genuine . . .' 'I had many visits with Shaw and his family which I enjoyed greatly . . . it certainly would not be far fetched to state that the Shaws were my real parents' . . . 'Now if anyone ever had influence over me it was Shaw . . .'(Snodgrass, 1982: 26, 33, 171), and he recalls on the occasion of Shaw's death in 1955, through a condolence note to his wife, the occasion of their first meeting where 'instinctively I knew him as a friend' (Snodgrass, 1982: 3).

Such relationships can be found in more recent studies too. In *Mema's House*, which tells the tales of a Mexican, the author, Nanick Prieur, writes: 'Mema' was 'a door opener and an eye opener . . . my host, my cook, my driver and my bodyguard. And he was, and still is, one of the closest friends I have' (Prieur, 1998: vii). The study focuses on him and his house, home to many homosexual and transvestite boys whose stories are also told throughout the book. Likewise, in the study of Mohammed by Pat Caplan (1997), there is clear evidence throughout of a strong bond and closeness between researcher and researched. In the opening discussion, Caplan discusses with Mohammed such matters as authorship (see Chapter 8), confidentiality and even the payments of royalties – and how she and Mohammed would split the proceeds. Throughout it is clear that Mohammed has great faith in Caplan and views her as a very good friend.

In all these cases we find something like *a methodology of friendship*, of building a quite special relationship founded partly on research goals but equally on friendship. Yet as these 'friendship tales' become increasingly revealed and advocated, the problems that they can bring should be addressed. As a number of feminists have recently noted, all is not so well with turning research into a friendship. For 'as researchers and participants get acquainted, establish trust and friendship, they become vulnerable to misunderstanding, disappointment and invaded privacy. It can lead amongst other things to false intimacies, fraudulent friendships, a deceptiveness over equal relationships, and a masking of power' (Kirsch, 1999: 26).

Sexing research: erotic dimensions and the 'Lover Role'   We can take all this one stage further into slightly dangerous, controversial land. Here we turn to the hidden dimensions of romance, passion and sexuality that must impinge on much research, even if rarely spoken about. It is curious, not to say disingenuous, to find that most research is written as if such experiences quite simply never happen in people's lives. From fieldwork to life story research, as people come and go, nothing much ever seems to happen in the 'erotic dimension'. Just where is it? We can sense a little of this dimension (once again) from Malinowki's Diary – indeed the fact that he actually speaks of his own 'persistent and painful struggle against "lewd" and "impure" fantasies about Trobriand and missionary women, whom he "pawed" and perhaps more' (Newton, 1993: 6), gives a sign as to a deep undercurrent of research that has until very recently been consistently downplayed.

But a series of recent studies have started to make this erotic dimension more explicit. In a wonderful account of Kay, a lesbian in her eighties and one of her key informants at the lesbian community, Cherry Grove, Esther Newton makes her passion and involvement very clear:

> This morning I introduced myself to a woman of eighty plus whom I'd been wanting to meet, as she rolled toward me in her electric chair. Not only was she receptive, she clasped my arm in an intimate embrace and practically pulled me into her while we talked . . . and my heart quite turned over. Such are the perils of fieldwork . . . the beauty of it is I adore her even though I need her and have ulterior professional motives. (Newton, 1993: 12–14)

The closeness of this relationship blossoms over a number of years. In other instances such relationships have led directly to marriage. During her fieldwork in the West Indies, Gearing falls in love with her key informant:

> As we spent more time together, discussing our respective family histories, I came to trust him and began to see him as a person I cared for deeply, as well as a person to whom I was strongly attracted. I was also impressed by the sacrifices EC made to help me . . . [he] often brought me small gifts of food or flowers. . . . The combination of personal and professional attractions was

incredibly appealing, and actually impossible to resist. My intellectual excitement kept pace with my physical attraction as I learned more and more. (Gearing, 1995: 199).

Out of this 'erotic dimension' grew a deeper understanding of life in the West Indies. Others have argued that such sexual overt relations are necessary in many areas of fieldwork. Two minor classics – by Styles (1979) and Stewart (1972) show how personal sexual experiences of gay bath houses (Styles) and heterosexual brothels (Stewart) can help understand sexualities. Both these researchers argued that in order to understand what was going on sexually, you had to experience it! (And interestingly neither seem to have published much – or anything – after these initial studies: maybe it was enough to damage their careers?) In the wake of an explosion of 'sex research' around AIDS, one leading anthropologist, Ralph Bolton, positively advocated sex with respondents if what you wish to understand is sexuality. For him, 'information obtained post coitally . . . when people tend to relax and open up their lives, was always richer, more from the heart and more revealing than the data gathered in a more detached manner' (Bolton, 1995: 148).

Reflexivity, emotions and the researcher's self

All this takes us into the more intimate worlds of doing research. We start to see that the doing of life story research is also personal, interactional, emotional, embodied work that can have implications for the self of the researcher as well as the researched. How does the researcher present him- or herself? How is a relational self built up with the subjects of research? How is the interaction embodied? How are feelings presented and managed (cf. Coffey, 1999; Kleinman and Copp, 1993)?

In an earlier work on 'sexual life stories', I describe a situation of life story interviewing that I enter and then start to reflect on just why I did this and what it means. I will repeat a little of this here, as it starts to capture something of the reflexive process beginning. Here I describe my first encounter with a so-called 'foot fetishist', whom the research secretary named Jack.

> I travel to the North of England where I meet a young man in his early twenties in a hotel lobby. We go to my hotel room, and he tells me in enormous detail of his desire to be trod upon by women in high heels. As this happens, he fantasizes a dagger being plunged into his stomach. It is a long story, which takes me through his childhood memories of this and the 'driven' nature of his 'single' adult life. I record the conversation, and respond very sympathetically to him: he seems a nice enough man. Back at my university, the tape is transcribed and makes fascinating reading. The secretary [of the research] names him Jack (a pseudonym: but interestingly her husband is called Jack!). This transcript is sent to Jack, who comments profusely on it. A short correspondence is set up, and I send him a copy of a key book in this field: *The Sex*

Life of the Foot and Shoe. For the past ten years, the transcript and its commentary sits in my filing cabinet. I have lost contact with him. (Plummer, 1995a: 10)

And after this brief description – so much more could have been said – I continue asking questions of myself about what I was actually doing:

What brought me to seek out a man who wanted to talk about his 'unusual' sexual life? Why should I, in the name of Holy Social Science, want to coax anyone to tell me about their sexual lives? What brought him to the hotel room to tell me all about it? How could he produce such stories, and how did my 'tolerant' responses to him actively encourage him to tell a certain sort of story – he could sense very early on that I was not going to be shocked or censorious in any way. But didn't that make him say certain things rather than others? And to leave endless undetected absences? How much of his story was a performance of a dress rehearsal he had practised many times in solitude before? What, then, was the relationship of my transcribed interview to his actual life? And how was I to write this? In his voice, or in my voice, or in his voice through my voice, or even in my voice through his voice? And then, once read by others – including me and him – what multiple interpretations would it be open to? Would there perhaps be a correct reading which would finally get us all to the truth of such foot fetishists? Or would it be used as an occasion for condemnation, or curiosity, or simple titillation, or as a guide for someone else to locate their sexual nature? What would it do to Jack once published? And indeed, what has it done to him since it has *not* been published, but sits unread in a filing cabinet? And so it goes on. The questions proliferate. I became more and more aware of these questions at the time of doing the research, and they slowly incapacitated me. Just what *are* these sexual stories gathered for research? (Plummer, 1995a: 12)

Now, some years later, I could take this questioning even further – this kind of 'reflexivity' just scrapes the surface! I could ask about my sense of self as I approach the hotel, whilst I am in it, and after I leave. Did I not perhaps feel a little apprehensive or even scared of meeting a stranger in this way (yes, I certainly did!). Did I not feel something of a 'deceiver' in doing this research – he has got nothing out of it, after all, except a copy of a book and a chance to tell his story? Did I like the man, or not; did I perhaps even 'fancy him' (not that I can recall!). How did my feelings show through – were they 'stiff and starchy' (as I know I can be) 'easy going', or 'smooth/charming' (as I can also sometimes be!). And what-ever my feelings were, how might this have shaped what we both said. And what did he think of me – some silly university bloke who knew something, a sympathetic listener, just an interviewer: why should he even care? Was there a 'kindness between strangers' or was there a lurking hostility and mutual distrust? And how did all this play into my more general life? Again, it could go on . . . and on.

Emotion worlds Susan Krieger, in a series of studies and observations, has pondered just how she 'had a right to say something that was mine':

so much social science cuts off from the author, and we feel we often have no right at all to bring ourselves and our feelings about our work into the study. In several works, of which *The Mirror Dance* (1983), *Social Science and the Self* (1991), and *The Family Silver* (1996) are the most famous, Krieger has laboured to find ways in which she can do research and yet allow her own presence and experiences to be felt. Thus, in *The Mirror Dance*, she documents some of the problems of trying to write up a number of intensive interviews with lesbians in a small community around the themes of privacy, identity, community. Even though this is a much more initmate study than most, she found that her problem was not 'lack of distance' but 'too much distance': she was too estranged from her data and the people she studied. Putting herself back in, seeing personally her year's participation with the group she studied, meant an active emotional re-engagement process in which an understanding of her own self, worked through over time, helped clarify her 'data'.

Drawing upon some of these studies, it may help for the researcher to ponder more their own emotional and self worlds as they do their research. For instance, they could ask:

- Before: Amazingly our feelings and self nearly always get written out of the studies. But think of such questions as: why am I doing this study – do I have an axe to grind, do I have a passion? And if so, how do I feel this, and how might it shape my work? What kind of person am I to do this kind of work, and what may it say about who I like, don't like, situations I am willing to go in?
- During: Do I like the person I am interviewing, or not. Maybe, in worst case scenarios, I actively dislike them – or, maybe, I am even 'falling in love' with them?
- After: How do I feel about the work, the field notes, the transcripts, the analysis? The later meetings etc.

These are pretty banal and obvious questions, but they remain ones that are almost wholly hidden from the research process.

Ethics and morality in research

In his book *Doing Documentary Work* (1997), Robert Coles (whose major works includes the five volume *Children of Crisis*) spends much time ruminating on the moral and psychological tensions of doing such research. Of course, the goals of such study are usually entirely laudable: someone needs to tell this story well and humanely. But there is a niggle: all this borders on the abusive and the exploitative. What gives any social scientist (or any journalist for that matter) the right to invade another's life, gather up their tale, and then leave: telling (and often selling) their story to others? It is indeed a strange pratice when described like this.

Bluntly, what, if anything, do we owe those we have 'studied', whose lives we have gone on to document? Should we, for instance, send back the writing, the photography, the film once it is completed? If so, at what stage of that work's development . . .? Should we pay our informants for all the time and effort put into making a film or working with a photographer, or an interviewer? Should we share our royalties, our artists fees, our monetary rewards or prizes with the subject of our documentary project, or share them with a group or fund whose purpose it is to address the 'particular problem' we have presented? Then there is the problem of exploitation . . . is it 'exploitative' to do documentary work, to arrive on a given scene, ask for people's co-operation, time, energy and knowledge, do one's 'study' or 'project', and soon enough, leave, *thank yous* presumably extended. How can we do such work honorably . . .? (Coles, 1997: 76–7)

Coles's students feel this angst too: as one of them (a photographer) says of trying to get in to a home to take some photos:

I'll be sitting there in someone's home – I've interrupted their life, the nerve of me! – and I think to myself, this is wrong. Why don't I take a polite 'No' politely, and leave? Why am I being so conniving? That's the word I should use! Why *should* that family let me hang around? I use that phrase as it means I'll be a fly on the wall, and their already difficult life won't be made any worse, but it's not true, and I know it's not true, and they do, too. I suppose I could try to bribe them, pay them. But that's not right – or is it? Why shouldn't they be paid? They're poor and they need the money, and I'll get something out of this, that's certain . . . we get recognition, and we build our lives up, our careers – and they, there's nothing in it for them. They put up with us! . . . (Coles, 1997: 82–3)

This student goes on for several pages worrying about what he is doing – Coles calls it 'his conscience, his soul'; and it is good to hear such worries. In my experience, remarkably few students think like this and raise such issues. Research is something that is just done and the ethics of the matter are largely disregarded. I find this very worrying – not least when whole courses on research methods can bypass such critical concerns. My aim now is to probe a little into some of these ethical issues. I start with a crude listing of seven concerns, before moving on to consider the broader worries they raise.

1 *Ownership and intellectual property rights*   The first question sounds silly: 'Who owns the life being studied?' And put as bluntly as this, the answer must be clear – it is the person who tells the tale, whose life it is, who should own the 'story'. But so often this is clearly not the case. Along comes the social scientist to get the tale; all goes well and a good story appears; but then the researcher says goodbye and publishes the tale. Now it belongs to the researcher, and often becomes wholly cut off from the life of the teller. Quite rightly, this has provoked increasing outrage from 'subjects' who are beginning to fight back and resist this process. In a

celebrated case at the 1973 International Congress of Anthropology and Ethnological Sciences, flying teams of angry young African anthropologists rushed from session to session with a message that went like this:

> You, sir or madam, spent fifteen months studying my village, published two books about 'your' people, and never sent us so much as a copy of either book or helped us in any way to profit from what you learned! (cited in Finnegan, 1992: 216)

This sounds extreme, but it is everywhere in social science. When people respond to a large survey and their voices are quoted in texts, who owns this? When people show their letters, or photos, or diaries to researchers, and these are then extensively used, who owns them? And when someone tells their life story which then becomes a book by someone else – *The Polish Peasant* by Thomas and Znaniccki who owns this?

We have entered the growing and important debates about voice, ownership and 'intellectual property rights'. How to get copyright permission to use other voices? To whom to attribute authorship in publication? How to recognize the rights and obligations found in all research – not least with respect to remuneration.

2 Confidentiality With many life documents the issue of confidentiality is an acute one: stories of lives by their very nature usually render the authors recognizable. Often, texts reveal a discussion with life history subjects as to just how far this confidentiality should be maintained (e.g. Caplan, 1997: 1–4). And ultimately many life histories do explicitly reveal their informants – presumably with their consent, sometimes with their encouragement(?). Thus, Ralph Samuels's (1981) study of the life of Arthur Harding has Harding's photograph on the cover of the book (as well as many other photographs inside); Allport's *Letters from Jenny* (1965) has photographs of Mrs Masterson and other participants in the story opposite the title page; whilst the story of *I, Rigoberta Menchú* (1984) led to her ultimately being awarded a Nobel laureate: she became world famous as a result of the publication of her life story. (Her sequel included a photograph of herself; Menchú, 1998.) Nevertheless, many probably make a clear claim to guarantee anonymity. Thus names are changed, places are shifted and sometimes a few 'fictional' events are added to prevent intimates of the subject suspecting. Just how far one can go in such modifications without making a nonsense of the goal of some kind of authenticity, becomes a key point. Nevertheless, such blanket guarantees of confidentiality are rarely enough to prevent a dedicated pursuer of identity tracking down the original subject. Fifty years after the original study, Clifford Shaw's 'Jack Roller' in Chicago was located for a re-interview in Los Angeles (Snodgrass, 1982), and after only a month's detective work Oscar Lewis's 'Children of Sanchez' (1961) were tracked down by a reporter (Diener and Crandall, 1978: 103).

The research guarantee of confidentiality to the subject may, ironically, also be threatened by the subject's own self-publicity. Years ago, an interviewee of mine who I maintained contact with for several years until his death, would repeatedly remind me of my need to safeguard his security and confidences – only to proceed to tell his friends and acquaintances all about his involvement in the research! Indeed, these friends would then talk to me about this involvement, and I would be placed in the curious position of pretending not to know what they meant. My wall of silence was constantly threatened by the subject's babbling declarations. In the end, I had to stop researching this subject as confidentiality was an impossibility. A similar problem befell Klockars with Vincent Swaggi, the fence:

> I told Vincent that I would not reveal his identity unless it meant that I was going to jail if I did not, and he told me that he really could not expect me to do more. These contingencies notwithstanding Vincent could just not resist a little advance publicity. He told everybody – judges, lawyers, politicians, prosecutors, thieves, hustlers and most of his good customers. He started this word of mouth publicity campaign a full year before the book was released. (Klockars, 1977: 214)

This classic issue of confidentiality can also be raised posthumously. In the celebrated case of Diane Wood Middlebrook's experience of writing a biography of Anne Sexton, a poet who killed herself in 1975, she was allowed access by Sexton's therapist to some 300 tapes – tapes which revealed, amongst other things, her sexual abuse by another therapist. A controversy rightly followed whether such private material should really have been made available to the biographer – though Middlebrook has made a strong defence of her practice, based on what she feels Sexton would have approved (Middlebrook, 1996). The issue of confidentiality is always cited as one of the obvious worries of research: but it remains rife with problems, and needs very careful consideration before, during and after the research.

3 Honesty and the scandals of life stories As in life, so in research, 'honesty' would seem to be a fairly basic requirement! So a minimal canon of 'science' might well be seen as suggesting that the researcher should be as accurate, painstaking and honest as possible. Life histories, for example, should just not be 'made up' – this may be the novelist's domain, but the social scientist should accurately describe a real life. Yet in science generally there is enough evidence to suggest that outright falsification does occur sometimes. Social science research contains a curious dark history of accusations of cheating, lying, deceptions and plagiarism which is still to be written. When a typical student reads about research findings in their studies, they usually take them at face value. But they should not. For some of the biggest and most famous of studies have been accused of treacherous deception. Indeed, there are a growing number of 'research scandals' which suggest researchers do not follow these basic rules. Some seem very serious – for instance, the controversy around the work of Sir Cyril Burt on intelligence testing where it has been suggested that the world-renowned scientist faked most of his data, invented co-authors and fabricated results to negate critics! A huge controversy followed (Joynson, 1989). The celebrated sex researcher Alfred Kinsey's studies have been the butt of a number of exposés, some suggesting he was gay, others proposing he was a sado-masochist, still others suggesting he encouraged paedophilia (Gathorne-Hardy, 1998; Jones, 1997). In another famous case, the 'Hitler Diaries' which were discovered during the 1980s – purportedly revealing much about Hitler's life – were soon disclosed as 'fakes' (Hamilton, 1991). More mildly, it has been suggested that Margaret Mead's widely cited and ground breaking studies of lives in Samoa (*Coming of Age in Samoa*) were conducted by a woman who could not speak the language of the people and visited them only a few times (Freeman, 1984).

Three 'life story scandals' are worthy of note because they have become so very famous in the academic community (and outside). The first is the classic, highly influential *Roots* by Alex Haley (1977). This was not just a best-selling book, but also a widely watched television series throughout the world. It was an important book for blacks in North America as it told their story – of slavery, of migration, of past lives. It charted Haley's ancestry from The Gambia through his slave roots and on into modern times – through the eyes of Kunta Kinte, a slave boy brought to America. And it gave its author Alex Haley a Pulitzer Prize and made him a millionaire. But in 1978, there was a five week plagiarism trial which suggested that Haley had copied some 80 passages from a slave novel of the 1960s (*The African* by Harold Courlander). The charges were settled out of court; but after this there were accusations of key figures not having lived, of Haley's planting responses to interviewed people, of numerous errors that implied much had been fabricated, that many of the records showed errors in the lineage: and so forth. All these accusations led to a concern that Haley had got away with all this because the 'liberal reception' was so strong that it simply could not be challenged. For some, the controversies still continue (Noble, 1993).

Another famous but contested life story was that of Don Juan told by Carlos Castaneda (Castaneda, 1968). In 1973, Carlos Castaneda received his PhD in anthropology from the University of California at Los Angeles for presenting the life stories of an old Yacqui Mexican Indian sorcerer, Don Juan, who espoused a philosophy of ascetic mysticism and became Castaneda's 'master'. Castaneda walked the Sonoman desert with Don Juan whilst he told his story. The new young scholar was introduced to a world of hallucinogenic plants and psychedelic drugs, alternative realities and shamans – the 'Yacqui Way' – recorded in voluminous field notes and interviews (that later were not available for inspection!). The thesis became a best-seller – as *The Teachings of Don Juan* – and Castaneda went on to write further popular works – *A Separate Reality, Journey to Ixtlan, Tales of Power, The Second Ring of Power* – developing a cult following, especially amongst the hippies of the time. Praised and read by many, his work has become something of a cause célèbre in academic circles, where Castaneda has been accused of fraud and deception. At the time of its publication, there were suspicions; although he was awarded his PhD, nobody seems to have seen the original material for the study and many experts reviewing the book (the leading anthropologists Edmund Leach and Weston Le Barre among them) have been scathing and dismissive, suggesting little connection between the book and the Yacqui tradition. More recently, Richard de Mille's compilations of commentaries in his *The Don Juan Papers* (1990) amasses much evidence to suggest that the whole project was a hoax. He claims that the evidence contradicts itself; that there is a lack of convincing detail (and sometimes even 'implausible detail') and that much of the text sounds like it comes from the books and works of others (over 200 literary influences have been cited as shaping this text). For example: 'during nine years of collecting plants and hunting animals with Don Juan, Carlos learns not one Indian name for any plant or animal' (De Mille, 1990: 19); the environmental descriptions of the Sonoran desert he lived in do not ring true; they go wandering in the desert in the most extreme temperatures which 'only the utterly inexperienced or foolhardy' would do (p. 35). In general, the stories do now seem to be nearer to fiction than an anthropological science making truth claims! But defenders even go so far as to say that the truth itself does not matter: what Castaneda conveys is a deep subjective experience, an alternative reality. And in this lies its anthropological merit! Oddly, though, even if some of these studies are deceptions, this does not immediately diminish their value for analysis. The leading qualitative researcher David Silverman (1975), for example, analysed Castaneda's 'text' as a case of cultural construction independent of its truth content.

Most recently, the story of *I, Rigoberta Menchú* (introduced in Chapter 2) has caused concern. Recall that it is claimed that this major study had local impact in shifting Guatemalan politics and has also become a 'symbol' of the international human rights movement. This is largely because of Rigoberta Menchú's claims both to be a key spokesperson for all oppressed indigenous American peoples, and for her vivid portrayals of the torture and slaughtering of her people and family at the hands of the Guatemalan government. It has the ring of truth for all colonized, exploited, indigenous people. But some have claimed that there are many worrying aspects to her account. There is a worry about the role Elisabeth Burgos-Debray (1984) (known to be politically committed to the left) played in constructing a text that was claimed to have been the voice of a 23-year-old Guatemalan woman, when she had only been speaking Spanish for three years, and the ensuing conflict between both people. There is the concern Menchú acknowledges in the text, that she must keep the 'secrets' of her culture. There is a problem about the role of 'the Guatemalan guerrillas' in the conflict – the guerrillas are depicted as siding with the Indian people but in practice their role was more complicated, with support varying by region, and with the suggestion that guerrillas were to blame for at least some of the violence. There is a concern that parts of the story may have been invented. There are signs of inflation. There is a concern about Menchú's own subsequent role back in Guatemala – seemingly spending little time there (*Newsweek*, 21 June 1999). And so the controversy goes on and on. Most of this is flagged in a controversial study of Menchú's story by David Stoll (1999) – a book which has itself become the cause of much debate and worry. Disregarding the validity of such claims, what seems to be most at issue here is the way in which such stories can be used by different shades of the political spectrum. It reminds us that life stories have work to perform: they are never just stories. And we need always to look at the contrasting political roles they can play.

4 *Deception* A related form of dishonesty arises with deception. In psychology this dilemma raises its head most frequently when research subjects are not told the true nature of the experiment – some suggest this may be between 20 and 40 per cent of all studies (Diener and Crandall, 1978: 74). In sociology, the dilemma appears where the researcher conceals his or her identity and 'cons' their way into a new group – an issue that is often dubbed the overt/covert debate (see Erikson, 1967). Life history research can rarely involve such direct and blatant deceptions – it is hard to see how a subject could be persuaded to hand over his or her letters, diaries, or provide a detailed life story without being told about the research in some way (albeit death may lead to their posthumous abuse). But deceptions of a lesser nature can and will occur all along the way. Thus, for example, the general description given of the research may leave out some key issues – indeed to tell the subject precisely what it is you are looking for may bias the outcome quite substantially. Further, different accounts of the research may have to be presented to different groups. In one of my own studies, for example, of sexual minorities, we produced four different statements about the goals and aims of the research – for the subjects, for colleagues, for general enquiries and for outside friends. None of these accounts actually lied, they merely emphasized different aspects of the research. For issues of confidentiality, sometimes researchers must partially deceive their readership. Thus two of our respondents had occupations that were unique and rendered them as 'minor celebrities': to reveal this would be to reveal their identity, yet not to reveal it would be to distort the picture.

In the classic study of *The Profesional Thief*, Edwin Sutherland's thief, Chic Conwell, is for example described as having died in 1933

(Sutherland, 1967: vii), but it appears that he lived at least until the 1940s, remaining friendly with 'the Doctor' (as he called Sutherland). Again, little lies like this may help to protect the subject from possible legal or social hassles. Karl Klockars faced a similar problem when he discovered this his professional fence (Vincent Swaggi) was also an informant – 'the greatest undercover agent in the country' – and that through this informant role he had received some police protection. To have explicitly revealed this in the book would have been to expose Swaggi to his own underworld: as Swaggi remarked, 'you tell about that and I'll have every gang in the country gunning for me' (Klockars, 1977: 212). To get round this problem, Klockars made oblique references in the text and footnotes – 'I felt obliged to make the truth opaque to all but the most vigorous readers'. Ironically, by 1977 Klockars did seem willing to reveal all. So perhaps a case can be made for such deceptions, providing the social scientist keeps documentation of them, and makes them public when the risk of informant damage has ceased.

5 **Exploitation** Perhaps the most crucial ethical problem in life history research is that of *exploitation*. Consider again what life histories are usually about: a subject is asked by a sociologist to give up hours – often hundreds of hours – of his or her life to tell their story. It might be very painful and involve a great deal of effort. And at the end of it all – for reasons of confidentiality – the subject must remain anonymous while the sociologist publishes. Hence *The Jack Roller* is 'by Clifford Shaw', *The Professional Fence* is 'by Carl B. Klockars', and *Being Different* is 'collected, compiled, and edited with an introduction and conclusion by Robert Bogdan'. Worse, it may even be the case that the researcher takes all the royalties. The case of *I, Rigoberta Menchú* became something of a cause célèbre when the author, Elisabeth Burgos-Debray, was denounced by the subject. Rigoberta claimed 'That is not my book . . . It is a book by Elisabeth Burgos. It is not my work; it is a work that does not belong to me morally, politically, or economically' (Stoll, 1999: xi). And certainly there have been prosecutions over such alleged abuses: the mother of one 'case study' – that of Genie, a 'wild child' found at the age of 13 to be living in complete isolation and subsequently studied in detail by psychologists – filed a suit against the researchers on the grounds that private and confidential information had been disclosed for 'prestige and profit' and that Genie had been subjected to 'unreasonable and out-rageous' testing (Curtiss, 1977; Pines, 1981: 34). It is estimated that total damages could be around $500,000! In this case, exploitation of the sub-ject has clearly become an issue and maybe it is time for the researchers to confront the problem of their subjects' rights. For, unlike the researcher, the respondents will not usually be able to gain status or prestige for their story, since it will usually be published anonymously. It seems fair, therefore, that for their work they should be entitled to material reward. This might be through informal means (buying meals, giving presents

and so forth), but it is perhaps advisable to establish their rights more formally. Spradley, for example, explicitly contracted one of his life history subjects (James Sewid):

> When it became apparent that the edited transcripts might become a published book, I decided to safeguard Mr. Sewid's rights by making him a full partner who signed the contract with Yale University Press. He shared equally in all royalties and, with me, had the right to decide on crucial matters of content. (Spradley, 1979: 36)

With such explicit 'contracts' the risk of exploitation is reduced.

6 *Informed consent*   One of the most frequently named ethical criteria for research is that of *'informed consent'* (cf. The British Sociological Association in Barnes, 1979: 105): respondents in research should know that they are involved in a research undertaking and roughly what this research is about. With sociological life histories this is usually the case, and although it is perfectly possible for a researcher to listen to somebody's tale and record it secretly, 1 am unaware of this happening. With raw documents, however, like letters and diaries, the chances of an invasion of privacy do increase. Were Mrs Masterson's letters given by her to Allport for analysis? The answer is no (Allport, 1965: vi). So how, if she were alive, would she feel about her private letters being published and discussed? (You might like to ask how you would feel about your own private letters being treated like this.)

In photography and documentary film the right to comment would appear paramount, since respondents are immediately recognizable and irrevocable damage could thus be done to them. But to ask them for permission is surely also to invite them to pose, to present a good front for the camera (Barnes, 1979: 144; cf. Harper, 1978). Wiseman poses a solution to this dilemma: he always takes pictures without asking permission. Then, as he says, 'I go up to someone and say, "We just took your picture and it's going to be for a movie . . . Do you have any objection?" If they have any objection, I don't use the material. I either ask just before the shooting or immediately after' (Wiseman, 1971: 320).

7 *Hurt and harm*   A final worry is the *hurt and harm* that may befall the subjects through the researcher's activities. Social science has produced many instances where communities have been upset by community studies on them – feeling they have been misrepresented; or where individual people feel they have told a story in good faith only for it to result in a kind of damaging or sensational exposure (some case studies of this can be found in Caroline Brettell's collection, *When They Read What We Write* (1993). Sometimes damage can be done just by rumour and gossip – even when not true. But there are major studies – Arthur Vidich and Joseph Stein's *Small Town in a Mass Society* (1958), Oscar Lewis's

Children of Sanchez (1961), Nancy Scheper-Hughes's *Saints, Scholars and Schizophrenics* (1979) (the latter two both being about Irish communities) – which have been targets of full-scale attack. Vidich was pilloried in a town carnival; Lewis was taken to court by the Mexican Geographical and Statistical Society; and a village schoolmaster said to Scheper-Hughes:

> It's not your science I am questioning, but this: don't we have the right to lead unexamined lives, the right not to be analysed? Don't we have a right to hold on to an image of ourselves as different to be sure, but as innocent and unblemished all the same? (quoted in Brettell, 1993: 13)

Now in the hands of a seasoned researcher, there has to be a hope that these things can be avoided – that there is a deep awareness of the complicated ethical involvement research brings to bear on a subject's life: telling their stories could literally destroy them – bring them to suicidal edges, murderous thoughts, danger. More modestly, they may be severely traumatized. The telling of a story of a life is a deeply problematic and ethical process in which researchers are fully impli-cated. In the hands of a novice researcher – and especially say a student rushing in to gather a life story for a dissertation – such awareness may be very thin and the damage that could be done, enormous.

This harm cannot be masked by simply assuming that the researcher is a 'nice guy', a good human being just doing the best they can. Maybe – hopefully – the researcher is. But in practice life story research always means you are playing with another person's life: so you had better be careful. Very careful indeed. For – and despite protestations from some researchers who want to make it more equal – there is always an asym-metrical relation between researcher and researched: as Peneff remarks, 'life stories appear not to call into question the privileges carried by the interviewer's social group' (Simeoni and Dani, 1995a: 4–5). And these privileges are great indeed.

As we have seen in earlier discussions of 'voice', it is usually the researcher who narrates the other's life and this brings its own worries. As Judith Stacey, in a classic of feminist ethnography, remarks:

> The research product is ultimately that of the researcher. With very rare exceptions it is the researcher who narrates, who 'authors' the ethnography . . . a written document structured primarily by *a researcher's purposes*, offering *a researcher's interpretations*, registered in *a researcher's voice*. (Stacey, 1988: 22; emphasis added)

And the trouble is that when we write about others – and especially if it purports to be their story and often told in their (edited) words – they have been brought (by us) to say it, and in the saying of it their lives may have been changed. To speak of traumas hitherto unnamed – of child abuse, of rape, of holocaust survival, of undiagnosed illness, of coming out as a transvestite – is to solidify and consolidate in words a kind of a life. And for this – in a way – the researcher becomes responsible.

Yet it goes further: for as we write it down for them or with them, so we solidify their lives in ways they ultimately may not wish. And more, when they come to read it – if they do – how will they feel about it? Today, in a month, or in twenty years? I know, for instance, of one young gay man who boldly told his story when he was young, but who was horrified to find it 'following him around' twenty years on! For others will read the story too . . . and in the process be alarmed, upset, or learn things they really did not want to know. Telling a tale may hover deeply over your life (and the lives of others), casting its spell and playing out its role for many years. It may never go away, and even become the life as lived – as one takes on a celebrity role (cf. Menchú above). All this is what one writer has nicely called 'the afterlife of the life history': *'Afterlife* makes the point that the life history process continues beyond the crystallization of the narrative into text to encompass audience response to the published work, reflections on its construction as a text, as well as its impact on the lives of its narrator and collector' (Blackman, 1992: 2). To this we may also add that it can have an impact on the lives of friends and families.

Consider the case told by Amia Lieblich. She gathered life stories on a Kibbutz – some of which are people from the same family. The stories are then given back to their tellers to read. What she found was that in the reading of other kin's stories, there can be sad surprises. You learn what others think and say about you by reading the stories that they tell. As she writes:

> An older women, Genia, who also read the first draft was the person I respected more than any other member of the kibbutz. After the joint meeting with all the 'readers', Genia asked to see me in private. 'I am shocked' she said, 'I cried so much' . . . she explained what caused her all this pain were the stories of her two daughters, which were included in the book. I realised that both of them said in so many words that Genia had been a 'bad mother'. During their childhood she dedicated all her time to the affairs of the kibbutz whilst they felt neglected and rejected. Although remorseful tears were shed in our conversation, Genia did not ask me to change a word in her or her daughters' narratives because she accepted their authenticity . . . (Lieblich, 1996: 181)

The human sciences need to be made human. The potential harm and damage, the sheer intrusiveness into someone else's life, the bare-faced cheek to believe that one can simply tell another's story, the uncritical self-satisfaction of telling another's story, the frequent arrogance of 'colonizing' their world view – all this needs to be considered. And indeed it is – as more and more subjects of life stories hear the stories of their lives gathered by others. As Rosaldo says the 'natives [are] talking back' (cf. Rosaldo, 1986). And this, rightly, has made it increasingly hazardous for life stories to be gathered. Indeed, over the past couple of decades the risk of the subjects of biographies taking authors and publishers to court with expensive law suits has seriously increased – as have the difficulties in gaining access to some people's lives, and the threat of physical and verbal abuse. The life historian or the biographer is now often an unwelcome guest in many people's lives (cf. Smith, 1999)

Positioning ethics

So far I have done little more than raise dilemmas. We have rummaged through a minefield of ethical traps. What suggestions does social science make for attempting to deal with such concerns? For some time – and at the broadest of levels – two positions have been regularly outlined as baselines for ethical positions in social research: the *ethical absolutist* and the *situational relativist* (cf. Denzin, 1978a; Klockars and O'Connor, 1979, pt 1). In many ways, this mirrors much wider debates in contemporary moral theory between the universalists and the situationalists, a debate that is often linked to a male voice and a different voice (where the former makes universalistic and abstract claims whilst the latter suggests a more embedded, situated, and ironic turn); and between communitarians and liberals (where the former champion common community values and the latter champion individual rights). I will return to this later, but will first try to get these two positions fairly clear.

Ethical absolutists are usually universalists and communitarians. They seeks to establish firm principles which should guide all social research – 'the risks to subjects must be outweighed by potential benefits', for example, or there must be 'informed consent' (cf. Klockars, 1977: 203). Such principles often get encoded in professional charters, like those of the British Sociological Association, or the American Anthropological Association. And they become the ground rules of various ethical committees and institutional review boards. They are seen as absolutely necessary to protect both the community and the researcher. All professionals within the research community should have their code of ethics, every piece of research should be 'vetted' for its ethical principles, and failure to follow them could well be grounds for litigation and expulsion from a professional body. Minimally, according to Gesa Kirsch, researchers must usually:

- obtain informed consent in writing from participants;
- make sure that participation is entirely voluntary; that is, participants must be allowed to withdraw from the research at any time without any negative repercussions;
- inform participants of any risks involved in the research and ensure that potential risks and benefits are proportional;

- protect the confidentiality of all participants;
- ensure that participants' well-being, reputations, and employment are not affected by their participation in the research (or lack thereof);
- ensure that selection of participants is equitable (Kirsch, 1999: 41–2).

Situational relativists, in contrast, suggest that the ethical dilemmas of the social scientist are not 'special' but coterminous with the problems of living in everyday life. As in life these days, there can be no fixed and absolutely binding guidelines. Rather, ethics have to be produced creatively in the concrete situation at hand. To live an ethical life is a process of decision making in situations, drawing from culture and history, and not a pattern of just 'following rules'. Any attempt to legislate this morality could simply degenerate into mindlessness, rigidity or   as with many professionals   a monopolistic front that perpetuates privileges and elites (those with a higher morality(!) than ordinary mortals). As Elliot Liebow remarked of his own research with life stories of homeless women:

> I tried to bring the same ethics to fieldwork that I try to bring to any other part of my life, and this effort seemed to work reasonably well. It would have been wrong for me to misrepresent myself to the women and conceal my purpose, but it would be equally wrong to do that with anyone else. (Liebow, 1993/5: 327)

The argument here suggests, then, that researchers are familiar with ethical decisions in their daily lives and need no special research rule book.

Both sides have their weaknesses. If, for instance, as the absolutists usually insist, there should be 'informed consent', it may leave relatively privileged groups under-researched (since they will say 'no') and underprivileged groups over-researched (they have nothing to lose and say 'yes' in hope) (cf. Duster et al., 1979; Lofland, 1976). If the individual conscience is the guide, as the relativists insist, the door is wide open for the unscrupulous – even immoral – researcher. But as in so many debates, it may be that this is a false polarity. Individual decision taking around ethical concerns could surely take place within wider frameworks of guidance?

In conclusion: narratives of research ethics and communities of research stories

Social science, like life, is shot through with personal, political and ethical dilemmas – and life history research is no exception to this. Maybe nowadays there is a much greater need for researchers to turn explicitly to current debates in ethical and moral theory as part of their research training. At the minimum, for example, research needs to take on board issues surrounding what could be called the five great ethical principles of current times:

- The principle of respect, recognition and tolerance for persons and their differences.
- The principle of promoting the caring of others, what has been called, following many feminists, 'an ethic of care'.
- The principle of expanding equalities, fairness and justice.
- The principle of enlarging spheres of autonomy, freedoms and choice.
- The principle of minimizing harm.

Of course, for some philosophers, these principles are often seen to be incommensurate, incompatible and insufficient. Thus, Selma Sevenhuijsen suggests ways in which the ethics of care is at odds with the ethics of justice:

> An ethics of care involves different moral concepts: responsibilities and relationships, rather than rules and rights. Second, it is bound to concrete situations rather then being formal and abstract. And thirdly, the ethics of care can be described as a moral activity, the 'activity of caring', rather than a set of principles which can be simply followed. The central question in the ethics of care – how to deal with dependency and responsibility – differs radically from that of rights ethics: what are the highest normative principles and rights in situations of moral conduct? (Selma Sevenhuijsen, 1998: 107)

Now whilst I can agree with the importance she attaches to the ethics of care, the way she phrases this is such as to recreate all the old antinomies again. Why is everything so mutually exclusive? Why must it be that care and rights are at odds? A strange language is used – she places responsibilities with care, whereas it is often seen as the other side of rights. Why can one not have high principles alongside situational ethics?

It seems to me that each of the above principles could be quite helpful as starting points in guiding researchers through their 'moral mazes'. But only as starting points. Subsequently any ethical debates need to start becoming grounded in the day-to-day practices and narratives.

Post-modern ethics?   But more. It may be that as society takes a more postmodern turn – full of fragmentations, risks, collapsing of grand narratives etc. – so these dilemmas will become both more numerous and more self-consciously taken. It may be that we have to live more and more with ambiguity, difficult decisions, and a certain openness to change in the world. Zygmunt Bauman writes of all this as the emergence of a new kind of ethics – *a postmodern ethics*, where the important issue starts to become a greater awareness of making ethical choices in every part of a life, and of the profoundly ambivalent nature of these choices. Bauman's is absolutely not a claim for any kind of relativism, but rather for a kind of a return to 'the great issues of ethics – like human rights, social justice, balance between peaceful cooperation and personal self-assertion, synchronization of indviudal conduct and collective welfare – [which] have lost nothing of their topicality'. But, says Bauman, 'they only need to be seen, and dealt with, in a novel way' (Bauman, 1993: 4). For him, the contemporary ethical position must recognize ambivalence, non-rationality, the aporetic, the non-universalizable, and the irrational. This is not an 'anything goes' stance, but rather one in which ethical matters are constantly deliberated upon as part of a deliberative society (Bauman, 1999). An aporetic situation now exists whereby contradictions and tensions cannot be overcome – they have to be lived with in struggle and disagreement. And 'human beings are morally ambivalent' (1993: 10).

This change in the modes of arguing in moral debates may be seen as a shift

from	*to*
a given content	a way of thinking (a process, ambivalence)
abstract principles and philosophies	actual, stories, narrative
general rules/universals	situated
given by authorities	struggling with the self

What would surely help in this task is a clearer discussion of such issues amongst all researchers, discussions that do not always depend upon abstract principles like those I have described above, but which all take seriously the stories that researchers provide of their own situated ethical problems and decision makings. We need stories and narratives of research ethics to help fashion our own research lives, and to see the kinds of broader principle (like the five suggested above) which they can then draw upon. We need these stories to be taught on 'research courses' (rather than the formalists' dry protocols which convey little of real research). By and large, researchers do not follow binding universal rules; their ethics may draw from such rules but it surely applies them in situated contexts; and so there is much to learn from hearing these narratives of research ethics. Throughout this book I have drawn from fragments of such stories – of researchers talking about their ethical choices – which I hope may be further extended and developed. Researchers' autobiographies, auto/ethnography, and 'research tales from the field' all provide a rich source of such stories from which we can learn.

My aim in this chapter has been to chart some of the personal and ethical issues that researchers confront, and to lay out some paths to resolution through a postmodern ethics, which may well involve care, justice, recognition, equality and minimal harm. But these are only opening comments. In the end, I have to conclude in the same way as Maurice Punch's excellent review of the whole field: 'This area is a swamp, and . . . I have provided no map. Each individual will have to trace his or her own path' (Punch, 1994: 94). To this I may only add that the narratives of others may prove to be of some assistance.

Guide to further reading

On **reflexivity in social science**, see Rosanna Hertz (ed.), *Reflexivity and Voice* (1997); Amanda Coffey, *The Ethnographic Self: Fieldwork and the Representation of Identity* (1999); Judith Okely and Helen Callaway (eds), *Anthropology and Autobiography* (1992). On the recent feminist influence on much of this, see Marjorie DeVault, *Liberating Method: Feminism and Social Research* (1999); M.M. Fonow and J.A. Cook (eds), *Beyond Methodology: Feminist Scholarship as Lived Research* (1991); Gloria Bowles and R.D. Klein, *Theories of Women's Studies* (1983); Helen Roberts, *Doing Feminist Research* (1981); and Liz Stanley and Sue Wise's *Breaking Out* (1983) and *Breaking Out Again* (1993). On wider influences, see Linda Tuhiwai Smith, *Decolonizing Methodologies* (1999); Patti Lather, *Getting Smart: Feminist Research and Pedagogy with/in the Postmodern* (1991); Henry Giroux, *Border Crossings: Cultural Workers and the Politics of Education* (1992).

Classics of personal reflection include W.F. Whyte, *Street Corner Society* (1943/1993 4th edn) especially appendix (and see also the analyses of it made in *Journal of Contemporary Ethnography*, 1992). The interplay of researcher and researched is brought out very clearly in a recent classic, Pat Caplan's *African Voices, African Lives* (1997). More general personal reflections of social scientists can be found in such works as Adams and Preiss (1960), Berreman (1962), Vidich et al. (1964), Powdermaker (1967), Freilich (1970), Wax (1971), Bell and Newby (1977) and Roberts (1981) and Berger (1990). A recent account of tales from the field is Annette Lareaa and Jeffrey Schultz's *Journeys Through Ethnography: Realistic Accounts of Fieldwork* (1996). In anthropology, anthologies of personal experiences in the field include Don D. Fowler and Donald L. Hardesty's *Others Knowing Others: Perspectives on Ethnographic Careers* (1994). An intriguing collection of essays on *Fieldnotes* (edited by Roger Sanjek, 1990) provides many insights into anthropologists' lives.

Several recent anthologies have discussed the **role of sex and the researcher**. See Don Kulick and Margaret Wilson (eds), *Taboo: Sex, Identity and Erotic Subjectivity in Anthropological Fieldwork* (1995); Ellen Lewin and William L. Leap (eds), *Out in the Field: Issues in Fieldwork and Ethnography* (1996); Fran Markowitz and Michael Ashkenazi (ed.), *Sex, Sexuality and the Anthropologist* (1999). A brief review of issues can be found in Amanda Coffey's *The Ethnographic Self* (1999: ch. 5). In the growing writing in this area, Esther Newton's short piece 'My best informant's dress: the erotic equation in fieldwork', in *Cultural Anthropology*, 1993, 8: 2–23 shines out as does Kath Weston's *longslowburn* (1998).

On **the uses of personal experience**, see Carolyn Ellis and Michael Flaherty (eds), *Investigating Subjectivity* (1992) and on emotions and fieldwork see Sherryl Kleinman and Martha A. Copp's book with that title (1993) and Deborah Lupton's *The Emotional Self* (1998); see also Gillian Bendelow and Simon J. Williams (eds), *Emotions in Social Life* (1998) and Candace Clark, *Misery and Company* (1997).

The issue of **research ethics in general** is discussed in many places. A general account is Maurice Punch's *The Politics and Ethics of Fieldwork* (1986), as well as his 'Politics and ethics in qualitative research' in Denzin and Lincoln's *Handbook of Qualitative Research* (1994: 83–97). A feminist account is Gesa E. Kirsch's *Ethical Dilemmas in Feminist Research* (1999). Other statements and analyses include Martin Bulmer's *Social Research Ethics* (1982), E. Diener and R. Crandall's *Ethics in Social and Behavioural Research* (1978), and J.A. Barnes's *Who Should Know What?* (1979). Classically, ethical dilemmas in life history research have been discussed in Carl Klockars's (1977) 'Field ethics for the life history', which is an explicit formal commentary, and in Ruthellen Josselson's edited collection *Ethics and Process in the Narrative Study of Lives* (1996). Annabel Faraday and Ken Plummer's article 'Doing life histories' (1979) has a section on the ethics of their research. See also Raymond Lee's insightful *Doing Research on Sensitive Topics* (1993).

There are a number of **accounts of ethical controversies within the social sciences** in general. See, for instance, Derek Freeman's *Margaret Mead and Samoa* (1984); Laud Humphreys's *Tea Room Trade* (1970) (especially the ethics appendix); Stan Cohen and Laurie Taylor's *Psychological Survival: the Experience of Long-term Imprisonment* (1981). One of the big controversies centres around Elisabeth Burgos-Debray's *I, Rigoberta Menchú: An Indian Woman in Guatamala* (1984), which was given a very controversial re-interpretation in David Stoll's *Rigoberta Menchú and the Story of All Poor Guatemalans* (1999). The controversy is debated in the *New York Times Review of Books* (18 April 1999: 29), *Times Higher Education Supplement* (17 September 1999), *Newsweek* (21 June 1999) and by Stoll (1999). Many papers on 'truth and Castaneda' can be found in Richard de Mille's *The Don Juan Papers: Further Castaneda Controversies* (1990). See also the attack on postmodernism in Alan Sokal and Jean Bricmont's *Intellectual Impostures* (1998) and Russ Meyer's *Genie: A Scientific Tragedy* (1994).

There are now quite a number of **'narratives of ethics'** written by practitioners. Robert Coles's *Doing Documentary Work* (1997) is very valuable. Otherwise, there are useful introductions and appendices to various studies, such as Ruth Lewis's introduction to *Living the Revolution* (O. Lewis et al., 1977), James Agee's *Let Us Now Praise Famous Men* (1965) and Elliot Liebow's *Tell Them Who I Am* (1993).

11 Truth, Value and Memory in Life Stories

What then have I to do with men, that they should hear my confessions – as if they could heal all my infirmities – a race, curious to know the lives of others, slothful to amend their own? Why seek they to hear from me what I am; who will not hear from Thee what themselves are? And how know they, when from myself they hear of myself, whether I say true; seeing no man knows what is in man, but the spirit of man which is in him? But if they hear from Thee of themselves, they cannot say 'The Lord lieth'. For what is it to hear from Thee of themselves, but to know themselves? And who knoweth and saith 'It is false' unless himself lieth? But because charity believeth all things, I also Oh Lord, will in such wise confess unto Thee, that men may hear, to whom I cannot demonstrate whether I confess truly; yet they believe me, whose ears charity openeth unto me' . . .

(Saint Augustine, *Confessions*, Book Ten)

We are thrust into the darkness of the universe. We try to create worlds to live within and to spin our stories through time so that we and our world are constantly being recreated, retold, revised. We are creating ourselves and being created in our stories.

(Miller Mair, 1989: 80)

In 1997, Benjamin Wilkomirski's much acclaimed Holocaust story *Fragments: Memories of a Childhood (1939–1948)* was published in Germany. Immediately identified as 'one of the great works of the Holocaust', as a poetical masterpiece, this personal story told the experiences of a young Jewish boy in the concentration camps of Majdanek and Auschwitz as he *remembers* experiencing the horrors of these camps. Soon the book was translated into some 12 languages and won a number of literary awards. As the adult Wilkomirski travelled widely to promote the book, he would visibly break down before his audience whilst revisiting the extreme traumas of his early life. And yet a little while later a number of commentators found much to doubt in the book – indeed claimed Wilkomirski had never been in the camps, had lived his early days in a Swiss orphanage, had been adopted into a wealthy family, and was not Jewish. A dossier denouncing the book was produced and the German publishers decided to withdraw the hardback edition. At the time of writing this, the controversy is gathering pace. In early 2000, Wilkomirski was stripped of a literary award he had been given in 1997 (the Jewish

Quarterly Literary Prize) and Picador, his English publisher, decided to withdraw the book too. It seems likely that the book is indeed a work of fiction – a very good one – written by a man who is himself severely traumatized and self-deceiving. So what is to be made of its claims? What can we make of life stories that are fabricated? What are we to make of memory if it is so self-deluding? If the power of a life story lies in its telling, maybe we should give up social science and turn to good fiction? And if life stories can be shown to be 'lies' or 'false memories', what is the point of collecting them? In this closing chapter, I look first at some of the problems increasingly recognized around 'memory sites', before turning to the wider issues of 'truth'.

The problem of memory

> Memory makes us, we make memory.
>
> (Elizabeth Tonkin, 1992: ch. 7)

> Memory forms the fabric of human life, affecting everything from the ability to perform simple, everyday tasks to the recognition of the self. Memory establishes life's continuity; it gives meaning to the present, as each moment is constituted by the past. As the means by which we remember who we are, memory provides the very core of identity.
>
> (Marita Sturken, 1997: 1)

Since all life story work is selective work, 'memories' are often seen as a major path to this selection and life stories become 'memory books' (Terkel, 1970). Indeed, since life stories 'dig over the past', they always entail issues of recall and memory. But as a person tells their story, in what ways are they remembering their past? Is the story being told partly a function of how good a memory is? Are life stories really just sedimented memories? A very simple view might think so. But once we start to look at what we know of 'memory', and the enormous interest taken in the topic of 'memories' in recent years, not just by psychologists but by historians and cultural critics, the answers become much more complex. For recent studies of holocaust 'survivors', Vietnam War veterans, Gulf War traumas, AIDS, child sexual abuse and Alzheimer's disease have all served to make 'memory' a much more problematic idea.

Life story work involves recollecting, remembering, re-discovering, along with the active processes of memorializing and constructing history. Life memories are nested and enveloped in their habitus – their environment of assumptions and languages – through which they make sense and can be told (cf. Bourdieu, 1984; Tonkin, 1992: 106–7). As Frisch vividly puts it:

What happens to experience on the way to becoming memory? What happens
to experiences on the way to becoming history? As an era of intense collective
experience recedes into the past what is the relationship of memory to
historical generalization? (Frisch, 1998: 33)

Oral history in particular may be seen as a 'powerful tool for discovering, exploring and evaluating the nature of the historical memory –
how people make sense of their past, how they connect individual
experience and its social context, how the past becomes part of the
present, and how people use it to interpret their lives and the world
around them' (Frisch, 1990: 188). Yet 'memory' may have its downside.
Once composed, the story can become 'freeze dried text'. If it is written
down, placed in a muesum, turned into a book (as many memories are),
then it can 'freeze' the story – making a process and experience become a
fixed event. It may serve ironically to lose other ways of telling the story
or the life. 'Memory' may reify the life into something it is not.

For our purposes, I wish to suggest that 'memory' may work on a
number of interconnected levels caught in a series of terms for different
kinds of 'memories'. First, there is what most people would readily
recognize as *psychological, individual personal memory* where the focus is
upon what a person can recall, how well they can recall it (which often
varies by time of day, mental tiredness and the like) along with various
failures to recall – the most extreme versions being pathologies like
Alzheimer's disease. In most respects, this is the most trod path, with a
long literature of critiques and debates. It is often captured in the metaphor of a 'storehouse', where memories are more or less piled up and
become more or less accessible. For Freud, all our memories are shaped
by the repressed unconscious and need great effort to be brought back
into consciousness. In general, within this view, life histories are concerned with dredging up the memories from the past. (An introduction
to some of these ideas may be found in Janice Haaken, 1999: Part 1.)

Yet this relatively straightforward view has recently been under siege.
Now, 'memory' starts to be seen as much less of an inner psychological
phenomenon, and much more of a socially shared experience. It could
be, for instance, that 'memories' are simply our most habitually told
stories, our best stories. It is what we have said so often that we literally
come to believe it as true (even when not). What is recalled the first time
may structure and shape the experience, turning it into a 'memory habit'
and a kind of fact. Long afterwards, when the event has been lost, what
we are left with is only this 'habit', this 'story'. Vaclav Havel, recalling
war time experiences, comments:

Twenty or thirty years ago, in the army, we had a lot of obscure adventures,
and years later we tell them at parties, and suddenly we realize that those two
very difficult years of our lives have become lumped together into a few
episodes that have lodged in our memory in a standardized form. And are

always told in a standardized way, in the same words. But in fact that lump of memories has nothing to do with our experience of those two years in the army and what it has made of us. (cited in Clendinnen, 1999: 33)

This, then, may be seen as leading to a second kind of memory: *narrative memory*, where the focus is on the narratives that people tell about their past, and where highly selective stories dredged from the past somehow seem to have taken on a life of their own. They are somewhat akin to what Gordon Allport once called 'autonomous motives', whereby he designated that whatever 'motives' may have initiated a conduct in the first place, these same 'motives' ultimately came to be ruled by laws unto themselves – by motives which, so to speak, take on their own life. Likewise, memories often become 'our best stories', the stories we tell so often that we come to believe them as true. Clearly, this version of memory fits well with the current interest in story telling and narratives. Our narratives are our memories. Jerome Bruner captures it well when he says that 'I believe that the ways of telling stories and the ways of conceptualizing that go with them become so habitual that they finally become recipes for structuring experience itself, for laying down routes into memory, for not only guiding the life narrative up to the present but directing it into the future' (Bruner, 1987: 31).

A sense of narrative leads us to a third form of memory – *collective memory*, where the focus now moves beyond individuals and is placed upon 'the social frameworks of memory'. For the Durkheimian sociologist Maurice Halbwachs (1877–1945) – the most distinguished proponent of this view – 'no memory is possible outside frameworks used by people living in society to determine and retrieve their recollections' (Halbwachs, 1992: 43). Thus, life stories can only be told once a societal framework becomes available for them to be told: stories of North American Blacks 'up from slavery', of gay men and lesbians 'coming out' or indeed of 'victims of sexual abuse' can only be told once a social framework has emerged which helps organize them and make them more accessible. Many stories and histories simply cannot be told when the social frameworks are not there. And here the local community, and a sense of belonging to a culture, may become keys to unlocking such 'frames'. The closely linked *'cultural memory'* indicates what has come to be taken as important within a culture (and by implication what has not, what has been lost), and it does so frequently through artefacts – 'cultural products imbued with cultural meaning' (Sturken, 1997: 3). This might include things like the AIDS Memorial Quilt, film and documentary evidence around the Vietnam War, or the creation of specific monuments and museums (like the United States Holocaust Memorial Museum in Washington, or the Gay Memorial Pink Triangle in Amsterdam). These 'cultural objects' help shape much of these 'collective memories'. Part of this may be *'generational memory'*, which highlights the ways in which memories become identified with events that happened generations earlier . . . 'to encompass the memories which individuals have of their own families' history, as well as more general collective memories about the past' (Hareven, 1996: 242). Thus, it could be suggested that the late Alex Haley's book (and subsequent highly successful TV drama) *Roots: The Saga of an American Family*, which documented the search for Black America's roots in Africa, helped lay down frameworks and the craft of genealogy in which others could start to locate or 'construct' their own 'black', 'slave' memories. Nowadays there are even web sites that help you to do this. Likewise, 'memories' of important world events (political, economic, religious etc.) as well as 'local catastrophes' (floods, fires etc.) can become structured through generations, with people referring back 'disproportionately to a time when the respondents were in their teens or early twenties' (Schuman and Scott, 1989). Again, as the memory is claimed for a particular group so it may become hardened, solidified, the 'true memory' (when it is usually only one of many possibilities, the others becoming lost).

What becomes clearer and clearer in all this must be the idea that memory is no simple 'psychological faculty' from within – it is shaped through and through by setting, society, culture. Memories come to depend upon what we might call *'memory sites'* and *'technologies of memory'* (Sturken, 1997: 9) – film, photos, books, museums, video, news-letters, badges, ribbons etc. – which help give this memory a shape. And this helps us sense another closely allied form of memory which has been called *popular memory*. Memory here is 'a term which directs our attention not to the past but to the *past–present relation'* (Popular Memory Group, 1998: 78). The focus is on memory as a form of 'political practice' which helps 'give voice' to stories that have either never been told or which have been lost, returning such memories to their communities where they may be reworked for the present. Here are the memories of class, traditional communities, oppressed minorities, indigenous peoples, the colonized, the marginalized, the depressed and oppressed. Often they can be heard surfacing in the practice of 'consciousness raising' – starting with the student movement in the 1960s but achieving 'spectacular success in the women's movement' of the 1970s. Here, according to Sara Evans (1980), women found new spaces to speak collectively about their personal experiences – of rape, housework, abortion, wife battering, work, pregnancy, bodies and the like; and found role models, friendship networks and new senses of self which helped give a collective shape to their 'memories'. One woman's previously silenced story led to another woman's story: memories became political.

Several further distinctions could be drawn. *'Autobiographical memories'* are the memories built up around a life. *'Primary memories'* are those of people who live through certain events and remember them in a certain manner whilst *'secondary memories'* involve the 'critical work [performed] on primary memory, whether by the person who initially had the relevant experience, or more typically by an analyst', or some other (see

Dominick La Capra, 1998: 20–1). *'Postmemory'* categorizes the experience of those who grow up dominated by narratives that preceded their birth, whose own belated stories are evacuated by the stories of the previous generation shaped by traumatic events' (Hirsch, 1997: 22). *'Transformative remembering'* suggests a dynamic process of remembering – not simply memory – whereby 'the recollection of an event . . . serves as a psychological marker from an early to a later form of self-knowledge'. It implies a kind of dynamic shaping insight behind the organization of later memories (Haaken, 1999). There are, then, many kinds of social 'memories' that need to be considered in understanding a life.

Memorializing lives

In a major way, the telling of life stories and the production of 'documents of life' can, in effect, be seen as a process of memorializing folk. Lives are turned into 'memories' through a social process and become 'sites' where the life can be found. Thus the AIDS Quilt 'consists of an ever-growing number of three-by-six foot panels, each of which memorializes an individual who died from AIDS' (Sturken, 1997: 183). By 1996 there were some 40,000 panels from twenty-nine countries – still only a small proportion of those who had died from AIDS across the world. But each panel tells its own story – from friends, families and lovers; builds on its own materials – clothing, condoms, champagne glasses; and becomes a key site of politics, healing and 'remembrance' in the AIDS epidemic. Likewise, in the rapidly expanding field of holocaust studies which I briefly mentioned in Chapter 2, there has been a prolific outpouring of 'writing and recording' of the testimonies of holocaust survivors. Stored in archives, embedded in monuments and museums, published in a huge flow of 'Holocaust Studies', they constitute a massive social process of what we again might call 'the memorialization of life stories'. The holocaust does undoubtedly bring to the fore many of the key issues in understanding memory. What is involved in remembering here? Is it, for example, a traumatic and repressed moment from the 1940s that is brought to the surface; and if so, how does this most extraordinarily painful recalling take place? What lies in the actual memories – so much suffering is hard to begin to describe? And is the provision of thousands of such testimonies a way of providing and maintaining for the future a critical exchange between past, present and future? Whatever it is, there is clearly no simple memory at work here. Indeed, for some, such memories have a potential for being overly exploitative; there may be too much 'selling of the holocaust' (Cole, 1999). Others suggest we may be remembering it too much: there may be a 'surfeit of memory' (Maier, 1993). The memories may impose a unity on certain communities, essentializing the past and the life, making it actually harder to see what was really going on.

Practices of truth in life story telling

Here, then, we are back to the old problems that have always been posed by life story writing and reading: how can the story be evaluated? How can we tell a 'good' story from a 'bad' one? Must they be 'true' to be of any worth? And what might 'truth' mean? Are all stories equally valid or are there important ways of distinguishing between them? As we saw in Chapter 4, these are classic, and largely unresolved, problems running all the way through auto/biographical history (cf. Mandelbaum, 1967; Marcus, 1994; Stanley, 1992).

Although, as we saw in Chapter 7, many have gone in pursuit of the 'validity' or 'real truth' about the life, the problem of the link between lives, life narratives and fiction/truth has been placed squarely on the intellectual agenda. Simple distinctions might initially be drawn between the 'naive realist accounts' of a life (where the story deeply reflects the life) and 'naive interpretive accounts' (where the story is no more than an interpretation), with many shades between. But this is simple indeed. These days, I believe that most life story researchers would accept that we can never get at a simple, real truth about a life through a life story; that we can never get at a simple 'historical truth' through an oral history; or that any researcher can have a straightforward, superior access to knowledge about another's life. As a leading proponent of this view, Jerome Bruner claims:

> an autobiography is not and cannot be a way of simply signifying or referring to a 'life as lived'. I take the view that there is no such thing as a 'life as lived' to be referred to. On this view, a life is created or constructed by the act of autobiography. It is a way of construing experience – and of reconstruing and reconstructing it until our breath and our pen fails us. Construal and reconstrual are interpretive . . . Obviously, then, there is no such thing as a 'uniquely' true, correct or even faithful autobiography. (Bruner, 1993: 38–9)

If we accept, as I think we must, that all life stories are composed – that the stories of our lives are indeed constructed, fabricated, invented, made up – this does not mean that all the stories we hear have to be seen as equally valid or invalid, truthful or deceptive. We can differentiate. To say that lives are invented is not to force us down some extreme path where anything at all can be said about a life. Indeed, I believe it is just the opposite: to recognize that lives are constructed means that we then need to search out ways for evaluating just what it is that is being constructed. The leading Italian oral historian, Allessandro Portelli, for example, recognizes that life stories are not and cannot be objective: they are always 'artificial, variable and partial'. But at the same time this does not weaken them. We may even know that some statements are factually wrong: and yet 'such "wrong" statements [may] still [be] psychologically "true" and . . . this truth may be equally as important as factually reliable accounts' (Portelli, 1998: 72, 68). He provides a striking example through the stories surrounding the death of a young Italian steelworker, Luigi Trastulli, killed in an anti-NATO demonstration outside his factory. In relaying the story of his life, communists focused on his heroism and bravery; conservatives on the need for order; others saw him as a martyr shot against the wall – a crucified hero; and still others disputed the timing of the incident as being in 1953 (Portelli, 1991). Different narratives shaped the experience as told: which one is right? This may not in the end matter: for each account dangles from a feeling mood, a perspective, a point of view. I am reminded here of the Japanese film *Rashamon* (by Jingo Minoura, 1951), which opens with a violent scene of a bandit attacking a nobleman in the forest – to be followed by four very different 'stories' about the event. It is a classic literary device: to recognize that stories are told from different points of view which have their own truth at the time of telling.

We need, then, various criteria for appraising the different connections between multiple life stories, human experiences, narrative structures and 'truth'; we need to connect to contrasting philosophies of knowledge; and we need to draw out ways of distinguishing different kinds of life stories based on their truth claims. There have been a number of attempts to do just this. We have already seen the earliest attempt of John Dollard to provide criteria for a life history in a book of that name (1935). Seven unifying criteria are provided for the appraisal of any particular life history (see Chapter 6). Likewise, Herbert Blumer listed several criteria in his analysis of *The Polish Peasant* (see Chapter 6). In the main, these early studies provide traditional criteria which may be seen as less suitable these days. Thus one quite recent study argues that:

> The 'old' criteria for evaluation of research were basically reliability, validity, objectivity and replicability . . . [yet] narrative materials – like reality itself – can be read, understood, and analysed in extremely diverse ways . . . reaching alternative narrative accounts is by no means an indication of inadequate scholarship but a manifestation of the wealth of such material and the range of sensitivities of different readers . . . (Lieblich et al., 1998: 171)

Nevertheless, these same authors go on to ask: 'How can we distinguish a good study from a bad one?' and proceed to suggest four possible criteria that work for them. These are *width* (the comprehensiveness of evidence); *coherence* (the creation of a complete and meaningful picture); *insightfulness* (the sense of innovation and originality in the story); and *parsimony* (the ability to provide an analysis based on a small number of concepts and linked to elegance and aesthetic appeal). Others have provided similar listings. Thus, Norman Denzin suggests four standards of truth: *sincerity, subjective truth, historical truth* and *fictional truth* (Denzin, 1989: 23). Whilst more recently, Catherine Kohler Riessman has suggested a further four criteria: *persuasiveness* – which asks if the interpretation is reasonable and convincing (which depends therefore on the writing skills of the author and the sensitivity of the audience, and not veracity at all); *coherence* – which relates to the global, local and thematic concerns 'to make [the description] as thick as possible'; *correspondence* and *pragmatism* (Riessman, 1993: 64–9). Some of these I will discuss below, as I examine this problem further.

Six ways to tell a 'true story'?

The most apparent approach to evaluating life stories and sensing their truth can be found in an orthodox *positivist* approach: the aim would be to get the story told of the life actually to represent what is going on in the life as closely as possible. Drawing from a so-called 'correspondence theory of truth', and highlighting the issues of validity raised in Chapter 6, the aim would be to match key events described in the life story with key events in the outside world. It is the historian's method – cross-checking and scrutinizing with other data. Birth dates are checked with birth certificates; school records are checked with the school; marriage, health, work can all often be checked upon. This is fine for the measurable world of 'objective events', but it becomes harder when attention is turned to what life stories are best at: the inner, more subjective worlds of feelings, thoughts, emotions. These cannot be so easily matched. And it is here that some life story writers have turned to notions of sincerity and authenticity. Indeed, two classic studies – Thomas and Znaniecki (1958) and Shaw (1966: 47) – both suggest 'sincerity' as a key issue. Shaw, for example, in writing of the delinquent Stanley, thinks that the numerous contacts he had with the boy, as well as a matching with official records etc., means that the sincerity of Stanley 'cannot be questioned' (1966: 47 footnote). Throughout this book, problems with this positivist approach have been highlighted. Of course, there is much value in capturing these more 'objective' features of a life, but there are clear limitations too.

A second closely linked approach would come from the position of *realism*: the aim would be to take the surface tale of the life as told and make it go much deeper – theoretically and conceptually. Here the turn is to a transcendental reality over and above narrative and thought which is capable of being grasped largely through an adequate theoretical apparatus which takes into account ontology – the nature of the reality of a society (or in this case, 'a person'). The classical works of psychoanalysis, psycho-history and psychobiography can furnish many examples of this more realist mode, where the depths of what makes a life work may be found in the unconscious realm. The task of the theory is to dig this out, so the life story becomes more and more 'real'. (A variant of this is also found in the grounded theory approach of letting many life stories fill out a wider reality: see Miller, 2000.)

This approach to 'realism' in social science is very different from the realist approach used in literary theory. Here the rich descriptions of

reality – as in Balzac or Dickens – lead to a realist novel in its own right;
with Freud and others the rich descriptions are always in need of 'deep
theorizing' which transcends the limit of what has been told. In any
event, this approach to truth will make strong claims that a life story
does indeed harbour an objective reality, but one which needs much
theoretical work to bring to the surface.

A third version of truth is strongly connected to the *interpretive*
paradigm: the aim is to gain enhanced understanding from the story. A
number of feminists have taken this as a main task of life story work. The
Personal Narratives Group, a feminist group working in the late 1980s in
the USA, suggest that 'truths' refer to 'the multiplicity of ways in which a
[woman's] life story reveals and reflects important features of her
conscious experiences and social landscape, creating from both her
essential reality' (Personal Narratives Group, 1989: 14). As they continue:
'When people talk about their lives, people lie sometimes, forget a little,
exaggerate, become confused, get things wrong. Yet they are revealing
truths . . . the guiding principle . . . could be that all autobiographical
memory is true: it is up to the interpreter to discover in which sense,
where, and for what purpose' (Personal Narratives Group, 1989: 261,
197). This is not far removed from the classic statement of the goals of life
history research articulated in the 1920s by Thomas and Znaniceki when
they insisted that life stories help provide access to subjective realities.

Closely linked to this is the *narrative* theory of truth: the aim here is to
examine the features of the narrative structure which enable us to grasp
its workings. Donald P. Spence, for example, has distinguished between
'narrative truth' and 'historical truth', with the latter seeing truth being
dug out of the past but the former seeing that life story is done in the
present. As we have seen in the previous chapter, narratives have stories,
plots, characters, themes and genres; 'memory' organizes sequences,
events, time; conversations have definite flows and coherence; unities are
searched for; mnemotechnic devices – landscapes, music, objects – help
provide structures and sites for reclaiming the past. The focus here, then,
is on the narrative organization of the life and it is appraised through
these terms. Here the life story is fully recognized as a narrative, told in
the present about a past, and the appreciation of the story comes from
sensing its linkages to what Elizabeth Tonkin has called 'the representations of pastness' – and the ways people recall different aspects of their
past (Tonkin, 1992: 1–4). The modes in which we come to say and organize our senses of 'pastness', often through the language of 'memory',
become very central (see below).

A fifth version may be called the *aesthetic* theory of truth, and it
proposes yet another set of criteria. The aim here lies much more with
the elegance and beauty with which the story is told – not the harshness
of realism or the technicalities of positivism but the beauty of the
subjective. Starting with Goethe's *Dichtung und Wahrheit* (Fiction and
Truth), much 'autobiographical' writing has been more concerned with

conveying the story as a writing form, even if some parts are made up and others glossed over. It is a theory which puts the life story alongside 'great literature' to be read for its own joy, pleasure and education. It is closely linked to the story as a form of rhetoric, a form of speech designed to persuade. James Bennett (1981), in a powerful analysis of criminal 'oral histories', suggests their rhetorical function. He argues that no delinquent oral history probably ever appeared before AD 1800, and so the form itself tells us something about the time and place. Why did it emerge there and then? For Bennett, oral histories come to be written because they start to find an audience who can be persuaded through these 'histories', 'speeches' and 'advocacies' of the need for reform and change. The intentions of their collectors (authors) were often to change the attitudes of the rich and the middle classes, and to provide ammunition for reformers: their function was political and moral. Indeed, arguably, this is not just true of delinquent life stories. As Gordon Allport once said, 'social progress may come about through the employment of vivid stories of personal experience' (Allport, 1942: 40).

This is closely linked to the *pragmatic* function of life stories: here the aim becomes to see just how life stories are put to use and what their impact and consequences are. We can start to look at the value of the story – to the teller, to the listener, to the group, to society, to history? And the value may change at different times. As Robert Atkinson claims:

> Life stories . . . can guide us, stage by stage, through the entire life course . . . can affirm, validate, and support our own experience in relation to those around us . . . can bring us face to face with an ultimate mystery . . . can render a cosmology, an interpretive total image of the world, that is in accord with the knowledge of the time, a world view that makes sense of the universe around us. (1998: 9–10)

In what follows, I turn to this pragmatic value in a little more detail.

The pragmatics of life stories: putting the stories to good use

To tell the story of a life may be at the heart of our cultures: connecting the inner world to the outer world, speaking to the subjective and the objective, establishing the boundaries of identities (of who one is and who one is not); crossing 'brute being' – embodied and emotional – with 'knowing self' – rational and irrational; making links across life phases and cohort generations; revealing historical shifts in a culture; establishing collective memories and imagined communities; telling of the concerns of their time and place. Often the call to stories is a moral call (Coles, 1989; Plummer, 2000). In short, life stories can bridge cultural history with personal biography. What matters to people keeps getting told in their stories of their life.

We can see life stories working their way through a series of *circles*: *self*, *others*, *community*, *the whole society*. Starting at the most basic level, life stories perform their work for the life of the *self*. Indeed, people who tell the story of their lives usually find it has given them some coherence, some sense of their developmental path, an understanding perhaps of how some key life crises have developed, a sense of who is important in their life, a story of the meaning of a life itself! An individual's story has the power to tie together past, present and future in his or her life. It is a story that is able to provide unity and purpose (Linde, 1993; McAdams, 1985: 18; McAdams, 1993). This is no small claim – and at its most extreme it is the common injunction to 'know thyself' which brings almost a mystical, religious comprehension. Yet it can often fail: leaving a life in fragments, incoherences, bits (cf. Barthes, 1984). Indeed, postmodern accounts of the self seem to sense that this is becoming more and more common (cf. Gergen, 1991).

Moving beyond this, life stories also work to inform *others*: as Robert Atkinson says, when you listen to another's life story, you might ask yourself: 'What do I have to learn from the experience? What does *this* life story mean from the perspective of my own life experience? What do I see of my own life in this life story? What can I learn from it to tell my own story more effectively?' (Atkinson, 1998: 71). And going still further, life stories can ultimately be used to illustrate the workings of a wider community or whole society. Unique lives can make bridges to wider social concerns and help illuminate the 'myths we live by'. At the most general level, then, life stories may be seen as helping us see ourselves, others, life around us, and ultimately the universe (Campbell, 1991).

Life stories and their therapeutic role

One of the striking new turns in the uses of life histories and narratives has been their development within medicine and therapy. Of course, ever since Freud and earlier, the focus upon understanding the dynamics of an individual case or life has always been a prime concern. Freud's work is littered with famous 'life stories' – Dora, Little Hans, the Wolf Man and so on. But until fairly recently the goals of such work have been largely to use the life to 'read off' signs and symptoms presented as the real underlying dynamic of the repressed unconscious at work. The task was one of narrative reconstruction, of finding the historical truth of the person in their life.

Yet we can also approach the life story as a narrative that helps give unity and understanding to a life in the here and now. Thus, the inchoate stuff and flow of day-to-day life is turned into a rich life narrative which helps give coherence, shape and form to the life; and from which vantage point the life may be lived more fully and clearly. From many angles – illness narratives, trauma and abuse narratives, crisis narratives, coming out narratives, ageing and reminiscence narratives – the power of the story to hold together a potentially fragile life starts to be seen. I will give three brief examples.

First, as we have seen, in much *psychotherapy* a major divide can be found between those who hear the story as symptomatic of an underlying problem (as in classical psychoanalysis) and those who hear the 'story as told' as formative in its own right. In either view, the therapy situation can be seen as one in which the patient/subject is asked to provide a story of their own life; but the response of the analyst is very different. Freud went in search of historical truth – an archaeological dig into the unconscious; others such as Spence (1982) go in search of 'narrative truth', which is 'what we have in mind when we say that such and such is a good story'. Thus, therapy starts to become the creation of stories which people can live with. For Roy Schafer (1992) pyschoanalysis is an active, constructive event where clients/patients are involved in producing storylines of their lives, often coming from well-known stories: the self story narrative is the key, around which the therapist can build dialogues (see McLeod, 1997; Miller, 2000; White and Epston, 1990).

A second striking therapeutic use of life stories and narratives is within *medicine*. A core example of this can be found in Arthur Kleinman's influential *The Illness Narratives* (1988), which deals with a series of life narratives focusing on distressing illnesses – chronic pain, AIDS, dying, colostomy. The stories are told within the full richness of a life, and are seen as ways of making sense and giving meaning to deeply disturbing experiences. Kleinman distinguishes the bodily disease from the socially located illness, and suggests that doctors hitherto have given too much primacy to the former, neglecting the needs patients have for making sense of their lives and illness, learning from the narratives of illness that others have provided. Pain on its own needs a sense-making frame, which patients should be encouraged to find. As he says:

> The illness narrative is a story the patient tells, and significant others retell, to give coherence to the distinctive events and long-term course of suffering. The plot lines, core metaphors, and rhetorical devices that structure the illness narrative are drawn from cultural and personal models for arranging experiences in meaningful ways and for effectively communicating those meanings. Over the long course of chronic disorder, these model texts shape and even create experience. The personal narrative does not merely reflect illness experience, but rather it contributes to the experience of symptoms and suffering . . . (Kleinman, 1988: 49)

He provides an opening checklist of the kinds of questions that could be asked of a patient:

> What is the cause of the disorder? Why did it have its onset precisely when it did? What does the illness do to my body? What course is it following now, and what course can I expect it to follow in the future? What is the source of

improvements, and exacerbations? How can I control the illness, its exacerbations and its consequences? What are the principal effects the illness has had
on my (our) life? What do I most fear about this illness? What treatment do I
wish to receive? What do I expect of the treatment? . . . such questions are not
asked simply to gain information. They are deeply felt. The facial expression,
the tone of voice, posture, body movements, gait, and, especially, the eyes
expose the emotional turmoil that is so much part of the long-term experience
of chronic illness. (Kleinman, 1988: 43–4)

In an elegant study of the narratives of illness and the powerful roles
they play in dealing with illness, Arthur Frank has suggested three major
stories in which the ill try to find themselves. Two are common enough
and well recognizable: he calls them the 'Restitution Narrative' and the
'Quest Narrative'. The former implies the ill person will get well again:
'Yesterday I was healthy, today I'm sick, but tomorrow I'll be healthy
again' (Frank, 1995: 77). A remedy will be found and it plays a key role in
the plot. Quest Narratives, by contrast, are tales of a journey – a passage,
a voice finding itself, a personal tale is told in which whatever the illness
is, the person can come to terms with it. They do not always imply the
person will get better, but there will be a coming to terms with the
illness. Against these two common narratives, Frank also finds a third
narrative which is far less welcomely heard: it is what he calls the 'Chaos
Narrative'. It speaks the unspeakable about illness: life may never get
better, troubles go to 'bottomless depths', everything is out of control.
This narrative may even be an anti-narrative as the chaos of a life and its
illness may not even be able to get into words, let alone plots and stories.
This is the wounded story teller (Frank, 1995).

A third illustration concerns *the elderly* and involves *'reminiscence work'*.
In the 1960s, Butler and others started to suggest the importance of
'reminiscence' and 'life reviews' in the lives of the elderly. The act of
purposely remembering can play a signifcant role in helping to create a
coherent and unitary self (cf. Meyerhoff). With the 'greying of the
population' and the growing importance of the elderly ending their lives
inside nursing homes, getting their life stories told can perform many
valuable functions. The recognition of this has recently had something of
the momentum of a social movement. A pioneer in this field, Joanna
Bornat (1989), has traced the origins of this movement in the UK to three
sources: the academic growth of oral history, the spread of community
publishing – such as the Centerprise Publishing Project in Hackney,
London (with books like Dot Starn's *When I was a Child*, published in
1973; cf. Bornat, 1989: 20) – and the development of ideas in psychology
around recall and memory enabling almost everyone to become an oral
historian of some kind. (The UK organization Help the Aged produced a
tape–slide show in 1981 called 'Recall' to facilitate this.)

Yet in all these therapeutic tasks, we must be careful. Jaber Gubrium,
for instance, whilst listening to the life stories of elderly people in

'Florida Manor', can sense, tellingly, that many lives never achieve a coherence – that many 'elderly faces' may reveal the fragments of stories past whilst being unable to find connections with (an often diseased) present. As he says at the close of his book of life stories: 'There is little overall evidence that affairs are ultimately settled, sundered ties finally repaired, transgressions at last righted or accounted for, or preparations for the future or the afterlife completed' (Gubrium, 1993: 188).

Life stories in education

Life histories also have a strong affinity with education, teaching, learning. Although story telling in education is often not taken seriously – much too lightweight and enjoyable – recently there have been many and major claims as to its significance. Thus, the political philosopher Benjamin R. Barber – in his influential book on education, *An Aristocracy of Everyone* (1992) – claims that 'education is systematic storytelling'; a host of moral philosophers have suggested that narratives of our lives may be the most appropriate ways of 'educating the senses' (e.g. Hannah Arendt, Alastair MacIntyre, Richard Rorty, Martha Nussbaum and others); and books such as Noblit and Dempsey's *The Social Construction of Virtue* (1996) have suggested that schools may well be the depositories of oral histories of the good life. In any event, life stories and education are firmly on the agenda for making the world more understandable, for here 'the universal [may be] found as it should be, in the concrete' (Nisbet, 1976: 213). 'The particular [may be] the only path to the general, but cannot itself be comprehended outside of the general' (Lifton, 1973: 19). The life history provides an ideal vehicle for the educator to sway to and fro between life's specifics and theory's generalities. There are many ways that life stories can be put to good use in education. Written biographies of others and students can become organizing points in a course; research projects can gather a life story (again, of themselves or others). Adjuncts can be used: video can be made use of in fieldwork and life history interviews can be brought to the class for dissection; photographs can be taken and the images discussed; diaries can be kept and analysed. (For some useful discussion of the role of life stories in education, see especially Carol Witherell and Nel Noddings, 1991.)

Life stories in policy, politics and change

Robert Park had a clear view that 'the life history method should work a quiet catharsis of comprehension' (Matthews, 1977: 163). Park's main area of practical activity, race relations, convinced him that the best source of change was 'intimate acquaintance with the problem itself' through the personal document; he asserted, '[there is] no other technique for improvement of race relations in which I have any confidence whatsoever' (p. 163). He continued:

My own experiences prove that there is nothing which has so completely transformed the attitudes of people towards each other as these intimate life histories, of which Booker Washington's *Up From Slavery* is the most striking example. For this reason, we have put more emphasis on the collection of materials of this kind, than we have put on formal statistics ... Such a study ... will achieve the ends for which this investigation was undertaken without the necessity of making any appeal, argument or special pleas for anyone. (Park, quoted in Matthews, 1977: 163)

Park is arguing for a painstaking grasping of the other person's viewpoint and seems to believe that once people of good will are exposed to such concrete details (and they must be details) of individual human predicaments, they will come in their good will to grasp what needs to be done about the situation and bring about change within it. This view talks of a mode of approaching problems but does not of itself take a clearly political stance. The affinity seems to lie with libertarianism, but this approach can, notoriously, be allied to the right or the left. There can be documentaries of celebration as well as documentaries of critique – as has been well demonstrated in studies of American documentaries (see Stott, 1977: chs 10 and 13). Nevertheless, in the hands of so many practitioners, it is undoubtedly a tool of critical attack (Denfield, 1974; Kriseberg, 1975: ch. 3). Over and over again then, in life history research we find the straining towards 'a catharsis of comprehension', to overcome that 'certain blindness' of which all human beings are victim. Robert Bogdan's (1974) depiction of Jane Fry, the transsexual, affords once again a good illustration. Traditionally, transsexualism has been viewed as a sickness; what the 200 pages of Jane Fry's own story allow us to see is that it is an intelligible, even reasonable, experience for her. It accords her a credence which challenges the words and worlds of the clinic practitioner. 'Jane accepts her gender feelings for what they are, that is, she takes them for granted. The professionals, however, see them as immature verbalizations of character disorder, a castration anxiety, a psychotic profile and part of the repertoire for the resolution of core conflicts' (Bogdan, 1974: 215). Bogdan continues:

We see glaring contradictions between Jane's definitions and those of the professionals. The many pages of Jane's story that have preceded this discussion have acquainted us with Jane's vocabulary and views before confronting those of the experts. Having spent more time with her and having more first hand information about her than all the professionals whose comment had been presented here we are in a position to look at them more sceptically and to give the patient's perspective more credence. Seldom are we given an opportunity to see in such detail the position of the client juxtaposed with that of the professional – be the client a juvenile delinquent, a retardate, a welfare recipient or a transsexual.

He continues further:

The professional is seldom effectively challenged, and more rarely are the assumptions based on his training and experience publicly examined or questioned. Jane's perspective enables us to question inductively diagnostic labels, psychological constructs and the way mental illness and various forms of so-called deviant behaviour are conceptualized. (Bogdan, 1974: 217)

Jane Fry's story is not an isolated example of this 'catharsis of comprehension' or more strongly what Bogdan refers to as 'the politics of perspective'. Thus Chic Conwell, Sutherland's 'Professional Thief', shows how the whole criminal justice system is open to bribery and corruption – and how the thief would 'have to have a very beautiful imagination to believe he will get justice in a court where at other times he has his cases fixed and where perhaps at the moment the other side has the fix in' (Sutherland, 1967: 199). Harry King, Chambliss's 'Box Man', finds the 'square john' straight world much less honest than his criminal world – 'there was more thieves, cheaters, racketeers on society's side of the fence than there was on the criminal side' (Chambliss, 1972: 132). William Tanner Spradley's 'Drunk', describes how he was robbed by the police (Spradley, 1970: 14). And a dying man, Archie, writes:

I had finished playing games with others on the subject of my illness and my dying. In refusing, I may come across as hostile; in fact, I probably did recently with the neurologist; but I will not forfeit my own well being while her [sic] or anybody else plays out a role. Virtually nothing is known medically about my disease; there is no treatment for it; my body tells me more accurately about my symptoms than any physician can tell at this point. I do not deny that the skill and technical knowledge of the physicians are invaluable in many situations, but in some, in my own, his role is a very limited one and I do not intend to aggrandise it; our society rewards medical practitioners entirely out proportion to their specific value in society . . . (Hanlan, 1979: 37)

And so the stories could continue, giving flesh and bones to the injustices and indignities of the world where so frequently in social science there is only bland and horrible jargon that serves to over-distance from the issues, to conceal and mystify what is actually occurring in the social world. It is clear then from the above, and from many of the arguments in this book, that a central thrust of personal document research is to enable voices to be heard that are usually silenced: the victims of what Becker (1971) calls a 'hierarchy of credibility' can come through to others on their own terms, slowly puncturing the 'certain blindness' that enshrouds all human beings. Not, of course, that it is only the underdogs whose voices can be heard in personal documents. For such research has a fundamentally democratizing thrust to it: each person has a life and a story to tell. Before the tape recorder or the camera all, however momentarily, are equal. Thus, when Wiseman is accused of presenting a sympathetic view of the oppressive police in his film *Law and Order*, he can retort:

I would certainly never agree that the only view that the film presents is of the cop as a nice guy. What I really object to is the view that the cop, as a human being, is really any different from anybody else. I don't believe it's true; I may have believed it was true before I spent six weeks with them, but I certainly don't believe it now. The ease with which some people can classify large groups of people as either being groovy or just pigs escapes me. (Wiseman, 1971: 325)

All voices need hearing: it is just that some are heard less often than others. The social scientist can, through personal documents, play a minor role of advocacy (cf. Lifton, 1972; Weber and McCall, 1978).

'Quality' assessment: a role in the evaluation process?   If there has been one telling buzz phrase of the late twentieth century it has to have been 'Quality Assessment' – or TQA ('total' quality assessment) – and it is matched by the rise of what we could call 'the quality assurance industry'. Taking its cue from big business, it has entered the world of care, health, education and welfare as well. More and more, governments insist that enormous amounts of time should be given to procedures of quality evaluation. At its very best, it can be a skilled and refined procedure to assist organizations to improve. But much more frequently its assumptions and practices work directly against many of the humanistic assumptions advocated within this book. Instead of sensing the life in all its subjective ambiguity, a series of shorthand devices, appraisals, forms, charts, checklists, focus groups and quick responses are sought. All of these militate against the very process of understanding what is going on.

In his sensitive and moving account of elderly nursing homes, Jaber Gubrium has collected what he calls 'life narratives' and juxtaposed them with the ideas of quality assessment. He talks of the importance of people telling their life narratives in nursing homes, and of the recognition of the importance of this by practitioners and evaluators. He senses how the stories they tell cannot be neatly captured and frozen in time because their 'horizons of meaning' shift, such that the meaning of the home and indeed their life itself is constantly changing in the older person's mind. It may well matter what time of day it is, who he or she is speaking to, what medications have recently been taken, and indeed what the rest of their life has been like – the sense to them of what has been important and what has not. Their own sense of an inner world may place little – or a lot – of significance on the home. And this may change all the while. Nobody hence can capture this straightforwardly. As Gubrium says:

this book examines the subjective meaning of the nursing home's quality of care and quality of life. A sample of residents have been given the opportunity to tell their stories, to speak of life and convey in their own terms the meaning of the qualities in their facilities in relation to the significant matters of long stays. Meanings are presented from residents' points of view, revealing where and, if so how the qualities of their lives figure in. It is a bottom up rather than a top down look and shows how what may be deemed adminstratively the qualities of care and life do not reflect what the qualities appear to be to care receivers. (1993: xv)

Daley has also written a scathing attack on the numerous rounds of assessment situations found in American society (and all western capitalist societies), each of which is blind to a narrow conception of people's abilities 'in psychiatric hospital where one can observe patients put down by the medical model, industry where one can see employees and managers put down by the personnel model, and in the study of bureaucratic operations, where one can watch students or employees being processed' (Daley, 1971: xiii). In each case a narrow look prohibits a concern with life as a whole – people are 'viewed through a filter of assumptions denying much of their potential, dignity and individuality' and an overall sense of where they have come from, where they are going to, what matters to them, is amputated, ignored or denied. Drawing from the psychological models of Allport and Maslow, Daley argues that 'The ultimate criterion of truth about an individual' can only be gleaned from a life history:

> A man's [sic] life is to him the most obvious and overwhelming of all realities. Traces of his past are his constant companions; as for his future do not most people act as if they will live indefinitely? It is therefore most surprising that there should be any question whether life is a substantial enough form of fact to provide data for an assessment system. Perhaps what has so long delayed the evolution of a life history assessment system, has been the undeniable problems of a person's life as an awesome, intricate, beautifully complex phenomena [sic], much too complex for the simple descriptive procedures preferred by assessment psychologists in the past. (Daley, 1971: 28)

In conclusion: the moral call of stories

At the heart of the liberal-humanist tradition is the concern with a human life story. And in understanding a life and in listening to the lives of others are laid bare the struggles around morality and ethics that help organize any culture. Telling the stories of a life not only enables us to see pathways into a culture, but it also provides us with prescriptions for living the ethical life, even in these postmodern times (cf. Bauman, 1993). I am certainly not saying here that such a path leads us to any clear foundational views of ethics; indeed, it does not. But it does leads us to see lives as moral struggles, embedded in specific contexts, shaped by particular conventions of time and place. The moral tales of a life are always collectively embedded in various communities and traditions, they do not arise out of nowhere (see Box 11.1).

BOX 11.1 EVALUATING LIFE STORIES IN THE MEDIA

How to make sense of the multiple life story tellings that are found in all kinds of media – from 'great literature' to 'docusoaps'? How may the watchers and the readers come to assume a more critical stance in relation to the life story tellings they are given? Here are some starting questions to ponder.

What are the moral dimensions of the story? Life stories are moral tales which show moral life at work. They show how ethical dilemmas are worked out in everyday lives – facing all the ambivalence, contradiction, stress and situatedness of living a life (and are thereby much less interested in abstract philosophical debates around ethics). Life stories embody *grounded moralities and ethics*. So when we read or hear a life story, we can ask: what are the moral dramas here and how are they being resolved?

Does the life story **create new cultural insights**? Most life stories are soaked in conventions – they can easily become repetitive or stylized stories that give little insight. There are some stories that have been told once too often. One thing we might start looking for are life stories that are awash in imagination and originality, and which inform us about 'cultures' in new and challenging ways. There have been 'experiments in autobiography' for a long while now; so simply playing with the bits – like Nietzsche, Barthes, Sartre – actually no longer constitutes newness. It is a cliché that lives are 'constructed' and need deconstructing. We probably know enough about new forms: what is needed is new contents. Stories that have not yet been told.

How far does the story reveal its own **reflexivity**? We need to see how the person telling the story – the self – is part of the analysis. Some life stories may be tidied up as 'confessional narratives': what is needed is more of a reflexive telling.

How can we locate **voices, authorships and ownerships** in the life story? Who is telling the story, who is helping to tell the story (the coaxers, the coachers), and who owns the story? Can we really hear the many voices in the text or are they being silenced by the author? Whose voice is dominant? Who is written out? Indeed, who may be demeaned and belittled by the telling of this life?

Who are the **Others**. Can life stories describe that which is not 'them' without fostering an outsider, a marginal group, an 'other'. How can the distance between those studied and those studying be narrowed? Some popular forms like the 'video diary' seem to be making successful moves in this direction – where the story is assembled through the life of the filmers themselves. AIDS autovideo seems to be one area where people with AIDS have not been rendered outsiders but become more and more part of the video work.

Crucial in these days of 'relativist charges', can life stories be made accountable to **practices of truth**. What are the truth claims being made through the story – realist, pragmatic, aesthetic, interpretivist, positivist? How are strategies at work to suggest a certain kind of truth and discredit others; and what overall judgements are being made. What are the different ways of establishing truths within the life story?

Try to be attentive to the **array of dimensions** that the life story tries to capture. Is the 'life' done too swiftly, recorded too lightly, written up too simply? There has to be an immersion in language, in context, in mood, in identities, in bodies, in emotions. Tales that overstate the rational and stay outside of the languages and feelings of those studied are not likely to be very valuable.

What is the connectedness of the story? What is its **embeddedness and location in time and space**. Too much story telling hangs suspended in mid air and stories that become disembedded from their local histories and wider contexts tell only a very small part of the story.

Source: abridged from Plummer, 1999

I am suggesting then, at the end of this book, that matters of ethics and morals enter into the very act of telling a life. The call to the telling of our lives then goes much deeper than its simply being 'a perfect sociological method' (as W.I. Thomas argued), or a good tool for the ethnographic imagination. As many writers have long known, the telling of stories – and especially life stories – goes to the heart of the moral life of a culture (Coles, 1989). That is: people try through their life stories to give some coherence, some point to their existence, even when this fails. In one sense such stories all become 'ethical tales', struggling to show the different choices that people have faced and how they dealt with them. In doing this, they start to provide pragmatic guides to the ways in which a culture organizes its ethical practices. And this is a concern that moves right across the lifespan – from the moral tales told by little children to the reminiscing of the elderly (e.g. Bornat, 1994; Gubrium, 1993); from the stories told in men's lives to those told in women's (e.g. Connell, 1995; Gilligan et al., 1990); from the tales of the 'normal' to those of the 'different' (e.g. Bogdan, 1974). Life stories have been at the heart of many recent issues – from AIDS and cancer to Kosovo and Israel: personal tales work their way. There is not a concern here with abstract systems of morality, but rather with the lived experiences of lives.

And it is in these stories that people struggle to tell, that they reveal, as probably nowhere else, the moral worlds they construct; and these in turn help to provide markers and guidelines to that culture's moral life. Looking at the tales told around and in a school – always rich in stories both formal and less formal – can guide a person into the moral life of a school (Noblit and Dempsey, 1996; Witherell and Noddings, 1991). Listening to feminist-inspired autobiographies can lead to a better understanding of moral textures and social change in the public sphere (Lara, 1998). And reading the tales of black autobiography – including the slave narratives – can help in the political and moral formation of a Black Public Sphere (Black Public Sphere Collective, 1995). Life stories perform major moral work: this is their challenge and their promise. We tell and 'construct'; we hear and 'remember'; and all the time we are assembling ethical worlds. In a famous epigraph, Hannah Arendt once remarked that 'All sorrows can be borne if you put them in a story or tell a story about them'. Of all our stories, life stories are probably the most powerful at doing this.

Guide to further reading

On **memory**, see Paul Connerton, *How Societies Remember* (1989); Elizabeth Tonkin, *Narrating Our Pasts: The Social Construction of Oral History* (1992); and Marita Sturken, *Tangled Memories: The Vietnam War, the AIDS Epidemic and the Politics of Remembering* (1997), which as well as providing valuable case material of war and AIDS, has a well-organized bibliography on 'memory' and related issues. A useful overview of the 'state of the field' in 1998 was Jeffrey Olick and Joyce Robbins 'Social Memory Studies' (1998). There are several journals in this field, but see especially *History and Memory: Studies in Representations of the Past*, published twice a year by Indiana University Press (Volume 1, 1988).

The **general value of life stories** is discussed in Robert Atkinson's *The Life Story Interview* (1998). The central value of life histories as an adjunct to phenomenological work is discussed in an article by L.C. Watson, 'Understanding a life history as a subjective document' (1976): it argues the central link to hermeneutics (not discussed in this text), outlines eleven descriptive categories 'for a framework of understanding' and then applies them to the life of a 32-year-old Guajiro woman, Bianca Gonzalez. Wider discussions of the value of documents may be found in Allport's *The Use of Personal Documents* (1942); and in Gottschalk et al., *The Use of Personal Documents* (especially Robert Angell's contribution) (1942).

On the **therapeutic value of life stories**, the most readable introduction is Arthur Kleinman's *The Illness Narratives: Suffering, Healing and the Human Condition* (1988); and a very valuable review of the whole field here is John McLeod's *Narrative and Psychotherapy* (1997). Key texts include Miller Mair's *Beyond Psychology and Psychotherapy: A Poetics of Experience* (1989); Roy Schafer's *Retelling a Life: Narration and Dialogue in Psychoanalysis* (1992); Donald Spence's *Narrative Truth and Historical Truth: Meaning and Interpretation in Psychoanalysis* (1982) and Michael White and David Epston's *Narrative Means to Therapeutic Ends* (1990).

On the **elderly**, see the work of Joanna Bornat, Peter Coleman's *Ageing and Reminiscence Processes* (1986), and James Birren et al. (eds), *Aging and Biography* (1996). An opening selection of studies on life stories and the elderly would include Barbara Myerhoff's *Remembered Lives: The Work of Ritual, Storytelling and Growing Older* (1992); Paul Thompson et al.'s *I Don't Feel Old* (1990), Jaber Gubrium's *Speaking of Life* (1993) and Kenyon and Randall's *Restorying Our Lives* (1997).

On **teaching and life history**, see the special issue of *Sociology* (Vol. 27, No. 1) on Biography and Autobiography in Sociology, which has a section showing how life stories may be used in teaching and research. On radical approaches to teaching and education, useful sources are Patti Lather, *Getting Smart: Feminist Research and Pedagogy with/in the Post-modern* (1991) and Henry Giroux, *Border Crossings: Cultural Workers and the Politics of Education* (1992). More classically, see Noblit and Dempsey, *The Social Construction of Virtue* (1996), Benjamin Barber's *An Aristocracy of Everyone* (1992) and Carel Witherell and Nel Noddings, *Stories Lives Tell: Narrative and Dialogue in Education* (1991).

12 Epilogue: Critical Humanism in a Post-modern World

The writing on the wall is legible enough. The European Text, more of a museum prospectus these days than a gospel, is taken to task from within and without. It is made responsible for colonizing the past. It is labelled ethnocentric by guilt-ridden Europeans and irrelevant by those excluded from the European text. Its universalism is treated as oppressive on the one hand and impotent on the other . . . And yet, there seems to be no viable alternative to the restoration of the text of interpretation and the universal hermeneutic community through the revitalization of (European) humanism . . .

(Agnes Heller and Ferenc Fehér, 1991: 561–2)

Holding on to the promises of the modern age is very difficult in a time of fragmentation. Yet while each of us lives in his or her own village, we live in a global village too . . . It is a mark of the vitality of modernism despite its undertakers that the struggle for human rights is global, that the sciences are everywhere, that democracy attracts our energies and loyalties . . .

(Howard Radest, 1996: 47–8)

There is an illusive centre to this contradictory, tension-ridden enter-prise that seems to be moving further and further away from grand narratives, and single overarching ontological, epistemological and methodological paradigms. This centre lies in *the humanistic com-mitment of the qualitative researcher to study the world always from the perspective of the interacting individual.* From this simple commitment flow the liberal and radical politics of qualitative research. Action, feminist, clinical, constructivist, ethnic, critical and cultural studies researchers all unite on this point. They all share the belief that a politics of liberation must always begin with the perspectives, desires and dreams of those individuals and groups who have been oppressed by the larger ideological, economic and political forces of a society or a historical moment.

(Norman Denzin, in Denzin and Lincoln, 1994: 575; emphasis added)

As I have suggested throughout the book, a view which takes the human being as an embodied, emotional, interactive self, striving for meaning in wider historically specific social worlds and an even wider universe, is not a bad, even humbling, starting place for the 'human sciences'. And that to listen attentively to the stories people tell of their lives is, equally, not a bad take-off point for doing 'human research'. Whilst they each bring a long history of different usages and meanings – as Chapter 4 tried to show – as generic terms, they do head us toward some important starting points and issues.

And yet these days 'life stories' 'the human being' and 'humanism' are thoroughly contested terms. A very specific, narrow, 'westernized' version has simultaneously been made dominant and then been heavily discredited. Indeed, the twentieth century witnessed attacks on 'humanism' from all sides. Behaviourists claimed it was too subjective. Religions – old and new – claimed it was too materialist. Pessimists saw the history of the twentieth century unfolding as evidence of man's accelerating inhumanity to man along with the end of progress thus enshrined. 'Deconstructionists' saw 'man' as a 'fiction' (and a gendered one at that!), claimed the 'death of the author', and reconstructed 'him' as 'subjectivities' found in 'discourse', 'regimes of truth', and 'technologies of the self'. Indeed, with the arrival of the postmodern, 'human beings' and 'humanism' are seen as 'master narratives' whose day is over. All in all, humanism and all it stands for has become a dirty word. As the prominent anthropologist Clifford Geertz would have it:

> [t]he Western conception of the person as a bounded, unique, more or less integrated, motivational and cognitive universe, a dynamic centre of awareness, emotion, judgement and action, organized into a distinctive whole and set contrastively against other such wholes and against a social and natural background is, however incorrigible it may seem to us, a rather peculiar idea within the context of the world's cultures. (Geertz, 1983)

Or again, as the feminist anthropologist Lila Abu-Lughod notes in her book *Writing Women's Worlds*:

> There are certainly good reasons to be wary of [a] philosophy that has masked the persistence of systematic social differences by appealing to an allegedly universal individual as hero and autonomous subject; that has allowed us to assume that the domination and exploitation of nature by man was justified by his place at the centre of the universe; that has failed to see that its 'essential humanism' has culturally and socially specific characteristics and in fact excludes most humans; and that refuses to understand how we as subjects are constructed in discourses attached to power. (Abu-Lughod, 1993: 28)

Given such damning attacks from such a wide range of sources, why should I wish to retrieve the term and make a defence? At the simplest level, I would argue that we need it because we have little else. Indeed, Lila Abu-Lughod herself – after making such scathing remarks – goes on to make a plea for a 'tactical humanism'. As she says, 'humanism continues to be in the West the language of human equality with the greatest moral force. I do not think we can abandon it' (1993: 28). At the start of a new century, then, it seems to me that it is time for a reconsideration of this language. Indeed, one core thesis of this book is to reconsider the old arguments about the importance of looking at lives in all their differences and generalities as a prime goal for the human sciences; and that this 'looking' is predicated upon a kind of humanism which needs clarifying. 'Differences' may have been insufficently recognized in some of the humanisms of the past.

The anti-humanist project

Let me be clear first about the claims made against 'humanism', and suggest that generally they demean a complex, differentiated term into something far too simple. Why has 'humanism' become the enemy-in-our-midst, a term 'used by its critics to identify everything they think is wrong with the modern world' (Johnson, 1994: vii)? The longstanding attacks from theologies, from behavioural psychologies and from certain kinds of philosophers are well known. But the more recent attacks have denounced 'humanism' as a form of white, male, western, elite domination and colonization which is being imposed throughout the world. This loose but important cluster of positions – usually identified with a postmodern sensibility – would include multicultural theorists, post-colonialists, many feminists, queer theorists and anti-racists, as well as post-structural theorists! Of course, it is a grouping which traditionalists and conservatives would not even start to take seriously. But for me, this forward looking contemporary thought is vital for change; and yet it is generally united in its opposition to the humanist project.

One key object of attack is what N.J. Rengger has called 'High Humanism' (1996: 29), a position which defends all the classical canons of the west in art, literature, music etc. In general, there are three things which seem to especially worry the critics. First, there is the worry that humanists propose some kind of common and hence universal 'human being' or self: a common humanity – an ontological position that senses an essential and common human nature. This universalism is held to blind us to wider differences and positions in the world. Second, there is a concern that humanists see this 'self' or humanity as a powerful, actualizing and autonomous force in the world – a theory of action that puts the individual agent at the centre of the universe. In contrast to the first worry over universalism, this results in a critique of the overt individualism of the theory and of the ways in which this individualism is a result of the Enlightenment project which is not to be found in other societies. Far from being a positive, this is seen to lead, morally, to a dangerous self-absorption, narcissism and selfishness; and, politically, to justify the excesses of the free markets of a *laissez-faire capitalism*. And thirdly, the critics are concerned that this 'humanism of self-actualization' turns itself into a series of moral and political claims about progress through a liberal and democratic society, ultimately a progress which champions the development of Enlightenment thought and the western ideal. Here the concern turns to the ways in which much humanism, far from being a liberatory force, has served as a blanket ideology to justify all manner of oppression – from holocausts to colonialism to wars. Hence the most general principles of modern humanism – a universal, unencumbered 'self', a belief in the power of unique autonomous individuals, and the linkage to the 'modern' western liberal project – are seen as betraying an ethnocentric and colonizing (even totalitarian) impulse. This humanism is both racist and misogynist and has served as a major dominating discourse to organize imperialism, the colonization of whole societies, and the totalitarianisms of the twentieth century. People outside of this western hegemony are necessarily co-opted into it. There are strong 'romantic' tones behind this worship of the self, which are only a few steps away from racist and European 'Superman' overtones. These ideas of the human subject are distinctly 'western' and bring with them a whole series of ideological assumptions about the centrality of the white, western, male, middle class/bourgeois position – hence it becomes the enemy of feminism (human has equalled male), ethnic movements (human has equalled white superiority), gays (human has equalled heterosexual) and all cultures outside of the western Enlightenment project (human has equalled the middle class west).

There are myriad strands in these critical arguments and I cannot rehearse them all here. Michel Foucault, the French philospher of ideas who was extremely influential during the 1980s and 1990s, is often seen as a key spokesperson for them. His theory develops an influential critique of Enlightenment thought and the rise of the individual subject, suggesting that far from being an emancipatory project 'humanism' is one in which subjugations of all kinds can be found . . .

> The modern individual – objectified, analysed, fixed – is a historical achievement. There is no universal person on whom power has performed its operations and knowledge, its enquiries. Rather, the individual is the effect and object of a certain crossing of power and knowledge. He [sic] is the product of the complex strategic development in the field of power and the multiple development in the human sciences. (Foucault, 1979b: 159–60)

The 'Human Subject' becomes a western invention. For Foucault, 'there is no point of dreaming of a time when knowledge will cease to depend on power; this is just the way of reviving humanism in a utopian guise' . . . we should not be deceived by all the Constitutions framed throughout the world since the French Revolution, the Codes written and revised, a whole continuous and clamorous legislative activity: these were the forms that made an essentially normalizing power acceptable' (Foucault, 1979b: 144; Gordon, 1980: 52). Foucault sees our human subjectivities as constituted in and through a spiral of power–knowledge discourses. From the discourses of psychiatry, sexology, criminology, medicine and the whole of the humanities, the 'modern individual' has been invented. But it is not a progress or a liberation – merely a trapping on the forces of power.

But if Foucault is one voice, there are many influential others. Feminisms of various kinds, for instance, have suggested how the 'human' of humanism is a bourgeois white male, and that emancipation has largely meant his emancipation: a different model was needed for women.

> It is no accident that the symbolic system of the family of man – and so the essence of woman – breaks up at the same moment that networks of connection among people on the planet are unprecedently multiple, pregnant and complex. 'Advanced capitalism' is inadequate to convey the structure of this historical moment. In the 'Western' sense, the end of man is at stake. It is no accident that woman disintegrates into women in our time. (Haraway, 1991: 160)

And from the postcolonial movement, Aimé Césaire critiques the so-called humanist involvement of the west:

> They [colonizers] talk to me about progress, about achievements, diseases cured, improved standards of living. I am talking about societies drained of their essence, cultures trampled underfoot, institutions undermined, lands confiscated, religions smashed, magnificent artistic creations destroyed, extraordinary *possibilities* wiped out. (Césaire, 1972: 23–4; emphasis in original)

And at its boldest, all-encompassing postmodern turn, we find with Baudrillard that the human becomes a counterfeit hyper-real simulation, a false representation inhabiting a world of its own, the real human confused with the model; and with Lyotard we find someone who declares the end of all our grand narratives, of which perhaps humanism has to have been the grandest of all. As he says, so famously:

> I will use the term modern to designate any science that legitimates itself with reference to a metadiscourse of this kind making an explicit appeal to some grand narrative. Such as the dialectics of Spirit, the hermeneutics of meaning, the emancipation of the rational or working subject, or the creation of wealth . . . I define postmodern as incredulity towards metanarratives. The narrative loses its function, its great hero, its great dangers, its great voyages, its great goal. (Lyotard, 1984: xxiv)

Over and over again, and usually with due reason, the voices clamour to announce the death of humanism.

Weakening the critique

And yet, despite these many and serious objections to humanism, there is a long history of diverse forms of humanisms in world history and the object of attack is usually a very limited 'Eurocentric' one, often an invention of critics. Early humanists of the pre-Renaissance movement – like Erasmus – did not find their humanism incompatible with religion; any more than the existence of an Islamic humanism or Buddhist humanism. Indeed, Alfred McLung Lee – champion of a humanistic sociology – sees it everywhere:

> Humanism has figured in a wide range of religious, political and academic movements. As such it has been identified with atheism, capitalism, classicism, communism, democracy, egalitarianism, populism, nationalism, positivism, pragmatism, relativism, science, scientism, socialism, statism, symbolic inter-actionism, and supernaturalism, including versions of ancient paganisms, Hinduism, Buddhism, Judaism, Roman Catholicism, Protestantism and Mohammedanism. It has also been rationalized as being opposed to each of these. It has served as an ingredient in movement against each. And these terms do not at all suggest all of humanism's ideological and social associ-ations. (Lee, 1978: 44–5)

It seems to be one of those words that can mean all things to all people. More: it is also clear that the attack is usually waged at a high level of generality in itself – between, for instance, Sartre and Heidegger most famously – where specifics of what constitutes the human are often seriously overlooked. And more curiously, it is also clear that many of the opponents of humanism can be found wanting to hold on to some version of humanism at the end of their critique. Indeed, it is odd that some of the strongest opponents lapse into a kind of humanism at different points of their argument. For instance, Edward Said – a leading postcolonial critic of western style humanism – actually urges another kind of humanism 'shorn of all its unpleasantly triumphalist weight' (Said, 1992: 230), whilst Aimé Césaire (quoted above) actually sees the enemy as a 'pseudo-humanism', implying that humanism still matters and that it is actually just the recent, western conception of humanism that should be objected to, not the word itself or indeed its apparent wide meanings. Likewise, the anthropologist Lila Abu-Lughod – again cited above and so clearly aware of the deficiencies of humanism – actually writes and champions a mode of humanism (she calls it 'tactical human-ism') as more or less the best vision we have.

Others, maybe less critical, go even further and suggest that the claims of multiculturalism actually depend upon a tacit pact with western democratic assumptions. Thus the liberal political scientist Benjamin Barber can say:

> Think for a moment about the ideas and principles underlying anticanonical curricular innovation and critical multiculturalism: a conviction that indi-viduals and groups have a right to self-determination; belief in human equality coupled with a belief in human autonomy; the tenet which holds that domi-nation in social relations, however grounded, is always illegitimate; and the

principle that reason and the knowledge issuing from reason are themselves socially embedded in personal biography and social history and thus in power relations. Every one of these ideas is predominantly the product of Western Civilization. (Barber, 1992: 147)

Likewise with feminism. Whilst many feminists espouse a hatred of humanism for its seeming equation with 'man' (and liberalism), many of the earliest writings were clearly humanist inspired – from Mary Wollstonecraft to Simone de Beauvoir. Indeed, in an important, neglected study, the Australian feminist Pauline Johnson has very gently and systematically argued that *'feminism is a humanism'* (1994: x; emphasis added). For her, feminism – in its many shades – has actually been infused with a kind of radical humanism – 'a historical project born of conscious value choices and the vagaries of critical, social and political movements' (Johnson, 1994: xi). She hints clearly at the problem that comes with humanism in a striking passage:

Modern humanism is pinned on a dilemma which invades its very core. It recognizes that modern humanism is caught in a paradoxical relation between the universalistic character of its own aspirations and the always particularistic, culture bound terms in which these universalizing claims are raised. Radical humanism is, . . . distinguished both by its determination to defend the ideas of modern humanism as contingent, historical values and by its efforts to grasp the consequences which this recognition of its historically contingent character must have for the 'cause' of modern humanism itself . . . (Johnson, 1994: 135)

Indeed, at the start of the twenty-first century, there have been many signs that the critique of humanism which pervaded the previous century has started to be reinvigorated. More and more contemporary commentators – well aware of the attacks above – go on to make some kind of humanist claims. It would not be hard to find signs of humanism in the works of Cornell West, Jeffrey Weeks, Martha Nussbaum, Seyla Benhabib, Nancy Fraser, Anthony Giddens, Zygmunt Bauman, Agnes Heller, Jürgen Habermas, Mikhail Bakhtin and many others: none of whom I have space to consider in a brief epilogue like this!

A human conception: for a pragmatic critical humanism

To recap and to be clear. What I have hoped to start to achieve in this book is a restoration of a language of humanism for social science. Of course, there are many who have never given this language up. But it is also the case that many have, in the wake of the postmodern imagination. I am trying to show that often the claims of anti-humanists have rested upon an overly simplified view of humanism that many humanists have already relinquished. The view of a simple 'unitary' human being is just not sustainable. Moreover, frequently even this self-same postmodernism re-imports humanistic assumptions back into its work without acknowledging them. And I have been trying to do this because the core of this book is to continue with a defence of a methodology – personal documents, life stories and the like – that takes humanism, the humanities and the human being as its, albeit highly fractured, baseline.

It should by now be very clear that the humanism which I am talking about is *not* the solitary, unencumbered self of much liberal theory – not a simple, self-actualizing individual. Quite the contrary, given what has been said above, 'the human being' (or self, person, agent, subject, personhood) of the 'critical humanism' I am trying to locate has a number of differing characteristics to this solitary isolated individual. I call it 'critical' precisely because it stands in critical opposition to earlier overstated assumptions of unitary human beings.

Briefly, this 'human being' that life stories aim to describe is always an embedded, dialogic, contingent, embodied, universal self with a moral (and political character). Thus, humans are:

1   *Embedded.* Human beings cannot be understood if they are taken out of the contexts of time and space of which they are always a part. Thus the 'human being' is not a universal empty signifier: rather 'it' is always stuffed full of the culture and the historical moments of which it is a part, and this history and culture is always in process and changing. Human beings 'nest' in a universe of contexts. To talk otherwise is to engage in the 'myth of the universal man'. As the historian David Hackett Fischer has nicely put it:

> The fallacy of the universal person falsely assumes that people are intel-lectually and psychologically the same in all times and places and circumstances . . . People, in various times and places, have not merely thought different things. They have thought them differently. It is probable that their most fundamental cerebral processes have changed through time. Their deepest emotional drives and desires may themselves have been transformed. Significant elements of continuity cannot be understood without a sense of the discontinuities too . . . (Fischer, 1971: 204)

2   *Symbolic, dialogic, inter-subjective with selves.* Language and symbolic communication is central to human beings, yet it is not a solitary or monologic language. Humans are never alone (except perhaps in extreme psychotic situations, but even here there may be a sense of others), and are dialogic, inter-subjective (i.e. with others and not simply subjective), and have selves that are capable of reflexivity, reflectivity. Humans can and do communicate with themselves and others, critically because (as Mead has it) they have selves. Human beings are able to take the roles of others, imaginatively and

sympathetically, and chart their own actions in relations to these others. They live in worlds reflected in and through others and their languages. And more: they are able through language to hold conversations with others. Of course, other animals can do this too – but not in the same complex fashions which lead to cultures and histories. Most especially, human beings as part of their selfhood and dialogic character can become story tellers. They are 'homo narrans', the narrators of their own lives, both interpersonally and internally.

3   *Contingent*. Human beings are surrounded throughout their lives by chance, fateful moments, contingencies. Agnes Heller draws out the philosophical metaphor that 'man is thrown into the world' and argues that:

> *The modern person is a contingent person* . . . Contingency is one of the main constituents of the human condition, for nothing in our genetic equipment predetermines us to be born in precisely such and such an age, in such and such a social condition, caste, class and the like . . . the modern person is born as a cluster of possibilities without telos . . . [and] it must choose the framework, the telos, of his or her life . . . (Heller, 1990: 5–6)

4   *Dually embodied and symbolic*. Human beings are both animals and creatures with great symbolic potential. They are, in the words of Ernest Becker, 'little gods who shit'. Thus, whilst humanism must examine the ways in which humans develop massive symbolic and meaningful worlds – how man is engaged in a search for meaning – it should never overlook the embodied and animalistic nature of this experience. Unlike some past humanisms, this cannot sever the human being from the wider animal kingdom – nor even would it place the human being at the centre of the animal world. Rather, human beings are part of this wider animal world – and, again, contingent upon it.

5   *Universal*. To say this is not to contradict the above. There is a continuous tension between the specificities and variety of humanities at any time and place, and the universal potentials which are to be found in all humans. Quite what these universals may be is a matter of dispute: the liberal, humanist feminist philosopher Martha Nussbaum (1999: 41), for example, suggests a long list of 'human capabilities' like 'bodily health and integrity', senses, imagination, thought; emotions; practical reason; affiliation; concern for other species; play; control over one's environment; and life itself'. To this I might add the crucial self-reflexive process – a process of communication – which is central to the way we function. This is just one listing: there are many others (e.g. Donald E. Brown, 1991). The point is to recognize both universal capacities along with diversity and specificity.

6   *With a moral (ethical, political) character*. Another abiding feature of human lives has to be the question: 'how to live a life?' Human

cultures drip with moral and ethical problems, and are organized through and within circuits of power. Of course, such issues can be avoided: but overwhelmingly they are the stuff of human cultures – the webs of meaning through which lives get organized. We are talking about the potentials for lives – individually and collectively – to become more and more enriched, varied and fruitful.

Postmodernism has brought a strong critique of traditional notions of the human and humanism. In its most sceptical, cynical, ludic and despairing forms, it will remain resolutely anti-humanist. But in some of its more affirmative, open, critical and political versions, it can easily be accommodated with most (if not all) of what I have said above. The telling of a life can be both a humanistic and postmodern project.

Guide to further reading

A short guide to a number of these debates linked to modernity and humanism can be found in N.J. Rengger's *Retreat from the Modern: Humanism, Postmodernism and the Flight from Modernist Culture* (1996). Modern humanism may be best represented by: Ferenc Fehér, 'Between relativism and fundamentalism: hermeneutic as Europe's mainstream political tradition', *Thesis Eleven*, 1988, 22: 79–81, and reprinted in Agnes Heller and Ferenc Fehér, *The Grandeur and Twilight of Radical Universalism* (1991); Agnes Heller, *A Philosophy of Morals* (1990); Martha C. Nussbaum, *Sex and Social Justice* (1999); Pauline Johnson, *Feminism as Radical Humanism* (1994); and Howard B. Radest, *Humanism with a Human Face: Intimacy and the Enlightenment* (1996). John Gibbins and Bo Reimer's discussion on *The Politics of Postmodernity* (1999) draws upon a distinction between sceptical and affirmative postmodernisms, which could be a useful way ahead.

Appendix   New Technologies/New Sources/ New Archiving in Life Story Work

Using new technologies

'Hi-Tech' changes in social research of all kinds are now well on their way. Chapter 4 hinted at major changes ahead in the gathering of life stories and their social impact; whilst Chapter 7 suggested at times how they may impact the research process. The past decade has seen the arrival of many new information technologies – from the now ubiquitous word processor and e-mail to web sites and 'software packages' – which can assist in qualitative research in general and life story research in particular. It is very likely they will change the field enormously in the next few years. They will help in the writing of life stories and in their organization, editing, coding, conceptualizing, writing up and presenting, as well as finally archiving. They will become major resources for hyperlinking and making connections across different forms of data.

Broadly, we can distinguish various uses which include the following.

1   The use of IT as a simple mechanism for data retrieval. Here there are all kinds of web sites where personal documents have been stored and are available for the researcher. In the course of writing this book, for instance, I searched for information on the life story data for Alex Haley's influential *Roots* and found some 1,500 web sites where it appears! A short listing of some relevant web sites is provided at the end of this appendix.

2   The use of *Computer Assisted Qualitative Data Analysis Programs (CAQDAS)*. Here are programmes designed specifically to 'handle' soft data. They take three major forms:

- text retriever – allowing basic searches and sortings of data
- code and retrieve packages – allowing texts to be organized and codes allocated
- theory-building software – allowing texts to be sorted and coded and then move to a higher level of concept and theory-building.

At the broadest level, the data from a life story (or other qualitative strategy) is typed on disk under regular file headings and stored. It is then systematically coded through the software, using various layers of coding. There are now a good number of such programs available, each with relative merits. For more details, look at the websites for

The Ethnograph	http://www.QualisResearch.Com
NUD*IST	http://www.qsr.com.au
Atlas	http://www.atlasti.de
etc.	

Sage Publications distribute some of the major programs, including The Ethnograph, NUD*IST and Atlas, and information can be accessed via http://www.sagepub.co.uk/scolari

Further details on these kinds of programs can be found on Computer Assisted Qualitative Data Analysis Software Networking Project (CAQDAS) which is based at the University of Surrey: http://www.soc.surrey.ac.uk/caqdas

3   The use of word processing as a tool for data collection and analysis. For the less technologically minded, it does seems that a good word processing package can do the job as well as many of the more specific programs, provided the researcher does not want to attain very high levels of sophistication (and a lot of the work described in this book would not find such 'treatment' really appropriate). Stanley and Temple (1995) have described this more simple process:

1   use word processing files
2   set line and page margins
3   run a macro to line number the text on screen and hard copy
4   save and print a line numbered hard copy of text (back up as appropriate)
5   create a working copy of original by saving with a different name
6   photocopy line copy – at least once
7   read – to analyse
8   work manually on working hard copy, mark up themes, words etc.
9   and so on.

They continue with points similar to these, showing that it is possible to adapt simple word processing skills to organizing and analysing the data . . . For more information on the use of IT, see the Socinfo Guide: SOSIG, *The Internet for Social Scientists*   http://sosig.esrc.bris.ac.uk/training/issnltr.html

A note on archives and life story work

In recent years, and certainly since the publication of the first edition of this book, there has been a steady and growing interest in the issues surrounding the archiving of life story materials and qualitative research in general. Once the researcher has done his or her work and written up their study, what is to happen to the data? There are many horror stories, for instance, of researchers just throwing away their materials, or stashing them in old boxes under beds and in attics to be found on their deaths! The issue becomes: What should happen to this data? How might it be stored and preserved once the research is over? For what purposes could it be re-used (for assessment of validity of past studies, enhance secondary data analysis, for follow up studies)? Who should this then be accessible to?

A number of specialist archives have now been set up. In some countries there are extensive libraries of folklore collections (e.g. in Finland). In the UK this includes the National Sound Archive (based at the British Library), The Royal Institute's Film and Photo Libraries, the Mass Observation archive (at University of Sussex) and, perhaps most significantly, Qualidata (based at the University of Essex). But there are also a number of more local-based archives – women's archives, gay and lesbian archives, local history groups etc. Throughout the world, this can usually be quite easily tracked by a key name website search.

On archiving, there is extensive documentation of issues to be found in the work of the ESRC's Qualidata (Sociology Department, University of Essex, UK), where, under the directorship of Paul Thompson and the management of Louise

Corti, an extensive array of reports has been produced. Below are listed a number of potentially useful starting points and archival resources:

Qualidata

http://www.essex.ac.uk/qualidata/

The Essex Archive for Qualitative Data – called Qualidata. A lot of useful information about archiving and good links to a lot of archives.

Glen Elder Web Page

http://www.cpc.unc.edu/projects/lifecourse/index.html

A useful site for those interested in life course development. It describes some of the major researches in the USA.

http://www.bl.uk/index.html

Takes you into the British Library, where you can find, amongst so many things, *The National Sound Archive*. With the right browsers, you can listen to oral history tapes . . .

Oral history

Oral History At Columbia University

http://www.cc.columbia.edu/cu/libraries/indiv/oral/

One of the major sites.

Oral History Society (UK)

http://www.essex.ac.uk/sociology/oralhi3.htm

Web site for oral history organizations (check, may be out of date): based at Essex.

British Library National Sound Archive

www.bl.uk./collections/sound-archive

Mass Observation Archive (Sussex)

http://www.sussex.ac.uk/library/massobs/homearch.html

Oral History Assosciation (USA)

http://omega.dickinson.edu/organizations/oha/

Center for Oral History, University of Connecticut

http://www.oralhistory.uconn.edu

Oral History Index

http://www.vcmha.org/oralhist.html

RRLC (Rochester Regional Library Council) Guidelines for Oral History Interviews
http://www.rrlc.org/hrac/oralhis.html

'The Century Speaks'

www.bbc.co.uk/education/history/oral.shtml

A BBC oral history archive.

Some life story collections

The Fortunoff Collection

http://www.library.yale.edu/testimonies/homepage.html

A collection of more than 4,000 witnesses and survivors of the Holocaust.

The Shoah Collection

http://www.vhf.org/

More than 200,000 hours of video tapes. This 'Spielberg' project is the largest collection of personal documents in the world.

Alex Haley websites

http://www.blackfamilies.com/living/family_relationships/alex_haley.html

This provides a good entrance point both to the work of Alex Haley, and also to the task of constructing one's own genealogy.

http://www.public.asu.edu/~metro/aflit/haley/index.html

The best access to the work of Alex Haley.

Family histories

http://www.4evercdmemories.com/

through which you can organize family histories on CD:

Diaries

The Open Diary
http://www.opendiary.com/
(an interactive on line diary community)

Film and video collections

British Universities Film and Video Council

http://www.bufvc.ac.uk/

This is the home of the British collection and it can provide good reference materials on film, television programmes and video.

Documentary films

http://www.documentaryfilms. net/site.html

Some more specific web sites

The Garbage Project
http://wacky.ccit.arizona.edu/-bara/gbg-in-1.htm

The popular magazine *Biography* has a web site at:
http://biography.com

Other web site resources

Life documents can be found everywhere on the internet, and are a significant resource. Because they can change rapidly, however, and are often closed, a long list of such websites has not been included in this book. In many ways, the best way to find sites is to 'surf'. Below are some interesting sites and other sources – that were functioning as the book went to press.

General gateways to sociology

There are many 'sociology' sites which are very wide-ranging. Not only are there links to a wide array of sociology sites and organizations, there are also links to key sociology associations and sociology departments throughout the world. The following were very useful as first entries at the time of going to press:

http://www.pscw.uva.nl/sociosite/
http://www.princeton.edu/~sociolog/links.html
http://www.socioweb.com/~markbl/socioweb/

Theory links

Symbolic Interactionism. This is the home page of the Society for the Study of Symbolic Interaction. At last look, it had not been updated for a while.
http://sun.soci.niu.edu/~sssi/

The Foucault Files
http://www.qut.edu.au/edu/cpol/foucault/

For the journals: see
Sociological Research Online
http://www.socresonline.org.uk/socresonline/3/2/1.html
(which would give you Vol. 3, No. 2).

There are also now numerous books which list web sites. See:

Milson Henry (ed.) (1999) *IT in the Social Sciences: A Student Guide to the Information and Communication Technologies.* Oxford: Blackwell.
The Hutchinson Directory of Web Sites (1999) Oxford: Helicon Publishing.
Gibbs, G.R. (1997) *SocInfo Guide to IT*, 4th edn. Stirling: University of Stirling.

Bibliography

Abercrombie, N., Hill, S. and Turner, B.S. (1986) *Sovereign Individuals of Capitalism*. London: Allen and Unwin.

Ablon, J. (1985) *Little People of America: Myths and Methods*. New York: Praeger.

Abu-Lughod, L. (1993) *Writing Women's Worlds: Bedouin Stories*. Berkeley, CA: University of California Press.

Adams, R.N. and Preiss, J.J. (1960) *Human Organization Research: Field Relations and Techniques*. Homewood, IL: Dorsey Press.

Adler, A. (1929) *The Case of Miss R: The Interpretation of a Life Story*. New York: Greenberg.

Adler, P.A. and Adler, P. (1987) *Membership Roles in Field Research*. London: Sage.

Adler, P.A. and Adler, P. (1994) 'Observational techniques', in N.K. Denzin and Y. Lincoln (eds), *Handbook of Qualitative Research*. London: Sage. ch. 23.

Agar, M. (1996) *The Professional Stranger*, 2nd edn. London: Academic Press.

Agee, J. and Evans, W. (1965) *Let Us Now Praise Famous Men: Three Tenant Families*. London: Peter Owen.

Agger, B. (2000) *Public Sociology: From Social Facts to Literary Acts*. New York: Rowman and Littlefield.

Akeret, R.V. (1973) *Photoanalysis: How to Interpret the Hidden Psychological Meaning of Personal and Public Photographs*. New York: Wyden.

Albrecht, G.L. (1985) 'Videotape safaris: entering the field with a camera', *Qualitative Sociology*, 8 (4): 325–44.

Allen, S.L. (ed.) (1994) *Media Anthropology: Informing Global Citizens*. London: Bergin and Garvey.

Allport, G.W. (1942) *The Use of Personal Documents in Psychological Science*. New York: Social Science Research Council.

Allport, G.W. (1962) 'The general and the unique in psychological science', *Journal of Personality*, 30 (3): 405–22.

Allport, G.W. (ed.) (1965) *Letters from Jenny*. London: Harcourt Brace Jovanovich.

Altheide, D.L. (1996) *Qualitative Media Analysis*. London: Sage.

Althusser, L. (1969) *For Marx*. Harmondsworth: Penguin.

Althusser, L. (1976) 'Reply to John Lewis', in *Essays in Self Criticism*. London: New Left Books.

Anderson, N. (1961) *The Hobo*. Chicago: University of Chicago Press. (First published in 1923.)

Anderson, N. (1975) *The American Hobo: An Autobiography*. Leiden: E.J. Brill.

Angell, R.C. (1942) 'A critical review of the development of the personal document method in sociology 1920–1940', in L. Gottschalk, C. Kluckhohn and R. Angell (eds), *The Use of Personal Documents in History, Anthropology and Sociology*. New York: Science Research Council. pp. 177–232.

Angell, R.C. and Freedman, R. (1953) 'The use of documents, records, census materials and indices', in L. Festinger and D. Katz (eds), *Research Methods in the Behavioural Sciences*. New York: Holt, Rinehart & Winston. pp. 300–26.

Ashmore, M. (1989) *The Reflexive Thesis*. Chicago: University of Chicago Press.

Atkins, T.R. (1976) *Frederick Wiseman*. New York: Simon and Schuster.

Atkinson, P. (1990) *The Ethnographic Imagination: Textual Constructions of Reality.* London: Routledge.

Atkinson, P. (1992) *Understanding Ethnographic Texts.* London: Sage.

Atkinson, P. (1999) 'Voice and unvoiced: Review Essay', *Sociology*, 33 (1): 191–6.

Atkinson, R. (1998) *The Life Story Interview.* London: Sage.

Bain, R. (1930) 'Review of the Jack Roller', *Annals of the American Academy of Political and Social Science*, Issue No. 151.

Bakan, D. (1969) *On Method.* San Francisco, CA: Jossey–Bass.

Bakan, D. (1996) 'Some reflections about narrative research and hurt and harm', in R. Josselson (ed.), *Ethics and Process in the Narrative Study of Lives.* London: Sage (Vol. 4 of *The Narrative Study of Lives* series). pp. 3–8.

Ball, M.S. and Smith, G.W.H. (1992) *Analysing Visual Data.* London: Sage.

Banish, R. (1976) *City Families: Chicago and London.* New York: Pantheon.

Banks, A. and Banks, S.P. (eds) (1998) *Fiction and Social Research: By Ice or Fire.* London: AltaMira.

Barber, B. (1992) *An Aristocracy of Everyone: The Politics of Education and the Future of America.* New York: Oxford University Press.

Barbo, B. (1987) *The Walking Wounded: A Mother's True Story.* Lindborg, KS: Carlsons.

Barker, R. and Wright, H. (1951) *One Boy's Day.* New York: Harper and Row.

Barnes, J.A. (1979) *Who Should Know What? Social Science Privacy and Ethics.* Harmondsworth: Penguin.

Barthes, R. (1967) *Writing Degree Zero.* London: Cape.

Barthes, R. (1975) *Roland Barthes by Roland Barthes.* Paris: Editions du Seuill. (New York: Farrar, Strauss and Giroux, 1977; Berkeley, CA: University of California Press, 1994.)

Barthes, R. (1977) 'The death of the author', in *Image–Music–Text.* Glasgow: Fontana/ Collins. (Originally published in French, 1968.)

Barthes, R. (1984) *Camera Lucida.* London: Fontana.

Basting, A.D. (1998) *The Stages of Age: Performing Age in Contemporary American Culture.* Ann Arbor, MI: University of Michigan Press.

Bateson, G. and Mead, M. (1942) *Balinese Character*, Vol. II. New York: New York Academy of Science.

Bateson, M.C. (1989) *Composing a Life.* New York: Penguin.

Bauman, Z. (1993) *Postmodern Ethics.* Oxford: Blackwell.

Bauman, Z. (1999) *In Search of Politics.* Cambridge: Polity.

Baumeister, R. (1986) *Identity: Cultural Change and the Struggle for Self.* Oxford and New York: Oxford University Press.

Becker, H.S. (1963) *Outsiders: Studies in the Sociology of Deviance.* New York: The Free Press of Glencoe.

Becker, H.S. (1966) 'Introduction' to *The Jack Roller*, by Clifford Shaw, in H.S. Becker (1971) *Sociological Work.* London: Allen Lane.

Becker, H.S. (1971) *Sociological Work: Method and Substance.* London: Allen Lane.

Becker, H.S. (1974) 'Photography and sociology', *Studies in the Anthropology of Visual Communication*, 5: 2–26.

Becker, H.S. (1979) 'Do photographs tell the truth?', in T.D. Cook and C.S. Reichardt (eds), *Qualitative and Quantitative Methods in Evaluation Research.* Beverly Hills, CA: Sage. pp. 99–117.

Becker, H.S. (1986) *Writing for Social Scientists.* Chicago: University of Chicago Press.

Becker, H.S. (1996) *The Tricks of the Trade.* Chicago: University of Chicago Press.

Belk, R. (1995) 'Studies in the new consumer behaviour', in D. Miller (ed.), *Consumption: A Review of New Studies.* London: Routledge. pp. 58–94.

Bell, C. and Newby, H. (eds) (1977) *Doing Sociological Research.* London: Allen and Unwin.

Bell, L. (1998) 'Public and private meanings in diaries: researching family and childcare', in J. Ribbens and R. Edwards (eds), *Feminist Dilemmas in Qualitative Research*. London: Sage. pp. 72–86.

Bell, M.M. (1994) *Childerley: Nature and Morality in a Country Village*. Chicago: University of Chicago Press.

Bellah, R., Madsen, R., Sullivan, W., Swidler, A. and Tipton, S. (1985) *Habits of the Heart: Individualism and Commitment in American Life*. New York: Harper and Row.

Bendelow, G. and Williams, S.J. (eds) (1998) *Emotions in Social Life*. London: Routledge.

Benjamin, W. (1955) *Illuminations*. London: Fontana.

Benjamin, W. (1990) 'The Work of Art in the Age of Mechanical Reproduction', reproduced from *Illuminations* in J. Hanhardt, *Video Culture: A Critical Investigation*. Rochester, NY: Visual Studies Workshop Press.

Bennett, J. (1981) *Oral History and Delinquency: The Rhetoric of Criminology*. Chicago: University of Chicago Press.

Benstock, S. (ed.) (1988) *The Private Self: Theory and Practice of Women's Autobiographical Writings*. London: Routledge.

Berg, B. (1998) *Qualitative Research Methods for the Social Sciences*, 3rd edn. London: Allyn and Bacon.

Berger, B. (1990) *Authors of Their Own Lives: Intellectual Autobiographies by Twenty American Sociologists*. Berkeley, CA: University of California Press.

Berger, J. (1972) *Ways of Seeing*. Harmondsworth: Pelican.

Berger, J. (1980) *About Looking*. London: Writers and Readers Cooperative.

Berger, M. (1977) *Real and Imagined Worlds: The Novel and Social Science*. London: Harvard University Press.

Berger, P. (1966) *Invitation to Sociology*. Harmondsworth: Penguin.

Berreman, G. (1962) *Behind Many Masks*. Ithaca, NY: Cornell University Press/Society for Applied Anthropology.

Bertaux, D. (ed.) (1981) *Biography and Society. The Life History Approach in the Social Sciences*. Beverly Hills, CA: Sage.

Bertaux, D. and Bertaux-Wiame, I. (1981) 'Life stories in the bakers' trade', in D. Bertaux, *Biography and Society. The Life History Approach in the Social Sciences*. Beverly Hills, CA: Sage. pp. 169–90.

Bertaux, D. and Kohli, M. (1984) 'The life story approach: a continental view', *Annual Review of Sociology*, 10: 215–37.

Bierstedt, R. (ed.) (1969) *Florian Znaniecki on Humanistic Sociology*. Chicago: University of Chicago Press.

Billig, M. (1987/1996 2nd edn) *Arguing and Thinking: A Rhetorical Approach to Social Psychology*. Cambridge: University of Cambridge Press.

Birren, J.E., Kenyon, G.M., Ruth, J.G., Schroots, J. and Svensson, T. (eds) (1996) *Aging and Biography: Explorations in Adult Development*. New York: Springer.

Bjorklund, D. (1999) *Interpreting the Self: Two Hundred Years of American Autobiography*. Chicago: University of Chicago Press.

Black Public Sphere Collective (eds) (1995) *The Black Public Sphere: A Public Culture Book*. Chicago: University of Chicago Press.

Blackman, M.B. (1992) 'Introduction: the afterlife of the life history', *Journal of Narrative and Life History*, 2 (1): 1–9.

Blauner, B. (1987) 'Problems of editing "first-person" sociology', *Qualitative Sociology*, 10 (1): 46–64.

Blauner, B. (1989) *Black Lives, White Lives: Three Faces of Race Relations in America*. Berkeley, CA: University of California Press.

Blumer, H. (1933) *Movies and Conduct*. New York: Macmillan.

Blumer, H. (1939/1979) *Critiques of Research in the Social Sciences: I: An Appraisal of Thomas and Znaniecki's The Polish Peasant in Europe and America*. New York: Social Science Research Council (2nd edn, with a new introduction, New Brunswick, NJ: Transaction Books).

Blumer, H. (1969) *Symbolic Interactionism*. Englewood Cliffs, NJ: Prentice-Hall.

Blumer, H. and Hughes, E.C. (1980) 'Reminiscences of classic Chicago', *Urban Life*, 9: 251–81.

Blythe, R. (1969) *Akenfield*. London: Allen Lane.

Bogardus, E.S. (1926) *The New Social Research*. Los Angeles: Press of Jesse Ray Miller.

Bogdan, R. (1974) *Being Different: The Autobiography of Jane Fry*. London: Wiley.

Bogdan, R. and Taylor, S. (1975) *Introduction to Qualitative Research Methods: A Phenomenological Approach to the Social Sciences*. London: Wiley. (3rd edn 1998.)

Bogue, D.J. (ed.) (1974) *The Basic Writings of Ernest W. Burgess*. Chicago: Community and Family Study Center, University of Chicago.

Bolton, R. (1995) 'Tricks, friends and lovers: erotic encounters in the field', in D. Kulick and M. Wilson (eds), *Taboo: Sex, Identity and Erotic Subjectivity in Anthropological Fieldwork*. London: Routledge. pp. 140–67.

Borenstein, A. (1978) *Redeeming the Sin: Social Science and Literature*. New York: Columbia University Press.

Bornat, J. (1989) 'Oral history as a social movement: reminiscence and older people', *Oral History*, 17 (2): 16–30.

Bornat, J. (ed.) (1994) *Reminiscence Reviewed: Perspectives, Evaluations, Achievements*. Buckingham: Open University Press.

Boswell, J. (1950 edn) *London Journal 1762–3*. New York: McGraw Hill.

Botkin, B.A. (1945/1994) *Lay My Burden Down. A Folk History of Slaves*. New York: Delta.

Bouchard, T. (1976) 'Unobtrusive methods: an inventory of uses', *Sociological Method and Research*, 4: 267–300.

Bourdieu, P. (1984) *Distinction: A Social Critique of the Judgement of Taste*. Cambridge, MA: Harvard University Press.

Bourdieu, P. (1988) *Homo Academicus*. Stanford, CA: Stanford University Press.

Bourdieu, P. and Wacquant, L. (1992) *An Invitation to Reflexive Sociology*. Chicago: University of Chicago Press.

Bourdieu, P. et al. (1999) *The Weight of the World: Social Suffering in Contemporary Society* (trans. P.P. Ferguson et al.). Cambridge: Polity Press.

Bowen, E.S. (Laura Bohanan) (1954) *Return to Laughter*. New York: Harper.

Bowles, G. and Klein, R.D. (1983) *Theories of Women's Studies*. London: Routledge

Bradbury, M. (1996) *The Atlas of Literature*. London: De Agostini.

Bramson, L. (1961) *The Political Context of Sociology*. Princeton, NJ: Princeton University Press.

Brettell, C.B. (1993) *When They Read What We Write: The Politics of Ethnography*. London: Bergin and Garvey.

Brook, J. and Boal, I.A. (eds) (1995) *Resisting the Virtual Life: The Culture and Politics of Information*. San Francisco: City Lights.

Brown, D.E. (1991) *Human Universals*. New York: McGraw–Hill.

Brown, R.H. (1977) *A Poetic for Sociology: Toward a Logic of Discovery for the Human Sciences*. Cambridge: Cambridge University Press.

Bruner, J. (1986) *Actual Minds, Possible Worlds*. Cambridge, MA: Harvard University Press.

Bruner, J. (1987) 'Life as narrative', *Social Research*, 54 (1): 11–32.

Bruner, J.S. (1990) *Acts of Meaning*. Cambridge, MA: Harvard University Press.

Bruner, J. (1993) 'The autobiographical process', in R. Folkenflik (ed.), *The Culture of Autobiography: Constructions of Self Representation*. Stanford, CA: Stanford University Press. pp. 38–56.

Bruyn, S.T. (1966) *The Human Perspective in Sociology: The Methodology of Participant Observation*. Englewood Cliffs, NJ: Prentice–Hall.

Bryman, A. and Burgess, R.G. (eds) (1994) *Analysing Qualitative Data*. London: Sage.

Bulmer, M. (ed.) (1978) *Mining and Social Change. Durham County in the Twentieth Century*. London: Croom Helm.

Bulmer, M. (ed.) (1982) *Social Research Ethics*. London: Allen and Unwin.

Bulmer, M. (1984) *The Chicago School of Sociology*. Chicago: Chicago University Press.

Burgess, B. (1994) *In the Field*. London: Allen and Unwin.

Burgess, E.W. (1941) 'An experiment in the standardization of the case study', *Sociology*, 4: 329–48.

Burgess, E.W. (1945) 'Research methods in sociology', in G. Gurvitch and W.E. Moore (eds), *Twentieth Century Sociology*. New York: The Philosophical Library Inc. pp. 20–40.

Burgess, R. (ed.) (1984) *Field Research: A Sourcebook and Field Manual*. London: Allen and Unwin.

Burgin, V. (ed.) (1982) *Thinking Photography*. London: Macmillan.

Burgos-Debray, E. (ed.) (1984) *I, Rigoberta Menchú: An Indian Woman in Guatemala*. London: Verso.

Burke, K. (1945) *A Grammar of Motives*. New York: Prentice–Hall.

Burnett, J., Vincent, D. and Mayall, M. (eds) (1984) *The Autobiography of the Working Class: An Annotated, Critical Bibliography*. Brighton: Harvester.

Butler, J. (1990) *Gender Trouble: Feminism and the Subversion of Identity*. New York: Routledge.

Butler, R.N. (1963) 'The life-review: an interpretation of reminiscence in the aged', *Psychiatry*, 26: 63–76.

Butterfield, S. (1974) *Black Autobiography in America*. Amherst, MA: University of Massachusetts Press.

Calder-Marshall, A. (1963) *The Innocent Eye: The Life of R.J. Flaherty*. London: W.H. Allen.

Callen, M. (1987/1990) *Surviving and Thriving with Aids*. New York: PWA Coalition.

Campbell, J. (1991) *The Power of Myth*. NewYork: Anchor/Doubleday Paperback.

Caplan, P. (1997) *African Voices, African Lives: Personal Narratives from a Swahili Village*. London: Routledge.

Capote, T. (1966) *In Cold Blood*. London: Hamish Hamilton.

Carey, J.T. (1975) *Sociology and Public Affairs*: Vol. 16, *The Chicago School*. (Sage Library of Social Research.) Beverly Hills, CA: Sage.

Carlson, M. (1996) *Performance: A Critical Introduction*. London: Routledge.

Carroll, J. (1993) *Humanism: The Wreck of Western Culture*. London: Fontana.

Castaneda, C. (1968) *The Teachings of Don Juan*. Harmondsworth: Penguin.

Castells, M. (1998) *The Information Age*, 3 vols. Oxford: Blackwell.

Cavan, R.S. (1928) *Suicide*. New York: Russell and Russell.

Cavan, R.S. (1929) 'Topical summaries of current literature: interviewing for life history material', *American Journal of Sociology*, 15: 100–15.

Cavan, R.S., Hauser, P.M. and Stouffer, S.A. (1930) 'A note on the statistical treatment of life history material', *Social Forces*, 9: 200–3.

Césaire, A. (1972) *Discourse on Colonialism*. New York: Monthly Review Press (and excerpted in P. Williams and L. Chrisman (eds) (1998) *Colonial Discourse and Post-Colonial Theory: A Reader*. Brighton: Harvester Wheatsheaf).

Chalasinski, J. (1981) 'The life records of the young generation of Polish peasants as a manifestation of contemporary culture', in D. Bertaux. (ed.), *Biography and Society. The Life History Approach in the Social Sciences*. Beverly Hills, CA: Sage. pp. 119–31.

Chamberlain, M. and Thompson, P. (1998) *Narrative and Genre*. London: Routledge.

Chamberlayne, P., Bornat, J. and Wengraf, T. (2000) *The Turn to Biographical Methods in Social Science: Comparative Issues and Examples*. London: Routledge.

Chambers, R. (1998) *Facing It: AIDS Diaries and the Death of the Author*. Michigan: University of Michigan Press.

Chambliss, B. (1972) *The Box Man; A Professional Thief's Journal* (by H. King as told to and edited by B. Chambliss). New York: Harper and Row.

Chaplin, E. (1994) *Sociology and Visual Representation*. London: Routledge.

Chasnoff, S. (1996) 'Performing teen motherhood on video: autoethnography as counterdiscourse', in S. Smith and J. Watson (eds), *Geting a Life: Everyday Uses of Autobiography*. Minneapolis, MN: University of Minnesota Press. pp. 108–33.

Cicourel, A.V. (1964) *Method and Measurement in Sociology*. New York: The Free Press.

Clark, C. (1997) *Misery and Company*. Chicago: University of Chicago Press.

Classen, Constance (1993) *Worlds of Sense. Exploring the Senses in History and Across Cultures*. London: Routledge.

Clendinnen, I. (1999) *Reading the Holocaust*. Cambridge: Cambridge University Press.

Clifford, J. and Marcus. G.E. (1986) *Writing Culture: The Poetics and Politics of Ethnography*. Berkeley, CA: University of California Press.

Clough, P.T. (1992) *The End(s) of Ethnography: From Realism to Social Criticism*. London: Sage.

Coffey, A. (1999) *The Ethnographic Self: Fieldwork and the Representation of Identity*. London: Sage.

Coffey, A. and Atkinson, P. (1996) *Making Sense of Qualitative Data: Complementary Research Strategies*. London: Sage.

Cohen, S. and Taylor, L. (1976) *Escape Attempts*. London: Allen Lane. (2nd edn, London: Routledge, 1992.)

Cohen, S. and Taylor, L. (1977) 'Talking about prison blues', in C. Bell and H. Newby (eds), *Doing Sociological Research*. London: Unwin.

Cohen, S. and Taylor, L. (1981) *Psychological Survival: The Experience of Long-term Imprisonment*. Harmondsworth: Penguin.

Cohler, B.J. (1982) 'Personal narratives and the life course', *Life Span Development and Behaviour*, 4: 205–38.

Cole, T. (1999) *Selling the Holocaust*. London: Routledge.

Coleman, P. (1986) *Ageing and Reminiscence Processes: Social and Clinical Implications*. New York: Wiley.

Coles, R. (1968) *Children of Crisis*. London: Faber.

Coles, R. (1973) *Erik H. Erikson: The Growth of His Work*. London: Souvenir Press.

Coles, R. (1989) *The Call of Stories: Teaching and the Moral Imagination*. Boston, MA: Houghton-Mifflin.

Coles, R. (1997) *Doing Documentary Work*. Oxford: Oxford University Press.

Coles, R. and Coles, J.H. (1978) *Women of Crisis: Lives of Struggle*. New York: Delacorte Seymour Lawrence.

Collier, J. Jr and Collier, M. (1986) *Visual Anthropology: Photography as a Research' Method*, 2nd edn. Albuquerque, NM: University of New Mexico.

Collins, P.H. (1990) *Black Feminist Thought: Knowledge, Consciousness and the Politics of Empowerment*. London: Unwin Hyman. (Reprinted Routledge, 1991.)

Connell, R.W. (1995) *Masculinities*. Cambridge: Polity Press.

Connerton, P (1989) *How Societies Remember*. Cambridge: Cambrdge University Press.

Converse, J.M. and Schuman, H. (1974) *Conversations at Random. Survey Research as Interviewers See It*. London: Wiley.

Cook, K.K. (1991) 'Filling the dark spaces: breast cancer and autobiography', *Auto/ Biography Studies*, 6 (1): 85–94.

Coser, L. (1978) 'American trends', in T. Bottomore and R. Nisbet (eds), *A History of Sociological Analysis*. London: Heinemann.

Cottrell, L.S., Hunter, A. and Short, J.F. (1973) *Ernest Burgess on Community, Family and Delinquency*. Chicago: University of Chicago Press.

Cox, E. (1990) *Thanksgiving: An Aids Journal*. New York: Harper and Row.

Coxon, A.P.M. (1996) *Between the Sheets: Sexual Diaries and Gay Men's Sex in the Era of AIDS*. London: Cassell.

Crapanzano, V. (1985) *Tuhami: Portrait of a Moroccan*. Chicago: University of Chicago Press.

Crapanzano, V. (1986) 'Hermes dilemma: the masking of subversion in ethnographic description', in J. Clifford and G.E. Marcus, *Writing Culture: The Poetics and Politics of Ethnography*. Berkeley, CA: University of California Press. pp. 51–77.

Cresswell, J.W. (1998) *Qualitative Inquiry and Research Design: Choosing among Five Traditions*. London: Sage.

Cressey, D.R. (1953) *Other People's Money*. Glencoe, IL: The Free Press; 2nd edn (1973), Motclair, NJ: Patterson Smith.

Curry, T. and Clarke, A.C. (1977) *Introducing Visual Sociology*. Dubuque, IA: Kendall/ Hunt.

Curtiss, S. (1977) *Genie: A Psycholinguistic Study of a Wolf Child*. London: Academic Press.

Daley, A. (1971) *Assessment of Lives: Personality Evaluation in a Bureaucratic Society*. London: Jossey–Bass.

Danahay, M.A. (1996) 'Professional subjects: prepacking the academic CV', in S. Smith and J. Watson (eds), *Geting a Life: Everyday Uses of Autobiography*. Minneapolis, MN: University of Minnesota Press. pp. 351–67.

Dandekker, C. (1990) *Surveillance, Power and Modernity*. Cambridge: Polity Press.

Davidoff, L. (1979) 'Class and gender in Victorian England: the diaries of Arthur J. Munby and Hannah Cullwick', *Feminist Studies*, 5: 87–141.

Davies, C.A. (1999) *Reflexive Ethnography: A Guide to Researching Selves and Others*. London: Routledge.

Davis, C. and Gates, H.L. (eds) (1985) *The Slave's Narrative*. Oxford: Oxford University Press.

Dawe, A. (1978) 'Theories of social action', in R. Bottomore and R. Nisbet (eds), *A History of Sociological Analysis*. London: Heinemann. pp. 362–417.

de Beauvoir, S. (1974) *All Said and Done*. London: Andre Deutsch and Weidenfeld and Nicolson. pp. 1–2.

De Mille, R. (ed.) (1990) *The Don Juan Papers: Further Castaneda Controversies*. Belmont, CA: Wadsworth.

Denfield, D. (ed.) (1974) *Streetwise Criminology*. Cambridge, MA: Schenkman.

Denzin, N.K. (1970) *Sociological Methods: A Source Book*. London: Butterworth.

Denzin, N.K. (1978a) *The Research Act*, 2nd edn. Chicago: Aldine.

Denzin, N.K. (1978b) *Studies in Symbolic Interaction: A Research Annual*, Vol. I. Greenwich, CT: JAI Press.

Denzin, N.K. (1979) *Studies in Symbolic Interaction: A Research Annual*, Vol. II. Greenwich, CT: JAI Press.

Denzin, N.K. (1989) *Interpretive Biography*. London: Sage.

Denzin, N.K. (1991) *Images of Postmoden Society: Social Theory and Contemporary Cinema*. London: Sage.

Denzin, N.K. (1992) *Symbolic Interactionism and Cultural Studies: The Politics of Interpretation*. Oxford: Blackwell.

Denzin, N.K. (1995) *The Cinematic Society: The Voyeur's Gaze*. London: Sage.

Denzin, N.K. (1996) 'Prophetic pragmatism and the postmodern: a comment on Maines', *Symbolic Interaction*, 19 (4): 341–56.

Denzin, N.K. (1997) *Interpretive Ethnography: Ethnographic Practices for the 21st Century*. London: Sage.

Denzin, N.K and Lincoln, Y. (eds) (1994) *The Handbook of Qualitative Research*. London: Sage.

Derrida, J. (1976) *Of Grammatology*. Baltimore, MD: Johns Hopkins University Press.

DeVault, M.L. (1999) *Liberating Method: Feminism and Social Research*. Philadelphia: Temple University Press.

Devereux, G. (1967) *From Anxiety to Method in the Behavioural Sciences*. The Hague: Mouton and Co.

Dewey, J. (1991) *The Later Works of John Dewey, 1925–1953*. A.S. Sharpe (ed.). Carbondale and Edwardsville, IL: Southern Illinois Press.

Dickens, D.R and Fontana, A. (1994) *Postmodernism and Social Inquiry*. London: UCL Press.

Dickstein, M. (ed.) (1998) *The Revival of Pragmatism*. London: Duke University Press.

Diener, E. and Crandall, R. (1978) *Ethics in Social and Behavioural Research*. Chicago: University of Chicago Press.

Dilthey, W. (1923/1988) *Introduction to the Human Sciences*. London: Harvester Wheatsheaf.

Dollard, J. (1935) *Criteria for the Life History: with Analysis of Six Notable Documents*. New Haven, CT: Yale University Press.

Douglas, J.D. (1967) *The Social Meanings of Suicide*. Princeton, NJ: Princeton University Press.

Douglas, J.D. (1976) *Investigative Social Research: Individual and Team Field Research*. Beverly Hills, CA: Sage.

Douglass, F. (1845/1982) *Narrative of the Life of Frederick Douglass, An American Slave*. Harmondsworth: Penguin Classic.

Dowsett, G.W. (1996) *Practicing Desire: Homosexual Sex in the Era of AIDS*. Stanford: University of Stanford Press.

Drake, M. (ed.) (1973) *Applied Historical Studies*. London: Methuen.

Dukes, W.F. (1965) 'N=1', *Psychological Bulletin*, 64 (1): 74–9.

Dunaway, D. and Baum, W.K. (eds) (1996) *Oral History: An Interdisciplinary Anthology*, 2nd edn. London: AltaMira Press.

Duneier, M. (1992) *Slim's Table: Race, Respectability and Masculinity*. Chicago: University of Chicago Press.

Duneier, M. (1999) *Sidewalk*. New York: Farrar, Straus and Giroux.

Dunn, G. (1992) *Thinking Across the American Grain: Ideology, Intellect and the New Pragmatism*. Chicago: University of Chicago Press.

Duster, T., Matza, D. and Wellman, D. (1979) 'Field work and the protection of human subjects', *American Sociologist*, 14: 136–42.

Dyk, W. (1938) *Son of Old Man Hat*. New York: Harcourt Brace Jovanovich.

Edgerton, R.B. and Langness, L.L. (1974) *Methods and Styles in the Study of Culture*. San Francisco, CA: Chandler and Sharp.

Edwards, D. (1997) *Discourse and Cognition*. London: Sage.

Elder, G.H. (1974) *Children of the Great Depression: Social Change in Life Experience*. Chicago: University of Chicago Press.

Elder, G. (1985) 'Perspectives on the life course', in G. Elder (ed.), *Life Course Dynamics: Trajectories and Transitions, 1968–1980*. Ithaca, NY: Cornell University Press. ch. 1.

Ellis, C. (1991) 'Emotional Sociology', in N.K. Denzin (ed.), *Studies in Symbolic Interaction*. Greenwich, CT: JAI Press.

Ellis, C. (1995) *Final Negotiations: A Story of Love, Loss and Chronic Illness*. Philadelphia: Temple University Press.

Ellis, C. and Bochner, A.P. (eds) (1996) *Composing Ethnography: Alternative Forms of Qualitative Writing*. London: Sage.

Ellis, C. and Flaherty, M.G. (eds) (1992a) 'Telling and performing personal stories: the constraints of choice in abortion', in *Investigating Subjectivity: Research on Lived Experience*. London: Sage. ch. 4.

Ellis, C. and Flaherty, M.G. (eds) (1992b) *Investigating Subjectivity: Research on Lived Experience*. London: Sage.

Ellis, J. (1988) *Documentary Idea: A Critical History of English Language Documentary Film and Video*. Hemel Hempstead: Prentice–Hall.

Elsbree, L. (1982) *The Rituals of Life: Patterns in Narratives*. London: Kennikat Press.

Emerson, R.M., Rachel, F. and Shaw, L. (1995) *Writing Ethnographic Field Notes*. Chicago: University of Chicago Press.

Emmison, M. and Smith, P. (2000) *Researching the Visual*. London: Sage.

Erikson, E.H. (1959) *Young Man Luther*. London: Faber.

Erikson, E.H. (1968) *Identity: Youth and Crisis*. London: Faber.

Erikson, E.H. (1977) *Childhood and Society*. St Albans: Triad/Paladin.

Erikson, K.T. (1967) 'A comment on disguised observation in sociology', *Social Problems*, 14: 366–73.

Erikson, K.T. (1973) 'Sociology and the historical perspective', in M. Drake (ed.), *Applied Historical Studies*. London: Methuen. pp. 13–30.

Erikson, K.T. (1976) *Everything in its Path: Destruction of Community in the Buffalo Creek Flood*. New York: Simon and Schuster.

Erikson, E. (1982) *The Life Cycle Completed: A Review*. New York: WW Norton. pp. 58–9.

Ermarth, M. (1978) *Wilhelm Dilthey: The Critique of Historical Reason*. Chicago: University of Chicago Press.

Evans, S. (1980) *Personal Politics: The Roots of Women's Liberation in the Civil Rights Movement and the New Left*. New York: Vintage.

Faraday, A. and Plummer, K. (1979) 'Doing life histories', *Sociological Review*, 27 November: 773–92.

Faris, E. (1937) *The Nature of Human Nature and Other Essays in Social Psychology*. London: McGraw-Hill.

Fetterman, D.M. (1989) *Ethnography: Step by Step*. London: Sage.

Fiedler, J. (1978) *Field Research: A Manual for Logistics and Management of Scientific Studies in Natural Settings*. London: Jossey–Bass.

Fielding, N. and Lee, R. (1991) *Using Computers in Qualitative Research*. London: Sage.

Fine, G.A. (ed.) (1995) *A Second Chicago School? The Development of Post War American Sociology*. Chicago: University of Chicago Press.

Finnegan, R.H. (1992) *Oral Traditions and the Verbal Arts: A Guide to Research Practices*. London: Routledge.

Fischer, D.H. (1971) *Historians' Fallacies*. London: Routledge and Kegan Paul.

Flick, U. (1998) *An Introduction to Qualitative Research*. London: Sage.

Folkenflik, R. (ed.) (1993) *The Culture of Autobiography: Constructions of Self Representation*. Stanford, CA: Stanford University Press.

Foltz, T.G. and Griffin, W. (1996) 'She changes everything she touches: ethnographic journeys of self discovery', in C. Ellis and A. Bochner (eds), *Composing Ethnography: Alternative Forms of Qualitative Writing*. London: Sage. pp. 301–28.

Fonow, M.M. and Cook, J.A. (eds) (1991) *Beyond Methodology: Feminist Scholarship as Lived Research*. Bloomington, IN: Indiana University Press.

Fontana, A. and Frey, J.H. (1994) 'Interviewing', in N.K. Denzin and Y. Lincoln (eds), *Handbook of Qualitative Research*. London: Sage. pp. 361–76.

Fothergill, R.A. (1974) *Private Chronicles: A Study of English Diaries*. London: Oxford University Press.

Foucault, M. (1977) *Discipline and Punish*. London: Allen Lane.

Foucault, M. (1978) *I, Pierre Rivière, Having Slaughtered My Mother, My Sister and My Brother . . .* Harmondsworth: Penguin.

Foucault, M. (1979a) 'What is an author!', *Screen*, 20: 13–35.

Foucault, M. (1979b) *The History of Sexuality*, Vol 1. London: Allen Lane.

Foucault, M. (1980) *Herculine Barbin: Being the Recently Discovered Memoirs of a Nineteenth Century French Hermaphrodite*. New York: Pantheon.

Fowler, D.D. and Hardesty, D. (1994) *Others Knowing Others: Perspectives on Ethnographic Careers*. Washington, DC: Smithsonian Institute.

Fox, K.V. (1996) 'Silent voices: a subversive reading of child sexual abuse', in C. Ellis and A. Bochner (eds), *Composing Ethnography: Alternative Forms of Qualitative Writing*. London: Sage. pp. 330–56.

Frank, A.W. (1995) *The Wounded Storyteller: Body, Illness and Ethics*. Chicago: University of Chicago Press.

Frazier, C.E. (1976) *Theoretical Approaches to Deviance*. Columbus, Ohio: Charles E. Merrill.

Frazier, E.F. (1967) *Negro Youth at the Crossways: Their Personality Development in the Middle States*. New York: Schocken Books. (First published 1940.)

Freeman, D. (1984) *Margaret Mead and Samoa*. Harmondsworth: Penguin.

Freilich, M. (ed.) (1970) *Marginal Natives: Anthropologists at Work*. London: Harper and Row.

Freud, S. (1910/1963) *Leonardo da Vinci and a Memory of his Childhood* (trans. A. Typson). Harmondsworth: Penguin Books.

Freud, S. (1925) 'Analysis of a phobia in a five year old boy', *Collected Papers*, Vol. 2. London: Hogarth Press. pp. 149–289.

Freud, S. (1976) *The Interpretation of Dreams*. The Penguin Freud Library, Vol. 4. Harmondsworth: Pelican.

Freud, S. (1977) *Case Histories: 'Dora' and 'Little Hans'*. The Penguin Freud Library, Vol. 8. Harmondsworth: Penguin.

Friday, N. (1976) *My Secret Garden*. New York: Pocket Books.

Friday, N. (1977) *My Mother, My Self*. New York: Dell Publishing.

Friedan, B. (1963) *The Feminine Mystique*. New York: Dell Publishing.

Friedman, L. (1999) *Identity's Architect: A Biography of Erik H. Erickson*. New York: Scribner.

Frisch, M. (1990) *A Shared Authority: Essays on the Craft and Meanings of Oral and Public History*. Albany, NY: State University of New York Press.

Frisch, M. (1998) 'Oral history and hard times: a review essay', in R. Perks and A. Thompson (eds), *The Oral History Reader*. London: Routledge. pp. 29–37.

Fry, C.L. (1934) *The Technique of Social Investigation*. New York: Harper and Bros.

Frye, N. (1988) *On Education*. Toronto: Fitzhenry and Whiteside.

Gagnon, J. and Simon, W. (1973) *Sexual Conduct: The Social Sources of Human Sexuality*. Chicago: Aldine.

Gamson, J. (1998) *Freaks Talk Back: Tabloid Talk Shows and Sexual Non-Conformity*. Chicago: University of Chicago Press.

Garfinkel, H. (1967) *Studies in Ethnomethodology*. Englewood Cliffs, NJ: Prentice–Hall.

Gathorne-Hardy, J. (1998) *Sex, the Measure of All Things: A Life of Alfred C. Kinsey*. London: Chatto and Windus.

Gearing, J. (1995) 'Fear and loathing in the West Indies: research from the heart (as well as the head)', in D. Kulick and M. Wilson (eds), *Taboo: Sex, Identity and Erotic Subjectivity in Anthropological Fieldwork*. London: Routledge. pp. 186–216.

Geertz, C. (1973) *The Interpretation of Cultures*. New York: Basic Books.

Geertz, C. (1983) *Local Knowledge: Further Essays in Interpretive Anthropology*. New York: Basic Books.

Geertz, C. (1988) *Works and Lives. The Anthropologist as Author*. Stanford, CA: Stanford University Press.

Gergen, K. (1991) *The Saturated Self*. New York: Basic Books.

Gergen, K. (1999) *An Invitation to Social Construction*. London: Sage.

Gershuny, J. and Sullivan, O. (1998) 'The sociological uses of time-use diary analysis', *European Sociological Review*, 14: 69–85.

Gibbins, J. and Reimer, B. (1999) *The Politics of Postmodernity: An Introduction to Contemporary Politics and Culture*. London: Sage.

Gibbons, F. and Moss, S. (1999) 'Fragments of a fraud', *Guardian*, 15 October, p. 2.

Giddens, A. (1986) *The Constitution of Society*. Cambridge: Polity Press.

Giddens, A. (1991) *Modernity and Self-Identity*. Cambridge: Polity Press.

Giele, J.Z. and Elder, G.H. (eds) (1998) *Methods of Life Course Research: Qualitative and Quantitative Approaches*. London: Sage.

Gilbert, N. (ed.) (1993) *Researching Social Life*. London: Sage.

Gilligan, C. (1982) *In a Different Voice*. Cambridge, MA: Harvard University Press.

Gilligan, C., Brown, L. and Rogers, A. (1990) 'Psyche embedded', in A.I. Rabin, R.A. Zucker, R. Emmons and S. Frank (eds), *Studying Persons and Lives*. New York: Springer. pp. 86–147.

Giroux, H. (1992) *Border Crossings: Cultural Workers and the Politics of Education*. London: Routledge.

Gittings, D. (1998) *Madness in its Place: Narratives of Severall's Hospital 1913–1997*. London: Routledge.

Gittings, D. (1979) 'Oral history, reliability and recollection', in L. Moss and H.

Goldstein (eds), *The Recall Method in Social Surveys*. London: University of London, Institute of Education. pp. 82–99.

Gittings, R. (1978) *The Nature of Biography*. London: Heinemann.

Glaser, B.G. and Strauss, A. (1967a) *Awareness of Dying*. London: Weidenfeld & Nicolson.

Glaser, B.G. and Strauss, A. (1967b) *The Discovery of Grounded Theory*. Chicago: Aldine.

Glaser, B.G. and Strauss, A. (1968) *Time for Dying*. Chicago: Aldine.

Glaser, E. and Palmer, L. (1991) *The Absence of Angels*. New York: Putnam's Sons.

Glassner, B. and Hertz, R. (eds) (1999) *Qualitatative Sociology as Everyday Life*. London: Sage.

Gluck, S. Berger and Patai, D. (eds) (1991) *Women's Words: The Feminist Practice of Oral History*. London: Routledge.

Gluck, S. Berger, Ritchie, D. and Eynon, B. (1999) 'Reflections on oral history in the new millennium', *Oral History Review*, 26 (2): 1–28.

Goffman, E. (1959) *The Presentation of Self in Everyday Life*. Harmondsworth: Penguin.

Goffman, E. (1961) *Asylums*. Garden City, NY: Doubleday (Penguin edition, 1968).

Gold, R.L. (1958) 'Roles in sociological field observation', *Social Forces*, 36: 217–23.

Golden-Biddle, K. and Locke, K.D. (1997) *Composing Qualitative Research*. London: Sage.

Goode, D. (1994) *A World Without Words: The Social Construction of Children Born Deaf and Blind*. Philadelphia: Temple University Press.

Goodson, I. (1992) *Studying Teachers' Lives*. London: Routledge.

Gorden, R.L. (1969) *Interviewing: Strategy, Techniques, and Tactics*. Homewood, IL: Dorsey Press.

Gordon, C. (ed.) (1980) *Michel Foucault: Power/Knowledge – Selected Interviews and Other Writings, 1972–1977*. Brighton: Harvester Press.

Gottschalk, L., Kluckhohn, C. and Angell, R. (1942) *The Use of Personal Documents in History, Anthropology and Sociology*. New York: Science Research Council.

Gouldner, A. (1962) 'Anti-minotaur: the myth of a value free sociology', *Social Problems*, 9 (3): 199–213.

Gouldner, A. (1971) *The Coming Crisis of Western Sociology*. London: Allen Lane.

Greenberg, G. (1994) *The Self on the Shelf: Recovery Books and the Good Life*. Albany, NY: State University of New York Press.

Grele, R. (ed.) (1975) *Envelopes of Sound: Six Practitioners Discuss the Method, Theory and Practice of Oral History and Oral Testimony*. Chicago: Precedent Publishing.

Griffin, S. (1979) *Rape: The Power of Consciousness*. New York: Harper and Row.

Gubrium, J.F. (1993) *Speaking of Life: Horizons of Meaning for Nursing Home Residents*. New York: Aldine de Gruyter.

Gubrium, J.F. and Buckholdt, D.R. (1977) *Toward Maturity*. London: Jossey–Bass.

Gubrium, J.F. and Holstein, J.H. (1997) *The New Language of Qualitative Method*. Oxford: Oxford University Press.

Gubrium, J.F. and Lyncott, R.J. (1985) 'Alzheimer's disease as biographical work', in W.A. Peterson and J. Quadagno (eds), *Social Bonds in Later Life*. London: Sage. pp. 349–68.

Gurvitch, G. and Moore, W.E. (1945) *Twentieth Century Sociology*. New York: The Philosophical Library Inc.

Gusfield, J. (1976) 'The literary rhetoric of science', *American Sociological Review*, 41: 16–34.

Haaken, J. (1999) *Pillars of Salt: Gender, Memory and the Perils of Looking Back*. New Brunswick, NJ: Rutgers University Press.

Habermas, J. (1989) *The Transformation of the Public Sphere*. Cambridge: Polity Press. (Originally published in German, 1962.)

Halbwachs, M. (1992) *On Collective Memory* (edited and translated by L.A. Coser). Chicago: University of Chicago Press.

Haley, A. (1976/1977) *Roots: The Saga of an American Family*. New York: Doubleday/ London: Hutchinson.

Halle, D. (1993) *Inside Culture: Art and Class in the American Home*. Chicago: University of Chicago Press.

Hamiliton, C. (1991) *The Hitler Diaries: Fakes that Fooled the World*. Lexington, KY: University of Kentucky Press.

Hammersley, M. and Atkinson, P. (1995) *Ethnography: Principles in Practice*, 3rd edn. London: Routledge.

Handley, C.S. (1997) *Annotated Bibliography of Diaries*, 4 vols. Aldeburgh: Hanover Press. (Also available in CD-Rom.)

Hanhardt, J. (1986/1990) *Video Culture: A Critical Investigation*. Rochester, NY: Visual Studies Workshop Press.

Hanlan, A.J. (1979) *Autobiography of Dying*. New York: Doubleday.

Hareven, T. (1996) 'The search for generational memory', in D.K. Dunaway and W.K. Baum (eds), *Oral History: An Interdisciplinary Anthology*. London: AltaMira Press.

Haraway, D. (1991) *Simians, Cyborgs and Women: The Reinvention of Nature*. New York: Routledge.

Harding, S. (1991) *Whose Science? Whose Knowledge? Thinking from Women's Lives*. Milton Keynes: Open University Press.

Hardy, F. (ed.) (1946) *Grierson on Documentary*. London: Collins.

Harper, D. (1978) 'At home on the rails: ethics in a photographic research project', *Qualitative Sociology*, 1: 61–77.

Harper, D. (1982) *Good Company*. Chicago: University of Chicago Press.

Harper, D. (1987) *Working Knowledge: Skill and Community in a Small Shop*. Chicago: University of Chicago Press.

Harper, D. (1994) 'On the authority of the image: visual methods at the crossroads', in N.K. Denzin and Y. Lincoln (eds), *Handbook of Qualitative Research*. London: Sage. pp. 403–12.

Haslam, C. and Bryman, A. (eds) (1994) *Social Scientists Meet the Media*. London: Routledge.

Haug, F. (ed.) (1983/1987) *Female Sexualization: A Collective Work of Memory*. London: Verso.

Hazlett, J.D. (1998) *My Generation: Collective Autobiography and Identity Politics*. Madison, WI: University of Wisconsin Press.

Heider, K.G. (1976) *Ethnographic Film*. Austin, TX: University of Texas.

Heller, A. (1990) *A Philosophy of Morals*. Oxford: Blackwell.

Heller, A. and Fehér, F. (1991) *The Grandeur and Twilight of Radical Universalism*. New Brunswick, NJ: Transaction Books.

Henny, L. (1986) 'Trend report: theory and practice of visual sociology', *Current Sociology* (Special issue), 34 (3).

Henry, M. (ed.) (1999) *I.T. in the Social Sciences: A Student's Guide to the Information and Communication Technologies*. Oxford: Blackwell.

Heraclitus (1960 edn) *The PreSocratics* (ed. Philip Wheelwright). Indianapolis, IN: Bobbs Merrill.

Herman, N.J. and Reynolds, L.T. (eds) (1994) *Symbolic Interaction: An Introduction to Social Psychology*. New York: General Hall.

Hertz, R. (ed.) (1997) *Reflexivity and Voice*. London: Sage.

Hersey, J. (1972) *Hiroshima*. Harmondsworth: Penguin.

Hewitt, J.P. (1994) *Self and Society*, 6th edn. Boston, MA: Allyn and Bacon.

Heyl, B.S. (1979) *The Madam as Entrepreneur. Career Management in House Prostitution*. New Brunswick, NJ: Transaction Books (2nd edn 2000).

Hillis Miller, J. (1990) 'Narrative', in F. Lentricchia and T. McLaughlin, *Critical Terms for Literary Study*. Chicago: University of Chicago Press.

Hine, L. (1977) *America and Lewis Hine*. New York: Aperture.

Hinkle, R.C. (1980) *Founding Theory of American Sociology, 1881–1915*. London: Routledge and Kegan Paul.

Hirsch, M. (1997) *Family Frames: Photographs, Narrative and Postmemory*. London: Routledge.

Hobbs, D. and May, T. (1993) *Interpreting the Field: Accounts of Ethnography*. Oxford: Oxford Universty Press.

Hockings, P. (1995) *Principles of Visual Anthropology*, 2nd edn. New York: Mouton de Gruyter.

Holliday, R. (1999) 'The comfort of identity', *Sexualities*, 2 (4): 475–91.

Holstein, J. and Gubrium, J. (1995) *The Active Interview*. London: Sage.

Holstein, J. and Gubrium, J.F. (2000) *The Self We Live By*. Cambridge: Cambridge University Press.

Holt, H. (1906/1990) *The Life Stories of (Undistinguished) Americans as Told by Themselves*. London: Routledge.

Homans, G.C. (1949) 'The strategy of industrial sociology', *American Journal of Sociology*, 54: 330–7.

Homans, G.C. (1967) *The Nature of Social Science*. New York: Harcourt, Brace and World.

hooks, b. (1992) 'Revolutionary black women', in *Black Looks: Race and Representation*. London: Turnaround.

Hoskins, J. (1998) *Biographical Objects: How Things Tell the Stories of People's Lives*. London: Routledge.

Hoyle, J. (1991) *Mark: How a Boy's Courage in Facing Aids Inspired a Town*. South Bend, IN: Langford/Diamond Communications.

Hughes, H.M. (ed.) (1961) *The Fantastic Lodge: The Autobiography of a Girl Drug Addict*. Boston, MA: Houghton-Mifflin.

Humphreys, L. (1970) *Tea Room Trade*. Chicago: Aldine.

Humphries, S. and Gordon, P. (1992) *Out of Sight: The Experiences of Disability 1900–1950*. London: Channel Four Publications.

Irvine, L. (1999) *Co-Dependent Forevermore: The Invention of Self in a Self Help Group*. Chicago: University of Chicago Press.

Jackson, B. (1972) *Outside the Law: A Thief's Primer*. New Brunswick, NJ: Transaction Books.

Jackson, B. (1977) *Killing Time: Life in the Arkansas Penitentiary*. New York: Cornell University Press.

Jackson, B. (1978) 'Killing time: life in the Arkansas Penitentiary', *Qualitative Sociology*, 1: 21–32.

Jackson, D. (1990) *Unmasking Masculinity: A Critical Autobiography*. London: Unwin.

Jackson, M. (1989) *Paths Toward a Clearing: Radical Empiricism and Ethnographic Inquiry*. Bloomington, IN: Indiana University Press.

Jacobs, J. (1974) *Sun City: An Ethnographic Study of a Retirement Community*. New York: Holt, Rinehart & Winston.

Jacobs, L. (1979) *The Documentary Tradition*. London: W.W. Norton.

Jahoda, M., Lazarsfeld, P. and Zeisel, H. (1972) *Marienthal: The Sociography of an Unemployed Community*, 2nd edn. London: Tavistock.

James, W. (1899/1913) *Talks to Teachers on Psychology: And to Students on some of Life's Ideals*. London: Longman Green.

James, W. (1902/1952) *The Varieties of Religious Experience: A Study in Human Nature*. New York: Longman Green.

James, W. (1907/1955) *Pragmatism*. New York: Meridian Books.

James, W. (1997) *The Writings of William James: A Comprehensive Edition* (edited with an introduction and new preface by J.J. McDermott). Chicago: University of Chicago Press. (Originally published by Random House, 1967.)

Janowitz, M. (ed.) (1966) *W.I. Thomas on Social Organization and Social Personality*. Chicago: University of Chicago Press.

Jansen, S.C. (1980) 'The stranger as seer or voyeur: a dilemma of the peep-show theory of knowledge', *Qualitative Sociology*, 2 (3): 22–55.

Jelinek, E.C. (ed.) (1980) *Women's Autobiography: Essays in Criticism*. Bloomington, IN: Indiana University Press.

Johnson, C. and Taylor, Y. (eds) (1998) *I Was Born A Slave*, Vols 1 and 2: *An Anthology of Classic Slave Narratives*. London: Payback.

Johnson, J. (1990) *Selecting Ethnographic Informants*. London: Sage.

Johnson, Pauline (1994) *Feminism as Radical Humanism*. San Francisco: Westview.

Jones, J.H. (1997) *Alfred C. Kinsey: A Public/Private Life*. New York: W.W. Norton.

Josselson, R. (ed.) (1996) *Ethics and Process in the Narrative Study of Lives*. London: Sage (*The Narrative Study of Lives*, Vol. 4.)

Josselson, R. and Lieblich, A. (eds) (1993–) *The Narrative Study of Lives* (series). London: Sage.

Joynson, R.B. (1989) *The Burt Affair*. London: Routledge.

Juhasz, A. (1995) *AIDS TV: Identity, Community and Alternative Video*. Durham, NC: Duke University Press.

Juhasz, A. (1999) 'It's about autonomy, stupid: sexuality in feminist video', *Sexualities*, 2 (3): 333–42.

Junker, B.H. (1960) *Field Work: An Introduction to the Social Sciences*. Chicago: University of Chicago Press.

Kaku, M. (1998) *Visions: How Science Will Revolutionize the Twenty First Century*. Oxford: Oxford University Press.

Karp, D.A. (1996) *Speaking of Sadness: Depression, Disconnection and the Meanings of Illness*. Oxford: Oxford University Press.

Kastenbaum, R., Derbin, V., Sabatini, P. and Artt, S. (1972) '"The Ages of Me": toward personal and interpersonal definitions of functional aging', *Aging and Human Development*, 2 (2): 197.

Kegan, R. (1982) *The Evolving Self*. Cambridge, MA: Harvard University Press.

Kenyon, G.M. and Randall, L.W. (1997) *Restorying Our Lives: Personal Growth Through Autobiographical Reflection*. London: Praeger.

Kessler, S.J. and McKenna, W. (1978) *Gender: An Ethnomethodological Approach*. London: Wiley.

Kimmel, D.C. (1989) *Adulthood and Aging: An Interdisciplinary, Developments View*. New York: Wiley.

Kinsey, A.C., Pomeroy, W.B. and Martin, C.E. (1948) *Sexual Behaviour in the Human Male*. London: W.B. Saunders.

Kirsch, G.E. (1999) *Ethical Dilemmas in Feminist Research: The Politics of Location, Interpretation and Publication*. Albany, NY: State University of New York Press.

Kleinman, A. (1988) *The Illness Narratives: Suffering, Healing and the Human Condition*. New York: Basic Books.

Kleinman, S. and Copp, M.A. (1993) *Emotions and Fieldwork*. London: Sage.

Klockars, C.B. (1975) *The Professional Fence*. London: Tavistock.

Klockars, C.B. (1977) 'Field ethics for the life history', in R.S. Weppner (ed.), *Street Ethnography*. London: Sage. pp. 201–27.

Klockars, C.B. and O'Connor, F.B. (eds) (1979) *Deviance and Decency: The Ethics of Research with Human Subjects*. London: Sage.

Kluckhohn, C. (1942) 'The personal document in anthropological science', in L. Gottschalk, C. Kluckhohn and R. Angell, *The Use of Personal Documents in History, Anthropology and Sociology*. New York: Science Research Council. pp. 79–176.

Kohli, M. and Meyer, J.W. (1986) 'Social structure and social construction of life stages', *Human Development*, 29: 145–80.

Kotre, J.N. and Hall, E. (1999) *Seasons of Life: The Dramatic Journey from Birth to Death*. Ann Arbor, MI: Ann Arbor Paperbacks.

Kramer, L. (1989) *Reports from the Holocaust*. New York: St Martin's Press.

Krieger, S. (1983) *The Mirror Dance: Identity in a Women's Community*. Philadelphia: Temple University Press.

Krieger, S. (1991) *Social Science and the Self*. New Brunswick, NJ: Rutgers University Press.

Krieger, S. (1996) *The Family Silver: Essays on Relationships Among Women*. Berkeley, CA: University of California Press.

Kriseberg, B. (1975) *Crime and Privilege: Toward a New Criminology*. Englewood Cliffs, NJ: Prentice–Hall/Spectrum.

Kulick, D. and Wilson, M. (eds) (1995) *Taboo: Sex, Identity and Erotic Subjectivity in Anthropological Fieldwork*. London: Routledge.

Kulick, D. (1999) *Travesti: Sex, Gender and Culture among Brazilian Transgendered Prostitutes*. Chicago: University of Chicago Press.

Kvale, S. (1996) *InterViews*. London: Sage.

La Capra, D. (1998) *History and Memory after Auschwitz*. London: Cornell University Press.

Lane, H. (1977) *The Wild Boy of Aveyron*. London: Allen and Unwin.

Langer, L. (1991) *Holocaust Testimonies: The Ruins of Memory*. New Haven, CT: Yale University Press.

Langness, L.L. (1965) *The Life History in Anthropological Science*. London: Holt, Rinehart & Winston.

Langness, L.L. and Frank, G. (1981) *An Anthropological Approach to Biography*. Novato, CA: Chandler and Sharp.

Lara, M.P. (1998) *Moral Textures: Feminist Narratives in the Public Sphere*. Cambridge: Polity Press.

Lareaa, A. and Schultz, J. (1996) *Journeys through Ethnography: Realistic Accounts of Fieldwork*. Boulder, CO: Westview Press.

Lasch, C. (1979) *The Culture of Narcissism*. New York: Norton.

Lather, P. (1991) *Getting Smart: Feminist Research and Pedagogy with/in the Postmodern*. London: Routledge.

Lee, A.M. (1978) *Sociology for Whom?* New York: Oxford University Press.

Lee, R.M. (1993) *Doing Research on Sensitive Topics*. London: Sage.

Lemert, C. (1997) *Social Things: An Introduction to the Sociological Life*. Lanham, MA: Rowman and Littlefield.

Lentricchia, F. and McLaughlin, T. (eds) (1990) *Critical Terms for Literary Studies*. Chicago: University of Chicago Press.

Lepenies, W. (1988) *Between Literature and Science: The Rise of Sociology*. Cambridge: Cambridge University Press.

Lesy, M. (1973) *Wisconsin Death Trip*. New York: Pantheon.

Lesy, M. (1976) *Real Life: Louisville in the Twenties*. New York: Pantheon.

Lesy, M. (1982) *Bearing Witness: A Photographic Chronicle of American Life, 1850–1945*. New York: Pantheon.

Levi, P. (1947/1987) *If This Is a Man*. London: Abacus.

Levi, P. (1986, 1988) *The Drowned and the Saved*. London: Michael Joseph.

Levine, D.N. (ed.) (1971) *George Simmel on Individuality and Social Forms*. Chicago: University of Chicago Press.

Levinson, D.J., Darrow, C.N., Klein, E.B., Levinson, M.H. and McKee, B.J. (1978) *The Seasons of a Man's Life*. New York: Knopf.

Levinson, D.J., Darrow, C.N., Klein, E.B., Levinson, M.H. and McKee, B.J. (1996) *The Seasons of a Woman's Life*. New York: Knopf.

Levi-Strauss, C. (1966) *The Savage Mind*. London: Weidenfeld.

Lewin, E. and Leap, W. (eds) (1996) *Out in the Field: Issues in Fieldwork and Ethnography*. Champaign, IL: University of Illinois Press.

Lewis, J. and Fraser, M. (1996) 'Patches of grief and rage: visitor responses to the NAMES Project AIDS Memorial Quilt', *Qualitative Sociology*, 19 (4): 433–51.

Lewis, O. (1959) *Five Families*. New York: Basic Books.

Lewis, O. (1961) *Children of Sanchez: Autobiography of a Mexican Family*. New York: Random House.

Lewis, O. (1964) *Pedro Martinez: A Mexican Peasant and His Family*. London: Secker and Warburg.

Lewis, O. (1965) *La Vida: A Puerto Rican Family in the Culture of Poverty*. New York: Random House.

Lewis, O. (1979a) *A Death in the Sanchez Family*. London: Secker and Warburg.

Lewis, O. (1979b) *Anthropological Essays*. New York: Random House.

Lewis, O., Lewis, R. and Rigdon, M. (1977) *Living the Revolution: An Oral History of Contemporary Cuba*, Vol. 1, *Four Men*. London/Urbana, IL: University of Illinois Press.

Lieblich, A. (1996) 'Some unforeseen outcomes of conducting narrative research with people of one's own culture', in R. Josselson (ed.), *Ethics and Process in the Narrative Study of Lives*. London: Sage (Vol. 4 of *The Narrative Study of Lives* series). pp. 172–84.

Lieblich, A., Tuval-Mashiach, R. and Zilber, T. (1998) *Narrative Research: Reading Analysis and Interpretation*. London: Sage.

Liebow, E. (1967) *Tally's Corner*. Boston, MA: Little, Brown.

Liebow, E. (1993) *Tell Them Who I Am: The Lives of Homeless Women*. New York: Penguin.

Lifton, R. (1972) 'Experiments in advocacy research', in J.H. Masserman (ed.), *Research and Relevance*. Vol. XXI, *Science and Psychoanalysis*. New York: Grune and Stratton.

Lifton, R.J. (1973) *Home from the War*. New York: Simon and Schuster.

Light, P.C. (1988) *Baby Boomers*. Ontario: Penguin Books.

Lincoln, Y.S. (1995) 'The Sixth Moment: emerging problems in qualitative research', *Studies in Symbolic Interaction*, 19: 37–56.

Linde, C. (1993) *Life Stories: The Creation of Coherence*. Oxford: Oxford University Press.

Lindesmith, A. (1947, rev. 1968) *Opiate Addiction*. Chicago: University of Chicago Press.

Lofland, J. (1974) 'Styles of reporting qualitative field research', *American Sociologist*, 9 (Aug): 101–11.

Lofland, J. (1976) *Doing Social Life*. London: Wiley.

Lofland, J. and Lofland, L. (1995) *Analyzing Social Settings: A Guide to Qualitative Observation and Analysis*, 3rd edn. Belmont, CA: Wadsworth.

Lofland, L. (1980) 'Reminiscences of classic Chicago: The Blumer–Hughes Talk', *Urban Life*, 9 (3): 251–81.

Loizos, P. (1993) *Innovation in Ethnographic Film – From Innocence to Self Consciousness*. Chicago: University of Chicago Press.

Lomax, H. and Casey, N. (1998) 'Recording social life: reflexivity and video methodology', *Sociological Research Online*, 3 (2): http://www.socresonline.org.uk/socresonline/3/2/1.html

Lukes, S. (1973) *Individualism*. Oxford: Blackwell.

Lundberg, G.A. (1926) 'Case work and the statistical method', *Social Forces*, 5: 61–5.

Lundberg, G.A. (1941) 'Case studies v. statistical methods – an issue based on misunderstanding', *Sociometry*, 4: 379–83.

Lupton, D. (1998) *The Emotional Self*. London: Sage.

Lury, C. (1998) *Prosthetic Culture: Photography, Memory and Identity*. London: Routledge.

Lyman, S.M. and Scott, M.B. (1975) *The Drama of Social Reality*. Oxford: Oxford University Press.

Lynd, R.S. (1939) *Knowledge for What?* Princeton, NJ: Princeton University Press.

Lyotard, J.F. (1984) *The Postmodern Condition*. Minneapolis, MN: University of Minnesota Press.

Maas, S. and Kuypers, J.A. (1974) *From Thirty to Seventy: a 40 Year Longitudinal Study of Adult Life Styles and Personality*. London: Jossey–Bass.

Macionis, J. and Plummer, K. (1998) *Sociology: A Global Introduction*. Hemel Hempstead: Prentice–Hall.

Madge, C. (1963) *The Origin of Scientific Sociology*. London: Tavistock.

Maines, D.R. (1993) 'Narrative's moment and sociology's phenomena: toward a narrative sociology', *Sociological Quarterly*, 34 (1): 17–38.

Maines, D. (1996) 'On postmodernism, pragmatism and plasterers: some inter-actionist's thought and queries', *Symbolic Interaction*, 19 (4): 323–40.

Mair, M. (1989) *Beyond Psychology and Psychotherapy: A Poetics of Experience*. London: Routledge.

Makkreed, R. (1975) *Dilthey: Philosopher of the Human Studies*. Princeton, NJ: Princeton University Press.

Malcolm, J. (1990) *The Journalist and the Murderer*. New York: Knopf.

Malinowski, B. (1922) *Argonauts of the Western Pacific*. London: Routledge and Kegan Paul.

Malinowski, B. (1929) *Sexual Life of Savages in North Western Melanesia*. New York: Harcourt, Brace and World.

Malinowski, B. (1967) *A Diary in the Strict Sense of the Term*. London: Routledge and Kegan Paul.

Mandelbaum, M. (1967) *The Problem of Historical Knowledge. An Answer to Relativism*. London: Harper and Row.

Mann, C. and Stewart, F. (2000) *Internet Communication and Qualitative Research: A Handbook for Researching Online*. London: Sage.

Mann, S. (1992) *Immediate Family*. New York: Aperture.

Manning, P. (1982) 'Analytic induction', in R. Smith and P. Manning, *Qualitative Methods*. Ballinger Publishing; reproduced in K. Plummer (1991) *Symbolic Inter-action*, Volume 2. Aldershot, Edward Elgar. pp. 401–30.

Marcus, G.E. (1994) 'What comes (just) after "Post"? The case of ethnography', in N.K. Denzin and Y. Lincoln (eds), *Handbook of Qualitative Research*. London: Sage. pp. 563–74.

Marcus, L. (1994) *Auto/biographical Discourses: Theory, Criticism, Practice*. Manchester: Manchester University Press.

Markham, A.N. (1999) *Life Online: Researching Real Experience in Virtual Space*. London: AltaMira Press.

Markowitz, F. and Ashkenazi, M. (eds) (1999) *Sex, Sexuality and the Anthropologist*. Urbana, IL: University of Illinois Press.

Marsden, D. and Duff, E. (1974) *Workless. Some Unemployed Men and Their Families*. Harmondsworth: Penguin (reprinted with a new introduction, 1982).

Marshall, G. (1981) 'Accounting for deviance', *International Journal of Sociology and Social Policy*, I (1): 17–45.

Mass Observation (1943/1987) *The Pub and the People*. London: The Cresset Library.

Mathieson, C.M. and Stam, H.J. (1995) 'Renegotiating identity: cancer narratives', *Sociology of Health and Illness*, 17 (3): 283–306.

Matthews, F. (1977) *Quest for an American Sociology: Robert E. Park and the Chicago School*. Montreal: McGill–Queens University Press.

Mattingly, C. (1998) *Healing Dramas and Clinical Plots: The Narrative Structure of Experience*. Cambridge: Cambridge University Press.

Matza, D. (1969) *Becoming Deviant*. Englewood Cliffs, NJ: Prentice–Hall.

McAdams, D. (1985) *Power, Intimacy and the Life Story*. New York: Guilford Press.

McAdams, D. (1993) *The Stories We Live By: Personal Myths and the Making of the Self*. New York: Guilford Press.

MacClancy, J. and McDonagh, C. (eds) (1996) *Popularizing Anthropology*. London: Routledge.

McCloskey, D. (1985) *The Rhetoric of Economics*. Madison, WI: University of Wisconsin.

McCracken, G. (1988) *The Long Interview*. London: Sage.

McDonald, K. and Cousins, M. (eds) (1996) *Imagining Reality: The Faber Book of the Documentary*. London: Faber and Faber.

McKeon, K. (1987) *The Origins of the English Novel, 1600–1740*. Baltimore, MD: Johns Hopkins University Press.

McLeod, J. (1997) *Narrative and Psychotherapy*. London: Sage.

McQuire, S. (1998) *Visions of Modernity*. London: Sage.

Mead, M. (1964) 'Anthropology and the camera', in W. Morgan (ed.), *The Encyclopedia of Photography*, Vol. 1. New York: Greystone.

Meatyard, R.E. (1974) *The Family Album of Lucybelle Crater*. New York: The Book Organization.

Meehl, P. (1951) *Clinical v. Statistical Prediction: A Theoretical Analysis and Review of the Evidence*. Minneapolis, MN: University of Minnesota.

Menchú, R. (ed. by E. Burgos-Debray) (1984) *I, Rigoberta Menchú: An Indian Woman in Guatemala*. London: Verso.

Menchú, R. (1998) *Crossing Borders*. London: Verso.

Merton, R.K. (1988) 'Some thoughts on the concept of sociological biography', in M. White Riley (ed.), *Sociological Lives*. London: Sage. pp. 17–21.

Merton, R.K. (1968) *Social Theory and Social Structure*. London: Collier Macmillan.

Messerschmidt, J.W. (2000) *Nine Lives: Adolescent Masculinities, the Body and Violence*. Boulder, CO: Westview Press.

Meyer, R. (1994) *Genie: A Scientific Tragedy*. New York: Harper Perennial.

Michigan Law Review (1989) 'The law and story telling', Special Issue, vol. 87 (8).

Middlebrook, D.W. (1996) 'Telling secrets', in M. Rhiel and D. Suchoff (eds), *The Seductions of Biography*. London: Routledge.

Miller, D. (ed.) (1995) *Acknowledging Consumption: A Review of New Studies*. London: Routledge.

Miller, N. and Morgan, D. (1993) 'Called to account: the CV as an autobiographcial practice', *Sociology*, 27 (1): 133–43.

Miller, R.L. (2000) *Researching Life Stories and Family Histories*. London: Sage.

Mills, C.W. (1940) 'Situated actions and vocabularies of motive', *American Science Review*, V: 904–13.

Mills, C.W. (1959/1970) *The Sociological Imagination*. Harmondsworth: Penguin.

Misch, G. (1951) *A History of Autobiography in Antiquity* (trans. E.W. Dickes), 2 Vols. Cambridge, MA: Harvard University Press.

Mitchell, W.J. (1992) *The Re-Configured Eye: Visual Truth in the Post-Photographic Era*. Cambridge, MA: MIT Press.

Molotch, H. (1994) 'Going out', *Sociological Forum*, 9 (2): 22–39.

Monette, P. (1992) *Borrowed Time: An AIDS Memoir*. New York: Avon Books.

Money, J.W. (1987) *To All the Girls I Loved Before: An AIDS Diary*. Boston, MA: Alyson.

Moran, J.M. (1996) 'Wedding Video and its generation', in M. Renov and E. Suderburg (eds), *Resolutions: Contemporary Video Practice*. Minnesota, MN: University of Minnesota Press. pp. 360–81.

Morgan, D. (1998) 'Sociological imaginings and imagining sociology: bodies, auto/ biographies and other mysteries', *Sociology*, 32 (4): 647–63.

Morris, B. (1994) *The Anthropology of the Self: The Individual in Cultural Perspective*. London: Pluto Press.

Morrison, B. (1997) *As if*. London: Granta Books.

Morrison, B. (1998) *Too True*. London: Granta.

Morse, J.M. (1994) 'Designing funded qualitative research', in N.K. Denzin and Y.S. Lincoln (eds), *Handbook of Qualitative Research*. London: Sage. pp. 220–35.

Mowrer, E.R. (1927) *Family Disorganization*. Chicago: University of Chicago Press.

Musello, C. (1979) 'Family photography', in J. Wagner (ed.), *Images of Information: Still Photography in the Social Sciences*. Beverly Hills, CA: Sage. pp. 101–18.

Myerhoff, B. (1978) *Number Our Days*. New York: Touchstone.

Myerhoff, B. (1992) *Remembered Lives: The Work of Ritual, Storytelling and Growing Older*. Ann Arbor, MI: University of Michigan Press.

Nardi, P. (1990) 'AIDS and obituaries: the perpetuation of stigma in the press', in D. Feldman (ed.), *Culture and Aids*. New York: Praeger. pp. 159–68.

Nardi, P., Sanders, D. and Marmor, J. (1994) *Growing up before Stonewall: Life Stories of Some Gay Men*. London: Routledge.

National Press Photographers Association (1978) *The Best of Photojournalism*. London: Orbis Publishing.

Nelson, K. (ed.) (1998) *Narratives from the Crib*. Cambridge, MA: Harvard University Press.

Neumann, M. (1998) 'Collecting ourselves at the end of the century', in C. Ellis and A. Bochner (eds), *Composing Ethnography: Alternative Forms of Qualitative Writing*. London: Sage. pp. 172–98.

Newton, E. (1993) 'My best informant's dress: the erotic equation in fieldwork', *Cultural Anthropology*, 8: 2–23.

Nichols, B. (1991) *Representing Reality: Issues and Concepts in Documentary*. Bloomington, IN: Indiana University Press.

Nisbet, R. (1976) *Sociology as an Art Form*. London: Heinemann.

Noble, N. (1993) 'Uncovering roots', *Village Voice*, 23 February.

Noblit, G. and Dempsey, V.O. (1996) *The Social Construction of Virtue: The Moral Life of Schools*. Albany, NY: New York University Press.

Nungesser, L.G. (1986) *Epidemic of Courage: Facing AIDS in America*, New York, St Martin's Press.

Nussbaum, M. (1999) *Sex and Social Justice*. Oxford. Oxford University Press.

Okely, J. and Callaway, H. (eds) (1992) *Anthropology and Autobiography*. New York: Routledge.

Olick, J.K. and Robbins, J. (1998) 'Social memory studies from "collective memory" to the historical sociology of mnemonic practices', *Annual Review of Sociology*, 24: 105–40.

Olney, J. (1972) *Metaphors of Self: The Meanings of Autobiography*. Princeton, NJ: Princeton University Press.

Olney, J. (ed.) (1980) *Autobiography: Essays Theoretical and Critical*. Princeton, NJ: Princeton University Press.

Olney, J. (1985) '"I Was Born": slave narratives, their status as autobiography and as literature', in C. Davis and H.L. Gates (eds), *The Slave's Narrative*. Oxford: Oxford University Press.

Olney, J. (1998) *Memory and Narrative: The Weave of Life-Writing*. Chicago: University of Chicago Press.

Orne, M.T. (1962) 'On the social psychology of the psychological experiment', *American Psychologist*, 17: 776–83.

Palmer, V.M. (1928) *Field Studies in Sociology: A Student's Manual*. Chicago: University of Chicago.

Park, R.E. and Burgess, E.W. (1921, 1969) *Introduction to the Science of Sociology: Including the Original Index to Basic Sociological Concepts*. Chicago: University of Chicago Press.

Parke, C.N. (1996) *Biography: Writing Lives*. New York: Twayne.

Parker, T. (1962) *The Courage of His Convictions*. London: Hutchinson.

Parker, T. (1963) *The Unknown Citizen*. London: Hutchinson.

Parker, T. (1965) *Five Women*. London: Hutchinson.

Parker, T. (1967) *A Man of Good Abilities*. London: Hutchinson.

Parker, T. (1969) *The Twisting Lane*. London: Hutchinson.

Parker, T. (1995) *The Violence of Our Lives: Interviews with Life Sentence Prisoners in America*. London: HarperCollins.

Parker, T. (1996) *Studs Terkel: A Life in Words*. New York: Henry Holt and Co.

Parker, T. (1999) *Criminal Conversations*. London: Routledge.

Pascal, R. (1960) *Design and Truth in Autobiography*. London: Routledge and Kegan Paul.

Pastore, J.L. (ed.) (1993) *Confronting AIDS through Literature: The Responsibilities of Representation*. Chicago: University of Illinois Press.

Peabody, B. (1986) *The Screaming Room: A Mother's Journal*. New York: Avon Books.

Pearson, C. (1988) *Goodbye, I Love You*. New York: Jove.

Pepys, S. (1970 edn) *The Diary of Samuel Pepys: A New and Complete Transcription* (edited by R. Latham and W. Matthews), Vols 1–9. London: Bell.

Perks, R. (1990) *Oral History: An Annotated Bibliography*. London: British Library National Sound Archive.

Perks, R. (1995) *Oral History: Talking About the Past*. London: Historical Association.

Perks, R. and Thompson, A. (eds) (1998) *The Oral History Reader*. London: Routledge.

Personal Narratives Group (eds) (1989) *Interpreting Women's Lives: Feminist Theory and Personal Narratives*. Bloomington, IN: Indiana University Press.

Pettiway, L. (1996) *Honey, Honey, Miss Thang*. Philadelphia: Temple University Press.

Pettiway, L. (1997) *Working It: Women Living through Drugs and Crime*. Philadelphia: Temple University Press.

Phillips, D.L. (1971) *Knowledge from What? Theories and Methods in Social Research*. Chicago: Rand McNally.

Phillips, D.L. (1973) *Abandoning Method*. London: Jossey–Bass.

Pines, M. (1981) 'The civilizing of Genie', *Psychology Today*, 15 (9): 28–34.

Platt, J. (1996) *A History of Sociological Research Methods in America, 1920–1960*. Cambridge: Cambridge University Press.

Plummer, K. (1979) 'Misunderstanding labelling perspectives', in D. Downes and P. Rock (eds), *Deviant Interpretations*. Oxford: Martin Robertson.

Plummer, K. (1990a) 'Herbert Blumer and the life history tradition', *Symbolic Interaction*, 13 (2): 125–45.

Plummer, K. (1990b) 'Staying in the empiricial world', *Symbolic Interaction*, 13 (2): 155–61.

Plummer, K. (ed.) (1991) *Symbolic Interactionism*, 2 vols. Aldershot: Edward Elgar.

Plummer, K. (1995a) *Telling Sexual Stories: Power, Change and Social Worlds*. London: Routledge.

Plummer, K. (1995b) 'Life story research', in J. Smith, R. Harré and L. Van Langhove (eds), *Rethinking Methods in Psychology*. London: Sage. pp. 50–64.

Plummer, K. (ed.) (1997) *The Chicago School*, 4 Vols. London: Routledge.

Plummer, K. (1999) 'The "ethnographic society" at century's end: clarifying the role of public ethnography', *Journal of Contemporary Ethnography*, 28 (6): 641–9.

Plummer, K. (2000) 'Symbolic interactionism at the end of the twentieth century' in Bryan Turner (ed.), *The Blackwell Companion to Social Theory*, 2nd edn. Oxford: Blackwell. pp. 193–222.

Polkinghorne, D.E. (1988) *Narrative Knowing and the Human Sciences*. Albany, NY: State University of New York Press.

Ponsonby, A. (1923) *English Diaries: A Review of English Diaries from the Sixteenth to the Twentieth Century with an Introduction on Diary Writing*. London: Methuen.

Popular Memory Group (1998) 'Popular memory: theory, politics method', in R. Perks and A. Thompson (eds), *The Oral History Reader*. London: Routledge. pp. 75–86.

Portelli, A. (1991) *The Death of Luigi Trastulli and Other Stories: Form and Meaning in Oral History*. Albany, NY: State University of New York Press.

Portelli, A. (1998) 'What makes oral history different?' in R. Perks and A. Thompson (eds), *The Oral History Reader*. London: Routledge. pp. 63–74.

Porter, K. and Weeks, J. (eds) (1994) *Between the Acts: Lives of Homosexual Men 1885–1967*. London: Routledge.

Poster, M. (1990) *The Mode of Information*. Cambridge: Polity Press.

Powdermaker, H. (1967) *Stranger and Friend: The Way of an Anthropologist*. London: Secker and Warburg.

Preston, J. (1989) *Personal Dispatches: Writers Confront AIDS*. New York: St Martin's Press.

Prieur, A. (1998) *Mema's House: On Transvestites, Queens and Machos*. Chicago: University of Chicago Press.

Prus, R. (1996) *Symbolic Interaction and Ethnographic Research*. Albany, NY: State University of New York Press.

Punch, M. (1986) *The Politics and Ethics of Fieldwork*. London: Sage.

Punch, M. (1994) 'Politics and ethics in qualitative research', in N.K. Denzin and Y. Lincoln (eds), *The Handbook of Qualitative Research*. London: Sage.

Quinney, R. (1996) 'Once my father travelled West to California', in C. Ellis and A.P. Bochner (eds), *Composing Ethnography: Alternative Forms of Qualitative Writing*. London: Sage. ch. 14.

Rabin, A.I., Zucker, R.A., Emmons, R.A. and Frank, S. (eds) (1990) *Studying Persons and Lives*. New York: Springer.

Radest, H.B. (1996) *Humanism with a Human Face: Intimacy and the Enlightenment*. London: Praeger.

Radin, P. (ed.) (1926) *Crashing Thunder: The Autobiography of an American Indian*. New York: D. Appleton and Co.

Ragin, C.C. and Becker, H.S. (1992) *What is a Case? Exploring the Foundations of Social Inquiry*. Cambridge: Cambridge University Press.

Rainer, T. (1978) *The New Diary: How to Use a Journal for Self Guidance and Expanded Creativity*. Los Angeles: J.P. Tarcher.

Rainer, T. (1998) *Your Life as Story*. New York: Penguin Putnam.

Rapport, N. (1997) *Transcendent Individual: Towards a Literary and Liberal Anthropology*. London: Routledge.

Rathje, W. and Murphy, C. (1992) *Rubbish! The Archaeology of Garbage*. New York: HarperCollins.

Raushenbush, R.W. (1979) *Robert E. Park: Biography of a Sociologist*. Durham, NC: Duke University Press.

Rawick, G.P. (ed.) (1971–9) *The American Slave: A Composite Auto-biography*. London/Westport, CT: Greenwood Press.

Read, P. (1994/1998) 'Presenting voices in different media: print, radio and CD Rom', in R. Perks and A. Thompson (eds), *The Oral History Reader*. London: Routledge. pp. 414–20.

Reed-Danahay, D.E. (ed.) (1997) *Auto/Ethnography: Rewriting the Self and the Social*. Oxford: Berg.

Reinharz, S. (1979) *On Becoming a Social Scientist*. San Francisco, CA: Jossey–Bass.

Reinharz, S. (1992) *Feminist Method in Social Science*. Oxford: Oxford University Press.

Rengger, N.J. (1996) *Retreat from the Modern: Humanism, Postmodernism and the Flight from Modernist Culture*. Exeter: Bowerdean Publishing.

Renov, M. and Suderburg, E. (1996) *Resolutions: Contemporary Video Practices*. Minnesota: University of Minnesota Press.

Rettig, R., Torres, M. and Garrett, G. (1977) *Manny: A Criminal Addict's Story*. Boston, MA: Houghton–Mifflin.

Ribbens, J. (1998) 'Hearing my feeling voice? An autobiographical discussions of motherhood', in J. Ribbens and R. Edwards (eds), *Feminist Dilemmas in Qualitative Research*. London: Sage. pp. 24–38.

Rich, A. (1976) *Of Woman Born: Motherhood as Experience and Institution*. New York: W.W. Norton.

Richardson, L. (1990) *Writing Strategies: Reaching Diverse Audiences*. London: Sage.

Richardson, L. (1992) 'Resisting resistance narratives: a representation for communication', *Studies in Symbolic Interactionism*, 13: 77–82.

Richardson, L. (1998) *Fields of Play: Constructing an Academic Life*. New Brunswick, NJ: Rutgers University Press.

Riemer, J.W. (1977) 'Varieties of opportunistic research', *Urban Life*, 5 (4): 467–77.

Riesman, D. and Glazer, N. (1952) *Faces in the Crowd: Individual Studies in Character and Politics*. New Haven, CT: Yale University Press.

Riesman, D., Denney, R. and Glazer, N. (1950) *The Lonely Crowd: A Study of the Changing American Character*. New Haven, CT: Yale University Press.

Riessman, C.K. (1993) *Narrative Analysis*. London: Sage.

Riis, J.A. (1971) *How the Other Half Lives*. New York: Dover. (First published 1890.)

Riley, M.W. (1963) *Sociological Research: I: A Case Approach*. New York: Harcourt, Brace and World.

Riley, M. White (1998) 'A life course approach: autobiographical notes', in J.Z. Giele and G.H. Elder (eds), *Methods of Life Course Research: Qualitative and Quantitative Approaches*. London: Sage. pp. 28–51.

Ritchie, D. (1995) *Doing Oral History*. New York: Twayne.

Ritchin, F. (1990) *'In Our Own Image': The Coming Revolution in Photography*. New York: Aperture.

Ritzer, G. (1995) *The McDonaldization of Society*, 2nd edn. London: Pine Forge.

Ritzer, G. (1997) *Postmodern Social Theory*. New York: McGraw-Hill.

Roazen, P. (1979) *Freud and His Followers*. Harmondsworth: Penguin. (Originally published by A. Knopf, 1975.)

Roberts, H. (ed.) (1981) *Doing Feminist Research*. London: Routledge and Kegan Paul.

Rock, P. (1979) *The Making of Symbolic Interactionism*. London: Macmillan.

Ronai, C.R. (1992) 'A reflexive self through narrative: a night in the life of an erotic dancer', in C. Ellis and M.G. Flaherty (eds), *Investigating Subjectivity: Research on Lived Experience*. London: Sage. ch. 5.

Ronai, C.R. (1996) 'My mother is mentally retarded', in C. Ellis and A.P. Bochner (eds), *Composing Ethnography: Alternative Forms of Qualitative Writing*. London: Sage. ch. 3.

Rosaldo, R. (1986) *When Natives Talk Back: Chicano Anthropology Since the Late 1960s*. Tucson: University of Arizona.

Rosaldo, R. (1989) *Culture and Truth: The Remaking of Social Analysis*. London: Routledge.

Rosenthal, A. (1971) *The New Documentary in Action: A Casebook in Film Making*. Berkeley, CA: University of California Press.

Rosenwald, G. and Ochberg, R.L. (eds) (1992) *Storied Lives: The Cultural Politics of Self Understanding*. New Haven, CT: Yale University Press.

Rousseau, J.J. (1781/1953) *The Confessions*. Harmondsworth: Penguin.

Rubin, H. and Rubin, I. (1995) *Qualitative Interviewing: The Art of Hearing Data*. London: Sage.

Rubin, L. (1972) *Worlds of Pain: Life in the Working Class Family*. New York: Basic Books.

Rubin, L. (1983) *Intimate Strangers: Men and Women Together*. New York: Harper.

Rubin, L. (1990) *Erotic Wars: What Happened to the Sexual Revolution?* New York: Harper.

Rubin, L. (1997) *The Transcendent Child: Tales of Triumph over the Past*. New York: Harper Perennial.

Rubin, H.J. and Rubin, I.S. (1995) *Qualitative Interviewing: The Art of Hearing Data*. London: Sage.

Rucker, D. (1969) *The Chicago Pragmatists*. Minneapolis, MN: University of Minnesota Press.

Rugg, L.H. (1999) *Picturing Ourselves: Photography and Autobiography*. Chicago: University of Chicago Press.

Runyan, W.M. (1982/1984) *Life Histories and Psychobiography: Explorations in Theory and Method*. Oxford: Oxford University Press.

Ruskin, Cindy (1988) *The Quilt: Stories from the Names Project*. New York: Pocket Books.

Ruth, J.E. and Oberg, P. (1996) 'Essays of life: old age in life history perspective', in J. Birren, G.M. Kenyon, J.G. Ruth, J. Schroots and T. Svensson (eds), *Aging and Biography: Explorations in Adult Development*. New York: Springer. pp. 167–86.

Rymer, R. (1994) *Genie: A Scientific Tragedy*. New York: HarperCollins.

Sacks, O. (1986) *The Man Who Mistook His Wife for a Hat*. London: Picador.

Said, E. (1985) *Orientalism*. Harmondsworth: Penguin.

Said, E. (1992) *Edward Said: A Critical Reader*. Oxford: Blackwell.

Samuels, R. (1981) *East-End Underworld: Chapters in the Life of Arthur Harding*. London: Routledge and Kegan Paul.

Sanjek, R. (ed.) (1990) *Fieldnotes: The Makings of Anthropology*. Ithaca, NY: Cornell University Press.

Sarbin, T.R. (1986) *Narrative Psychology: The Storied Nature of Human Conduct*. London: Praeger.

Sartre, J.P. (1963) *Search for a Method*. New York: Knopf.

Sartre, J.P. (1964) *The Words*. New York: George Braziller.

Sartre, J.P. (1938/1965) *Nausea*. Harmondsworth: Penguin.

Sartre, J.P. (1970) 'Jean Paul Sartre: an interview', *New York Review of Books*, XIV (6): 22–31.

Sartre, J.P. (1981, 1987, 1989) *The Family Idiot: Gustave Flaubert, 1821–1857*, 3 Vols. Chicago: University of Chicago Press.

Satyamurti, C. (1988) *Selected Poems*. Oxford: Oxford University Press.

Schafer, R. (1981) 'Narration in the psychoanalytic dialogue', in W.J.T. Mitchell, *On Narrative*. Chicago: University of Chicago Press. pp. 25–50.

Schafer, R. (1992) *Retelling a Life: Narration and Dialogue in Psychoanalysis*. New York: Basic Books.

Schatzman, L. and Strauss, A. (1973) *Social Research in the Field: Strategies for a Natural Sociology*. Englewood Cliffs, NJ: Prentice–Hall.

Scheffler, I. (1974) *Four Pragmatists: A Critical Introduction to Peirce, James, Mead and Dewey*. London: Routledge and Kegan Paul.

Scheper-Hughes, N. (1979) *Saints, Scholars and Schizophrenics: Mental Illness in Rural Ireland*. Chicago: Chicago University Press.

Schuessler, K.F. (ed.) (1973) *On Analysing Crime*. Chicago: University of Chicago Press.

Schuman, H. and Scott, J. (1989) 'Generations and collective memory', *American Sociological Review*, 54 (June): 359–81.

Schwartz, G., Merten, D., Behan, F. and Rosenthal, A. (1980) *Love and Commitment*. Beverly Hills, CA: Sage.

Schwartz, H. and Jacobs, J. (1979) *Qualitative Sociology: A Method to the Madness*. London: Collier–Macmillan.

Scott, J. (1990) *A Matter of Record*. Cambridge: Polity Press.

Scott, J. (1998) 'Experience', in S. Smith and J. Watson (eds), *Women, Autobiography, Theory: A Reader*. Madison, WI: University of Wisconsin Press. pp. 57–71.

Scott, J. and Alwin, D. (1998) 'Retrospective versus prospective measurement of life stories in longtitudinal research', in J. Giele and G.H. Elder (eds), *Methods of Life Course Research*. London Sage. pp. 98–127.

Seale, C. (ed.) (1998) *Researching Society and Culture*. London: Sage.

Sechrest, L. (1979) *Unobtrusive Measurement Today*. San Francisco, CA: Jossey–Bass. (2nd edn 2000.)

Sedgwick, E.K. (1990) *Epistemology of the Closet*. Berkeley, CA: University of California Press.

Seidman, S. (1997) *Difference Troubles: Queering Social Theory and Sexual Politics*. Cambridge: Cambridge University Press.

Selden, R. and Widdowson, P. (1993) *A Reader's Guide to Contemporary Literary Theory*, 3rd edn. Hemel Hempstead: Harvester Wheatsheaf.

Semin, A., Garb, T. and Kuspit, D. (eds) (1997) *Christian Boltanski*. London: Phaidon.

Sennett, R. and Cobb, R. (1972) *The Hidden Injuries of Class*. New York: Random House.

Sennett, R. (1974) *The Fall of Public Man*. London: Cambridge University Press.

Settersten, R.A. and Mayer, K.U. (1997) 'The measurement of age, age structuring and the life course', *Annual Review of Sociology*, 23: 233–61.

Sevenhuijsen, S. (1998) *Citizenship and the Ethics of Care*. London: Routledge.

Sexton, J.D. (1981) *Son of Tecún Umán: A Mayan Indian Tells his Life Story*. Tucson, AZ: The University of Arizona Press.

Shalin, D.N. (1993) 'Modernity, postmodernism, and pragmatist inquiry: an introduction', *Symbolic Interaction*, 16 (4): 303–32.

Shattuc, J.M. (1997) *The Talking Cure: TV Talk Shows and Women*. London: Routledge.

Shaw, C. (1966) *The Jack Roller: A Delinquent Boy's Own Story*. Chicago: University of Chicago Press.

Shaw, C. and McKay, H.D. (1969) *Juvenile Delinquency and Urban Areas*, rev. edn. Chicago: University of Chicago Press.

Shaw, C.R. (1931) *The Natural History of a Delinquent Career*. Chicago: University of Chicago Press.

Shaw, C.R. (1938) *Brothers in Crime*. Chicago: University of Chicago Press.

Sheehey, G. (1995) *New Passages: Mapping Your Life Across Time*. New York: Ballentine.

Sheehey, G. (1998) *Understanding Men's Passages: Discovering the New Map of Men's Lives*. New York: Random House.

Shelston, A. (1977) *Biography*. London: Methuen.

Sheridan, D. (1993) 'Writing to the archive: mass-observation as autobiogaphy', *Sociology*, 27 (1): 27–40.

Sherman, S.R. (1998) *Documenting Ourselves: Film, Video and Culture*. Lexington, KY: University of Kentucky Press.

Shils, E. (1948) *The Present State of American Sociology*. Glencoe, IL: The Free Press.

Short, K. (ed.) (1981) *Feature Films as History*. London: Croom Helm.

Shostak, M. (1981) *The Life and Words of a !Kung Woman*. Cambridge, MA: Harvard University Press.

Showalter, E. (1979) 'Towards a feminist poetics', in M. Jacobus (ed.), *Women Writing and Writing about Women*. London: Croom Helm.

Shweder, R.A. (1998) *Welcome to Middle Age! (and Other Cultural Fictions)*. Chicago: University of Chicago Press.

Silverman, D. (1973) 'Interview talk: bringing off a research instrument', *Sociology*, 7 (1): 31–48.

Silverman, D. (1975) *Reading Castaneda: A Prologue to the Social Science*. London: Routledge and Kegan Paul.

Silverman, D. (1993) *Interpreting Qualitative Data: Methods for Analyzing Talk, Text and Interaction*. London: Sage.

Silverman, D. (2000) *Doing Qualitative Research: A Practical Handbook*. London: Sage.

Simeoni, D. and Diani, M. (eds) (1995a) 'Biographical research', *Current Sociology*, 43 (2/3).

Simeoni, D. and Diani, M. (eds) (1995b) 'Taking Jenny at her word', *Current Sociology*, 43 (2/3): 27–40.

Simmel, G. (1908/1950) 'The Stranger', in K.H. Wolff (ed.), *The Sociology of Georg Simmel*. Glencoe, IL: Free Press.

Simmel, G. (1977) *The Problems of the Philosophy of History: Epistemological Essays* (ed. G. Oakes). New York: The Free Press/Macmillan.

Simmons, L.W. (ed.) (1942) *Sun Chief: The Autobiography of a Hopi Indian*. New Haven, CT: Yale University/Institute of Human Relations.

Simonds, W. (1992) *Women and Self Help Culture: Reading Between the Lines*. New Brunswick, NJ: Rutgers University Press.

Smith, H.L. (Director) (1935) *The New Survey of London Life and Labour: Vol. IX, Life and Leisure*. London: P.S. King.

Smith, L.T. (1999) *Decolonizing Methodologies: Research and Indigenous Peoples*. Dunedin: University of Otago Press.

Smith, S. (1974) *Where I'm Bound: Patterns of Slavery and Freedom in Black American Autobiography*. Westport, CT: Greenwood Press.

Smith, S. and Watson, J. (eds) (1996) *Getting a Life: Everyday Uses of Autobiography*. Minneapolis, MN: University of Minnesota Press.

Smith, S. and Watson, J. (eds) (1998) *Women, Autobiography, Theory: A Reader*. London: University of Wisconsin Press.

Snodgrass, J. (1973) 'The criminologist and his criminal: the case of Edwin H. Sutherland and Broadway Jones', *Issues in Criminology*, 8 (1): 1–17.

Snodgrass, J. (1978) 'The Jack Roller at seventy: a fifty year follow-up of the delinquent boy's own story'. Paper presented at the American Society of Criminology meetings in Dallas, November 1978.

Snodgrass, J. and The Jack Roller (1982) *The Jack Roller at Seventy*. Lexington, MA: DC Heath/ Lexington Books.

Sokal, A. and Bricmont, J. (1998) *Intellectual Impostures: Postmodern Philosophers' Abuse of Science*. London: Profile Books.

Sontag, S. (1979) *On Photography*. Harmondsworth: Penguin.

Sorokin, P. and Berger, C. (1938) *Time Budgets of Human Behaviour*. Cambridge, MA: Harvard University Press.

Spence, D.P. (1982) *Narrative Truth and Historical Truth: Meaning and Interpretation in Psychoanalysis*. New York: Norton.

Spence, J. (1986) *Putting Myself in the Picture: A Political, Personal and Photographic Autobiography*. London: Camden Press.

Spence, J. and Holland, P. (1991) *Family Snaps: The Meaning of Domestic Photography*. London: Virago.

Spradley, J.P. (1969) *Guests Never Leave Hungry: The Autobiography of James Sewid, a Kwakiutl Indian*. London: Yale University Press.

Spradley, J.P. (1970) *You Owe Yourself a Drunk: An Ethnography of Urban Nomads*. Boston, MA: Little, Brown.

Spradley, J.P. (1979) *The Ethnographic Interview*. London: Holt, Rinehart & Winston.

Spradley, J. (1980) *Participant Observation*. New York: Holt, Rinehart & Winston.

Stacey, J. (1988) 'Can there be a feminist ethnography?', *Women's Studies International Forum*, 11 (1): 21–7.

Stanley, L. (ed.) (1984) *The Diaries of Hannah Cullwick*. London: Virago.

Stanley, L. (1992) *The Auto/Biographical I; Theory and Practice of Feminist Auto/Biography*. Manchester: Manchester University Press.

Stanley, L. (1996) 'Mass Observation's "Little Kinsey" and the British Sex Survey Tradition', in J. Weeks and J. Holland (eds), *Sexual Cultures*. London: Macmillan. pp. 97–114.

Stanley, L. and Temple, B. (1995) 'Doing the business? Evaluating software packages to aid the analysis of qualitative data sets', *Studies in Qualitative Methodology*, 5: 169–93.

Stanley, L. and Wise, S. (1981) *Breaking Out: Feminist Consciousness*. London: Routledge. (2nd edn, *Breaking Out Again*, 1993.)

Stasz, C. (1979a) 'Texts, images and display conventions in sociology', *Qualitative Sociology*, 2 (1): 29–44.

Stasz, C. (1979b) 'The early history of visual sociology', in J. Wagner, *Images of Information: Still Photography in the Social Sciences*. Beverly Hills, CA: Sage. pp. 119–36.

Stave, B.M. (ed.) (1999) 'Reflections on oral history in the new millennium', *Oral History Review*, 26 (2): Summer/Fall.

Steedman, C. (1986) *Landscape for a Good Woman*. London: Virago.

Steel, D. (1980) *Discovering Your Family History*. London: British Broadcasting Corporation.

Steichen, E. (1955) *The Family of Man*. New York: Museum of Modern Art.

Stein, A. (1997) *Sex and Sensibility: Stories of a Lesbian Generation*. Berkeley, CA: University of California Press.

Stein, A. and Plummer, K. (1994) '"I can't ever think straight": queer theory and the missing sexual revolution in sociology', *Sociological Theory*, (12) July.

Stein, G. (1933) *The Autobiography of Alice B. Toklas*. Harmondsworth: Penguin.

Stein, G. (1938/1985) *Everybody's Autobiography*. London: Virago.

Stewart, G. (1972) 'On first being a John', *Urban Life and Culture*, 1: 225–74.

Stoll, D. (1999) *Rigoberta Menchú and the Story of All Poor Guatemalans*. Oxford: Westview Press.

Stoller, R. (1974) *Splitting: A Case of Female Masculinity*. New York: Delta Books.

Stonequist, E.V. (1961) *The Marginal Man: A Study in Personality and Culture Conflict*. New York: Russell and Russell (first published 1931).

Stones, R. (1996) *Sociological Reasoning: Towards a Post-Modern Sociology*. London: Macmillan.

Stones, R. (ed.) (1998) *Key Sociological Thinkers*. London: Macmillan.

Stott, W. (1977) *Documentary Experience and Thirties America*. Oxford: Oxford University Press.

Stouffer, S.A. (1930) 'Experimental comparison of statistical and case history methods in attitude research'. Unpublished PhD dissertation, University of Chicago.

Straus, R. (1974) *Escape from Custody*. New York: Harper and Row.

Strauss, A. (ed.) (1964) *George Herbert Mead on Social Psychology*. Chicago: University of Chicago Press.

Strauss, A. (1953/1969) *Mirrors and Masks: The Search for Identity*. San Francisco, CA: The Sociology Press.

Strauss, A. (1987) *Qualitative Analysis for Social Scientists*. Cambridge: Cambridge University Press.

Strauss, A. and Corbin, J. (1994) 'Grounded theory methodology: an overview', in N.K. Denzin and Y.S. Lincoln (eds), *Handbook of Qualitative Research*. London: Sage. pp. 273–85.

Strauss, A. and Corbin, J. (1998) *Basics of Qualitative Research*, 2nd edn. London: Sage.

Strauss, A. and Glaser, B. (1977) *Anguish: A Case History of a Dying Trajectory*. Oxford: Martin Robertson.

Sturken, M. (1997) *Tangled Memories: The Vietnam War, The AIDS Epidemic and the Politics of Remembering*. Berkeley, CA: University of California Press.

Styles, J. (1979) 'Outsider/insider: researching gay baths', *Urban Life*, 8 (2): 135–52.

Sutherland, E.H. (1937) *The Professional Thief by a Professional Thief*. Chicago: University of Chicago/Phoenix Books. (2nd edn 1967.)

Taft, J. (1933) *Thirty One Contacts with a Seven Year Old Boy*. New York: Macmillan.

Tannenbaum, F. (1938) *Crime and Community*. New York: Columbia University Press.

Taylor, C. (1989) *Sources of the Self*. Cambridge, MA: Harvard University Press.

Terkel, S. (1968) *Division Street: America*. London: Allen Lane.

Terkel, S. (1970) *Hard Times: An Oral History of the Great Depression*. London: Allen Lane.

Terkel, S. (1974/1977) *Working*. Harmondsworth: Penguin.

Terkel, S. (1978) *Talking to Myself: A Memoir of My Times*. New York: Pocket Books.

Terkel, S. (1981) *American Dreams: Lost and Found*. London: Hodder and Stoughton.

Terkel, S. (1984) *The Good War*. New York: Pantheon.

Terkel, S. (1986) *Chicago*. New York: Pantheon.

Terkel, S. (1992) *Race*. New York: New Press.

Terkel, S. (1995) *Coming of Age*. New York: New Press.

Thomas, W.I. and Znaniecki, F. (1958) *The Polish Peasant in Europe and America*. New York: Dover Publications. (First published 1918–21; republished in 2 vols 1927.)

Thompson, E.P. (1978) *The Poverty of Theory and Other Essays*. London: Merlin Press.

Thompson, P. (1978) *The Voice of the Past: Oral History*. Oxford: Opus Books/Oxford University Press. (3rd edn 2000.)

Thompson, P., Itzin, C. and Abendstern, M. (1990) *I Don't Feel Old: The Experience of Later Life*. Oxford: Oxford University Press.

Thrasher, F. (1963) *The Gang. A Study of 1,313 Gangs in Chicago*, abridged edn. Chicago: University of Chicago. (First unabridged edn published 1926.)

Tonkin, E. (1992) *Narrating Our Pasts: The Social Construction of Oral History*. Cambridge: Cambridge University Press.
Travisano, R.V. (1999) 'Madness and I', *Studies in Symbolic Interaction*, 22: 49–63.
Trilling, L. (1972) *Sincerity and Authenticity*. London: Oxford University Press.
Trinh, Minh-ha (1989) *Women, Native, Other: Writing Postcoloniality and Feminism*. Bloomington, IN: Indiana University Press.
Turkle, S. (1996) *Life on the Screen: Identity in the Age of the Internet*. London: Weidenfeld & Nicolson.
Turner, R. (1953) 'The quest for universals in sociological research', *American Sociological Review*, 2A (June): 605–11; also in N.K. Denzin (1970) *Sociological Methods: A Source Book*. London: Butterworth. pp. 264–77.
Turner, R.E. (ed.) (1967) *Robert E. Park on Social Control and Collective Behaviour*. Chicago: University of Chicago Press.
Turner, V. (1981) 'Social dramas and stories about them', in W.J. Mitchell (ed.), *On Narrative*. Chicago: University of Chicago Press.
Ulmer, G. (1989) *Teletheory*. London: Routledge.
Vaillant, G.E. (1977) *Adaptation to Life*. Boston, MA: Little, Brown.
Valentine, C.A. (1968) *Culture and Poverty: Critique and Counter Proposals*. Chicago: University of Chicago Press.
Van den Hoonaard, W.C. (1997) *Working with Sensitizing Concepts: Analytical Field Research*. London: Sage.
Van der Kolk, B. and Van der Har, O. (1995) 'The intrusive past: the flexibility of memory and the engraving of trauma', in C. Carruth (ed.), *Trauma*. Baltimore, MD: Johns Hopkins University Press.
Van Maanen, J. (1988) *Tales of the Field: On Writing Ethnography*. Chicago: University of Chicago Press.
Vansina, J. (1965) *Oral Tradition: A Study in Historical Methodology*. London: Routledge.
Vansina, J. (1985) *Oral Tradition as History*. Madison, WI: University of Wisconsin Press.
Vasoli, R.H. and Terzola, D. (1974) 'Sutherland's professional thief', *Criminology*, 12: 131–54.
Vaz, K.M. (ed.) (1997) *Oral Narrative Research with Black Women*. London: Sage.
Vidich, A.J. and Stein, M.J. (1958) *Small Town in a Mass Society*. New York: Wiley.
Vidich, A.J., Bersman, J. and Stein, M.J. (eds) (1964) *Reflections on Community Studies*. New York: Wiley.
Vinitzky-Seroussi, V. (1998) *After Pomp and Circumstance: High School Reunion as an Autobiographical Occasion*. Chicago, IL: University of Chicago Press.
Wagner, J. (ed.) (1979) *Images of Information: Still Photography in the Social Sciences*. Beverly Hills, CA: Sage.
Wagner-Martin, L. (1994) *Telling Women's Lives: The New Biography*. New Brunswick, NJ: Rutgers University Press.
Walmsley, J. (1998) 'Life history interviewing with people with learning disabilities', in R. Perks and A. Thompson (eds), *The Oral History Reader*. London: Routledge.
Warner, L. (1963) *Yankee City*. New Haven: Yale University Press.
Washington, B.T. (1965) *Up From Slavery*. New York: Dodd, Mead.
Watson, J. (1968) *The Double Helix*. New York: Atheneum.
Watson, J. (1996) 'Ordering the family: genealogy as autobiographical pedigree', in S. Smith and J. Watson (eds), *Getting a Life*. Minneapolis, MN: University of Minnesota Press. pp. 297–323.
Watson, L.C. (1976) 'Understanding a life history as a subjective document: hermeneutical and phenomenological perspectives', *Ethos*, 4 (1): 95–131.
Watson, L.C. and Watson-Franke, M.B. (1985) *Interpreting Life Histories: An Anthropological Inquiry*. New Brunswick, NJ: Transaction Books.
Wax, R.H. (1971) *Doing Fieldwork*. Chicago: University of Chicago Press.
Webb, B. and Webb, S. (1932) *The Methods of Social Study*. London: Longman Green.

Webb, E.J., Campbell, D.T., Schwartz, R.D. and Sechrest, L. (1966) *Unobtrusive Measures: Non-reactive Research in the Social Sciences*. Chicago: Rand McNally.

Weber, G.H. and McCall, G.J. (1978) *Social Scientists as Advocates: Views from the Applied Disciplines*. London: Sage.

Weber, R. (1981) *The Literature of Fact: Literary Non-Fiction in American Writing*. Athens, OH: Ohio University Press.

Weintraub, K.J. (1978) *The Value of the Individual: Self and Circumstance in Autobiography*. Chicago: University of Chicago Press.

Wells, L. (ed.) (1997) *Photography: A Critical Introduction*. London: Routledge.

Wells, H.G. (1934) *Experiment in Autobiography*, 2 Vols. New York: Macmillan.

Werner, O. and Schoepfle, G.M. (1987) *Systematic Fieldwork*, vol. 1. *Foundations of Ethnography and Interviewing*. Newbury Park: Sage.

Weston, K. (1998) *longslowburn: sexuality and social science*. London: Routledge.

White, H. (1973) *Metahistory*. Baltimore, MD: Johns Hopkins University Press.

White, H. (1978) *Tropics of Discourse: Essays in Cultural Critique*. Baltimore, MD: Johns Hopkins University Press.

White, H. (1987) *The Content of the Form: Narrative Discourse and Historical Representation*. Baltimore, MD: Johns Hopkins University Press.

White, M. and Epston, D. (1990) *Narrative Means to Therapeutic Ends*. New York: W.W. Norton.

White, R. (1975) *Lives in Progress: A Study of the Natural Growth of Personality*, 3rd edn. New York: Holt, Rinehart & Winston.

White, R. (1991) *Ryan White: My Own Story*. New York: Dial Books.

Whyte, W.F. (1943) *Street Corner Society: The Social Structure of an Italian Slum*. Chicago: University of Chicago Press. (4th edn 1993.)

Wilkomirski, B. (1997) *Fragments: Memories of a Childhood (1939–1948)*. London: Picador.

Willard, W. (1983) *Argumentation and the Social Grounds of Knowledge*. Alabama: University of Alabama.

Willis, P. (1978) *Learning to Labour*. Hampshire: Gower.

Wilson, E. (1956) *A Piece of My Mind*. New York: Strauss and Cudahy.

Wilson, W.J. (ed.) (1993) *Sociology and the Public Agenda*. Newbury Park: Sage.

Wilson, W., Schwartz, P. and Ritzer, G. (1998) 'Engaging publics in sociological dialogue', *Contemporary Sociology*, 17 (5): 435–53.

Wiseman, F. (1971) 'Interview with Wiseman', in G.R. Levin, *Documentary Explorations*. New York: Doubleday. pp. 313–28.

Witherell, C. and Noddings, N. (eds) (1991) *Stories Lives Tell: Narrative and Dialogue in Education*. New York: Teacher's College, Columbia University.

Wolcott, H.F. (1990) *Writing Up Qualitative Research*. London: Sage.

Wolf, M. (1992) *A Thrice Told Tale: Feminism, Postmodernism and Ethnographic Responsibility*. Stanford, CA: Stanford University Press.

Wolfe, T. (1973) *The New Journalism*. New York: Harper and Row.

Wolff, J. (1981) *The Social Production of Art*. London: Macmillan.

Woolf, V. (1928) *Orlando: A Biography*. London: Hogarth Press.

Woolf, V. (1929) *A Room of Her Own*. London: Hogarth Press.

Woolf, V. (1978) *Moments of Being*. London: Granta.

Young, M.W. (1999) *Malinowksi's Kiriwina: Fieldwork Photography 1915–1918*. Chicago: University of Chicago Press.

Yow, V.R. (1994) *Recording Oral History: A Practical Guide for Social Scientists*. London: Sage.

Zavarzadeh, M. (1976) *The Mythopoeic Reality: The Post War American Non Fiction Novel*. Urbana, IL: University of Illinois Press.

Zetterberg, H.L. (ed.) (1956) *Sociology in the United States of America: A Trend Report*. Paris: UNESCO, Documentation in the Social Sciences.

Zimmerman, D.H. and Wieder, D.L. (1977) 'The diary diary–interview method', *Urban Life* (now *Journal of Contemporary Ethnography*), 5 (4): 479–97.

Znaniecki, F. (1934) *The Method of Sociology*. New York: Farrar and Rinehart.

Zola, I. (1982) *Missing Pieces: A Chronicle of Living with a Disability*. Philadelphia: Temple University Press.

Zorbaugh, H. (1965) *The Gold Coast and the Slum*. Chicago: University of Chicago Press.

Key Names and Titles Index

Subject Index

acquaintance role 209
action 4, 18, 37, 43, 185
action model of life story telling 41–2
action-structure debate 4–7
aesthetic theory of truth 241
'afterlife' of a life story 41, 225
age cohort generation 128
ageing 192
AIDS (HIV) 91, 95, 175
  critical videos 72
  diaries 2, 52, 95
  quilts 58, 235, 237
alcoholism 54, 133, 134, 137
Alzheimer's Disease 47
ambiguity 228–9
American Anthroplogical Association 226
American Journal of Sociology 60
analytic files 151
analytic induction 160, 163
anarchism, *see* libertarianism
anonymity in research 137
anti-humanism 257, 261
anti-narrative 245
anthropological film 76
anthropology 34, 38, 60, 68, 119, 178, 200, 206
archiving 122, 266
audiences 97, 172, 174, 198, 199
Augustine, St. 85, 90, 99, 101, 232
authority 68, 100, 177
authors 89, 180–1, 251
auto/biography, *see* Chapter 4
auto/ethnography 34, 35, 147, 115, 199

Balinese 61–3
Bedouin women 120, 174, 179
behaviourism 256
bias in research 155, 157, 208
biographical objects 43, 57–8, 75
biography 20, 22–3, 42, 43, 101, 207, 268
  classics 80
birth cohorts 128
black narratives 25, 31, 93, 158, 182, 219, 236, 268
body 11, 30, 61, 114, 263
British Sociological Association 223, 226

cancer journals 2
CAQDAS 265
career 194
case studies and histories 108, 109, 111, 112, 132, 163
central life themes 129
'characters' 188
Chicago School of Sociology Chapter 5, 85, 118
childhood fix narrative 193
children 2, 192
cinema verité 73
coaxing, coaching and coercing 42
cockfighting 44, 62
coding data 151
cohorts 126, 128
collective stories 30, 31, 165
collectivism, *see* individualism
coming out tales 2, 31, 91, 94–6
commodification 100
comprehensive life douments 26
concentration camps, *see* Holocaust narratives
confessionals 2, 56, 71, 84, 85, 96, 100, 101, 207, 232
confidentiality 217–18
consumption 58, 75
contingencies 194, 263
continuum of constructions 166, 179–80
continuum of representativeness 153
conversational analysis 150
conversational units 190
core files 151
counter-stories 72
covert research 221
creativity 14, 45, 88
criminal narratives 26–9, 106–7, 158, 160, 162, 248
'crisis of representation' 13, 171
criteria for life histories 46, 113
critical documentaries 68
critical humanism Chapter 12, 14, 15, 261, 262–4
critical life events 129
cultural memory 65
cyberdocuments 96, 98–100, 267–9
cyberstory telling 78

data, collection, storage, analysis, presentation Chapter 7, 149, 151, 168, 265–6
day as a unit of study 51
death, 131, 164
deception in research 155, 221, 222
deconstructionism 256
definition of the situation 40, 110, 114, 158
delinquency 26, 106, 31, 60, 91, 106–7, 113, 153, 160, 191
demand characteristics 156
democratic texts 182
depression 33
development research sequence 121
dialogic 262
diary 48–52, 74, 85, 268
diary-diary interview 51
diary research, forms of 49
'differences' 257
digital photography 99
disability 32–3, 37
documentary 67
documentary film 66–8, 70, 76
documents 17
docu-soaps 68
domain assumption 173
domestic servants 52
Don, the sun chief 38, 134
Dora 22, 243
drama 10–11, 200
dreams 4
'dross rate' 55
drug narratives 25, 134, 163
dying trajectories 131, 164

edited life document 27
editing 67, 150, 176–7
education 246
elderly 61, 126, 128, 245, 254
electronic mail 54
emotions 13, 214–5, 150
epiphanies 187, 194
epistemology 238–50
ethical absolutism 226
ethical narratives 91, 230
ethical theory 226–30
ethics Chapter 10, 14, 120, 215–27, 230, 263
ethics of care 228